THE
Expositor's
Bible
Commentary

with The New International Version

1, 2 THESSALONIANS • 1, 2 TIMOTHY • TITUS

THE
Expositor's Bible Commentary

with The New International Version

1, 2 THESSALONIANS • 1, 2 TIMOTHY • TITUS

Robert L. Thomas, Ralph Earle
& D. Edmond Hiebert

ZondervanPublishingHouse
Grand Rapids, Michigan

A Division of HarperCollins*Publishers*

General Editor:

FRANK E. GAEBELEIN

Former Headmaster, Stony Brook School
Former Coeditor, *Christianity Today*

Associate Editors:

J. D. DOUGLAS

Editor, *The New International
Dictionary of the Christian Church*

RICHARD P. POLCYN

1, 2 Thessalonians; 1, 2 Timothy; Titus
Copyright © 1996 by Robert L. Thomas, Ralph Earle, D. Edmond Hiebert

Requests for information should be addressed to:
Zondervan Publishing House
Grand Rapids, Michigan 49530

Library of Congress Cataloging-in-Publication Data

The expositor's Bible commentary : with the New International Version of the Holy Bible /
    Frank E. Gaebelein, general editor of series.
        p.   cm.
    Includes bibliographical references and index.
    Contents: v. 1–2. Matthew / D. A. Carson — Mark / Walter W. Wessel — Luke / Walter
L. Liefeld — John / Merrill C. Tenney — Acts / Richard N. Longenecker — Romans /
Everett F. Harrison — 1 and 2 Corinthians / W. Harold Mare and Murray J. Harris —
Galatians and Ephesians / James Montgomery Boice and A. Skevington Wood—Philippians,
Colossians, Philemon / Homer A. Kent Jr., Gurtis Vaughan, and Arthur A. Rupprecht—
1, 2 Thessalonians; 1, 2 Timothy; Titus / Robert L. Thomas, Ralph Earle, and D. Edmond
Hiebert—Hebrews, James / Leon Morris and Donald W. Burdick—1, 2 Peter;
1, 2, 3 John; Jude / Edwin A. Blum and Glenn W. Barker—Revelation / Alan F. Johnson
    ISBN: 0-310-20386-4 (softcover)
    1. Bible N.T.—Commentaries. I. Gaebelein, Frank Ely, 1899–1983.
BS2341.2.E96 1995
220.7-dc 00   94-47450
                                                                                                      CIP

Printed in the United States of America

96 97 98 99 00 01 / ❖ EPAC 10 9 8 7 6 5 4 3 2 1

CONTENTS

PREFACE

The title of this work defines its purpose. Written primarily by expositors for expositors, it aims to provide preachers, teachers, and students of the Bible with a new and comprehensive commentary on the books of the Old and New Testaments. Its stance is that of a scholarly evangelicalism committed to the divine inspiration, complete trustworthiness, and full authority of the Bible. Its seventy-eight contributors come from the United States, Canada, England, Scotland, Australia, New Zealand, and Switzerland, and from various religious groups, including Anglican, Baptist, Brethren, Free, Independent, Methodist, Nazarene, Presbyterian, and Reformed churches. Most of them teach at colleges, universities, or theological seminaries.

No book has been more closely studied over a longer period of time than the Bible. From the Midrashic commentaries going back to the period of Ezra, through parts of the Dead Sea Scrolls and the Patristic literature, and on to the present, the Scriptures have been expounded. Indeed, there have been times when, as in the Reformation and on occasions since then, exposition has been at the cutting edge of Christian advance. Luther was a powerful exegete, and Calvin is still called "the prince of expositors."

Their successors have been many. And now, when the outburst of new translations and their unparalleled circulation have expanded the readership of the Bible, the need for exposition takes on fresh urgency.

Not that God's Word can ever become captive to its expositors. Among all other books, it stands first in its combination of perspicuity and profundity. Though a child can be made "wise for salvation" by believing its witness to Christ, the greatest mind cannot plumb the depths of its truth (2 Tim. 3:15; Rom. 11:33). As Gregory the Great said, "Holy Scripture is a stream of running water, where alike the elephant may swim, and the lamb walk." So, because of the inexhaustible nature of Scripture, the task of opening up its meaning is still a perennial obligation of biblical scholarship.

How that task is done inevitably reflects the outlook of those engaged in it. Every biblical scholar has presuppositions. To this neither the editors of these volumes nor the contributors to them are exceptions. They share a common commitment to the supernatural Christianity set forth in the inspired Word. Their purpose is not to supplant the many valuable commentaries that have preceded this work and from which both the editors and contributors have learned. It is rather to draw on the resources of contemporary evangelical scholarship in producing a new reference work for understanding the Scriptures.

A commentary that will continue to be useful through the years should handle contemporary trends in biblical studies in such a way as to avoid becoming outdated when critical fashions change. Biblical criticism is not in itself inadmissible, as some have mistakenly thought. When scholars investigate the authorship, date, literary characteristics, and purpose of a biblical document, they are practicing biblical criticism. So also when, in order to ascertain as nearly as possible the original form of the text, they deal with variant readings, scribal errors, emendations, and other phenomena in the manuscripts. To do these things is essential to responsible exegesis and exposition. And always there is the need to distinguish hypothesis from fact, conjecture from truth.

The chief principle of interpretation followed in this commentary is the grammatico-historical one—namely, that the primary aim of the exegete is to make clear the meaning of the text at the time and in the circumstances of its writing. This endeavor to understand what in the first instance the inspired writers actually said must not be confused with an inflexible literalism. Scripture makes lavish use of symbols and figures of speech; great portions of it are poetical. Yet when it speaks in this way, it speaks no less truly than it does in its historical and doctrinal portions. To understand its message requires attention to matters of grammar and syntax, word meanings, idioms, and literary forms—all in relation to the historical and cultural setting of the text.

The contributors to this work necessarily reflect varying convictions. In certain controversial matters the policy is that of clear statement of the contributors' own views followed by fair presentation of other ones. The treatment of eschatology, though it reflects differences of interpretation, is consistent with a general premillennial position. (Not all contributors, however, are premillennial.) But prophecy is more than prediction, and so this commentary gives due recognition to the major lode of godly social concern in the prophetic writings.

THE EXPOSITOR'S BIBLE COMMENTARY is presented as a scholarly work, though not primarily one of technical criticism. In its main portion, the Exposition, and in Volume 1 (General and Special Articles), all Semitic and Greek words are transliterated and the English equivalents given. As for the Notes, here Semitic and Greek characters are used but always with transliterations and English meanings, so that this portion of the commentary will be as accessible as possible to readers unacquainted with the original languages.

It is the conviction of the general editor, shared by his colleagues in the Zondervan editorial department, that in writing about the Bible, lucidity is not incompatible with scholarship. They are therefore endeavoring to make this a clear and understandable work.

The translation used in it is the New International Version (North American Edition). To the International Bible Society thanks are due for permission to use this most recent of the major Bible translations. The editors and publisher have chosen it because of the clarity and beauty of its style and its faithfulness to the original texts.

To the associate editor, Dr. J. D. Douglas, and to the contributing editors—Dr. Walter C. Kaiser, Jr. and Dr. Bruce K. Waltke for the Old Testament, and Dr. James Montgomery Boice and Dr. Merrill C. Tenney for the New Testament—the general editor expresses his gratitude for their unfailing cooperation and their generosity in advising him out of their expert scholarship. And to the many other contributors he is indebted for their invaluable part in this work. Finally, he owes a special debt of gratitude to Dr. Robert K. DeVries, executive vice-president of the Zondervan Publishing House; Rev. Gerard Terpstra, manuscript editor; and Miss Elizabeth Brown, secretary to Dr. DeVries, for their continual assistance and encouragement.

Whatever else it is—the greatest and most beautiful of books, the primary source of law and morality, the fountain of wisdom, and the infallible guide to life—the Bible is above all the inspired witness to Jesus Christ. May this work fulfill its function of expounding the Scriptures with grace and clarity, so that its users may find that both Old and New Testaments do indeed lead to our Lord Jesus Christ, who alone could say, "I have come that they may have life, and have it to the full" (John 10:10).

FRANK E. GAEBELEIN

ABBREVIATIONS

A. General Abbreviations

A	Codex Alexandrinus	MT	Masoretic text
Akkad.	Akkadian	n.	note
א	Codex Sinaiticus	n.d.	no date
Ap. Lit.	Apocalyptic Literature	Nestle	Nestle (ed.) *Novum*
Apoc.	Apocrypha		*Testamentum Graece*
Aq.	Aquila's Greek Translation	no.	number
	of the Old Testament	NT	New Testament
Arab.	Arabic	obs.	obsolete
Aram.	Aramaic	OL	Old Latin
b	Babylonian Gemara	OS	Old Syriac
B	Codex Vaticanus	OT	Old Testament
C	Codex Ephraemi Syri	p., pp.	page, pages
c.	*circa,* about	par.	paragraph
cf.	*confer,* compare	‖	parallel passage(s)
ch., chs.	chapter, chapters	Pers.	Persian
cod., codd.	codex, codices	Pesh.	Peshitta
contra	in contrast to	Phoen.	Phoenician
D	Codex Bezae	pl.	plural
DSS	Dead Sea Scrolls (see E.)	Pseudep.	Pseudepigrapha
ed., edd.	edited, edition, editor; editions	Q	Quelle ("Sayings" source
e.g.	*exempli gratia,* for example		in the Gospels)
Egyp.	Egyptian	qt.	quoted by
et al.	*et alii,* and others	q.v.	*quod vide,* which see
EV	English Versions of the Bible	R	Rabbah
fem.	feminine	rev.	revised, reviser, revision
ff.	following (verses, pages, etc.)	Rom.	Roman
fl.	flourished	RVm	Revised Version margin
ft.	foot, feet	Samar.	Samaritan recension
gen.	genitive	SCM	Student Christian Movement Press
Gr.	Greek	Sem.	Semitic
Heb.	Hebrew	sing.	singular
Hitt.	Hittite	SPCK	Society for the Promotion
ibid.	*ibidem,* in the same place		of Christian Knowledge
id.	*idem,* the same	Sumer.	Sumerian
i.e.	*id est,* that is	s.v.	*sub verbo,* under the word
impf.	imperfect	Syr.	Syriac
infra.	below	Symm.	Symmachus
in loc.	*in loco,* in the place cited	T	Talmud
j	Jerusalem or	Targ.	Targum
	Palestinian Gemara	Theod.	Theodotion
Lat.	Latin	TR	Textus Receptus
LL.	Late Latin	tr.	translation, translator,
LXX	Septuagint		translated
M	Mishnah	UBS	The United Bible Societies'
masc.	masculine		Greek Text
mg.	margin	Ugar.	Ugaritic
Mid	Midrash	u.s.	*ut supra,* as above
MS(S)	Manuscript(s)	viz.	*videlicet,* namely

vol.	volume	Vul.	Vulgate
v., vv.	verse, verses	WH	Westcott and Hort, *The*
vs.	versus		*New Testament in Greek*

B. Abbreviations for Modern Translations and Paraphrases

AmT	Smith and Goodspeed,	LB	The Living Bible
	The Complete Bible,	Mof	J. Moffatt, *A New Trans-*
	An American Translation		*lation of the Bible*
ASV	American Standard Version,	NAB	The New American Bible
	American Revised Version	NASB	New American Standard Bible
	(1901)	NEB	The New English Bible
Beck	Beck, *The New Testament in*	NIV	The New International Version
	the Language of Today	Ph	J. B. Phillips *The New Testa-*
BV	Berkeley Version (The		*ment in Modern English*
	Modern Language Bible)	RSV	Revised Standard Version
JB	The Jerusalem Bible	RV	Revised Version — 1881–1885
JPS	*Jewish Publication Society*	TCNT	Twentieth Century
	Version of the Old Testament		New Testament
KJV	King James Version	TEV	Today's English Version
Knox	R.G. Knox, *The Holy Bible:*	Wey	*Weymouth's New Testament*
	A Translation from the Latin		*in Modern Speech*
	Vulgate in the Light of the	Wms	C. B. Williams, *The New*
	Hebrew and Greek Original		*Testament: A Translation in*
			the Language of the People

C. Abbreviations for Periodicals and Reference Works

AASOR	*Annual of the American Schools*	BAG	Bauer, Arndt, and Gingrich:
	of Oriental Research		*Greek-English Lexicon*
AB	*Anchor Bible*		*of the New Testament*
AIs	de Vaux: *Ancient Israel*	BC	Foakes-Jackson and Lake: *The*
AJA	*American Journal of*		*Beginnings of Christianity*
	Archaeology	BDB	Brown, Driver, and Briggs:
AJSL	*American Journal of Semitic*		*Hebrew-English Lexicon*
	Languages and Literatures		*of the Old Testament*
AJT	*American Journal of*	BDF	Blass, Debrunner, and Funk:
	Theology		*A Greek Grammar of the*
Alf	Alford: *Greek Testament*		*New Testament and Other*
	Commentary		*Early Christian Literature*
ANEA	*Ancient Near Eastern*	BDT	Harrison: *Baker's Dictionary*
	Archaeology		*of Theology*
ANET	Pritchard: *Ancient Near*	Beng.	Bengel's *Gnomon*
	Eastern Texts	BETS	*Bulletin of the Evangelical*
ANF	Roberts and Donaldson:		*Theological Society*
	The Ante-Nicene Fathers	BJRL	*Bulletin of the John*
ANT	M. R. James: *The Apocryphal*		*Rylands Library*
	New Testament	BS	*Bibliotheca Sacra*
A-S	Abbot-Smith: *Manual Greek*	BT	*Babylonian Talmud*
	Lexicon of the New Testament	BTh	*Biblical Theology*
AThR	*Anglican Theological Review*	BW	*Biblical World*
BA	*Biblical Archaeologist*	CAH	*Cambridge Ancient History*
BASOR	*Bulletin of the American*	CanJTh	*Canadian Journal of Theology*
	Schools of Oriental Research	CBQ	*Catholic Biblical Quarterly*

CBSC	Cambridge Bible for Schools and Colleges
CE	Catholic Encyclopedia
CGT	Cambridge Greek Testament
CHS	Lange: Commentary on the Holy Scriptures
ChT	Christianity Today
Crem	Cremer: Biblico-Theological Lexicon of the New Testament Greek
DDB	Davis' Dictionary of the Bible
Deiss BS	Deissmann: Bible Studies
Deiss LAE	Deissmann: Light From the Ancient East
DNTT	Dictionary of New Testament Theology
EBC	The Expositor's Bible Commentary
EBi	Encyclopaedia Biblica
EBr	Encyclopaedia Britannica
EDB	Encyclopedic Dictionary of the Bible
EGT	Nicoll: Expositor's Greek Testament
EQ	Evangelical Quarterly
ET	Evangelische Theologie
ExB	The Expositor's Bible
Exp	The Expositor
ExpT	The Expository Times
FLAP	Finegan: Light From the Ancient Past
GR	Gordon Review
HBD	Harper's Bible Dictionary
HDAC	Hastings: Dictionary of the Apostolic Church
HDB	Hastings: Dictionary of the Bible
HDBrev.	Hastings: Dictionary of the Bible, one-vol. rev. by Grant and Rowley
HDCG	Hastings: Dictionary of Christ and the Gospels
HERE	Hastings: Encyclopedia of Religion and Ethics
HGEOTP	Heidel: The Gilgamesh Epic and Old Testament Parallels
HJP	Schurer: A History of the Jewish People in the Time of Christ
HR	Hatch and Redpath: Concordance to the Septuagint
HTR	Harvard Theological Review
HUCA	Hebrew Union College Annual
IB	The Interpreter's Bible
ICC	International Critical Commentary
IDB	The Interpreter's Dictionary of the Bible
IEJ	Israel Exploration Journal
Int	Interpretation
INT	E. Harrison: Introduction to the New Testament
IOT	R. K. Harrison: Introduction to the Old Testament
ISBE	The International Standard Bible Encyclopedia
ITQ	Irish Theological Quarterly
JAAR	Journal of American Academy of Religion
JAOS	Journal of American Oriental Society
JBL	Journal of Biblical Literature
JE	Jewish Encyclopedia
JETS	Journal of Evangelical Theological Society
JFB	Jamieson, Fausset, and Brown: Commentary on the Old and New Testament
JNES	Journal of Near Eastern Studies
Jos. Antiq.	Josephus: The Antiquities of the Jews
Jos. War	Josephus: The Jewish War
JQR	Jewish Quarterly Review
JR	Journal of Religion
JSJ	Journal for the Study of Judaism in the Persian, Hellenistic and Roman Periods
JSOR	Journal of the Society of Oriental Research
JSS	Journal of Semitic Studies
JT	Jerusalem Talmud
JTS	Journal of Theological Studies
KAHL	Kenyon: Archaeology in the Holy Land
KB	Koehler-Baumgartner: Lexicon in Veteris Testament Libros
KD	Keil and Delitzsch: Commentary on the Old Testament
LSJ	Liddell, Scott, Jones: Greek-English Lexicon
LTJM	Edersheim: The Life and Times of Jesus the Messiah

MM	Moulton and Milligan: *The Vocabulary of the Greek Testament*		*Testament aus Talmud und Midrash*
MNT	Moffatt: *New Testament Commentary*	SHERK	*The New Schaff-Herzog Encyclopedia of Religious Knowledge*
MST	McClintock and Strong: *Cyclopedia of Biblical, Theological, and Ecclesiastical Literature*	SJT	*Scottish Journal of Theology*
		SOT	Girdlestone: *Synonyms of Old Testament*
NBC	Davidson, Kevan, and Stibbs: *The New Bible Commentary*, 1st ed.	SOTI	Archer: *A Survey of Old Testament Introduction*
NBCrev.	Guthrie and Motyer: *The New Bible Commentary*, rev. ed.	ST	*Studia Theologica*
		TCERK	Loetscher: *The Twentieth Century Encyclopedia of Religious Knowledge*
NBD	J. D. Douglas: *The New Bible Dictionary*	TDNT	Kittel: *Theological Dictionary of the New Testament*
NCB	*New Century Bible*	TDOT	*Theological Dictionary of the Old Testament*
NCE	*New Catholic Encyclopedia*		
NIC	*New International Commentary*	Theol	*Theology*
NIDCC	Douglas: *The New International Dictionary of the Christian Church*	ThT	*Theology Today*
		TNTC	*Tyndale New Testament Commentaries*
NovTest	*Novum Testamentum*	Trench	Trench: *Synonyms of the New Testament*
NSI	Cooke: *Handbook of North Semitic Inscriptions*		
NTS	*New Testament Studies*	UBD	*Unger's Bible Dictionary*
ODCC	*The Oxford Dictionary of the Christian Church*, rev. ed.	UT	Gordon: *Ugaritic Textbook*
		VB	Allmen: *Vocabulary of the Bible*
Peake	Black and Rowley: *Peake's Commentary on the Bible*	VetTest	*Vetus Testamentum*
PEQ	*Palestine Exploration Quarterly*	Vincent	Vincent: *Word-Pictures in the New Testament*
PNF1	P. Schaff: *The Nicene and Post-Nicene Fathers* (1st series)	WBC	*Wycliffe Bible Commentary*
		WBE	*Wycliffe Bible Encyclopedia*
		WC	*Westminster Commentaries*
PNF2	P. Schaff and H. Wace: *The Nicene and Post-Nicene Fathers* (2nd series)	WesBC	*Wesleyan Bible Commentaries*
		WTJ	*Westminster Theological Journal*
PTR	*Princeton Theological Review*	ZAW	*Zeitschrift für die alttestamentliche Wissenschaft*
RB	*Revue Biblique*		
RHG	Robertson's *Grammar of the Greek New Testament in the Light of Historical Research*	ZNW	*Zeitschrift für die neutestamentliche Wissenschaft*
		ZPBD	*The Zondervan Pictorial Bible Dictionary*
RTWB	Richardson: *A Theological Wordbook of the Bible*	ZPEB	*The Zondervan Pictorial Encyclopedia of the Bible*
SBK	Strack and Billerbeck: *Kommentar zum Neuen*	ZWT	*Zeitschrift für wissenschaftliche Theologie*

D. Abbreviations for Books of the Bible, the Apocrypha, and the Pseudepigrapha

OLD TESTAMENT

Gen	2 Chron	Dan
Exod	Ezra	Hos
Lev	Neh	Joel
Num	Esth	Amos
Deut	Job	Obad
Josh	Ps(Pss)	Jonah
Judg	Prov	Mic
Ruth	Eccl	Nah
1 Sam	S of Songs	Hab
2 Sam	Isa	Zeph
1 Kings	Jer	Hag
2 Kings	Lam	Zech
1 Chron	Ezek	Mal

NEW TESTAMENT

Matt	1 Tim
Mark	2 Tim
Luke	Titus
John	Philem
Acts	Heb
Rom	James
1 Cor	1 Peter
2 Cor	2 Peter
Gal	1 John
Eph	2 John
Phil	3 John
Col	Jude
1 Thess	Rev
2 Thess	

APOCRYPHA

1 Esd	1 Esdras
2 Esd	2 Esdras
Tobit	Tobit
Jud	Judith
Add Esth	Additions to Esther
Wisd Sol	Wisdom of Solomon
Ecclus	Ecclesiasticus (Wisdom of Jesus the Son of Sirach)
Baruch	Baruch
Ep Jer	Epistle of Jeremy
S Th Ch	Song of the Three Children (or Young Men)
Sus	Susanna
Bel	Bel and the Dragon
Pr Man	Prayer of Manasseh
1 Macc	1 Maccabees
2 Macc	2 Maccabees

PSEUDEPIGRAPHA

As Moses	Assumption of Moses
2 Baruch	Syriac Apocalypse of Baruch
3 Baruch	Greek Apocalypse of Baruch
1 Enoch	Ethiopic Book of Enoch
2 Enoch	Slavonic Book of Enoch
3 Enoch	Hebrew Book of Enoch
4 Ezra	4 Ezra
JA	Joseph and Asenath
Jub	Book of Jubilees
L Aristeas	Letter of Aristeas
Life AE	Life of Adam and Eve
Liv Proph	Lives of the Prophets
MA Isa	Martyrdom and Ascension of Isaiah
3 Macc	3 Maccabees
4 Macc	4 Maccabees
Odes Sol	Odes of Solomon
P Jer	Paralipomena of Jeremiah
Pirke Aboth	Pirke Aboth
Ps 151	Psalm 151
Pss Sol	Psalms of Solomon
Sib Oracles	Sibylline Oracles
Story Ah	Story of Ahikar
T Abram	Testament of Abraham
T Adam	Testament of Adam
T Benjamin	Testament of Benjamin
T Dan	Testament of Dan
T Gad	Testament of Gad
T Job	Testament of Job
T Jos	Testament of Joseph
T Levi	Testament of Levi
T Naph	Testament of Naphtali
T 12 Pat	Testaments of the Twelve Patriarchs
Zad Frag	Zadokite Fragments

E. Abbreviations of Names of Dead Sea Scrolls and Related Texts

CD	Cairo (Genizah text of the) Damascus (Document)
DSS	Dead Sea Scrolls
Hev	Nahal Hever texts
Mas	Masada Texts
Mird	Khirbet mird texts
Mur	Wadi Murabba'at texts
P	Pesher (commentary)
Q	Qumran
1Q,2Q,etc.	Numbered caves of Qumran, yielding written material; followed by abbreviation of biblical or apocryphal book.
QL	Qumran Literature
1QapGen	Genesis Apocryphon of Qumran Cave 1
1QH	*Hodayot* (Thanksgiving Hymns) from Qumran Cave 1
1QIsa[a, b]	First or second copy of Isaiah from Qumran Cave 1
1QpHab	Pesher on Habakkuk from Qumran Cave 1
1QM	*Milhamah* (War Scroll)
1QS	*Serek Hayyahad* (Rule of the Community, Manual of Discipline)
1QSa	Appendix A (Rule of the Congregation) to 1QS
1QSb	Appendix B (Blessings) to 1QS
3Q15	Copper Scroll from Qumran Cave 3
4QFlor	Florilegium (or Eschatological Midrashim) from Qumran Cave 4
4Qmess ar	Aramaic "Messianic" text from Qumran Cave 4
4QPrNab	Prayer of Nabonidus from Qumran Cave 4
4QTest	Testimonia text from Qumran Cave 4
4QTLevi	Testament of Levi from Qumran Cave 4
4QPhyl	Phylacteries from Qumran Cave 4
11QMelch	Melchizedek text from Qumran Cave 11
11QtgJob	Targum of Job from Qumran Cave 11

TRANSLITERATIONS

Hebrew

א = ʾ	ד = ḏ	י = y	ס = s	ר = r
בּ = b	ה = h	כּ = k	ע = ʿ	שׂ = ś
ב = ḇ	ו = w	כ = ḵ	פּ = p	שׁ = š
גּ = g	ז = z	ל = l	פ = p̄	תּ = t
ג = ḡ	ח = ḥ	מ = m	צ = ṣ	ת = ṯ
דּ = d	ט = ṭ	נ = n	ק = q	

(ה)◌ָ = â (h)	◌ָ = ā	◌ַ = a	◌ֲ = ᵃ
◌ֵי = ê	◌ֵ = ē	◌ֶ = e	◌ֱ = ᵉ
◌ִי = î	◌ֹ = ō	◌ִ = i	◌ְ = ᵉ (*if vocal*)
וֹ = ô		◌ָ = o	◌ֳ = ᵒ
וּ = û		◌ֻ = u	

Aramaic

ʾ b g d h w z ḥ ṭ y k l m n s ʿ p ṣ q r ś š t

Arabic

ʾ b t ṯ ǧ ḥ ḫ d ḏ r z s š ṣ ḍ ṭ ẓ ʿ ġ f q k l m n h w y

Ugaritic

ʾ b g d ḏ h w z ḥ ḫ ṭ ẓ y k l m n s ś ʿ ġ ṗ ṣ q r š t ṯ

Greek

α	—	a	π	—	p	αι	—	ai
β	—	b	ρ	—	r	αὐ	—	au
γ	—	g	σ,ς	—	s	ει	—	ei
δ	—	d	τ	—	t	εὐ	—	eu
ε	—	e	υ	—	y	ηὐ	—	ēu
ζ	—	z	φ	—	ph	οι	—	oi
η	—	ē	χ	—	ch	οὐ	—	ou
θ	—	th	ψ	—	ps	υι	—	hui
ι	—	i	ω	—	ō			
κ	—	k				ῥ	—	rh
λ	—	l	γγ	—	ng	‘	—	h
μ	—	m	γκ	—	nk			
ν	—	n	γξ	—	nx	ᾳ	—	ā
ξ	—	x	γχ	—	nch	ῃ	—	ē
ο	—	o				ῳ	—	ō

1 THESSALONIANS

Robert L. Thomas

1 THESSALONIANS

Introduction

1. Background
2. Unity
3. Authorship and Canonicity
4. Date
5. Place of Origin and Destination
6. Occasion
7. Purpose
8. Theological Values
9. Bibliography
10. Outline

1. Background

First Thessalonians is understood by many to be the earliest of the Pauline Epistles. One may see a special appropriateness in this because these five chapters reveal so much of Paul's mind and heart. They contain a number of his characteristic doctrinal emphases and show the depth of his feeling for the Christians in Thessalonica.

Having been hindered by divine intervention from going south into the province of Asia and north into Bithynia (Acts 16:6, 7), Paul arrived at Troas probably in late March or early April of A.D. 49. From Troas, the westernmost city of Asia Minor, he was directed in a vision to cross the Aegean Sea into Macedonia and to take the gospel there for the first time (Acts 16:9). That he did (Acts 16:10, 11) was one of the crucial events in history because through it the gospel moved to the west and the evangelization of Europe began. Arriving at the port of Neapolis after a two-day voyage, the missionary party of Paul, Silas, Luke, and Timothy left almost immediately on the single-day journey of ten miles toward the larger city of Philippi to the north.

The successful mission at Philippi (Acts 16:12–40) lasted about two months. Then, leaving Luke and possibly Timothy behind, Paul and Silas left Philippi under pressure from the city officials and went westward toward Thessalonica, a major center about one hundred miles or a five-day walk away. It must have been a painful journey because of what they had suffered while in prison at Philippi (Acts 16:22–24; 1 Thess 2:2). En route they followed the famous Egnatian Way, which crossed Macedonia from east to west, and passed through Amphipolis and then through Apollonia (Acts 17:1). These two cities were apparently not suitable points for evangelism, so Paul and Silas continued to Thessalonica, a city founded by the Macedonian general Cassander in 315 B.C. and named after the step-sister of Alexander the Great.

At Thessalonica they found the circumstances suitable for settling down to preach for a time. The city was of good size, perhaps only about a third smaller than Salonika, its present-day counterpart, which has a population of about 300,000. Its location was conducive to commerce. It had a good natural harbor at the head of Thermaic Gulf and east of the mouth of the Auxius River. Traffic to and from the rich agricultural plains in the interior fed through this port and in both directions on the Egnatian Way. The city attracted sufficient Jewish merchants of the dispersion to account for the presence of a well-established synagogue within it (Acts 17:1).

Thessalonica was a free city ruled by its own council of citizens. Since 146 B.C. it had been the seat of Roman government for all Macedonia, earning for itself the description "the mother of all Macedon." The city was administered by five or six "officials" known as "politarchs" (Acts 17:6). For some years the accuracy of this title in Luke's account of the events was questioned; now it is universally conceded on the basis of nineteen inscriptions that clearly show the use of "politarch" in Macedonian governmental organization.[1]

Paul thought of Thessalonica as the next suitable place for planting the gospel. The presence of a synagogue offered an obvious place to begin (Acts 17:1–4). So he pursued his approach of proving from the OT that the Messiah must suffer and be raised and that Jesus is this Messiah. In the meantime, he could readily follow his own trade of manufacturing the goat's-hair cloth that was a prominent part of the local economy (cf. Acts 18:3; 1 Thess 2:9; 2 Thess 3:8). For three consecutive Sabbaths Paul spoke in the synagogue, but met with the usual Jewish resistance. Luke's description of the events may be interpreted as meaning that the resistance forced him to leave the city immediately.[2] On the other hand, we may understand that he continued his work in the city for some time after it was terminated in the synagogue.[3]

Three points make the latter alternative more probable: (1) Paul engaged in gainful employment at Thessalonica (1 Thess 2:9; 2 Thess 3:8). Two to three weeks are not sufficient time for settling into a trade and freeing converts from the burden of supporting their missionaries. Besides, Paul used his working as proof of his self-sacrifice for them, something he could hardly have done during a limited stay. (2) Upon his departure from Thessalonica, he left a thriving church—not one still in the throes of separation from the local synagogue. Indeed, by the time he left, this church included many Gentiles fresh from their heathen idolatry (1 Thess 1:9). They could not have been won through a synagogue ministry. (3) Before leaving, Paul had received at least two special gifts from Philippi a hundred miles or five days away. It is difficult to crowd all this into two or three weeks.[4]

A good number of Jews, God-fearing Gentiles, and prominent women responded to the synagogue ministry, including Jason at whose home Paul was entertained (Acts 17:4–9). Many others, principally Gentiles, became Christians in the weeks following (1 Thess 1:9). Numbered among the converts in the city were probably Aristarchus and Secundus (Acts 19:29; 20:4; 27:2) and perhaps Gaius (Acts 19:29) and Demas (2 Tim 4:10). After approximately three months, the Christian assembly was of considerable size, and the Jews became unbearably jealous. So they instigated riots to force the politarchs to rule against the Christians, whom they accused of upsetting society and opposing Caesar's decrees (Acts 17:5–9). Jason and several other Christians were brought in for a hearing. The city officials, however, stood firm under pressure and eventually let Jason and the others go. Though not personally involved in this incident,

---

[1]J.A. Thompson, *The Bible and Archaeology* (Grand Rapids: Eerdmans, 1972), pp. 388, 389.

[2]Donald Guthrie, *New Testament Introduction* (Downers Grove, Ill.: Inter-Varsity, 1970), p. 568.

[3]George Ogg, *The Odyssey of Paul* (Old Tappan, N.J.: Revell, 1968), pp. 121, 122.

[4]Willi Marxen, *Introduction to the New Testament* (Philadelphia: Fortress, 1968), p. 33.

Paul, Silas, and perhaps Timothy (if by now he had joined them from Philippi) knew it was time to leave so as to avoid bringing additional hardship on their brothers in Christ (Acts 17:10).

From Thessalonica they traveled west for two and a half days (fifty miles) to Berea. Here their synagogue ministry was favorably received for about seven weeks. It might have continued even longer if adversaries from Thessalonica had not heard of their success and come to disrupt their preaching. At this point Paul was forced to go on to Athens, but since Silas and Timothy had not been so conspicuous, they were able to remain at Berea (Acts 17:11-15).

The Berean brothers conducted Paul all the way to Athens, going first to the nearby coast (Acts 17:14) and then catching a ship for a one-week voyage to the city. A three-hundred mile overland trip to Athens, as certain Western and Byzantine readings imply,[5] is not probable. Paul's physical condition and his personal safety were too much a concern for his escorts to have taken this risk.[6] The party probably arrived in Athens late in October, A.D. 49.

Paul gave the returning Bereans instruction to have Silas and Timothy join him immediately at Athens (Acts 17:15), which they did (1 Thess 3:1). The two were then sent back to Macedonia, Timothy's responsibility being to encourage the Thessalonian Christians and bring back a report about them. If Timothy joined Paul at Athens by late November, it would have been about three months since Paul had left Thessalonica. He had become quite concerned about the converts there and at great personal sacrifice commissioned Timothy to strengthen them and find out how they were faring under persecution (1 Thess 3:1-5). Silas was probably sent on a similar mission to Philippi.

While the two men were away, Paul had a relatively fruitless ministry at Athens (Acts 17:16-34). Leaving there, he went to another Achaian city, Corinth, where he enjoyed a spiritually prosperous eighteen-to-twenty-month ministry. If the stay in Athens was about two months, his arrival in Corinth must have been in December, A.D. 49, or January, A.D. 50. If we allow time for Timothy's round trip to Thessalonica on foot and also time for his ministry in Thessalonica, then he and Silas probably returned to Paul from Macedonia in the spring of A.D. 50 (Acts 18:5; 1 Thess 3:6, 7). Timothy's report on Thessalonica was so encouraging that Paul wrote 1 Thessalonians almost immediately.

Luke's accuracy in describing Thessalonian history has been questioned on three counts.[7] The claim that Acts does not account for the presence of Gentile converts fresh from idolatry (1 Thess 1:9) is met by observing that Acts allows for a longer ministry than just two or three weeks in the synagogue (Acts 17:1-9). Subsequently, Paul's ministry became more oriented to the Gentiles. It is also claimed that 1 Thessalonians 3:4 indicates no persecution in connection with the founding of the church, contrary to Acts 17:5-8. This objection can be met by questioning whether 3:4 as well as 1:6 and 2:14, does not mean that Paul and his helpers experienced such trouble from the beginning. Verse 4 of chapter 3 could just as well speak of tribulations continuing into the future as of their beginning in the future. A third objection to the account in Acts 17:1-9 concerns its limitation of the length of Paul's stay to the time necessary for three Sabbath appearances. First Thessalonians necessitates a much longer period. This is not a valid criticism, however, because, as shown above, Acts allows for the longer period.

---

[5]F.F. Bruce, *The Acts of the Apostles* (London: Tyndale, 1952), p. 330.
[6]Ogg, *Odyssey of Paul*, p. 124.
[7]Marxen, *Introduction to the New Testament*, pp. 32, 33.

2. Unity

The unity of 1 Thessalonians has not been strongly questioned. Minor objections have been raised to 2:14–16 or some part of it. This passage is suspected of being a gloss added after the siege of A.D. 70.[8] No manuscript basis can be found for this supposition, nor is it necessary to assign the words to anyone but Paul. His situation is sufficient to account for an uncharacteristic outburst against his fellow Jews. Also to see direct reference in 2:14–16 to Jerusalem's fall is unfounded.

Another question about the unity of the Epistle involves two thanksgivings (1:2ff.; 2:13ff.) and two prayers (3:11–13; 5:23). These supposedly signal the beginnings and endings of what were originally two epistles. However, the various schemes proposed for a division of 1 Thessalonians into two epistles have not been persuasive.[9]

3. Authorship and Canonicity

Pauline authorship of 1 Thessalonians has not been successfully challenged. Only extremists such as the Tübingen scholars have questioned it. Morton belongs in this category.[10] Ancient testimony favors Paul. The canons of Marcion and Muratori have the Epistle among Paul's works. Irenaeus quotes it by name, and Tertullian and Clement of Alexandria acknowledge it as Pauline. Its recognition as canonical came quite early throughout Christendom, as attested by its inclusion in the Old Latin and Old Syriac versions.[11]

4. Date

Paul's initial visit to Corinth probably terminated shortly after Gallio became proconsul in that city (Acts 18:11–18). An inscription at Delphi in central Greece dates a proclamation of Roman Emperor Claudius some time early in A.D. 52. The inscription calls Gallio proconsul of Asia at the time, probably meaning that he had begun his term in the summer of 51. Paul's trial before Gallio appears to have come when he was new to the city, because the Jewish accusers tried to take advantage of his inexperience (Acts 18:12, 13). Paul's departure from Corinth was therefore in the late summer or early fall of A.D. 51. Since he spent eighteen to twenty months in Corinth (Acts 18:11, 18), we may reckon that he arrived there from Athens late A.D. 49 or early A.D. 50.

Timothy joined him from Thessalonica a few months later (see Background). After Paul's departure from the Thessalonian city, news about the Christians there had spread far and wide (1 Thess 1:8, 9). Also, a number of converts to Christ had died (1 Thess 4:13). From the late summer of A.D. 49 till the spring of A.D. 50 is enough time for these things to have happened, as well as for Timothy to have completed his mission. Hence, we may place Paul's writing of 1 Thessalonians some time in the spring of A.D. 50.

---

[8]Moffat, EGT, 4:11, 29.

[9]Ernest Best, *A Commentary on the First and Second Epistle to the Thessalonians* (New York: Harper, 1972), pp. 30–35.

[10]A.Q. Morton and James McLemon, *Paul, the Man and the Myth* (New York: Harper, 1966), pp. 93, 94.

[11]Guthrie, *New Testament Introduction*, p. 567.

5. Place of Origin and Destination

In light of the foregoing discussion under "Background," there is little doubt that Paul was at Corinth when he wrote 1 Thessalonians (Acts 18:5; 1 Thess 3:6). Suppositions as to an Ephesian origin fail to explain the presence of all three men—Paul, Silas, and Timothy—when the letter was written. Silas is not known to have been with Paul and Timothy after the initial Corinthian mission (Acts 18:5).[12] As for the traditional destination of Thessalonica, it has never been seriously challenged.

6. Occasion

Elements of Timothy's report (1 Thess 3:6, 7) undoubtedly prompted Paul to write 1 Thessalonians. The most significant of these included (1) encouraging words as to the spiritual stamina of the Thessalonian converts in the face of fierce opposition (3:6–10), (2) an alarming report of efforts to undermine Paul's reputation and question his sincerity (2:1–12, 17–20), (3) confusion and discouragement in regard to the return of the Lord and the part of the dead in it (4:13–5:11), and (4) areas of individual and community life that needed improvement (4:1–12; 5:12–22).

7. Purpose

In response to Timothy's report, Paul had three chief aims in writing the Epistle: (1) to express satisfaction and thanks to God for the healthy spiritual condition of the church (1:2–10), (2) to make a strong case against the false insinuations against himself and his associates (2:1–3:13), and (3) to suggest specific ways in which already strongly Christian behavior of the Thessalonians could be improved as they continued to seek God-approved holiness (4:1–5:24).

8. Theological Values

The two Thessalonian Epistles contribute much toward our understanding of Paul's theological outlook. In them he touches briefly on a number of themes: the doctrine of inspiration and authority of Scripture (1, 2:13; 2, 2:15; 3:6, 17); the doctrine of one true God (1, 1:9) existing in three Persons (1, 1:1, 5, 6; 4:8; 5:19; 2, 1:1, 2; 2:13); the doctrine of Jesus Christ's deity (1, 3:11, 12; 2, 2:16, 17); the doctrine of salvation based on Christ's death (1, 4:14; 5:9, 10; 2, 2:13, 14) and the believer's union and identification with Christ (1, 1:1; 5:5; 2, 1:1); and the doctrine of sanctification as relates to personal purity (1, 4:3–8), love (1, 4:9, 10), vocational diligence (1, 4:11, 12; 5:12–15; 2, 3:6–15), motivation (1, 5:16–18), and other areas. Also by his example he teaches important lessons on discipling others (1, 2:1–12, 17–20; 3:1–5) and prayer (1, 3:11–13; 5:23, 24; 2, 1:11, 12; 2:16, 17; 3:5, 16).

Far and away the largest theological contribution of the Epistles lies in what they say about eschatology. Perhaps the best way to summarize this is to survey Paul's use in the Epistles of various terms and themes relating to the end time. "Coming" or "presence"

---

[12]Marxen, *Introduction to the New Testament*, pp. 33, 34.

(*parousia*) is the most frequent term, sometimes referring to an examination of Christians before the Father and Christ (1, 2:19; 3:13; 5:23), sometimes to the moment of the Lord's meeting Christians in the air (1, 4:15; 2, 2:1), and sometimes to Christ's triumphant conquest of "the lawless one" (2, 2:8). From all this the dead in Christ will not be excluded (1, 4:13–18). "Revelation" (*apokalupsis*) occurs only once (2, 1:7) and spans the entire period beginning with the Lord's coming from heaven for the saints till his appearance on earth to put down those who do not know God and those who do not obey the gospel of Christ. Between these two points is a time of God's "wrath" (*orgē*) on earth (1, 1:10; 2:16; 5:9). This outworking of God's "vengeance" (*ekdikēsis*) against earth's rebels (2, 1:8) is the initial phase of the day of the Lord and may come at any moment (1, 5:2, 3). It will mean "tribulation" (*thlipsis*) to the unrepentant (2, 1:6)—a "sudden destruction," comparable to a pregnant woman's labor pains, that will culminate in "eternal destruction" or separation from the returning Lord and his glory (1, 5:3; 2, 1:9). While suffering through the period of wrath, the rebels will unite in a great apostate movement (*apostasia*) and support the rise of a great figure who advocates opposition to God's laws (2, 2:3, 4). They will be captivated by his deluding words and activities (2, 2:9–11). His high point in opposing God will be the abomination "that makes desolate" (Dan. 12:11) in the rebuilt Jerusalem temple (2, 2:4).

The "righteous judgment" (*dikaia krisis*) of God assures a devastating penalty against the ungodly, but also guarantees that believers will be counted worthy of God's kingdom (*basileia*) (1, 5:24, 2, 1:5), find rest from hardships (2, 1:7) and experience salvation and glory in lieu of the terrible fate awaiting their persecutors (1, 1:10; 5:9; 2, 1:7, 10, 12; 2:13, 14). Hence, they have every reason to persevere because they anticipate a deliverer who at any moment may summon them to meet him in the air (1, 1:10; 4:15–17; 5:4, 9; 2, 1:4–10). Anticipating that the Lord will return soon does not, however, release Christians from their usual everyday responsibilities. On the contrary, they must continue working and providing for their own support (1, 4:11, 12; 5:14; 2, 3:6–15).

9. Bibliography

Auberlen, C.A., and C.J. Riggenbach. *The Two Epistles of Paul to the Thessalonians* (Lange's Commentary), tr. by John Lille, New York: Scribner, Armstrong and Co., 1868.

Bailey, John, and James Clark. "I and II Thessalonians," *IB*, Vol. 11, 1955.

Best, Ernest. *A Commentary on the First and Second Epistles to the Thessalonians* (Harper's New Testament Commentaries). New York: Harper and Row, 1972.

Charles, R.H. *Eschatology*. New York: Schocken Books, 1963.

Ellicott, Charles J. *St. Paul's Epistles to the Thessalonians*. London: Longman, Green, Longman, Roberts and Green, 1880.

Frame, James Everett. *The Epistles of St. Paul to the Thessalonians* (ICC). Edinburgh: T. & T. Clark, 1912.

Fuller, Reginald H. *A Critical Introduction to the New Testament*. London: Gerald Duckworth, 1966.

———. *The Mission and Achievement of Jesus*. Chicago: Alec R. Allenson, Inc., 1954.

Guthrie, Donald. *New Testament Introduction*. Downers Grove, Ill.: Inter-Varsity, 1970.

Hendriksen, William. *I and II Thessalonians* (New Testament Commentary). Grand Rapids: Baker Book House, 1955.

Hiebert, D. Edmond. *The Thessalonian Epistles. A Call to Readiness*. Chicago: Moody Press, 1971.

Hogg, C.F., and W.E. Vine. *The Epistles of Paul the Apostle to the Thessalonians*. Glasgow: Pickering and Inglis, 1929.

Jeremias, J. *Unkown Sayings of Jesus*, tr. by Reginald H. Fuller. New York: Macmillan, 1957.

Kümmel, W.G. *Promise and Fulfillment*, tr. by Dorothy M. Barton. Naperville, Ill.: Alec R. Allenson, Inc., 1957.

Lenski, R.C.H. *The Interpretation of St. Paul's Epistles to the Colossians, to the Thessalonians, to Timothy, to Titus and to Philemon.* Columbus, Ohio: The Wartburg Press, 1946.

Lightfoot, J.B. *Notes on the Epistles of St. Paul.* Grand Rapids: Zondervan (1957 reprint), 1895.

Lünemann, Gottlieb. *Critical and Exegetical Handbook to the Epistles of St. Paul to the Thessalonians* (Meyer's Commentary), tr. by Paton J. Gloag. Edinburgh: T. & T. Clark, 1885.

Manson, T.W. *Studies in the Gospels and Epistles.* Manchester: University of Manchester, 1962.

Marxen, Willi. *Introduction to the New Testament*, tr. by G. Buswell. Philadelphia: Fortress, 1968.

Milligan, George. *St. Paul's Epistles to the Thessalonians* (ICC). London: Macmillan, 1908.

Morris, Leon. *The First and Second Epistles to the Thessalonians* (NIC). Grand Rapids: Eerdmans, 1959.

Olshausen, Hermann. *Biblical Commentary on St. Paul's Epistles to the Galatians, Ephesians, Colossians, and Thessalonians.* Edinburgh: T. & T. Clark, 1851.

Perrin, Norman. *The New Testament, An Introduction.* New York: Harcourt Brace Jovanovich, 1974.

10. Outline

I. Salutation (1:1)

II. Thanksgiving for the Thessalonians (1:2–10)
  A. The Manner of Giving Thanks—Praying (1:2)
  B. The Circumstances of Giving Thanks—Remembering (1:3)
  C. The Cause for Giving Thanks—Knowing (1:4–10)
    1. The impressions of the missionaries (1:4, 5)
    2. The effect on the Thessalonians (1:6–10)
      a. Their transformation (1:6, 7)
      b. Their witness (1:8–10)

III. Vindication Before the Thessalonians (2:1–3:13)
  A. Vindication Through Methods (2:1–12)
    1. Preaching, replete with power (2:1, 2)
    2. Preaching, removed from untruth (2:3, 4)
    3. Preaching, reinforced by godly concern (2:5–12)
      a. Evidenced by the absence of lower motives (2:5–7a)
      b. Evidenced by the presence of higher motives (2:7b–12)
  B. Vindication Through Their Thanksgiving (2:13–16)
    1. For the ready acceptance of the Word of God (2:13)
    2. For their endurance under persecution (2:14–16)
  C. Vindication Through Their Separation (2:17–3:13)
    1. Desire to go to them (2:17–20)
    2. Sending Timothy to them (3:1–5)
    3. Delight over their progress (3:6–10)
    4. Seeking direction for them (3:11–13)

IV. Exhortation to the Thessalonians (4:1–5:22)
  A. Exhortation Regarding Personal Needs (4:1–12)
    1. Continual improvement (4:1, 2)
    2. Sexual purity (4:3–8)
    3. Filial love (4:9, 10)
    4. Individual independence (4:11, 12)
  B. Exhortation Regarding Eschatological Needs (4:13–5:11)
    1. The dead in Christ (4:13–18)
    2. The day of the Lord (5:1–11)
      a. The coming of the day (5:1, 2)
      b. Unbelievers and the day (5:3)
      c. Believers and the day (5:4–11)
  C. Exhortation Regarding Ecclesiastical Needs (5:12–22)
    1. Responsibilities to the leaders (5:12, 13)
    2. Responsibilities to all (5:14, 15)
    3. Responsibilities to oneself (5:16–18)
    4. Responsibilities to public worship (5:19–22)

V. Conclusion (5:23–28)
  A. Petition for the Thessalonians (5:23, 24)
  B. Reciprocation by the Thessalonians (5:25–27)
  C. Benediction (5:28)

Text and Exposition

I. Salutation

1:1

> [1]Paul, Silas and Timothy,
>
> To the church of the Thessalonians, who are in God the Father and the Lord Jesus Christ:
> Grace and peace to you.

1 This salutation follows the form Paul used in all his Epistles and is in the same style as that of other letters of his time. It contains three elements: the writer, the recipient, and the greeting or salutation proper.

The first element of this particular salutation contains not one, but three names: Paul, Silas (Silvanus), and Timothy. "Paul" is a Greek name meaning "little." In Acts Luke preserves the Hebrew name "Saul" up to the point of the apostle's encounter with the Roman official Sergius Paulus (Acts 13:9) and also when he reports Paul's calling himself "Saul" when he retold his experience on the Damascus Road (Acts 22:7, 13; 26:14).

Obviously absent is the official title "apostle" Paul used in all his other Epistles to churches except 2 Thessalonians and Philippians. A reasonable explanation of this is that no note of authority was necessary in letters addressed to the Macedonian churches, where his apostolic position never seems to have been questioned as it was elsewhere (e.g., Galatia, Corinth). This is not to say that there was no opposition to Paul in Thessalonica. On the contrary, that there was opposition is evident from his self-vindication (1 Thess 2–3). The opposition, however, never became overt as in other places and never specifically attacked his right to apostleship.

The second name included among the writers is that of Silas. The spelling found in v.1 is actually "Silvanus," probably the Roman transliteration of the Jewish name given the Greek transliteration "Silas." In Acts, Luke consistently uses "Silas" (Acts 15:22, 27, 32, 34, 40; 16:19, 25, 29; 17:4, 10, 14, 15; 18:5); Paul always uses "Silvanus" (2 Cor 1:19; 2 Thess 1:1). At any rate, this colleague of Paul was most likely a Jew by birth, a gifted prophet, and highly esteemed among the Jerusalem Christians (Acts 15:22, 32). That he inclined toward the Hellenistic wing of Palestinian Christianity is supported on several grounds, such as, his hearty concurrence with the Jerusalem Council's decision concerning Gentile believers (Acts 15:22–32), his Roman citizenship (Acts 16:37), and his being chosen as Paul's fellow worker on the second missionary journey (Acts 15:40–18:6). After the mission in Corinth, we find no further word of Silas's connection with Paul. He probably became associated with Peter, especially in the composition and sending of 1 Peter (1 Peter 5:12).

As an associate in the founding of the Thessalonian church, he endured cruel beatings, imprisonment, and pursuit by an angry mob (Acts 16:23–25; 17:5). Silas was known for his absolute reliability and his faithfulness in risking his life in the service of Christ (Acts 15:25–27).

Paul's other colleague at this time was Timothy. This young man, having helped in Philippi, had apparently remained behind when Paul had left that city (Acts 16:40). His name is not included in the account of the founding of the Thessalonian church (Acts 17:1–10), but he presumably joined Paul and Silas at Thessalonica later. (For further information about Timothy, see the commentaries on 1 and 2 Timothy.)

The second element in the salutation is the reference to the recipient of the letter—"the church of the Thessalonians who are in God the Father and the Lord Jesus Christ." *Ekklēsia* ("church," "assembly") was the term applied to many types of public gatherings in the ancient Roman world, whether civil or religious. From this general sense, which is found also in LXX, there developed the technical meaning of an assembly of believers in Christ. The development of a technical meaning did not come at once, however. In fact, the earliest occurrence of the word in Acts is in 5:11 (*ekklēsia* in TR at Acts 2:47 is not found in more reliable MSS). Some have suggested that by the time this first Epistle was written, the word was still general and needed qualifying ("in God the Father and the Lord Jesus Christ") to distinguish it from other assemblies in the city (Frame, pp. 68, 69). They argue in this connection that Paul saw no need to identify *ekklēsia* thus in his later salutations (cf. also 1 Thess 2:14). But, contrary to this explanation, James used the word at an earlier date (c. A.D. 47) without qualification (James 5:14).

Some have not admitted this narrower scope of *ekklēsia*, on the grounds that the NT church is merely a development of the OT church and that they find in Acts 7:38 and Hebrews 2:12 a technical use of *ekklēsia* for God's people in the OT (cf. Deut 4:10; 23:2 and elsewhere in LXX where the word depicts Israel as a community). This reasoning, however, does not allow for the special use of the word in the NT in its preponderant reference to people from all races in the body of Christ beginning with Pentecost. This people is always distinguished from Israel and her ongoing purpose in God's plan.

In general usage, *ekklēsia* had lost some of its etymological force of "called out." Yet there is good possibility that something of this meaning pertains to the special group composing the Christian church (Acts 15:14; Rom 9:24). They are "called out" from previous relationships so as to constitute a body with special relation to God (cf. 1 Cor 10:32).

Sometimes *ekklēsia* designates all Christendom and is a synonym for the body of Christ (Col 1:18, 24). At other times it is a particular assembly in a particular location (Rom 16:5; 1 Cor 16:19; Col 4:15). Elsewhere, as here, it denotes all the assemblies in a single city (Rom 16:1; 1 Cor 1:2).

"In God the Father and the Lord Jesus Christ" tells of the spiritual quality of the believers. The translation of the phrase by the relative clause "who are in God the Father" gives more particularized information as to which *ekklēsia* Paul addresses within the city. It is not a pagan or nonreligious assembly (cf. "God the Father"). It is not a Jewish assembly (cf. "the Lord Jesus Christ"). It is distinctly "in Christ Jesus" (2:14). Being in union with the Father and Christ meant a new sphere of life, on an infinitely higher plane.

It should not be overlooked that the deity of the Son is taught here. Combining "God the Father" and "the Lord Jesus Christ" under one preposition demonstrates Jesus' equality with the Father and consequently his deity. To deny this fact (Best, p. 63) is to approach v.1 in an unnatural way, especially in light of *kyriō* ("Lord"—frequently used in reference to deity) and *Christō* ("Christ"—the title of Israel's divine Messiah).

"Grace to you and peace" (the Greek word order) recalls the normal Greek and Hebrew greetings. Paul coined a slight variation to connote the deepened Christian meaning. *Charis* ("grace") goes beyond *chairein* ("greetings"; cf. Acts 15:23; 23:26; James 1:1) in highlighting unmerited benefits given by God to the believer in Christ. Through grace lost men are saved from their sins in the eyes of a holy God by a transaction completely free of charge. Grace, however, does not cease at the point of salvation. It continually issues in privileges. These the writer wishes for his readers.

One of these benefits is reflected in "peace" (cf. Judg 19:20) but with a deeper meaning than among the ancient Hebrews. Differences separating God from his creatures had for centuries worked against peaceful relationships, but with the entrance of grace in its fullness through the coming of Christ (John 1:17) the ultimate basis for resolving this conflict and establishing harmony between God and man was laid. Because of this harmony man can also enjoy inward wholeness and tranquility.

Notes

1 The adjectival function of ἐν θεῷ πατρὶ καὶ κυρίῳ Ἰησοῦ Χριστῷ (en theō patri kai kyriō Iēsou Christō, "in God the Father and the Lord Jesus Christ") could have been shown more clearly with τῇ (tē, "the [one]") introducing it. This would have made perfectly clear its relationship to τῇ ἐκκλησίᾳ (tē ekklēsia, "the church"). It is doubtful that the gen. Θεσσαλονικέων (Thessalonikeōn, "of the Thessalonians") is of sufficient import to carry the weight of this phrase. Without the article, however, the function is almost the same, the only difference being added emphasis on unity and closeness as the text stands (Lightfoot, pp. 7, 8; Milligan, p. 4; Frame, pp. 69, 70). An adverbial force for the phrase is dubious—i.e., understanding a word like χαίρειν (chairein, "greetings") or γράφουσι (graphousi, "writing") before the phrase. The former is excluded by the χάρις (charis, "grace") to follow. The latter idea of "writing in God the Father..." is unparalleled elsewhere in Paul.

The phrase ἀπὸ θεῷ πατρὸς ἡμῶν καὶ κυρίου Ἰησοῦ Χριστοῦ (apo theō patros hēmōn kai kyriou Iēsou Christou, "from God our Father and the Lord Jesus Christ") following εἰρήνη (eirēnē, "peace"), while finding support in a few strong MSS, cannot be accepted here (but cf. 2 Thess 1:2). The reading that closes v.1 with eirēnē finds stronger support geographically and chronologically among the witnesses. It is therefore preferred.

II. Thanksgiving for the Thessalonians (1:2–10)

A. The Manner of Giving Thanks—Praying

1:2

²We always thank God for all of you, mentioning you in our prayers.

2 It was Paul's practice to begin his letters by thanking God for his readers. The only exception is the letter to the Galatians, where indignation and disappointment ruled out gratitude. The Thessalonians, however, did not disappoint him. Paul found much in their lives to be grateful for. In fact, he kept on being grateful, as the present tense of the verb "thank" and the adverb "always" show. Paul was not alone in gratitude. The pronoun "we" includes Silas and Timothy as sharing his appreciation. The verb must be understood as genuinely plural because the names of Paul's two colleagues immediately precede it. Of course, the first person plural need not always refer to more persons than the writer. There is such a thing as the editorial "we" in Paul's style (cf. 2:18; 3:1).

By thanking God at the beginning of the epistle, Paul lifts the thought above the human level and rises above the conventional opening of letters of his time. He is not trying to win the Thessalonians over by rhetorical flattery (cf. 2:5). On the contrary, he is sincerely trying to give the ultimate credit to the One from whom spiritual progress comes. When Christians realize their complete dependence on God and keep this in clear focus, then and only then are they capable of moving on to greater spiritual exploits such as those spoken of later in this Epistle (Milligan, p. 5).

"All of you" expresses Paul's desire not to exclude any of the Thessalonian believers. Every single one of them, no matter how obscure, had certain qualities worth thanking God for.

The latter part of v.2 is the first of three participial phrases that elaborate on the thanksgiving. "Mentioning you in our prayers" tells how Paul and his colleagues expressed their thanks. *Mneian poiein* ("making mention") is never used by Paul except in conjunction with prayer. Making mention of his readers at prayer times enabled him not only to thank God for their progress, but also to intercede for their advancement in the gospel. The full meaning of "in our prayers" is "on the occasion of our prayers." Paul is pointing to the times when, as he prayed with Silas and Timothy, they had remembered the Thessalonian believers one by one with gratitude and intercession.

Notes

2 The case for connecting περὶ πάντων (*peri pantōn*, "for all") with μνείαν ποιούμενοι (*mneian poioumenoi*, "making mention") instead of with εὐχαριστοῦμεν (*eucharistoumen*, "we give thanks") is quite unimpressive, as the finite verb clause would be stripped of its major content in favor of the subordinate participial clause. Hence, a comma should come after ὑμῶν (*hymōn*, "you"), not after πάντοτε (*pantote*, "always").

B. *The Circumstances of Giving Thanks—Remembering*

   1:3

   ³We continually remember before our God and Father your work produced by faith, your labor prompted by love, and your endurance inspired by hope in our Lord Jesus Christ.

3 The *mnēmoneuontes* ("remembering") clause in v.3 tells us the occasion when Paul and his colleagues thanked God. This was whenever they recalled the threefold nature of the Thessalonians' progress—a recollection so frequent as to be "continual." Of course, Paul does not mean that they thought of nothing but the Thessalonians. He rather uses the hyperbolic "continually" to indicate intense interest.

The words "before our God and Father" show the sincerity of this remembrance in prayer. Some in the Thessalonian church had questioned Paul's motives in dealing with them. So at the very outset, he dispels this suspicion and confronts it more directly in chapters 2–3 (cf. "God is our witness," 2:5, and "You are witnesses, and so is God," 2:10; cf. 3:9). To interpret "before our God and Father" (which comes at the end of v.3 in the Greek word order) in connection with "hope in our Lord Jesus Christ," as some have done, is to see in the phrase the heavenly scene where Christian hope will be culminated. While favored by the Greek word order, this interpretation fails to explain why Paul would leave the relation of the phrase introduced by *emprosthen* ("before") to *elpidos* ("hope") so ambiguous when he could have clarified it by an additional article (*tēs*) before the preposition. Hence, the phrase is best taken as an adverbial modifier with *mnēmoneuontes* ("remembering"; NIV, "remember").

The substance of what Paul and his colleagues remember about the Thessalonians is summed up in three words: "work," "labor," and "endurance." In turn, these three reflect three qualities of Christian character: "faith," "love," and "hope." (For other appearances of this familiar combination of graces, see 5:8; 1 Cor 13:13; Gal 5:5, 6; Col 1:4, 5; Heb 6:10–12; 10:22–24; 1 Peter 1:21, 22.) The exact nature of the first expression, "work produced by faith," has been identified as being either direct missionary work (cf. 1:8), acts of goodness toward others (cf. 4:9, 10), or loyalty to Christ in the face of severe persecution (1:6; 3:3–4, 8; cf. Best, p. 68). Though the second possibility overlaps the "labor prompted by love," it is probably an overrefinement to eliminate any one of these three from the scope of "work produced by faith." Faith manifests itself on a very broad front, so "work" should be left as general as possible.

For Paul to appreciate works is not surprising. Even in Romans, so notable for its repudiation of any system of justification by works (Rom 3:20, 21, 28; 4:4–6), Paul finds occasion to speak of *ergon* as the essential fruit of the believing life (Rom 2:7; 13:3; 14:20; cf. 1 Cor 3:14; Eph 2:10; Titus 3:1). This emphasis sets him in alignment with James regarding Christian living and the absolute necessity of works' accompanying faith to prove its vitality (James 2:14–26). Indeed, wherever genuine faith is present, it works (Gal 5:6).

Ergou ("work") looks specifically at the work performed. It is the end product. Love's result, *kopou* ("labor"), approximates the meaning of *ergou* but with a distinctive connotation of extraordinary effort expended. Coupled with the product of faith, therefore, is the wearisome toil by which love expends itself. So great is its concern for the object that love does not stop with ordinary effort, but goes the second mile and even beyond for the sake of another. "Labor" sometimes expended itself in providing financial support to sustain a Christian outreach (1 Cor 4:12; 2 Thess 3:8; cf. 1 Thess 2:9). This idea, however, is not prominent in 1:3, where the labor is more distinctly spiritual service— either beneficial efforts to help the sick and hungry or intense devotion to spreading the gospel despite intense persecution (Hendriksen, p. 48), or both (cf. 1 Cor 3:8; 15:10, 58; 2 Cor 10:15; Gal 4:11; Phil 2:16; 1 Thess 3:5). As with faith, so with love, a broad application is probably best. However it showed itself, one thing is certain: a great spirit of self-sacrifice was present, because this is inseparable from Christian love.

The supreme example of such loving self-sacrifice comes from no less than God the Father (John 3:16; 1 John 4:10) and his Son Jesus (John 13:34; 15:12). This is no mere emotional response prompted by the desirability of, or affinity for, the person loved, though feeling certainly is not absent from it. It is ultimately traceable to the will of the one who loves. He determines to love and does so no matter what the condition of the one loved. Such is God's love for man and so must the Christian's love for others be if "labor" for their good is to result. Remembering this attainment of their readers, Paul and his helpers had additional cause for thanking God.

"Endurance" (*hypomonē*) is the third visible fruit that evoked thanksgiving. This is an aggressive and courageous Christian quality, excluding self-pity even when times are hard. Difficulties endurance must cope with consist of trials encountered specifically in living for Jesus Christ. Endurance accepts the seemingly dreary "blind alleys" of Christian experience with a spirit of persistent zeal. It rules out discouragement and goes forward no matter how hopeless the situation. Such endurance is possible only when one is "inspired by hope in our Lord Jesus Christ." "Hope" (*elpis*) is the only adequate incentive for this heroic conduct. Christian anticipation looks to future certainties surrounding the return of "our Lord Jesus Christ." This confidence about the future braces the child of God to face all opposition while persevering and continuing in the spread of the gospel. Jesus' return and the encouragement it is to believers are major themes in both Thessalonian Epistles (1 Thess 1:10; 3:13; 4:13–5:11; 5:23; 2 Thess 1:4, 7, 10; 2:16).

These three Christian virtues—faith, love, and hope—occupied a large place in early analyses of Christian responsibility. The expectation was that in every life faith would work (Gal 5:6; James 2:18), love would labor (Rev 2:2, 4), and hope would endure (Rom 5:2–4; 8:24, 25). This threefold balance probably arose even before Paul's doctrinal stance had matured and perhaps came from the teachings of Christ himself (A.M. Hunter, *Paul and His Predecessors* [London: SCM Press Ltd., 1961], pp. 33–35). Paul's Thessalonian readers had fulfilled this expectation in everyday experience. Upon every remembrance of this success, he and his companions were moved to express gratitude to God.

Notes

3 Whether to understand ἀδιαλείπτως (*adialeiptōs*, "continually") (v.2 of Gr. text) with the previous ποιούμενοι (*poioumenoi*, "making [mention]") clause or with the subsequent μνημονεύοντες (*mnēmoneuontes*, "remembering") presents a difficult choice. The connection of the adverb with prayer elsewhere in Paul (especially Rom 1:9; cf. 1 Thess 2:13; 5:17) argues for the former connection. The cognate adjective's relation to μνείαν (*mneian*, "remembrance") in 2 Tim 1:3 does the same. Yet its immediate juxtaposition with *mnēmoneuontes* and the presence of the ἐπί (*epi*, "on," "in" [v.2]) phrase as another temporal qualification of *poioumenoi* tip the balance in favor of rendering the adverb with v.3: "continually remember."

The ἔμπροσθεν (*emprosthen*, "before") phrase of v.3 resembles the one in 3:9 more than those in 2:19 and 3:13. The latter carry special local connotations because of the forensic nature of their contexts. The idea of personal presence is not required in contexts where the phrase is designed to bring solemnity of expression as here. Furthermore, to read "before our God and Father" with "hope in our Lord Jesus Christ" results in a cumbersome accumulation of phrases quite uncharacteristic of Paul (Best, p. 70). Hence the connection with *mnēmoneuontes* is preferred.

C. *The Cause for Giving Thanks—Knowing (1:4–10)*

1. *The impressions of the missionaries*

1:4, 5

⁴Brothers loved by God, we know that he has chosen you,
⁵because our gospel came to you not simply with words, but also with power, with the Holy Spirit and with deep conviction. You know how we lived among you for your sake.

4,5 The wisdom of beginning a new paragraph at v.4 seems debatable, for it is a third participial clause modifying the subject of *eucharistoumen* ("we thank") (v.2) and in parallel with the subordinate clauses of vv.2b, 3. If v.2b supplies the manner of thanksgiving and v.3 the occasion, v.4 gives its ultimate cause. Intuitive knowledge of the

Thessalonian believers' having been selected by God was the source of the missionaries' constant prayer of thanksgiving.

A touch of tenderness, the first of many in these two Epistles, punctuates Paul's acknowledgment of the election of the Thessalonians. "Brothers" denotes the spiritual brotherhood into which all disciples of the Lord Jesus have been inducted (cf. Matt 12:46–50; Mark 3:31–35; Luke 8:19–21). That this form of address, a partial carryover from Judaism (cf. Acts 2:29, 37; 3:17), became very frequent in early Christianity is attested by twenty-eight occurrences in these two Epistles. It fell into relative disuse during the third century (A. Harnack, *The Expansion of Christianity in the First Three Centuries* [London: Williams and Norgate, 1905], pp. 9, 10, 31, 32). The affectionate vocative "brothers" is intensified when "loved by God" is added to it. Only here is this exact phrase used, though its near equivalent, "loved by the Lord," describes these same readers in 2 Thessalonians 2:13. More often Paul uses *agapētoi* ("beloved," "loved"), the verbal adjective, rather than *ēgapēmenoi* ("beloved," "loved"), the participial form (e.g., 1 Cor 10:14, 15:58). But with the adjective only once does he identify God as the one who loves (Rom 1:7). The participle in the present verse lays more emphasis than the adjective on the active exercise of God's love as already consummated and resulting in a fixed status of being loved (perfect tense).

Though God is specifically identified as the agent in loving, the agent of choosing (*tēn eklogēn*, "he has chosen," NIV) is not named. However, the obvious inference is that God had chosen them. "Loved by God" is suitable assurance that he also chooses, since his love and election are inextricably bound together (Rom 11:28; cf. 11:5).

"He has chosen" stands for *eklogēn*. This is God's sovereign choice of certain individuals, including the Thessalonian believers, prior to Adam's appearance on earth (cf. Eph 1:4). Some would locate God's choice of the Thessalonians at their conversion or thereafter by defining the elect as "those who are continuing in faith and who are persevering in obedience" (Arnold E. Airhart, "I and II Thessalonians," *Beacon Bible Commentary* [Kansas City, Mo.: Beacon Hill Press of Kansas City, 1965], 9:443). Yet Paul speaks of their election as a thing of the past, not as dependent on any human response, whether initial faith or subsequent faithfulness. To deny the pretemporal nature of this selection makes the word refer to historical circumstances surrounding the Thessalonians' conversion to Christ. But this unnaturally forces on *eklogē* ("selection," "choosing") an inappropriate meaning (Hiebert, p. 51) and necessitates positing an unprecedented second phase of divine election. For Paul to write concerning a knowledge his readers already knew him to possess, i.e., the details of their conversion, is too much of a truism to carry the emphasis resting on v.4. It is much better to allow *eklogēn* a setting prior to history. Knowledge of this prior choice by God was the root of Paul's thanksgiving.

Paul cannot leave unproved so direct a statement regarding election. So vv.5–10 give two grounds for the knowledge just asserted. The former of these relates to the experience of the missionaries themselves (v.5). They had sensed an unusual divine moving such as occurred only in special cases.

Interpretations that have assigned *hoti* ("because," v.5) an epexegetic force (i.e., giving additional information) see vv.5ff. as detailing the historical occasion and manner of election. Most persuasive among the evidences for this interpretation is Paul's practice elsewhere of assigning an objective force to *hoti* wherever he utilizes the *eidenai ti hoti* ("know something that") combination, as he does in vv.4, 5 (Rom 13:11; 1 Cor 16:15; 2 Cor 12:3, 4; 1 Thess 2:1; cf. Acts 16:3) (Lightfoot, p. 12). Aside from the difficulty in making this understanding of *hoti* ("that") agree with meaning given *eklogēn* ("chosen") in v.4, this idea misconstrues vv.5ff. in that these verses do not primarily deal with the

Thessalonians' conversion experience. In fact, v.5 does not directly relate to the Thessalonians but rather to Paul and his colleagues and vv.6–10 go beyond the conversion experience and its immediate sequel. It is better, therefore, to favor a causal *hoti*. Paul does follow up *eidenai ti* with a causal *hoti* at times, as witnessed by Romans 8:28, 29, though admittedly his syntax there is not exactly analogous with the present passage.

Instead of writing, "We came to you," the apostle puts the messengers in the background by saying, "Our gospel came to you." The message deserved foremost attention. Eight times in two Epistles *euangelion* ("gospel") is used to refer to the good news of salvation through Christ. Once the "good news" is unqualified by any modifier (1 Thess 2:4). Three times it is called "the gospel of God" (1 Thess 2:2, 8, 9), God being the author of the gospel (ablative of source). Twice it is "the gospel of Christ [or our Lord Jesus]" (1 Thess 3:2; 2 Thess 1:8), Christ being named as topic of the gospel message (objective genitive). The other two occurrences (1 Thess 1:5; 2 Thess 2:14) use "our gospel," meaning "the gospel we preach" (subjective genitive). Paul makes no claim to having originated the gospel (cf. 1 Cor 15:1–11; cf. Hunter, *Paul and His Predecessors*, p. 15). He claims only to be a staunch proclaimer of the glad tidings from the Father concerning his Son.

This gospel made its way to the Thessalonians through the missionaries in a fourfold manner. It came, first of all, "with words" or, literally, "in word" (*en logō*). This is obvious, since words are basic to intelligent communication. But the gospel's coming was not "simply" in word; speaking was only a part of the whole picture. Their preaching was not mere hollow rhetoric but contained three other ingredients essential to the outworking of God's elective purpose.

The first is "power" (*dynamei* [dat.]). Not to be confused with *dynameis*, the plural of *dynamis*, which means "miracles" (1 Cor 12:10; Gal 3:5), the singular does not specify supernatural manifestations but neither does it exclude them. This verse primarily points to the inward power with which the speakers were filled as they gave the message, a power that might show itself in a variety of ways. This made the speakers aware of God's special involvement in the gospel and its presentation.

The second ingredient of the spoken word is a person, for the message came "with the Holy Spirit." This Person certainly was behind the power just named. Yet he is much greater and more versatile than just the subjective power he produces. He is part of the Godhead (contrast Best, p. 75; Turner, *Syntax*, Vol. III of Moulton's *Grammar of NT Greek* [Edinburgh: T. & T. Clark, 1963], p. 175). He supplies a sense of divine reality to the spoken message.

Growing out of his special activity is a third ingredient of the spoken word. "With deep conviction" (*plērophora pollē*) means that the preachers possessed perfect assurance as to the truth and effectiveness of their message. *Plērophoria*, at one point meaning "fullness," developed a NT connotation of "full assurance" or "confidence" (MM, pp. 519, 520). Such subjective certainty, sensed by Paul and his associates, served as a major ingredient of this first proof that these readers had been chosen by God.

"You know how we lived among you for your sake" draws on the Thessalonians' innate awareness of what Paul and Silas and Timothy became while with them, so as to substantiate what sort of inner transformation God had wrought. Throughout the Epistle Paul carries his readers along with him by such expressions as "you know how" (*kathōs oidate*), which he uses as a precaution against those who might disagree (cf. 2:2, 5; 3:4). The quality of life shown by the missionaries had in itself been sufficient vindication of their sincerity and of the message they preached. Their attitudes were completely unselfish ("for your sake").

Notes

4,5 The only difference in construction between Romans 8:28, 29 and the present use of εἰδέναι τι ὅτι (*eidenai ti hoti*, "to know something because") is the replacing of a noun (τὴν ἐκλογήν, *tēn eklogēn*) as direct object by an objective ὅτι (*hoti*, "that") clause. The second *hoti* in Romans 8:28, 29 is causal. Though not an exact parallel, the structure is similar enough to refute the generalization that Paul *always* follows *eidenai ti* with an objective *hoti*.

In v.5 two appearances of ἐν (*en* "in;" NIV, "with," "among")—before πληροφορίᾳ (*plērophoria*, "conviction") and before ὑμῖν (*hymin*, "you")—have weak MS support. The sense of the verse is not greatly affected by their absence.

2. The effect on the Thessalonians (1:6–10)

a. Their transformation

1:6, 7

> 6You became imitators of us and of the Lord; in spite of severe suffering, you welcomed the message with the joy given by the Holy Spirit.
> 7And so you became a model to all the believers in Macedonia and Achaia.

6,7 The second proof of election lies in the effect of the gospel on those evangelized (vv.6–10): (1) They "welcomed the message" and were converted. (2) They did so "in spite of severe suffering." (3) In difficult circumstances they had a joy that could only be "given by the Holy Spirit." (4) They rapidly became "imitators" of Paul and also the Lord. (5) They grew to a point of becoming a "model to all the believers in Macedonia and Achaia." So complete a transformation rapidly accomplished happens only when God's elective purpose is at work in people.

At the beginning of v.6 the *kai* ("and" or variants thereof) has not been translated. But here *kai* followed by *hymeis* ("you") means "and you on your part" and introduces a new point in Paul's explanation of how he knew God had chosen the Thessalonians (v.4). In a relatively short time they "became imitators." *Egenēthēte*, "became," is the same verb and tense as *egenēthēmen*, "we lived," in v.5. Now their life style was completely different from what it was before the gospel came to them, because their conversion led them to imitate Paul and his companions. Paul repeatedly encouraged this wholesome following of examples (1 Cor 4:16; 11:1; Gal 4:12; Eph 5:1; Phil 3:17; 4:9; 1 Thess 3:12; 2 Thess 3:7, 9). He did not hesitate to present himself as one to be copied, because he had patterned his own life after Christ's (1 Cor 11:1). So he added "and of the Lord" in 1:6. The notion of imitating God and Christ applies especially to *holiness* (1 Peter 1:15, 16), *love* (Matt 5:43–48; Luke 6:36; John 13:34; 15:12) and *suffering* (Matt 16:24, 25; Mark 10:38, 39; Luke 14:27; John 15:18–20; 1 Peter 2:18–21)—three areas touched upon later in Thessalonians: holiness in 3:13; 4:3, 7; love in 3:12; 4:9, 10; and suffering in 3:2–4.

Spiritual advance was possible for the Thessalonians only after they first "welcomed the message" preached by the missionaries ("words," v.5, and "message," v.6, both are from *logos* ["word"]). Even after their conversion, their response to the message was just as enthusiastic, though this reponse entailed "severe suffering." "Suffering" or "tribulation" (*thlipsis*) plays a large part in these letters (1 Thess 1:6; 3:3, 4, 7; 2 Thess 1:4, 6,

19

7) because persecution was so common (Acts 17:5-9) and grew so intense as to be comparable to the bitter opposition by the Jews against the Lord Jesus and the Judean church (1 Thess 2:14-16). There was no extreme to which Christ's enemies would not go in making life miserable for Christians. Yet instead of misery the Thessalonians displayed a "joy given by the Holy Spirit." Such a response defies natural explanation. The same One who gave Paul and his companions power for proclaiming the gospel (v.5) dwelt within those who received the gospel and transformed them with joy.

The greatest attainment for these new Christians was becoming for others what Paul and his companions had been for them (v.7). They had become "a model" to Christians throughout Greece. *Typon* ("model") suggests an exact reproduction. Christians in Philippi, Berea, Athens, Corinth, and elsewhere in the Grecian provinces of Macedonia and Achaia did well to look to Thessalonica.

Notes

6,7 Whether the aorist participle δεξάμενοι (*dexamenoi*, "welcoming") is antecedent to or simultaneous with ἐγενήθητε (*egenēthēte*, "you became") should be clarified. If it is simultaneous, the participial phrase defines the nature of their imitation (Frame, p. 82; Lightfoot, p. 14). Syntactically this is possible, but it results in much too narrow a definition of μιμηταί (*mimētai*, "imitators"). Doubtless the Thessalonians' cordial reception of the message (*logos*) was part of their imitation subsequent to conversion, but this could not exhaust it as the above discussion of "imitators" shows. It is thus preferable to assign an antecedent force to the aorist participal and understand the clause as "after you received the message. . . ."

Θλίψει (*thlipsei*, "suffering") is used rarely outside biblical Gr. Its secular usage as "pressure" quickly became more frequent in LXX and the NT and took on a metaphorical connotation of "affliction"—the lot of God's people in this world. In the NT it has a general usage referring to any tribulation suffered by Christians (1:6; John 16:33), but it also has a special eschatological force in reference to the period just before Christ's return (Matt 24:21; cf. Dan 12:1).

For Christ to be referred to as "the Lord" instead of "Jesus" is not nearly so difficult as Best makes it (Best, pp. 77, 78). Artificial schemes for distinguishing the image of Christ, supposedly constructed in the imagination of the early church, from the historical Jesus are unworthy of serious exegetical consideration by those who are convinced of the infallibility of Scripture.

The sing. τύπον (*typon*, "model") in v.7 is a more likely reading than the pl. τύποι (*typoi*) because of diversified geographical support among ancient sources. It is also the more difficult reading. A copier would hardly have changed a pl. to a sing., but the converse is not true.

b. *Their witness*

1:8-10

> ⁸The Lord's message rang out from you not only in Macedonia and Achaia—your faith in God has become known everywhere. Therefore we do not need to say anything about it, ⁹for they themselves report what kind of reception you gave us. They tell how you turned to God from idols to serve the living and true God, ¹⁰and to wait for his Son from heaven, whom he raised from the dead—Jesus, who rescues us from the coming wrath.

8-10 In describing how the Thessalonians were a model Christian community and giving further proof of the effect of the gospel on them, Paul gives another indication of their election (cf. v.4): their vigorous propagation of their faith. Using the same Greek term (*logos*) that is translated "words" in v.5 and "message" in v.6, Paul now adds an ablative *tou kuriou* ("of the Lord") to specify the source of the message. Their progress was remarkable in that what Paul and his companions had preached (v.5) and the Thessalonians had received (v.6), they were now sharing on the widest scale possible. *Ho logos tou kuriou* ("the word [NIV, "message"] of the Lord," an OT equivalent of the Lord's utterance; cf. Isa 38:4, 5) is used extensively in Acts to describe the spreading gospel message (Acts 8:25; 13:44, 48, 49; 15:35, 36; 16:32; 19:10, 20). Paul affirms that these converts played a substantial part in this ever-widening scope of Christian witness.

With Thessalonica as the starting point ("from you"), the message "rang out" (v.8) as brass instruments that keep on sounding. The figure is of an echo that continues indefinitely (perfect tense, *eksēchētai*, "rang out') and implies the persistence of the testimony over an ever-increasing expanse—"not only in Macedonia and Achaia . . . everywhere." Here Greece is viewed as a single territory rather than two separate provinces (cf. also v.7). This contrasts (*all'*, "but," a word implied by the dash but not translated in the NIV, though found in the Greek of v.8) with "everywhere" or "in every place" (*en panti topō*). So impressed is Paul with how far the gospel had progressed through the Thessalonians' faithful witness that he obviously indulges in a kind of hyperbole. "Everywhere" is clearly not worldwide in scope; in writing to the Romans some five years later, Paul implied that Spain had not yet been evangelized (Rom 15:19, 20, 24). (For similar Pauline hyperboles see Rom 1:8; 2 Cor 2:14; Phil 1:13; Col 1:6.) Part of the Thessalonians' outreach stemmed from their location on the Egnatian Way and the Thermaic Gulf with access by sea to the whole Mediterranean world (Milligan, p. 12; Lightfoot, pp. 15, 16; Hiebert, p. 64). But the largest factor was their diligence in communicating their faith to others. This was probably reported to Paul by Silas and Timothy on returning from Macedonia (Acts 18:5; 1 Thess 3:6) and by Aquila and Priscilla from as far as Rome (Acts 18:2).

So carried away with the Thessalonians' witness was Paul that instead of ending his sentence of v.8 in a grammatically acceptable way at *en panti topō* ("everywhere"), he added, "Your faith in God has become known." News of this believing relationship constituted part of "the Lord's message" that had issued from them. It had gone forth and remained (*ekselēluthen*, perfect tense) so that Paul and his companions did not need to speak of it, though Paul later referred to it (cf. 2 Cor 8:1, 2).

Instead of Paul's telling others what had happened in Thessalonica, others were giving him a twofold report about this Macedonian city. First, they described how Paul, Silas and Timothy had entered the city (cf. v.5). Second, this church had turned to God from idols (v.9). Here Paul, who most often refers in a positive way to conversion as believing (cf. 1:7) uses a word for turning away from error and toward God ("turned," *epistrepsate*; cf. Acts 14:15; 26:18, 20; 2 Cor 3:16). His mention of idols shows the Thessalonians' Gentile origin, since idol worship did not dominate the Jews after the Babylonian exile. At the same time, it raises the question as to whether these are the same "God-fearing Greeks" (Acts 17:4) who were among the original converts. Normal expectation would be for "God-fearers" to already have separated themselves from idolatrous paganism because of affiliation, though loose, with a Jewish synagogue. Yet their release from past darkness may not have been total till secured by their relationship to God through Jesus Christ. Also probably included were additional Gentile converts who had no previous contact with Judaism.

Two purposes in the Thessalonians' turning to God are given: "to serve [*douleuein*—a verb related to *doulos,* "slave"] the living and true God" (v.9) and "to wait for his Son from heaven" (v.10). Such service to God speaks of utter devotion and recognition of his rightful lordship over mankind. He alone is worthy of this, for he is "living," in contrast to lifeless idols, and "true," in contrast to counterfeit representations of himself.

The second purpose, "to wait for his Son from heaven," strikes a doctrinal note prominent throughout the remainder of the Epistle. Paul's second missionary journey as gauged by his preaching at Thessalonica and as reflected in these two Epistles stressed eschatological events surrounding the return of Jesus Christ from the Father's right hand in heaven (cf. Acts 17:7; 1 Thess 2:19; 3:13; 4:15; 5:2, 23; 2 Thess 2:1, 8). Primitive Christianity universally held that the resurrected and ascended Christ would return and their expentancy of this event implied its nearness (Best, p. 83). For Paul to include himself and his readers among those to be rescued from wrath at this future moment (cf. "us," v.10) shows that they expected this to happen before death. Had Jesus never been raised from the dead, he could never return, but since he had been raised, his future reappearance is guaranteed by that very resurrection (just as is his divine sonship, Rom 1:4).

It is not some mystical spirit but the historical personage "Jesus" who will return as rescuer ("who rescues," *ton rhuomenon,* is a timeless substantive denoting one of his characteristics) of living Christians from the period of divine wrath at the close of the world's present age of grace. Used technically, as it so frequently is in the NT, "wrath" (*orgēs*) is a title for the period just before Messiah's kingdom on earth, when God will afflict earth's inhabitants with an unparalleled series of physical torments because of their rejection of His will (Matt 3:7; 24:21; Luke 21:23; Rev 6:16, 17). That the wrath is pictured as "coming" or "approaching" carries out effectively the force of the present participle *erchomenēs.* It is already on its way and hence quite near (Frame, p. 89). Throughout the Epistle, the events of Jesus' future coming are imminent (cf. "we who are still alive, who are left," 4:15, 17). So near was the world to being plunged into an unexpected time of trouble (cf. 1 Thess 5:2, 3) that it was on the brink of disaster. Such was the outlook of early Christendom and such is always a proper Christian anticipation.

Rather than fearing this time, however, Christians find an incentive to persevere (cf. "endurance inspired by hope," 1:3), because for them it will mean rescue rather than doom. Not even the stepped-up persecution of Christ's followers that will mark this future period will touch them, for their deliverer will remove them from the scene of these dreadful happenings.

It has been accurately observed that much of the terminology in vv.9b, 10 differs from normal Pauline usage (Hiebert, p. 66; Best, pp. 85, 86). Whether these differences can be attributed to Paul's incorporation of reports from others (Hiebert, p. 66) or to his adoption of "a pre-Pauline statement of the Church's faith" (Best, p. 86) cannot be determined with certainty. Perhaps both explanations contain elements of truth. In this his earliest Epistle Paul may not as yet have formulated his own theological vocabulary as he did later and so may have been dependent on statements that came to him from others (cf. 1 Cor 15:1–5).

Notes

8 The ἐν τῇ (*en tē,* "in [the]") appearing before "Achaia" in some MSS should be omitted in agreement with most editors. Its omission is more difficult to explain, as a scribe would more

likely have added it intentionally from v.7 than omitted it unintentionally. Yet the omission is not so difficult as to be impossible. Two proper nouns governed by the same *en tē* (before "Macedonia") present Greece as a unit in contradistinction to ἐν παντὶ τόπῳ (*en panti topō*, "in every place").

Placing a full stop after κυρίου (*kyriou*, "Lord") or Ἀχαΐα (*Achaia*) (see NIV, v.8) is questionable. While we must grant that the sentence as it stands is irregular, it is not beyond Paul's impetuous style to write such an anacoluthon. His emotional makeup often prompted him to vary from usual syntax. Perhaps a preferable rendering of the verse would be, "For the Lord's message rang out from you not only in Macedonia and Achaia, but everywhere your faith toward God has become known, so that we do not need to say anything about it."

10 Not much can be concluded regarding Paul's use of the pl. οὐρανῶν (*ouranōn*, "heavens"), since he uses the noun's sing. and pl. about equally (eleven sing. and ten pl.). The Heb word for "heaven"—שָׁמַיִם (*šāmayim*)—is pl. and Paul knew a plurality of heavenly spheres (2 Cor 12:2), but in these same Epistles he conceives of Christ's return from a singular οὐρανοῦ (*ouranou;* cf. 1 Thess 4:16; 2 Thess 1:7; so Milligan, pp. 14, 15). Apparently these are two ways to think of heaven, either as its components or as a single entity.

It is quite possible that Paul substitutes τῆς ἐρχομένης (*tēs erchomenēs*, "the coming"; i.e., on its way) for John the Baptist's τῆς μελλούσης (*tēs mellousēs*, "the coming") (Matt 3:7; Luke 3:7) to show a greater degree of imminence. For John this wrath was not an "any-moment" possibility, even though quite near. For Paul, however, prophetic events to precede the wrath had now been fulfilled (cf. 1 Thess 2:15, 16). This future wrath should be distinguished from the present wrath of God currently being poured out against rebellious humanity (Rom 1:18–32).

III. Vindication Before the Thessalonians (2:1–3:13)

A. *Vindication Through Methods (2:1–12)*

1. *Preaching, replete with power*

2:1, 2

> ¹You know, brothers, that our visit to you was not a failure. ²We had previously suffered and been insulted in Philippi, as you know, but with the help of our God we dared to tell you his gospel in spite of strong opposition.

1,2 Having explained so fully why he and his colleagues were thankful (1:2–10), Paul now takes up one of the main purposes for writing the Epistle—a lengthy vindication of the missionaries' character and ministry (chs. 2–3). *Gar* ("for") in 2:1, though not translated in NIV, forms a bridge between the chapters. It marks 2:1–16 as an expansion of chapter 1—probably 1:5–10 especially, since 2:1–12 looks into Paul's coming to Thessalonica and his conduct there (cf. 1:5, 9a) and 2:13–16 turns our attention to the Thessalonians' response (cf. 1:6–8, 9b, 10).

Yet chapter 2 does not just go over the same ground. In chapter 1 Paul's coming and the peoples' response show a knowledge of election (1:4). But in chapter 2 the same themes establish Paul's defense against insinuations about his alleged ulterior motives.

The identity of Paul's Thessalonian opponents is a puzzle difficult to piece together. Suggestions have included heretical pseudo-apostles as found in Corinth and Galatia, Judaizers, spiritual enthusiasts, Gnostics, and Jews (Best, p. 16). Also whether they were within the church or outside it remains a mystery. A possible reconstruction sees the Jews as continuing adversaries of Paul, even after he left Thessalonica (cf. 2:14–16), for they were so intent on destroying the work he had started that they persistently hurled accusations at him and labeled him another self-seeking religious propagandist. How they distorted his teaching to accuse him of treason while he was yet in the city (Acts 17:7) shows an abiding animosity toward him. Subjected to a constant barrage of accusations, Thessalonian Christians may easily have begun to question Paul's sincerity. There is no evidence of organized opposition within the church, yet Timothy apparently brought back news (3:6) that some uncertainty had arisen within it as to whether Paul's concern for it was genuine. This is not to say that his relations with the readers of the Epistle were no longer cordial (cf. 3:6), but symptoms of estrangement had appeared that could have led to an open rift unless treated immediately.

In light of this development, Paul again addresses his readers affectionately ("brothers," v.1) and reminds them of conditions throughout his initial visit. Special concern that his readers recall certain matters for themselves is evident in the recurrence of "you know" (vv.1, 2, 5, 11; cf. "you remember," v.9, and "you are witnesses," v.10). In v.1 particularly he points to their awareness by the intensive *autoi*: "you yourselves know."

What they are called to witness regarding the "visit" or "entrance" (*eisodon*, cf. 1:9) is that it "was not a failure." "Failure" renders the Greek adjective *kenē*, whose meaning has received much discussion. Some have referred it to the results of their ministry (Best, pp. 89, 90), but this idea would have been conveyed by *mataios* (Milligan, p. 16; Ellicott, p. 15; Lightfoot, p. 18; Frame, p. 92). Another suggestion is "empty-handed," i.e., greedy for gain (Hendriksen, p. 60). The ideas of "false," i.e., under false pretenses, and "aimless," i.e., without specific purpose, have also been suggested (Hiebert, pp. 79, 80). The greatest probability, however, rests with assigning the word a qualitative force, "void of content," "empty," since v.2 in presenting the other side speaks of their boldness and earnestness in ministry. This conclusion also agrees with 1:5, of which the present section is a resumption. The character of their ministry "was" and continues to be (*gegonen*, 2:1, perfect tense) real and courageous.

The opposite of the empty ministry denied in v.1 is one where no obstacle or threat is sufficient to deter the speaker of God's gospel (2:2. In Philippi, Paul and Silas had been beaten and severely flogged; they had been put in prison with their feet in stocks (Acts 16:22–24) and possibly otherwise cruelly mistreated because they had rescued a slave girl in the name of Jesus Christ. They had also been insulted by being arrested unjustly, stripped of their clothes, and treated like dangerous fugitives. Their Roman citizenship had been violated, and for this Paul demanded restitution (Acts 16:37). Still staggering from these injuries and indignities, the two came to Thessalonica. Under such conditions, most people would have refrained from repeating a message that had led to such violent treatment, but not these men. With God's help, they mustered sufficient courage to declare in this new city their gospel from God. *Eparrēsiasametha*, "we dared," richly describes how they boldly spoke out despite the same potential dangers as faced in Philippi.

Here again they encountered "strong opposition." *Agōni*, represented in the text above by "opposition," pictures an athlete's struggle to gain first place in a race or contest. Paul's conflict may have been inward (cf. Col 2:1), but most likely it came from outward persecutions and dangers originated by his Jewish opponents (cf. Phil 1:30), since inner strivings cannot equal the tempo of persecution set earlier in v.2. Though Luke does not directly mention "strong opposition" in Thessalonica (Acts 17:1–10), it is clear from the present Epistle that such did come. In spite of it, however, Paul's inner help from God produced a continuing proclamation of the gospel. Such earnestness plainly shows sincerity.

Notes

1,2 προπαθόντες (*propathontes*, "having previously suffered") and ὑβρισθέντες (*hubristhentes*, "having been insulted") are preferably understood as concessive rather than temporal, even though the καί (*kai*, "and") preceding the former in TR is not genuine. The bold speech of the apodosis is attained despite the condition expressed in the protasis.

2. Preaching, removed from untruth
2:3, 4

> 3For the appeal we make does not spring from error or impure motives, nor are we trying to trick you. 4On the contrary, we speak as men approved by God to be entrusted with the gospel. We are not trying to please men but God, who tests our hearts.

3,4 Not only was the preaching of Paul and his companions filled with power and earnestness when they evangelized Thessalonica (vv. 1, 2), but wherever they went it was above suspicion of any kind (vv. 3, 4). The boldness just described was possible because ("for," v.3) God, who tests man's motives, had approved their fitness to preach the gospel.

"Appeal" hints at the gently persuasive form of Paul's preaching. Whether hortatory or consolatory, *paraklēsis* ("appeal") always addresses the will in quest of a favorable decision, but the intellect is not excluded. Persuasion, however, is of various types, both wholesome and otherwise. Paul and his fellow workers had apparently been accused of appealing on wrong grounds. The damage from this accusation he is quite anxious to repair.

First to be corrected was the claim that his appeal arose from "error" or self-delusion. *Planēs* ("error") at times has an active sense of "deceit," a meaning indistinguishable in the present verse from *dolō* ("trying to trick you"). Here, however, it should be assigned its passive meaning of "error" as usual in the NT. Paul's message agreed perfectly with truth.

He answers his opponents further in the matter of "impure motives" or "impurity" (*akatharsias*). Some have defended a general definition of "impurity" by saying that a more specialized sense of sexual impurity is too abrupt and out of place in the present discussion (Best, p. 93). They add that Paul is never accused elsewhere of this sin of immorality (Findlay, CGT, p. 37; Lenski, p. 246). Whatever specialization may lie in its scope, it is argued, is limited to covetousness (cf. 2:5), which at times allegedly is covered by *akatharsia* (Hauck, TDNT, 3:428–429). Yet a more restricted meaning of sexual impurity has much in its favor. A casual reference to such in this pagan environment would have shocked no one (cf. 4:3–8; Milligan, p. 18; Lightfoot, pp. 20, 21). Doubtless, Paul's enemies were attacking him on many fronts, including this sin so prevalent among traveling religious teachers. Constant use of *akatharsia* for sexual sins in all literature of the time is persuasive for giving it the same meaning here (Frame, p. 95). The apostle disclaims anything of this type as a motive for his missionary activities.

He further denies any attempt to use deceit so as to trick his listeners. He was neither guilty of self-deceit (*planēs*, "error") nor of deceiving others (*dolō*, "guile,"; NIV, "trying to trick you") though he was accused of doing so on more occasions than this (cf. 2 Cor 4:2; 12:16). He made no empty promises and followed no humanly devised schemes. In seeking intelligent decisions from his hearers, he presented facts in their true light.

The true state of the missionaries was one of openness and honesty to the point that an omniscient God had found them worthy to declare his gospel (v.4). To be "approved by God" (perfect tense, *dedokimasmetha*) entails a process of testing, success in completing the tests, and a consequent state of endorsement by God. After calling Paul on the Damascus road, God subjected him to necessary rigors to demonstrate his capability for his assigned task. Having thus prepared him, he committed to him the gospel message for proclamation among Gentiles such as these readers. On the basis of this commission, the missionary team spoke wherever they went. They did nothing superficial just "to please men." Ultimately, they sought God's approbation. This kind of goal excluded anything ulterior or hidden from the eyes of him "who tests our hearts." The scrutiny of a God, who is able to sound the depths of every thought (cf. Rom 8:27 as to God's awareness of all men's thoughts), is Paul's ultimate court of appeal in summoning evidence for his absolute sincerity.

3. *Preaching, reinforced by godly concern (2:5-12)*

a. *Evidenced by the absence of lower motives*

2:5-6

> ⁵You know we never used flattery, nor did we put on a mask to cover up greed—God is our witness. ⁶We were not looking for praise from men, not from you or anyone else.
> ⁶As apostles of Christ we could have been a burden to you. . . .

5-6. Godly concern for his listeners underscores more forcefully than anything else the legitimacy of Paul's missionary methods (2:5-12). In turning to discuss his sincere care, he initially dispenses with the notion that he was moved by lower motives. *Gar* ("for," untranslated in text above but introducing v.5 of Greek text) explains how his general policy (vv.3, 4) was applied in Thessalonica. As in vv.1, 2 and 3, 4 Paul begins in a negative vein by denying allegations against his character (vv. 5-7a) before presenting the true picture (vv.7b-12; cf. *alla*, which introduces the positive side in each case, vv.2, 4, 7).

In the first of three denials, he calls his readers to verify his complete abstinence from any word used for flattering purposes. The insidious practice of saying nice things to gain influence over others for selfish reasons is what *kolakeias* ("flattery") denotes in classical writings (Milligan, p. 19; Lightfoot, p. 23). Paul seeks their own confirmation that he "never" (*oute . . . pote*) was guilty of this.

Second, he denies putting on the kind of mask that greed wears. "A mask to cover up greed" (v.5) renders *pleonexias* ("greed") as an objective genitive and may imply that the missionaries were greedy, but did not seek to hide it. This is out of harmony with Paul's defense that would not admit to greed. A more appropriate sense comes from a subjective genitive, "a pretext such as covetousness would use" (Ellicott, p. 19; Milligan, p. 20). Only God could verify inner freedom from greed. So Paul calls on God as witness (*theos martys*, v.5). The greed of which he was accused includes more than just avarice or love of money, which would be *philargyria* (cf. 1 Tim 6:10). *Pleonexia* is self-seeking of all types, a quest for anything that brings self-satisfaction. It grows out of complete disinterest in the rights of others—an attitude foreign to Paul and his helpers.

Third, Paul disavows the desire for "praise from men" (v.6). *Doxa*, most frequently rendered "glory" in the NT, here carries its classical force of "good opinion" or "honor." The world of Paul's time was filled with wandering philosophers, prophets of other religions, magicians, false prophets, and others seeking not only financial gain, but also the prestige of a good reputation. Divine approval (cf. v.4), not public esteem, was what motivated Paul and his companions, whether in Thessalonica or elsewhere.

Grammatically, the first part of v.7, *dynamenoi en barei einai hōs Christou apostoloi* ("as apostles of Christ we could have been a burden to you"), goes with the preceding and is required to complete the sense of v.6. *Dynamenoi* is concessive, "though we could have been." Paul, Silas, and Timothy could legitimately have claimed the dignity associated with their apostolic office. (*Apostoloi* is used here in a nontechnical sense that covers others besides eyewitnesses of Christ's resurrection; cf. 2 Cor 8:23; Phil 2:25.) *En barei* ("a burden") has primary reference to apostolic dignity. Such a prestigious connotation is to be preferred over understanding a material burden as the meaning. Verse 9 implies the right of the servant of Christ to receive support from converts; but v.7a speaks of authoritative position, in contrast both to seeking "praise" as they might have done (v.6) and to giving "gentle" treatment as they actually did (v.7b). The important position of Paul and his colleagues as Christ's representatives earned for them the right to receive special respect, but they did not stand on this right. So this is further evidence that they were not prompted by lower motives.

Notes

5 The genitive κολακείας (*kolakeias*, "of flattery") with λόγῳ (*logos*, "word") has been analyzed in several ways: ablative of source, "a word that comes from flattery"; genitive of description, "a flattering word"; and genitive of apposition, "a word that is flattery." Yet a subjective genitive is more to the point: "the word that flattery uses," in that the other genitive πλεονεξίας (*pleonexias*, "of greed") is also subjective (Ellicott, p. 19; Lightfoot, p. 23; Frame, p. 97).

6 Ζητοῦντες ... δόξαν (*zētountes ... doxan*," looking for praise") is a participial phrase of manner describing how the missionaries did not undertake their Thessalonian ministry. Paul does not say he never received honor from men or that he had no right to receive it. He does, however, deny that he required such from his converts (Frame, pp. 98, 99).

7 Placing Χριστοῦ (*Christou*, "Christ") before ἀπόστολοι (*apostoloi*, "apostles") calls special attention to whose apostles they were. This was the key to the importance of their position. Apostleship in itself is meaningless apart from the prestige of the sender (Ellicott, p. 20).

b. *Evidenced by the presence of higher motives*

2:7b-12

> 7bbut we were gentle among you, like a mother caring for her little children. 8We loved you so much that we were delighted to share with you not only the gospel of God but our lives as well, because you had become so dear to us. 9Surely you remember, brothers, our toil and hardship; we worked night and day in order not to be a burden to anyone while we preached the gospel of God to you.
> 10You are witnesses, and so is God, of how holy, righteous and blameless we were among you who believed. 11For you know that we dealt with each of you as a father deals with his own children, 12encouraging, comforting and urging you to live lives worthy of God, who calls you into his kingdom and glory.

7b The godly concern of Paul and his helpers was proved by their higher motives (7b–12) as well as by their freedom from lower motives (5–7a). With the "but" of v.7, the apostle takes up a positive description the Thessalonians were bound to agree with because of their own observations—"you remember" (v.9); "you are witnesses" (v.10); "you know" (v.11). While intermingling with these Macedonians as equals (*en mesō hymōn*, "among you," is intensive), Paul and his helpers were gentle, not authoritarian (v.7). They put aside their rights of being respected and playing a dominating part and demonstrated the utmost tenderness, comparable to that of a mother nursing her own children. *Trophos* means a nurse, but often as here refers to the mother herself. "Her" (*heautēs*) is emphatic and marks this close relationship. The figure implies a special effort to protect and to provide for every need, even to the extent of great sacrifice.

8 The manner of gentle treatment was a willingness to "share with you not only the gospel of God but our lives as well." "We loved you so much" represents a rare word of uncertain derivation (*homeiromenoi*), but the general thrust is clear. The missionaries knew a constant "yearning for" (cf. Job 3:21, LXX) these people, so much so that they found it a continual delight (*eudokoumen*, "we were delighted") to share their whole being with them. "Lives" (*psychas*) conveys more than just their physical lives; in the depths of their being they cared "because [the Thessalonians] had become so dear" to them. An even stronger relationship of love developed as the ministry continued—a relationship like that of a nursing mother with her child.

9 Verse 9 recalls the long hours of extreme toil and hardship by which the missionaries supported themselves while preaching. *Gar* ("surely") looks back to "we were delighted to share ... our lives" (v.8; cf. Lightfoot, p. 26; Ellicott, p. 22). The gentleness of v.7 (Frame, p. 102) is too distant to be included through the *gar*, and the endearing close of v.8 (Lenski, p. 253) is too subordinate grammatically to merit support by this conjunction. So Paul is taking the single item of self-support as evidence of his broader concern for the Thessalonians.

"Toil" (*kopon*), translated "labor" in 1:3, emphasizes the fatigue they incurred in expending themselves, while "hardship" (*mochthon*) highlights external difficulties encountered in the process. As in 2 Thessalonians 3:8, the combination describes the apostles' efforts at providing their own upkeep, an example much needed by some they were writing to (1 Thess 4:11, 12; 5:14; 2 Thess 3:6–15). They worked at night as well as during the day while proclaiming the gospel (2:9b). Paul's work was probably tentmaking (Acts 18:3), though it may have been the production of tent material from animal hair or skins (Hiebert, pp. 98, 99). Part of a Jewish child's upbringing was learning a trade, and Paul was no exception to this. He received some financial help from the Philippian church while he was in Thessalonica (Phil 4:15, 16), but not enough to permit him to stop working. Apparently his wages were so low that he needed gifts to enable him to take some time off for preaching (Acts 18:5; Best, p. 104). Though missionary service includes the right to support from others (1 Cor 9:3ff.), Paul does not seem to have used that right in Thessalonica, Corinth (1 Cor 4:12; 2 Cor 11:8), Ephesus (Acts 20:34, 35), and elsewhere.

By this "around-the-clock" diligence Paul lifted the burden of support from his converts. His central purpose was to give them the gospel of God. From this nothing should detract, and making the gospel "free of charge" (1 Cor 9:18) eliminated charges of selfish motives.

10 Paul appeals to the Thessalonians as witnesses of "how holy, righteous and blameless we were among you who believed." God also is called to attest to whatever was hidden to human eyes. *Hosiōs* ("holily") highlights religious piety while *dikaiōs* ("righteously") pertains principally to moral conduct. From the negative side, Paul and his companions were "blameless," untainted by fault in their dealings. All this was for the sake of the believers (*tois pisteuousin*).

11 A further comparison (*kathaper*, translated "for" in NIV) enlivens Paul's expression of concern. Changing from a mother's tender care in v.8 to a new metaphor, Paul is now a father dealing with his own children individually (*hena hekaston hymōn*, "each of you"). Christians need fatherly teaching and advice as well as motherly care.

12 The fatherly treatment included encouragement, comfort, and urging. "Encouraging" (*parakalountes*) can in some contexts signify a note of comfort, but here it has the hortatory flavor of "admonishing." "Comfort" is covered by the second participle (*paramythoumenoi*). "Urging" (*martyromenoi*) adds a note of authority. These actions were more than mere requests. Their goal was a worthy life style. "Live lives" represents the figure of "walking around" (*peripatein*), a common way of designating conduct in both biblical and nonbiblical Greek (Best, p. 107). In reference to the Christian life, it relates primarily to the moral sphere. Conduct should be on the plane of God's standards.

The call of God into His kingdom and glory is an incentive to a high quality of life. The articular present participle *tou kalountos* ("calls," NIV) probably has a substantival force with little attention to a continuing call (cf. Best, pp. 107, 108; Hiebert, pp. 105, 106), since God's character as a caller is indicated by a comparable construction in 5:24 and Paul uses *kaleō* only in the aorist and perfect indicative, never in the present. This participle displays no duration but looks back to the initial call of these readers, which in Paul is always effectual (Lightfoot, p. 29). In one sense God's kingdom is already present (Matt 12:28; 13:1–52; Rom 14:17; 1 Cor 4:20; Col 1:13), but ultimate realization of the messianic kingdom with its future glory is in view here (cf. Acts 17:7). As frequently in the Thessalonian literature, those Paul is addressing are pointed to the bliss ahead as incentive to godly living now. "Glory" is that unhindered manifestation of God's presence in which believers will share (Rom 5:2; 8:18).

Notes

7 The textual choice between ἤπιοι (*ēpioi*, "gentle") and νήπιοι (*nēpioi*, "babies") is difficult. External evidence for *nēpioi* is much stronger than for *ēpioi*. Yet Paul never used νήπιος (*nēpios*, "baby") of himself, and a radical inversion of metaphor that transforms the apostle so quickly from a baby to a mother nurse is too violent even for Paul (cf. Gal 4:19, which only approaches this in suddenness). On the other hand, *ēpioi* is an appropriate sequel to v.7a. Understanding that the n of *nēpioi* could have arisen by dittography, *ēpioi* is slightly preferable. This dictates that a full stop be placed after ἀπόστολοι (*apostoloi*, "apostles"), a comma after ὑμῶν (*hymōn*, "you") and another full stop after τέκνα (*tekna*, "children"). This allows the comparative ὡς (*hōs*, "as") clause to amplify the *ēpioi* (Metzger, *The Text of the NT*, [New York: Oxford, 1968], pp. 230–233; Metzger, *A Textual Commentary of the Greek NT*, [New York: U.B.S., 1971], pp. 629–630; Hiebert, pp. 93–95).

8 Of the various suggested etymologies for ὁμειρόμενοι (*homeiromenoi*, "longing for") BAG, p.

29

568; Frame, p. 101; Lightfoot, pp. 25, 26), none has gained widespread acceptance. The verb's rarity makes it hard to trace. Nonetheless, the general meaning is clear from its context here, in Job 3:21 (LXX), and Psalm 62:2 (Symmachus).

Whether Paul received contributions from Philippi once or more than once is obscured by difficulty with the phrase καὶ ἅπαξ καὶ δίς (kai hapax kai dis, "both once and twice"; NIV, "again and again") in Philippians 4:16 (cf. 1 Thess 2:18). Either way, the effect on the meaning in the present context is not great (Best, p. 104). It does appear from the present discussion that Paul spent an extended period in this city in which case multiple offerings are very likely.

10 The force of the dative τοῖς πιστεύουσιν (tois pisteuousin, "the ones believing") is probably that of advantage. A locative of sphere is not probable. A dative of reference is too general. Since he emphasizes in this section such devotion to his readers, advantage provides the best analysis.

11, 12 It is possible to construe the three participles as indicatives, e.g., παρακαλοῦντες (parakalountes, "encouraging") as παρακαλοῦμεν (parakaloumen, "we encouraged") (Frame, p. 104). But the rarity of this in Paul argues against it. Rather than inserting a verb completely foreign to the context, such as "we dealt" or "we admonished," to govern ἕνα ἕκαστον (hena hekaston, "each one") (Lightfoot, pp. 28, 29), ἐγενήθημεν (egenēthēmen, "we were," v.10) can more naturally extend its force into vv. 11, 12 (Ibid.).

The articular present participle carries mainly a substantival sense (RHG, pp. 892, 1108, 1109). Hence, it is precarious to build anything on the progressive nature of the aktionsart of such as καλοῦντος (kalountos, "calling"; NIV, "who calls") since nothing in the context especially warrants it.

B. Vindication Through Their Thanksgiving (2:13-16)

1. For the ready acceptance of the Word of God

2:13

> 13And we also thank God continually because, when you received the word of God, which you heard from us, you accepted it not as the word of men, but as it actually is, the word of God, which is at work in you who believe.

13 Having already thanked God in 1:2, 3 for their progress, Paul now does so again by alluding to 1:5-10, which describes specifically how the Thessalonians so rapidly entered on a Christian way of life (1:6-10; cf. discussion of 2:1, 2). Now he cites their ready acceptance of the Word of God (cf. 1:6)—not in proof of their election as in chapter 1, but to show the reason for his sincere gratitude for them.

Because of the deep personal commitment he and his helpers had to the work at Thessalonica (dia touto, "because of this," untranslated in NIV, connects v.13 with vv.1–12), Paul could write, "We also thank God continually." "Also" here connotes "on our part." The missionary team's reaction to the Thessalonians' ready response to the word was incessant thanksgiving. The spotlight now shifts from the evangelizers (vv.1–12) to those evangelized (vv.13–16) (Milligan, p. 28; Lightfoot, p. 30; Frame, pp. 106, 107).

The cause of thanksgiving having already been given (vv.1–12, as stipulated by dia touto), hoti in v.13 does not add another cause ("because" in NIV), but rather introduces the content of thanksgiving ("we also thank God continually that. . . ."; so Best, pp. 109, 110). The prayer of thanks not only referred to an objective reception (paralabontes, "[having] received"), but also a subjective acceptance (edexasthe, "you accepted"). The latter, a wholehearted welcome, indicated their high estimate of God's word (Ellicott,

p. 27; Lightfoot, p. 30; Frame, p. 107). This was the word they had heard preached by the missionaries (*akoēs par' hēmōn*, "you heard from us"), but ultimately it was the word from God (*tou Theou*). To accentuate the word's ultimate source, Paul bluntly states that they were not accepting "the word of men" ("as" in NIV is not in the Greek text), but what it "actually" was—"the word of God." Their appraisal of what they heard was accurate. Here is indication of Paul's consciousness of his own divinely imparted authority (cf. 1 Cor 14:37). His preaching was not the outgrowth of personal philosophical meanderings, but was deeply rooted in a message given by God himself (cf. *logos*, 1:5, 6, 8). What had been delivered to him through others (e.g., 1 Cor 11:23; 15:1, 3) and from the Lord directly (e.g., 1 Thess 4:15), he passed on to others. Such traditions were in turn taught to still others. Some teachings, such as the Thessalonian Epistles, were in written form, and became part of the NT canon (cf. 2 Tim 2:2; 2 Peter 3:15, 16).

Once received, this Word of God becomes an active power operating continually in the believer's life. When it is at work in those "who believe," there is a change in behavior and constant fruitfulness.

Notes

13 To seek an antecedent of τοῦτο (*touto*, "this"; with διά = "because of this," "therefore") in 2:1 (Best, pp. 109, 110), in 2:1–4 (Frame, p. 106) or in the ὅτι (*hoti*, "that," "because") clause of 2:13 (Lenski, p. 262) misses the underlying motive of the present paragraph. A desire to vindicate his ministry continues to control Paul's reasoning through chapter 3. He thus presents thanksgiving as another indication of his guileless interest in them. *Touto* therefore sums up what vv.1–12 has told about the missionaries' self-giving ministry.

Ἐνεργεῖται (*energeitai*, "is at work") is middle voice. Used actively in the NT, it always describes supernatural activity, principally God's. Since it is middle here, however, "the word," not "God," is the antecedent of its subject ὅς (*hos*, "which") (Armitage Robinson, *Ephesians*, [London: James Clarke & Co.], pp. 241–247).

2. For their endurance under persecution

2:14–16

14For you, brothers, became imitators of God's churches in Judea, which are in Christ Jesus. You suffered from your own countrymen the same things those churches suffered from the Jews, 15who killed the Lord Jesus and the prophets and also drove us out. They displease God and are hostile to all men 16in their effort to keep us from speaking to the Gentiles so that they may be saved. In this way they always heap up their sins to the limit. The wrath of God has come upon them at last.

14 Some see "for" as confirming the continued working of God's word (v.13; Ellicott, p. 28) while others see it as confirming the fact of the Thessalonians' belief (v.13; Olshausen, *Biblical Commentary* [Edinburgh: T. & T. Clark, 1851], 7:415). It is best, though, to regard it as confirming the principal statement of v.13—their ready acceptance of the Word (Best, p. 112). Welcoming the Word and enduring sufferings because of it often go together (cf. 1:6). While the working of the Word continued (v.13) up to the point of Paul's writing, the stature of the Thessalonians as "imitators" had already been established in the past (*egenēthēte*, "you . . . became"; cf. *egenēthēte*, 1:6). Imitation "of God's churches in Judea" differs, however, from imitating Paul and the Lord (1:6). Deliberate imitation of sufferings for sufferings' sake is an unworthy Christian objective, but imitation of a Christian life style is legitimate and desirable. Persecution inevitably arises from the outside when a Christian patterns his life after the Lord.

Paul tenderly reminds these brothers that they were not the first to be afflicted. "God's churches in Judea, which are in Christ Jesus" had been the first and through faithful endurance had become an example of what Jesus had predicted about the suffering entailed in discipleship. Lest there be any doubt as to whom they were following, these are distinguished from all pagan assemblies by being identified as "God's" and from all Jewish churches by being specified as those "in Christ Jesus." Apparently the way these earliest Jewish Christians handled themselves had become widely known, even before Luke wrote Acts about A.D. 62. Paul's sympathy toward and harmony with Judean Christianity, whose bitter opponent he had been before conversion, is hereby assured, and the unity of all Christians, no matter what ethnic background or geographical locality, underlies this description of their common experience in suffering. Hearty acceptance of the Word, which is so often accompanied by adversity, is the very thing that insures one against falling away when adversity arises (cf. Matt 13:20, 21; Luke 8:13).

Both the Thessalonian churches and the churches in Judea suffered persecution from fellow-countrymen. For the Thessalonians these were predominantly Gentiles, though Jews also had been instrumental in stirring up opposition in that city (Acts 17:5-9). For the Judean churches, opposition had come from those of a Jewish background who, of course, were also strong advocates of the Jewish religion that Christianity so strongly threatened.

15,16 Mention of "the Jews" (v.14) furnishes Paul an occasion to digress slightly and deliver a violent criticism of this persecuting element among them. Such harsh language is markedly out of character for Paul as we know him from his other writings. He is renowned for his desire to see the salvation of these his blood relatives (Rom 9:1-3; 10:1), regardless of how much he had suffered personally at their hands (2 Cor 11:24, 26). So "un-Pauline" is the passage that some have supposed that all or part of it was added at a later time (Bailey, IB, 11:279, 280). Yet there is not the slightest shred of hard evidence for deletion. Exactly what provoked this sudden outburst cannot be known with certainty. An accumulation of hostile acts probably played a part. The writer had been chased out of Damascus (Acts 9:23-25) and Jerusalem (Acts 9:29, 30) by his own people not very long after his conversion. His message was rejected and his party driven out of Pisidian Antioch by them (Acts 13:45, 46, 50). At Iconium the Jews poisoned people's minds against Paul and Barnabas and ultimately forced them out (Acts 14:2, 5, 6). They made a special journey to Lystra to instigate an uprising that produced Paul's stoning and being left for dead (Acts 14:19). Jewish opposition continued to hound the missionary band into the second journey, specifically at Thessalonica, again producing Paul's exit (Acts 17:5, 10). Even now as Paul pens these words from Corinth, a united attack has been mounted against him by the city's Jewish residents (Acts 18:6, 12, 13). Couple with this the present plight of the Thessalonian Christians (1 Thess 3:3), ultimately traceable to Jewish opponents, and it is no wonder that Paul uses the occasion to recount their consistent opposition to the Lord Jesus.

The acme of the Jews' opposition is their part in the death of the Lord Jesus. Hence,

Paul places this crime first among their offences (v.15). By persuasion of the Jewish leaders, the Roman authorities crucified Jesus (John 19:16; 1 Cor 2:8). Though joint responsibility was shared by Gentiles and Jews (Acts 4:27), at this point Paul lays guilt for the crime on Israel. The aggravated nature of the injustice is implied by the way Paul separates *ton kyrion* ("the Lord") from the human name "Jesus" (*ton kyrion apokteinantōn Iēsoun*, "the Lord killing [i.e.,] Jesus"). It was none less than the exalted Lord of glory against whom this heinous crime was committed.

In the wording above, "the prophets" (v.15) are grouped with "the Lord Jesus" as murder victims of the Jews. This is a possible interpretation in that many, though not all, the OT prophets died in this way. Also, it is an oft-sounded note in biblical writings (1 Kings 19:10; Matt 23:31, 35, 37; Luke 13:34; Acts 7:52; Rom 11:3). More important in this connection is Jesus' parable of the vineyard in which killing some of the servants [prophets] is preliminary to killing the son (Matt 21:35-39; Mark 12:5-8). On the other hand, a very probable case can be made for connecting "the prophets" with "us" in this verse and translating "drove out the prophets and us" (Milligan, p. 30). If the parable of the vineyard furnishes a valid background, connecting "the prophets" here in v.15 with "the Lord Jesus" is unsatisfactory in that a chronological order is not observed and not all the servants in the parable are slain. Of greater import in the parable is the idea of the persecution of the servants [prophets]. In fact, Luke's account (Luke 20:9-16) does not even mention killing the servants. It is anticlimactic to name OT prophets in series after the Lord Jesus, but to list them alongside Paul's missionary band furnishes excellent reason for the past action of "drove ... out" (aorist participle, *ekdiōxantōn*), since it is doubtful that Paul in this generalized description is thinking only of the single instance of their being forced out of Thessalonica. Furthermore, it helps vindicate the missionaries by placing them alongside the honored OT prophets.

Paul concludes v.15 by listing two more characteristics of the Jewish antagonists. "They displease God and are hostile to all men." The former is clearly an understatement, since they were militantly opposed to God. Their zeal for God was not guided by knowledge (Rom 10:2). So by opposing God's Messiah so strenuously, they became God's adversaries. This could not help but produce hostility to all men—a hostility arising not from a supposed racial superiority, but one manifested in stubborn resistance to admitting Jesus' messiahship.

This is proved by their "effort to keep us from speaking to the Gentiles so that they may be saved" (v.16). The Jews were quite resistant to having Jesus' messiahship and saving work proclaimed among themselves (Acts 4:18-21; 5:27, 28, 40), but Paul's Gentile mission provoked even more indignation, because it implied God's forsaking of Israel (cf. Acts 13:46, 48-50; 17:4, 5; cf. also Rom 11:11, 25). The saving purpose of Gentile preaching was what the Jews sought to eliminate. "They always heap up their sins to the limit" is the outcome of killing the Lord Jesus and all their subsequent adverse actions. Grammatically, the sentence sees the Jews with this aim, but consciously it was God who contemplated the ultimate outcome (cf. Rom 1:20; so Milligan, p. 31; Ellicott, p. 31). The figure of "heap up" or "fill to the full" (*anaplērōsai*) points to a well-defined limit of sin appointed by divine decree. When this point is reached, divine chastisement becomes inevitable. After generations of repeated apostasies and rebellion, Israel had arrived. The climax had come especially with rejection of the Messiah himself, and their already-fixed judgment was biding its time till its direct consequences were released.

"The wrath of God" is none other than the eschatological wrath for which the whole world is destined just before Messiah's kingdom (cf. 1:10) (Reginald H. Fuller, *The Mission and Achievement of Jesus* [Chicago: Alec R. Allenson, Inc., 1954], p. 26). A more general definition, such as the present outpouring of wrath (Rom 1:18), cannot satisfy the wrath's definiteness (*hē orgē*, "the wrath") in a letter so eschatologically oriented as this (Best, p. 119). In bringing Paul's excursus regarding the Jews to its logical climax, the meaning required is the future day of wrath. It is, to be sure, God's wrath, though "of God" (supplied in NIV) is not in the Greek.

If the wrath is yet future, why does Paul speak of it as happening in the past (*ephthasen*, "has come")? The best explanation of the aorist tense of the verb comes from comparing the only other NT combinations of *phanō epi* ("come upon")—Matt 12:28; Luke 11:20—where Jesus speaks of the kingdom's arrival in comparable terminology. The unique force of this verb connotes "arrival upon the threshold of fulfilment and accessible experience, *not* the entrance into that experience" (K.W. Clark, "Realized Eschatology," JBL, [Sept 1940], 59:379). Just as the kingdom reached the covenant people at Christ's first coming without their enjoying "the experience ensuing upon the initial contact" (Ibid., p. 379), so the wrath that will precede that kingdom has come before the Jews' full experience of it. All prerequisites for unleashing this future torrent have been met. God has set conditions in readiness through the first coming and the rejection of Messiah by this people. A time of trouble awaits Israel just as it does the rest of the world, and the breaking forth of this time is portrayed as an "imminent condemnation" by *ephthasen ep'* ("come upon") (Ibid., p. 380). As soon as human conditions in the progress of God's program warrant, the Jews with the rest of the non-Christian world will be plunged into this awful future turmoil. "At last" should probably be replaced by the footnote alternative "fully," the latter meaning that the issue is now settled. The determination cannot be reversed, the obstinate blindness of the Jewish people furnishing obvious proof of this (cf. John 13:1 for this sense of *eis telos* ["the full extent"] to describe Christ's irrevocable love).

Notes

15 Additional support for associating τοὺς προφήτας (*tous prophētas*, "the prophets") with τὸν κύριον Ἰησοῦν (*ton kurion Iēsoun*, "the Lord Jesus") may be cited. The position of the initial καί (*kai*, "and") just before *ton kurion* accords better with a correlative force: "both the Lord Jesus and the prophets." Also Christ's association (in Acts 7:52) with the prophets in suffering adds to the case. The chief deficiency with making this connection, however, is that one cannot justify placing "the Lord Jesus" prior to "the prophets." This order is neither logical nor chronological. Coupled with the aorist tense of ἐκδιωξάντων (*ekdiōxantōn*, "chasing out"; NIV, "drove . . . out") which most likely would have been present tense if the missionaries alone were in view, the case for associating OT prophets with NT Christian disciples in this verse is more convincing (cf. Matt 5:12).

16 God's displeasure with the Jews was already evident in the teachings of Christ (Matt 21:43; 23:38; 24:15-28; 27:25; Mark 11:14, 20; Luke 21:5-24; 23:27-31). That ἡ ὀργή (*hē orgē*, "the wrath") was already being carried out as a foreshadowing of punishments to come has been one explanation for the definiteness of wrath in 2:16 (Hendriksen, p. 73). *Orgē* is also used of God's present anger with the Jews nationally in Rom 9:22 (Hogg and Vine, p. 49). It is impossible to deny a present manifestation of God's wrath against both Jews and Gentiles, but predominantly in the NT and in 1 Thess particularly, God's wrath refers narrowly to a specific future period of limited duration. Such a meaning is required in 2:16.

Explanations for the aorist ἔφθασεν (*ephthasen*, "has come") have been multiplied. Some have taken it as constative and historical, pointing back either to OT times (Lenski, pp. 273, 274) or to the crucifixion (Hiebert, p. 120; Lightfoot, p. 35) or to some event or events in the more recent past such as Jewish misfortunes under Caligula, Claudius, or even Titus. But the Epistle was written long before A.D. 70 (Moulton, *Grammar*, 1:135; Milligan, p. 32; W.G. Kümmel, *Promise and Fulfilment* [Naperville, Ill.: Alec R. Allenson, Inc., 1957], p. 106). Because of the eschatological force of ὀργή (*orgē* "wrath"), however, all these are untenable. Others have taken the aorist to be prophetic (R.H. Fuller, p. 26; Morris, p. 92). The prophetic aorist as a Greek parallel to the Hebrew prophetic perfect is an established usage, but it is expected more in a grammatical framework characterized by other Semitisms (cf. Luke 1:51-53). The best explanation is a constative aorist, pointing to a past arrival but an arrival only in a potential or positional sense. Such a potential presence of the wrath accords with the Epistle's emphasis on an imminent breaking forth of end time events, one of which is the well-known trouble of Israel before Messiah's return (Best, pp. 120-121).

C. Vindication Through Their Separation (2:17-3:13)

1. Desire to go to them

2:17-20

> 17But, brothers, when we were torn away from you for a short time (in person, not in thought), out of our intense longing we made every effort to see you. 18For we wanted to come to you—certainly I, Paul, did, again and again—but Satan stopped us. 19For what is our hope, our joy, or the crown in which we will glory in the presence of our Lord Jesus when he comes? Is it not you? 20Indeed, you are our glory and joy.

17 Turning from his digression about the Jews, Paul continues to stress deep feeling for the Thessalonians. He pictures himself in contrast ("but") to the persecutors just mentioned (2:14-16). The affectionate "brothers" prepares for heartfelt words about his leaving them—a painful experience because of a consuming attraction for them, like that of a child who has prematurely lost his parents (cf. *aporphanisthentes*, "were torn away from you"). This graphic word combines the idea of separation with the mental anguish accompanying it. After only a brief absence ("for a very short time"), he wants to be with them. "We made every effort" (*perissoteros espoudasamen*) conveys a depth of feeling amounting to zeal, a zeal heightened by separation. Added to this deep emotion already portrayed is his "intense longing" (*pollē epithumia*).

Paul's warm words about his feeling for the Thessalonians may reflect rumors that he did not really care for them. Apparently some had said he had no interest in coming back to them and had come the first time only to satisfy selfish ambition.

18 Therefore, as if he were not satisfied with his already-overwhelming expressions of his feeling toward the Thessalonians, Paul proceeds to proof of a longing to see them. It is his personal inclination and purpose ("we wanted"). Here Paul's use of *thelō* ("wish," "will") better accords with his strong desire to return to the Thessalonians than *boulomai*, which relates more to decision after deliberation. The tug on his heart is manifest in the words "certainly I, Paul." Though Timothy and Silas had already returned to Thessalonica, Paul's failure to do so did not come from lack of intention; he had attempted another visit several times.

What can hinder such intense desire? It must be nothing less than Satanic hindrance. The hindrance was probably not the demands of missionary work elsewhere, since it is not the enemy's purpose to encourage such work. Restraint by civil officials in Thessalonica and opposition from local Jews are other possibilities, but these would hardly be sufficient to prevent Paul's return. A more plausible identification of the hindrance might be his illness (cf. 2 Cor 12:7), even though this would require the "us" to refer only to Paul. Of course, Paul did not attribute all changes in plans to Satan. He saw some doors as being closed by God's intervention. In fact, it was the Spirit's intervention that had led to the gospel's original proclamation in Thessalonica and surrounding Macedonia (cf. Acts 16:6-10).

The real existence of a personal and supernatural devil is incontrovertible. His present activity in opposing God is only a foretaste of heightened opposition to be launched in the future through his special human representative just prior to Jesus' personal return to earth (2 Thess 2:3-12).

19 Paul's rhetorical questions tie the Thessalonians into Paul's anticipation of the Lord Jesus' coming and presence. They will bring him joy and be a victor's wreath for him to glory in at that future moment of truth. As always with Paul, this is a boasting or glorying in what God has done (cf. 1 Cor 1:31), not in personal accomplishment (Rom 3:27; 4:2; cf. 2 Cor 1:14; Phil 2:16).

Interrupting his own question, he anticipates the answer: "Is it not you?" The untranslated *kai* ("even") in this answer heightens the effect of his statement: Is it not [in fact] you?" This is Paul's answer to those who say he did not care for the Thessalonian Christians. The future event Paul is looking toward is identical with the appearance of every Christian before the *bema* ("judgment seat") of Christ (2 Cor 5:10), where the works of every Christian will be evaluated. Because of his converts' evident spiritual attainments, Paul feels that this will be an occasion of joy and victory.

"When he comes" translates the literal meaning—"in [or at] his presence [or coming]." Here the noun is *parousia*, which in extrabiblical Greek sometimes meant a ruler's visit to a certain place. *Parousia* comes from two words: "to be" and "present." It may point to the moment of arrival to initiate a visit or it may focus on the stay initiated by the arrival. In the NT the word applies to the return of Jesus Christ. The various facets of this future visit are defined by the contexts in which *parousia* appears. In this instance it is Jesus' examination of his servants subsequent to his coming for them (4:15-17) that is in view.

20 Finally, Paul declares that the Thessalonians are his "glory and joy." Not only will they be this when Christ returns; they are so right now. So he silences the insinuations about his lack of concern for his converts.

Notes

17 Δέ (*de*, "but," "now") at the beginning of v.17 has been understood by some as simply continuative, rather than adversative (Best, p. 124; Hiebert, p. 122). The great difference between the attitude closing the previous paragraph and the one described in this paragraph speaks more strongly in favor of contrast than continuation, (Frame, p. 117; Milligan, p. 33).

18 Morris, after rejecting the idea that ἅπαξ καὶ δίς (*hapax kai dis*, "once and twice"; NIV, "again and again") is a Latinism, finds its source in LXX. The English meaning most suitable for the idiom, he writes, is "more than once." This is better than "repeatedly," which is too strong, or

"once or twice," which is too weak (Leon Morris, ΚΑΙ ΑΠΑΞ ΚΑΙ ΔΙΣ, NovTest [1956]:1:205–208).

---

2. Sending Timothy to them

3:1-5

¹So when we could stand it no longer, we thought it best to be left by ourselves in Athens. ²We sent Timothy, who is our brother and God's fellow worker in spreading the gospel of Christ, to strengthen and encourage you in your faith, ³so that no one would be unsettled by these trials. You know quite well that we were destined for them. ⁴In fact, when we were with you, we kept telling you that we would be persecuted. And it turned out that way, as you well know.

⁵For this reason, when I could stand it no longer, I sent to find out about your faith. I was afraid that in some way the tempter might have tempted you and our efforts might have been useless.

1-5 Paul now sought another way to dull the pain of separation from his beloved Thessalonians. So he sent Timothy, a valuable companion and effective servant, to serve in his place and bring back word about their afflictions and satanic temptation (3:1-5).

1 Paul gives as his reason for doing this: "We could stand it no longer." "Stand" (*stegontes*, literally "cover") does not refer to concealment of his feelings. That is the very thing he does not do. Rather, the verb has the metaphorical meaning of "hold out against." He was at this point unable to continue in ignorance of how his precious converts were faring in persecution. His personal trials meant far less to him than those he suffered vicariously for his beloved in Christ.

Paul's sincerity is again demonstrated by his willingness to do without his cherished co-worker Timothy ("to be left by ourselves") in a strange city dominated by pagan philosophy and animosity toward the gospel (cf. Acts 17:16–34). But was Paul actually alone? Some have thought that "we" and "ourselves" imply Silas's presence even after Timothy's departure because plural pronouns elsewhere in the letter include others besides Paul (cf. 1:2; Best, p. 131; Hiebert, p. 132). Yet his use of "us" in 2:18 may well have been in a singular sense in light of the "I, Paul" in the same verse. Also, v.5 picks up the plural of v.1 with the singular "I." For Paul to have used "we" in v.1 in any other than a singular sense would have defeated his apologetic desire to express his loneliness. If his long-time companion Silas had still been in Athens, there would have been little deprivation in Paul's not having Timothy with him. He would not be "alone" (*monoi*, v.1) in the real sense of the word unless Silas too was away (Morris, *NIC*, pp. 98, 99).

2 Some are troubled by the problem of harmonizing Timothy's movements with those recorded in Acts 17–18. Luke does not speak of Silas's and Timothy's response to Paul's invitation to come to him quickly (Acts 17:15)—i.e., while he was still in Athens. He does, however, tell of their joining him after his move to Corinth (Acts 18:5). Some have therefore surmised that either this passage in 1 Thessalonians or the account in Acts is historically inaccurate. Yet the supposition is unnecessary. Both books are quite accurate. The reconciliation lies in Luke's decision to omit the visit of Silas and Timothy to Athens. Actually, they did come to Paul while he was in Athens and then were again sent to the Macedonian cities, Timothy going to Thessalonica in accordance with v.1. With Silas's

departure prior to or simultaneous with Timothy's departure, the apostle was subjected to an almost intolerable state of loneliness until their subsequent return (Acts 18:5; 1 Thess 3:6). And he was willing to endure this only for the sake of benefitting the Thessalonians and satisfying his thirst for news of them.

Timothy was valuable not only to Paul, but also to Christians more generally, for he was their "brother and God's fellow worker in spreading the gospel of Christ." Timothy was a spiritual brother in the truest sense and an effective servant of God, and for Paul to choose him to go to Thessalonica demonstrates again his genuine concern for the Christians there.

Timothy's mission was "to strengthen and encourage" them in their faith, as Paul himself usually did (Acts 14:22; 15:32, 41; 18:23; Rom 1:11; 16:25; 1 Thess 3:13; 2 Thess 2:16, 17; 3:3). Dependence on God in faith was their only recourse in adversity. They could remain faithful only as they let him supply inner strength. Paul had a continuing concern for the Thessalonians' faith (cf. 3:10).

3 Timothy told them not to be "unsettled by these trials." "Trials," more specifically "afflictions" or "tribulations" (*thlipsesin*), are the stiffest test of faith. Such is the lot of Christ's followers (e.g., John 16:33). Yet these trials are not to be identified with the end-time tribulation just before the Messiah's return (Best, p. 135), which will mark the culmination of God's wrath against the ungodly (Matt 24:21; 1 Thess 2:16; 5:9; 2 Thess 1:6). The trials Paul speaks of here are part of the church's immediate experience, some of them having already happened (cf. v.4).

"Unsettled" (*sainesthai*) describes a state of being shaken or disturbed. In some contexts the same word connotes being lured away through deceptive means, but its other meaning of "unsettled" or "disquieted" better suits this discussion.

Paul had already told them that trials are an inevitable part of Christian experience (3:3; cf. Acts 14:22). Timothy was to reinforce this warning.

4 Christians are marked out for trials. The repeated warnings about persecution had already been substantiated. Prior to the writing of 1 Thessalonians things had "turned out that way" (*egeneto*). So there could be no confusion with the end-time tribulation before the *parousia*, for these were the common day-by-day tribulations that befall the disciple just as they did the Master (cf. John 15:18–16:4).

5 In this situation, Paul, speaking now only of himself at this point ("I"; cf. v.1), was constrained to find out through Timothy the state of their faith. He knew that "the tempter" (Satan; cf. Matt 4:3) had been at work among them and that God permits the enemy this activity. What Paul did not know about the Thessalonians, however, was whether or not the tempter's solicitations had been successful, making his work and that of his colleagues "useless."

Notes

2 The reading συνεργόν τοῦ θεοῦ (*sunergon tou theou*, "God's fellow worker") is preferred by some in lieu of διάκονον τοῦ θεοῦ (*diakonon tou theou*, "God's servant") as being more difficult and best explaining the origin of the other readings (Metzger, *The Text of the NT*, pp. 241, 242). "God's fellow worker" is no more difficult than "God's servant," however, in view of 1 Cor 3:9.

Since superior MS support rests with *diakonon tou theou*, it is the more probable choice. Since *diakonon* later became a secondary ecclesiastical office, some copyist may have balked at applying this title to Timothy and substituted "fellow worker."

5 The distinction between the indicative ἐπείρασεν (*epeirasen*, "tempted") and the parallel subjunctive γένηται (*genētai*, "became"; NIV, "might have been") should be high-lighted. The fact of temptation no doubt existed; consequently, an indicative appears in the former clause. The issue of temptation was unknown, however, until the return of Timothy. A potential mood, the subjunctive, was therefore appropriate. Happily, the missionaries' labor was not "useless."

---

3. Delight over their progress

3:6–10

> **6**But Timothy has just now come to us from you and has brought good news about your faith and love. He has told us that you always have pleasant memories of us and that you long to see us, just as we also long to see you.
> **7**Therefore, brothers, in all our distress and persecution we were encouraged about you because of your faith. **8**For now we really live, since you are standing firm in the Lord. **9**How can we thank God enough for you in return for all the joy we have in the presence of our God because of you?
> **10**Night and day we pray most earnestly that we may see you again and supply what is lacking in your faith.

6–10 Timothy finally returned from his Thessalonian mission with an opposite report from what Paul had feared. This cheering news greatly encouraged Paul and moved him to thanksgiving and prayer.

6 "Just now" shows that Timothy's arrival from Thessalonica immediately preceded the composition of the Epistle and probably provided its chief motivation. This arrival is the same as that in Acts 18:5, when Timothy and Silas came at approximately the same time. This substantiates the earlier conclusion that Paul was actually separated from both Timothy and Silas for a time (cf. 3:1). Doubtless he was refreshed by the return of his two associates, though by now he had moved from Athens to Corinth, where new Christian fellowship had developed.

Rather than using a neutral verb in speaking of Timothy's report (cf. *apangellousin*, "they relate," 1:9), Paul chooses the verb usually reserved for gospel preaching (*euangelisamenou*, "bringing good news"). Only here and in Revelation 10:7 does it refer to anything other than the good news of salvation. That Paul places Timothy's report in this exalted category shows his high estimate of the Thessalonians.

The report was both spiritual and personal. Spiritually, they had progressed in faith and love; their trust in God had been sufficient for their difficulties. Yet room for improvement remained (cf. v.10). Likewise their progress in loving others was uplifting news, though even here there was also room for growth (cf. 3:12; 4:9, 10). The absence of hope from the triad of faith, love, and hope (cf. 1:3; 5:8) is not significant. Faith and love adequately describe wholesome Christian development (cf. Gal 5:6; Eph 1:15; 3:17; 6:23; Col 1:4; 2 Thess 1:3).

Timothy's report of the kindly feelings of the Thessalonians toward him ("pleasant memories," "long to see us") assured Paul that they had not written him off as an exploiter, disinterested in their welfare. They still maintained a warm spot for him, matching his own tender longing to see them (cf. 2:17; 3:10).

7 The report helped Paul in his adversity (cf. Acts 18:6, 9, 10, 12, 13). He faced physical privations ("distress," *anagkē*) and suffering inflicted by his antagonists ("persecution," *thlipsei*). Like all Christians (3:3, 4), he was called to suffer persecution (cf. 2 Tim 3:12). It was their faith that encouraged Paul. Since they were willing to depend on God for help against impossible obstacles, Paul himself had an additional incentive to do this; in fact, he regularly derived personal encouragement from other believers (Rom 1:12; 2 Cor 7:4, 13; Philem 7).

8 The news Timothy brought rejuvenated Paul—"for now we really live." This was not a mysterious "communication of life within the Christian community," growing out of a relationship sustained "in the Lord" (contra Best, pp. 142, 143). Paul had been given a new lease on life. To know they continued "standing firm in the Lord," unmoved by affliction and unshaken by his detractors, was enough to stimulate Paul to renewed activity.

9 The result was thanksgiving to God. Paul found words inadequate to express his appreciation for what had happened in their lives. The change in Paul's mood was radical; "all our distress and persecution" (*pasē tē anagkē kai thlipsei hēmōn*, 3:7) has now become "all the joy we have" (*pasē tē chara hē chairomen*) because of the steadfastness of the Thessalonians. His was no superficial happiness but heartfelt and sincere joy "in the presence of our God."

10 Along with his rejoicing, Paul prayed continually for the Thessalonians. "Night and day" does not mean once in the evening and once in the morning, nor that he did nothing else but pray. It rather points to the extreme frequency of his prayers, while "most earnestly" refers to the intensity of his prayers.

The thrust of Paul's petitions for the Thessalonians is twofold: first, "that we may see you" (cf. 2:18 and 3:6); second, "to supply what is lacking in your faith." This shows his desire to correct, restore, and equip them in respect to faith. They have already been commended for "their work produced by faith" (1:3). Yet they had room for additional growth, and Paul felt his presence could foster it.

Notes

7 Διά (*dia*) is more precisely tr. "through" than "because of," since it is followed by the genitive rather than the accusative case. Very rarely does the preposition with the genitive express cause, but it does quite frequently denote means, which is very appropriate in this context. Hence, faith is seen as the instrument through which encouragement is imparted.

8 It is rare for ἐάν (*ean*, "if") to be followed by a present indicative such as στήκετε (*stēkete*, "stand"), the reading preferred to the weakly attested present subjunctive in v.8. Paul's choice of a present indicative rather than a more normal aorist subjunctive has the effect of expressing certainty that his readers will continue to stand firm from this point on.

4. Seeking direction for them

3:11–13

> ¹¹Now may our God and Father himself and our Lord Jesus clear the way for us to come to you. ¹²May the Lord make your love increase and overflow for each other and for everyone else, just as ours does for you. ¹³May he give you inner strength that you may be blameless and holy in the presence of our God and Father when our Lord Jesus comes with all his holy ones.

11–13 A transitional "now" introduces a subject that is not unrelated to v.10, in which Paul had spoken of his two petitions for the Thessalonians. Here they are elaborated on. God is addressed indirectly in the third person, in keeping with an Epistle addressed to men (cf. 5:23; 2 Thess 2:16; 3:5, 16).

11 Paul recognizes the uselessness of personal efforts toward a revisit unless God "clears the way." At the moment, the path of return is untravelable (cf. 2:18), but Paul prays for the removal of the barriers. Two persons viewed as one (cf. John 10:30) possess power to open the way to Thessalonica once again; "our God and Father himself and our Lord Jesus" is the compound subject of a singular verb (*kateuthunai*, "may [He] clear")— probably an indication of the unity of the Godhead (Ellicott, p. 46). Even if the deity of Jesus is not to be seen in such a grammatical feature (Best, p. 147), it must be understood, since only God is worthy to be addressed in prayer. "Himself" (*autos*), the word with which Paul opens this prayer, very possibly refers to both Father and Son, once again implying the one essence of these two persons (cf. 2 Thess 2:16) (Frame, pp. 136, 137).

In any event, it is futile to argue that the early church only gradually came to look upon Jesus as God. Indeed this is a truth endorsed prior to Pentecost (cf. Matt 16:16) and one that is foundational to the church's existence (cf. Matt 16:18). The Father and Son in their unity can grant this request, which they eventually did. Paul returned to the Macedonian province approximately five years later (Acts 19:21; 20:1; 1 Cor 16:5; 2 Cor 2:13) and in all likelihood made a point of visiting Thessalonica.

12,13 Paul's second petition pertains to "what is lacking" in their faith (cf. v.10), specifically the outworking of that faith in a growing love. Since "Lord" refers to Jesus in vv.11, 13 and likewise in all Paul's writings for the most part, it is best interpreted in this way here.

12 The petition is offered to the Lord Jesus alone, as Paul seeks the enlargement (*pleonasai*) and abundance (*perisseusai*) of the Thessalonians. Combined, the two words mean "increase you to overflowing." Paul prays this for them, not because they lacked love (4:9, 10a; cf. 4:1a), but because continual increase in selfless devotion to others (*perisseusai*, ["overflow"] and *perisseuein mallon*, ["do so more and more," 4:10b]; cf. *perisseuēte mallon*, ["do this more and more," 4:1b]) is always a need for Christians.

In line with the consistent NT emphasis, the prime objects of love are fellow Christians ("each other"; cf. John 13:34, 35; Rom 13:8; 1 Thess 4:9; 1 Peter 1:22; 1 John 3:11, 23). But love also reaches beyond the circle of Christians to all other people ("everyone else"). Jesus warned against a narrow conception of one's "neighbor" (Matt 5:43–48; Luke 10:25–37; cf. Matt 19:19; 22:39; Mark 12:31). Daringly, Paul sets himself as a standard of love to be emulated ("just as ours does for you"), a step he could take only because of his imitation of Jesus (cf. 1:6), who is the ultimate standard (John 13:34; 15:12).

13 The goal of Paul's prayer for the Thessalonians is that the Lord will grant them "inner strength" to be "blameless" in holiness "in the presence of our God and Father" when the Lord Jesus returns. He looks forward to the time of final accounting. An overflow of love (v.12) is the only route to holy conduct in which no fault can be found (v.13). For unless love prevails, selfish motives inhibit ethical development by turning us toward ourselves and away from God and blameless living. The holiness that belongs to God is the ideal we must seek (cf. Lev 19:2; 1 Peter 1:16).

The final accounting Paul alludes to will take place in the personal "presence of our God and Father." The local force of *emprosthen* ("in the presence of") obtains whenever this preposition relates appearance before a judge (Matt 27:11; 25:32; Luke 21:36; 2 Cor 5:10; contrast 1 Thess 1:3; 3:9; 1 John 3:19) (cf. BAG, p. 256). Earlier Paul has made "our Lord Jesus" the judge at this scene (1 Thess 2:19). This is no contradiction. The unity of the Father and Son, just seen in v.11, allows a joint judgeship. The *bēma* of Christ (2 Cor 5:10) is also the *bēma* of God (Rom 14:10), because Christ in his present session is with the Father in his heavenly throne (Rev 3:21; cf. Rom 8:34; Heb 1:3; 10:12). This hearing will take place at the future "visit" (*en tē parousia*, "in the coming") of the Lord Jesus (cf. 2:19). For the Thessalonians Paul prays for a favorable verdict at that time.

Others present at this reckoning will be "all his holy ones." Their identity has been variously taken either as that of angels or of redeemed human beings, or both angels and redeemed human beings. The last possibility can be eliminated in that Paul would hardly include two such diverse groups in the same category. That angels alone are meant is unlikely in light of NT usage of *hagioi* ("holy ones"). Universally in Paul and perhaps the entire NT (Jude 14 is debatable) it is a term for redeemed humanity, though usage in LXX and later Jewish literature differs. The redeemed are elsewhere associated with Christ at his return (2 Thess 1:10). Since human beings are the objects of judgment and their holiness is what is in focus (cf. "blameless and holy"), it is entirely appropriate to identify "the holy ones" as other Christian people joined with the Thessalonian Christians before the *bēma* of God and Christ.

Certain matters about the time "when our Lord Jesus comes" require clarification. For example, what relation does this event bear to the predicted future wrath (1:10; 2:16; 5:9) and the meeting of the saints with the Lord in the air (4:15-17)? If this is Christ's coming (*parousia*) prior to the period of wrath, it is identifiable with the meeting of 4:15-17. This interpretation, however, encounters obstacles. "With all his holy ones" is one of them. The redeemed cannot come with him until he has first come for them. To interpret "all his holy ones" as the spirits of the dead in Christ is not a satisfactory answer to the difficulty because some of those in Christ will not yet have died. "All" would not therefore be accurate because of the exclusion of this latter group. Furthermore, the readers were not yet assured that their dead would participate in the *parousia* (Best, p. 153).

If this is Christ's coming after the wrath, difficulties of a different type are encountered. Foremost among these is a disregard for the contextual emphasis on the judgment of saints. By the time of his return to earth after the wrath, this reckoning will have already taken place in heaven (i.e., *emprosthen tou theou kai patros hēmōn*, "in the presence of our God and Father"). It is to Christ's earlier return in the air (4:15-17) that the *bema* of God and Christ relates.

In resolving this difficulty, we must consider the scope of *parousia* as indicated in these Epistles (see Introduction, pp. 233, 234). The complexity of the term *parousia* demands that it include an extended visit as well as the arrival initiating that visit. This is provided for adequately in the rarer meaning of *parousia*, "presence" (cf. 1 Cor 16:17; 2 Cor 10:10; Phil 2:12). Included in this visit is an evaluation of the saints (cf. 2:19; 5:23), which is the aspect in view here in v.13. This judgment cannot be completely dissociated from Christ's coming in the air (4:15–17), because this advent marks its initiation. Yet it must be conceived of as a session in heaven in some measure separate from the arrival itself. At this juncture the degree to which Christians have attained a "blameless and holy" character will be divinely ascertained.

Notes

11 Αὐτός (*autos*, "himself") introduces prayers of this type also in 5:23; 2 Thess 2:16; 3:16. It refers once to the Father alone (5:23) and once to the Lord Jesus alone (2 Thess 3:16). In 2 Thess 2:16 the subject is a compound one as in 3:11, but with the Son preceding the Father. This pattern of usage implies that the pronoun extends to both members of the compound subject. The sense is probably "our God and Father and our Lord Jesus himself" rather than "our God and Father himself."

A compound subject governing a sing. verb is well known, but this is ordinarily found only when the verb precedes or stands between the subjects (Turner, *Syntax*, pp. 313, 314). Aside from v.11 and 2 Thess 2:16, 17, the only time Paul has a sing. verb following a compound subject is 1 Cor 15:50, another instance where the two subjects constitute a unit. Hence, unity in the Godhead best explains the sing. κατευθύναι (*kateuthynai*, "may [he] clear") in v.11.

13 Ἔμπροσθεν (*emprosthen*, "in the presence of") at times has nonlocal connotations, as in 1:3 and 3:9 of this Epistle. Yet a judicial hearing requires actual proximity to the judge. So here the preposition requires a location before the Father in heaven.

IV. Exhortation to the Thessalonians (4:1–5:22)

A. *Exhortation Regarding Personal Needs (4:1–12)*

1. *Continual improvement*

4:1, 2

> ¹Finally, brothers, we instructed you how to live in order to please God, as in fact you are living. Now we ask you and urge you in the Lord Jesus to do this more and more. ²You know what instructions we gave you by the authority of the Lord Jesus.

1 Paul now urges the Thessalonians on to greater spiritual attainments outlined in 3:10–13. His exhortations, introduced by "finally" (*loipon oun*—"finally therefore"; NIV includes the *oun*, "therefore," in the "finally"), however, are logically based on more than 3:10–13. The drastic change to a new line of thought implies that all of chapters 2 and 3 are in view. "Since our relations with you have been such as they have, since we have labored so much among you, since you have suffered for the gospel's sake, since there is yet progress to be made, since we have maintained a continuing prayerful

interest in you, we ask you, brothers, and urge you in the Lord Jesus . . ." (Lightfoot, p. 51; Ellicott, p. 58; Frame, p. 141).

"Finally" shows that the series of admonitions launched here will be the final part of the letter. With Paul a final word may be brief (2 Cor 13:11; Phil 4:8; 2 Tim 4:8) or extended (Phil 3:1; 2 Thess 3:1) as here. "Brothers" again shows his tenderness in approaching delicate subjects.

The nature of Paul's appeal is conveyed in "ask" (erōtōmen) and "urge" (parakaloumen). Since erōtōmen is used alone later in these Epistles ("We ask," 2 Thess 2:1), it is best not to equate the two words, but to understand the former as a gentle, friendly request and the latter as an authoritative apostolic plea. Paul frequently uses parakaloumen ("urge") when turning from the didactic portions of his Epistles to the outcome of his teaching (e.g., Rom 12:1; Eph 4:1). Such urging is more than a request, but less than a command (Best, p. 155). It conveys a kind of diplomatic authority and is absent from Paul's sharpest Epistle, Galatians. The words "in the Lord Jesus" are the context of the exhortations that are to follow.

The Thessalonians had already been given instruction about how they must "live in order to please God." Paul again views the Christian life as a "walk" ("live," peripatein; cf. 2:12). He might have immediately requested compliance with earlier instruction, but in the Greek word order he interrupts himself before doing so, lest he appear to be condemnatory. As always he gives credit where it is due, in this case recognizing the substantial progress that has been made. (cf. his previous commendations—1:3, 6–10; 3:6, 8).

Yet the realization of the ultimate goal of pleasing God and receiving his commendation (3:13) entailed continual improvement. "Do this more and more" (perisseuēte), though referring to the overflow of love Paul had prayed for (3:12) and was to urge (4:10), here relates to other dimensions of the Christian life as well (4:3 ff.; cf. 3:10).

2 So Paul stimulates his converts' memory of what he and his companions had told them. He characterizes their previous ministry as a delivering of "commands" (parangelias; NIV, "instructions"). These were binding because they were given "by the authority of the Lord Jesus."

Notes

1 An established Hellenistic Gr. formula is illustrated here: (1) a verb in the first person, παρακαλοῦμεν (parakaloumen, "we urge"), (2) a vocative, (3) a prepositional phrase, ἐν Κυρίῳ Ἰησοῦ (en Kyriō Iēsou, "in the Lord Jesus"), and (4) substance of what is requested (cf. ἵνα [hina, "in order to"] clause) Bjerkelund, Parakalō, cited by Best, pp. 154, 155).

A second hina is required to resume the first because of the extraordinary length of the parenthesis begun at the first καθώς (kathōs, "as"). It is sometimes Paul's style to deviate from his initial structure in order to interject an additional thought. In this case the second hina marks his return to the thought he began with the first hina (Lightfoot, p. 52; Frame, p. 142; Milligan, p. 46).

2. Sexual purity

4:3-8

> [3]It is God's will that you should be holy; that you should avoid sexual immorality; [4]that each of you should learn to control his own body in a way that is holy and honorable, [5]not in passionate lust like the heathen, who do not know God. [6]and that in this matter no one should wrong his brother or take advantage of him. The Lord will punish men for all such sins, as we have already told you and warned you. [7]For God did not call us to be impure, but to live a holy life. [8]Therefore, he who rejects this instruction does not reject man but God, who gives you his Holy Spirit.

3 The Greek text uses a *gar,* "for instance," (untranslated in NIV) to introduce some needed exhortations about sexual behavior. Christian holiness, says Paul, requires total abstinence from *porneias* ("sexual immorality," "fornication"). The word requires broad definition here as including all types of sexual sins between male and female. A year or two earlier a Christian council in Jerusalem had ruled decisively on a related issue affecting Gentile Christians (cf. Acts 15:20). It is not clear whether the Thessalonians were guilty of fornication, so common among the pagans (v.5). Though Paul may have had in mind the temptation to indulge in it, his strong words probably imply some overt transgressions. Pagan moral corruption looked upon fornication either indifferently or favorably. That the Thessalonians slipped into it after their conversion would not have been strange (Ellicott, p. 51; H. A. W. Meyer, *Acts,* p. 61; Lightfoot, p. 53). While Paul had congratulated them on their faith (cf. 1:3), this does not mean that there was no occasional misbehavior, even this kind, within the church (cf. 1 Cor 1:4–9; 5:1–5; 6:12–20).

4 The positive side of holiness requires one to "learn to control his own body" or "learn to live with his own wife" (cf. footnote in NIV; also note below). Some have resolved the uncertainty over the exact meaning of the Greek by referring *skeuos* (literally, "vessel"; NIV, "body") to the human body, a meaning that seeks support from Paul's usage in Romans 9:22, 23 and 2 Corinthians 4:7. But this overlooks the figurative nature of this term from the ceramics trade in its other two contexts. It also strains the meaning of *ktasthai,* which can only with great difficulty be understood as "control." Taking *skeuos* to be a wife may therefore be preferable. *Ktasthai* may in this way be given its natural meaning of "acquire." Or it may mean "keep on acquiring" or "live with" in the sense of cultivating a wife's favor, i.e., the couple should not be unduly separated and thus strain their marital relationship (cf. 1 Cor 7:2–5). Use of *skeuos* as "wife" is loosely paralleled in 1 Peter 3:7. A wholesome marriage was thus Paul's antidote for "sexual immorality." "Holy and honorable" describe the way to maintain the right kind of marriage, holiness being due God (4:3; cf. 3:13) and honor due the wife (Lightfoot, p. 55).

5 The pagans (i.e., the Gentiles), those with no inkling of the law of Moses or Christian practice, know nothing of this holy and honorable behavior. Their guiding principle is "passionate lust" because they "do not know God." Such reprehensible behavior is a consequence of their refusal to respond to God's revelation of himself (Rom 1:18–32). "Who do not know God" is a familiar Pauline expression for the Gentile world (Gal 4:8;

2 Thess 1:8; cf. Ps 79:6; Jer 10:25). Once removed from that realm into the church of God (cf. 1 Cor 10:32), a believer is obligated to maintain much higher standards.

6 Wronging and taking advantage of a brother, probably a Christian brother, are other violations of holiness. Though some have taken "this matter" to be business dealings, the emphasis of the context shows it to be sexual transgression. (Business dealings would require a plural, *pragmata*, "matters"). To have relations with a woman outside marriage is not just a trespass against God's law. It also defrauds some fellow Christian who eventually will take this woman as his own wife, or perhaps has already done so—an especially heinous sin because the one robbed is a spiritual relative of the robber. Paul does not allude to the other injustice, which is quite obvious. The woman herself is an object of cruel abuse in such a situation. This too is especially repulsive in a Christian setting.

A reason for complying with the standards set forth in vv.4, 5 relates to the Lord Jesus' future punishment of "all such sins." (*Dioti*, "because" in Gr. NT, shows the verse to be motivational.) Paul is not speaking of a present vengeance (1 Cor 5:1-5; 11:30-32), but of the future judgment of Christians at the *parousia* (2:19; 3:13; 1 Cor 3:10-17)—a judgment to be carried out by Christ (John 5:22; 2 Cor 5:10) in association with God the Father (Rom 14:10; 1 Thess 3:13). Paul's initial expedition to Thessalonica had informed and solemnly warned them of these dire consequences. We do not know what prompted him to put in writing this admonition about judgment. Perhaps urgency required stern words.

7 Another reason for compliance is the nature of God's calling. As in 2:12, this is God's effectual call, mediated through gospel preaching (2 Thess 2:14). Those who, having been called, have responded have not been inducted into a life of sexual impurity, but into a holy life (cf. 3:13; 4:3, 4). They now belong to a community with values different from those of "the heathen" (v.5) among whom they formerly lived.

8 Still another reason for compliance with the standards set forth in vv. 4, 5 is that they are God-given. Therefore rejection of them means rejecting not man, but God, "who gives [us] his Holy Spirit," who is inseparable from the kind of holy living demanded in this paragraph. (The Greek word order places special emphasis on "holy.")

Notes

4 In v.4 ἑαυτοῦ (*heautou*, "himself"; NIV, "his own body") is emphatic in meaning and by position (Blass-Debrunner, p. 148; Turner, p. 190). This furnishes additional reason for referring σκεῦος (*skeuos*, "vessel") to a wife. "*His own* wife" is meaningful, but little is gleaned from one's controlling "*his own* body."

6 Deciding how τὸ μὴ ὑπερβαίνειν κ. τ. λ. (*to mē huperbainein k. t. l.*, literally, "not to go beyond ...") relates to the preceding infinitival clauses is not simple. It is probably not parallel to them because of its article. If it were the purpose of previous actions, the article would have been τοῦ (*tou*, "of the"). Hence, it probably reverts to ὁ ἁγιασμός (*ho hagiasmos*, "holiness") of v.3 and introduces an example of sanctification even more specific than that in vv.3b, 4. This is a sample of the social injustice of fornication (Ellicott, p. 53).

8 There is some MS support for an aorist participle δόντα (*donta*, "having given") rather than a present διδοντα (*didonta*, "giving"). Yet it is not nearly so strong as that for the present. The aorist probably was prompted by the customary NT practice of referring to the Spirit's initial coming to the believer. The present may refer to God's character as giver (Best, p. 172), or it may look on his giving as a perpetual fortifying against uncleanness (Lightfoot, p. 58). The latter is more suitable to the context.

---

3. Filial love

4:9, 10

> 9Now about brotherly love we do not need to write to you, for you yourselves have been taught by God to love each other. 10And in fact, you do love all the brothers throughout Macedonia. Yet we urge you, brothers, to do so more and more.

9,10 "Now about" (*peri de*) is a frequent Pauline formula for introducing a new subject (4:13; 5:1; cf. 1 Cor 7:1, 25; 8:1; 12:1; 16:1, 12). In Corinthians the formula indicates answers to written questions, but here Paul responds to different elements of Timothy's oral report about Thessalonica (1 Thess 3:6). In vv.9, 10a he acknowledges their practical compliance with a responsibility to "love the brothers." "Brotherly love" (*philadelphia*), an expression for attachment to one's blood relatives in secular speech, was taken over by Christianity because of the close ties within the spiritual family of God. Paul views further writing on the subject as superfluous in that they are "taught by God" to do it. "Taught by God" (*theodidaktoi*), a rare term, does not refer to any single teaching such as an OT passage (Lev 19:18), the teaching of Jesus (John 13:34), or a prophetic revelation to the church through Paul or anyone else. It rather describes a divine relationship through the indwelling Holy Spirit (4:8; cf. John 6:45). At conversion, believers become lifelong pupils as the Spirit bears inner witness to the love within the Christian family (cf. Rom 5:5; Gal 5:22). No external stimulus is necessary. Mutual love among Christians is an inbred quality.

Proof of this inner instruction was visible in the Thessalonian's love for all Christians of their province. Any contacts they had with churches in Berea and Philippi are unknown except for the implications of these verses. Very possibly, groups of believers had sprung up in other parts of the province since the beginning of Paul's Macedonian mission (Acts 16:9–12). With some allowance for Paul's hyperbolic "all," it is safe to assume that a goodly proportion of the believers in the province had been touched by the Thessalonians' unselfish concern. Otherwise, the missionary zeal reflected in 1:8 lacks clear substantiation.

As exemplary as the Thessalonians had been (1:3; 3:6), however, further progress remained a goal for them (3:12). Paul's repetition of v.1 in "we urge you, brothers, to do so more and more" (a number of the Greek words are identical or nearly so) shows v.10b to be a particularization of the general admonition of v.1. "More love" is always a potentiality for Christians because the ultimate, the example of Christ himself (John 13:34; 15:12), is infinite and can only be approached, not fully reached.

Notes

9 The verb ἐστε (*este*, "are"; NIV, "have been") is present in sense as well as form. It does not have a perfect force ("have been"). It was the Thessalonians' continuing experience after Paul's departure, just as much as while he was there, to be taught of God to love one another. Hence, "you yourselves *are* taught by God" more suitably represents the meaning.

4. Individual independence

4:11, 12

> ¹¹Make it your ambition to lead a quiet life, to mind your own business and to work with your hands, just as we told you, ¹²so that your daily life may win the respect of outsiders and so that you will not be dependent on anybody.

11,12 These verses stand in close grammatical connection with v.10b. Yet the logical connection is not immediately obvious (Ellicott, p. 58). From the subject of love, Paul apparently changes to something quite different—viz., the importance of industry and individual responsibility in Christian living. The two are not completely unrelated. Nothing disrupts the peace of a Christian community more than the unwillingness of members to shoulder their part of the responsibility for it (Hiebert, p. 180). To disturb tranquility violates the love that permeates a truly Christian community. More specifically, some members of the Thessalonian church appear to have taken advantage of the liberality of other Macedonian Christians (cf. 2 Cor 8:1–5) in accepting financial help while making no effort at self-support (Lightfoot, p. 60).

We do not know the reason for this idleness. Though Paul had already spoken out against the lack of industry ("just as we told you") and though he now writes of it again, the condition later grew worse (2 Thess 3:6–15). Since these two Thessalonian Epistles are so strongly eschatological, it is quite probable that the condition stemmed from their misapplying truths about the Lord's return to their daily living. Christians must never evade their daily responsibilities under the pretense of proclaiming or preparing for Christ's return. To do so is to distort this great hope.

11 That restlessness may have been a problem for the Thessalonians is implied by Paul's exhortation—"make it your ambition to lead a quiet life." Another exhortation, "mind your own business," implies that a meddlesome spirit that often goes with restlessness was troubling them. Busybodies were active (2 Thess 3:11) and needed a reprimand. But the exhortation goes beyond telling them to stay out of other people's affairs; it also implies the necessity of keeping one's own affairs in order. Still another exhortation, "work with your hands," implies that idleness was a problem among the Thessalonians. In a Greek culture that degraded manual labor, Christianity joined with Judaism in viewing it as an honorable pursuit. Most of the Thessalonian believers earned their living with their hands. Paul tells them to continue supporting themselves and thus avoid the pitfalls of idleness (Ellicott, p. 59; Frame, p. 162).

12 These exhortations find a twofold result. For their conduct to "win the respect of outsiders," the Christians in Thessalonica must eliminate restlessness, meddlesomeness,

and idleness (v.11). Even "outsiders," so called because they have no connection with Christ and hence are outside the family of God—cf. 1 Cor 5:12, 13; Col 4:5; 1 Tim 3:7—recognize winsome conduct. On the other hand, they are repelled by those who do not carry their share of social responsibility. Closely associated with the importance of a good testimony is the need not to "be dependent on anybody." Of course, independence in an absolute sense is neither possible nor even desirable. We must understand Paul's admonitions not to be dependent in the light of the situation described in vv.11, 12a.

Notes

11 καί (kai, "and") begins v.11 and connects φιλοτιμεῖσθαι (philotimeisthai, "to strive eagerly"; NIV, "make it your ambition"), πράσσειν (prassein, "to do"; NIV, "to mind") and ἐργάζεσαι (ergazesthai, "to work") in parallel with περισσεύειν (perisseuein, "to do so more and more," v.10). All are dependent on παρακαλοῦμεν (parakaloumen, "we urge," v.10). The need to apply perisseuein to the preceding topic of love and the radical subject change in v.11 require a new paragraph at v.11, even though grammatically vv.11, 12 are a unit with v.10b.

"Make it your ambition" applies only to "lead a quiet life" and does not carry its force over to "mind your own business" or "work with your hands." It appears most natural to apply the καθώς (kathōs, "just as") clause to all three responsibilities rather than just the last.

12 Μηδενός (mēdenos, "no one, nothing"; NIV, "not ... anybody") is probably masc., not neuter, in that a masc. focuses on an abuse of brotherly love more clearly and constitutes a better parallel to the masc. πρὸς τοὺς ἔξω (pros tous eksō, "of outsiders") in the other half of the clause.

B. Exhortation Regarding Eschatological Needs (4:13–5:11)

1. The dead in Christ

4:13–18

> 13Brothers, we do not want you to be ignorant about those who sleep, or to grieve like the rest of men, who have no hope. 14We believe that Jesus died and rose again and so we believe that God will bring with Jesus those who sleep in him.
> 15According to the Lord's own word, we tell you that we who are still alive, who are left till the coming of the Lord, will certainly not precede those who have fallen alseep. 16For the Lord himself will come down from heaven, with a loud command, with the voice of the archangel and with the trumpet call of God, and the dead in Christ will rise first. 17After that, we who are still alive and are left will be caught up with them in the clouds to meet the Lord in the air. And so we will be with the Lord forever.
> 18Therefore encourage each other with these words.

13–18 Another issue raised by Timothy's report requires clarification: the part of the Christian dead in Christ's parousia (his coming). Paul discusses this new subject in one of the classic NT passages on the Lord's return (vv.13–18). The lack of knowledge of the Thessalonians concerning the part their fellow Christians who had died will have when the parousia occurs led him to write this reassuring paragraph.

13 Paul's words "we do not want you to be ignorant" as usual mark what follows for special attention. Here they introduce the correction of false impressions (cf. Rom 11:25; 1 Cor 10:1; 12:1). The Thessalonians had concluded that "those who sleep" would miss the victories and glory of the Lord's return. "Those who sleep" (*tōn koimōmenōn*) is an expression chosen in lieu of the "the dead" (v.15) because of death's temporary nature for Christians (cf. 1 Cor 7:39; 11:30; 15:6, 18, 20, 51; cf. also John 11:11). Though the pagans used "sleep" as a metaphor for "death," it is especially appropriate for Christians because of their assured bodily resurrection. Paul had previously taught the Thessalonians about the resurrection. On the basis of the resurrection our Christian "hope" has objective reality. That this sleep refers to the physical body and not to man's spirit is clear for several reasons. Death for Paul did not mean a state of unconscious repose, but a condition of being with Christ (Phil 1:23). Also the expression "dead in Christ" (v.16) is meaningless in connection with soul sleep, for a nonexistent sleeper can hardly be in union with Christ. Paul viewed "those who sleep" as continuing their relationship with Christ in heaven while their bodies were in the grave. The essential issue is not the fact of bodily resurrection, but what part, if any, those so raised will play in the *parousia*.

Paul wanted to deliver his readers from the grief experienced by "the rest of men" (cf. "outsiders," v.12). Non-Christians sorrow out of pity for the departed who have ventured into an unknown realm. For Christians, however, there should be no sorrow on behalf of believers who are dead. Grief on behalf of the living and the loss sustained when a loved one dies is legitimate for Christians (Phil 2:27), but that kind of grief is not in view here. Those who have died are better off than those left behind and will be equal participants in future resurrection and the glory of Christ.

14 For Christians, relief from sorrow is related to what the future holds. Just as "Jesus died and rose again," so will "those who sleep in him" be raised when God brings them to heaven with Jesus at his *parousia*. The fact of Jesus' death and resurrection guarantees as its sequel the eventual resurrection of the dead in Christ. This is similar to the guarantee of his return in 1:10.

It is significant that Paul does not refer to Jesus' death as "sleep." The difference between Jesus' experience and that of believers is that he really endured actual separation from God for the world's sins. Because of his real death Christian death has been transformed into sleep (Milligan, p. 57).

Though we might expect Paul to write "God will raise" instead of "God will bring with Jesus," he used the latter because of an unexpressed connection in his mind between the two ideas. To be brought with Jesus presupposes rising from the dead as part of the process (v.16). This is what had been taught the Thessalonians. Yet their ultimate anticipation is not just that of being raised, but that of being "with Jesus" (4:14; cf. 4:17; 5:10). Beyond resurrection this is the consummating desire of Christians. But even more is in store for Christians. The words "God will bring" point to a continuing movement heavenward after the meeting in the air (v.17), until the arrival in the Father's presence (3:13; cf. John 14:2, 3). A more detailed analysis of the process follows (*gar*, v.15).

15–17 The authority that validates Paul's affirmation ("we believe") in v.14 is nothing less than "the Lord's own word" (*logou kyriou*, "the word of the Lord"; cf. 1:8). Various attempts have been made to identify this source more specifically. Some say Jesus spoke the words while on earth, their substance being recorded later in such places as Matthew 24:30, 31 and John 6:39, 40; 11:25, 26. Similarities between this passage in 1 Thessalonians and the gospel accounts include a trumpet (Matt 24:31), a resurrection (John 11:25,

26), and a gathering of the elect (Matt 24:31) (Robert Gundry, *The Church and the Tribulation* [Grand Rapids: Zondervan, 1973], pp. 104, 135). Yet dissimilarities between it and the canonical sayings of Christ far outweigh the resemblances (Olshausen, p. 138; Lightfoot, p. 65; Moffatt, p. 37; Hendriksen, p. 114). Some of the differences between Matthew 24:30, 31 and 1 Thessalonians 4:15-17 are as follows: (1) In Matthew the Son of Man is coming on the clouds (but see Mark 13:26; Luke 21:27), in 1 Thessalonians ascending believers are in them. (2) In the former the angels gather, in the latter the Son does so personally. (3) In the former nothing is said about resurrection, while in the latter this is the main theme. (4) Matthew records nothing about the order of ascent, which is the principal lesson in Thessalonians. Distinctions between this and the Johannine passages are just as pronounced, if not more so.

Another suggestion has it that this is a saying of Jesus not contained in the canonical Gospels. Acts 20:35 is cited as another quotation of a non-Gospel saying (Moffatt, p. 37). It is further speculated that a saying like this may have come as a sequel to Jesus' repeated predictions of his disciples' martyrdom (Matt 10:28; 24:9; Mark 8:34; 10:39, 40; 13:12, 13; John 16:2). Such could have raised the issue of the disadvantage in martyrdom as compared with surviving to the *parousia* (Jeremias, p. 67). Though possible, this suggestion is not probable. Because of its relevance to early Christian circumstances, such a saying of Jesus would hardly have been passed over by the Gospel writers (Milligan, p. 58).

For Paul to have claimed this special authority for his own personal utterances does not adequately explain the definiteness of the expression "the Lord's own word" (Best, p. 190). Or for him to have drawn the saying from a Jewish or early Christian apocalyptic writing is not likely. The closest extrabiblical approximation to 4:15-17 is 4 Esdras 7:28, but 4 Esdras came at the end of the first century or in the early second century, too late for Paul to have known it (R.H. Charles, *Apocrypha and Pseudepigrapha* [London: Oxford, 1913] 2:552-553).

"The Lord's own word," therefore, is probably a direct revelation to the church through one of her prophets, Paul himself or possibly some other. The NT prophet's function was to instruct and console believers (cf. v.18 with 1 Cor 14:31), utilizing predictions about the future in the process (Acts 11:27, 28; 21:11). Since these elements are prominent here and since 1 Corinthians 15:51 classifies this subject as "mystery" revelation, which is the character of prophetic utterances, this explanation of Paul's external authority is quite satisfactory (Best, pp. 191-193; Hiebert, pp. 196, 197). Nowhere in these Epistles are the addressees reminded of having heard this teaching previously, though they were fully informed about the day of the Lord (1 Thess 5:2). How they could have been uninformed about this detail of the *parousia* (v.13) is not disclosed. Conceivably it could have been a special revelation to Paul for the sake of answering their question through Timothy, or it might have been a revelation received at another time since Paul's departure from the city. Whenever it came, it was now the privilege of the Thessalonians to know certain details about departed believers' part in the *parousia*.

The first part of Paul's prophetic revelation in vv.15-17 tells what will not happen. Believers "who are still alive, who are left to the coming of the Lord," will not go to meet him before the dead in Christ do so (v.15). When Paul uses "we," he apparently places this event within his own lifetime. How then can it be explained that the *parousia* did not precede Paul's death? To theorize that Paul was mistaken and to consider biblical inspiration in the light of such errors (James Denney, *Expositors Bible* [Hodder and Stoughton, n.d.], pp. 175-177) is to ignore Paul's avoidance of date setting (1 Thess 5:1,

2). In view of Jesus' teaching about our not knowing the day or hour of his coming (Matt 24; 36; cf. Acts 1:7), surely Paul would not limit it to his own lifespan.

Another possibility is to understand the participles *zōntes* and *perileipomenoi* as being hypothetical and meaning "if we live, if we remain." Yet rarely, if ever, can attributive participles function in such an adverbial and conditional sense. Furthermore, this sense would hardly fit the same two words in v.17 (Best, p. 195).

Some have also been proposed that Paul used less-than-honest means to prepare the Thessalonians for the Lord's return. With a good motive he proposed a time limit, though he knew Christ's word to the contrary (Matt 24:36). Aside from Paul's rejection of the unethical practice of making the end justify the means (Rom 3:8), this proposal conflicts with 1 Thessalonians 5:1, 2.

Others have suggested that Paul simply establishes two categories—those alive and those asleep. Since he did not fit into the latter, he took his place with the former. His presence in one or the other is inconsequential, however (Ellicott, pp. 62, 63; Hogg and Vine, pp. 138–140; Hiebert, p. 196). By entertaining the possibility of his own death before the *parousia*, as he did elsewhere (2 Cor 5:9; Phil 1:21ff.; 2:17; 2 Tim 4:6), Paul could not have meant more than to establish two categories here (Auberlen and Riggenbach, p. 76). While somewhat plausible, this view fails to explain the emphatic *hēmeis* ("we," v.15) or tell us why Paul used the first person instead of the third (Best, p. 195).

More feasible is the solution that sees Paul setting an example of expectancy for the church of all ages (Lightfoot, p. 67). Proper Christian anticipation includes the imminent return of Christ. His coming will be sudden and unexpected, an any-moment possibility. This means that no divinely revealed prophesies remain to be fulfilled before that event. Without setting a deadline, Paul hoped that it would transpire in his own lifetime. Entertaining the possibility of his own death (2 Tim 4:6–8) and not desiring to contravene Christ's teaching about delay (Matt 24:48; 25:5; Luke 19:11–27), Paul, along with all primitive Christianity, reckoned on the prospect of remaining alive till Christ returned (Rom. 13:11; 1 Cor 7:26, 29; 10:11; 15:51, 52; 16:22; Phil 4:5). A personal hope of this type characterized him throughout his days (2 Cor 5:1–4; Phil 3:20, 21; 1 Tim 6:14; 2 Tim 4:8; Titus 2:11–13). Had this not been the Thessalonians' outlook, their question regarding the dead in Christ and exclusion from the *parousia* would have been meaningless. They were thinking in terms of an imminent *parousia*, expecting to see it before death (Best, p. 183). An intervening period of messianic woes or birthpangs was not their anticipation (Best, p. 184), for such intense persecution would have meant probable martyrdom, and in that case they would have had doubts about their own participation in the *parousia*. Hence, Paul believed and had taught his converts that the next event on the prophetic calendar for them was their being gathered to Christ.

This teaching about a future *parousia* that will be a cosmic and dateable event in world history is as valid for the twentieth century as it was for the first. It is not to be explained away as an event outside history because of the alleged limited cosmological framework of early Christian minds (cf. Best, pp. 360–370). Just as God intervened in history through his Son's first coming, so he will do at his return.

The principal assertion of v.15, then, concerns those who are alive and anticipating Christ's momentary return, as was Paul, and their relation to "those who have fallen asleep." The former group "will certainly not precede" the latter. This strong assertion alleviates the Thessalonians' apprehension about their dead.

The positive chronology of vv.16, 17 supports this strong statement (cf. the *gar* ["for"] at the beginning of v.16). Without any intermediary, "the Lord himself will come down from heaven" (v.16), where he has been since ascending to the Father's right hand. In so doing, he will issue "a loud command," such as one given by a person with authority.

The purpose is to awaken "those who have fallen asleep." Associated with the command will be "the voice of the archangel," probably Michael's (Jude 9) and "the trumpet call" (cf. 1 Cor 15:52). As a sequel to this movement from heaven, "the dead in Christ" will rise before anything else occurs. Far from being excluded from the *parousia*, they will be main participants in the first act of the Lord's return. This word of comfort must have brought great relief to the Thessalonians and it has certainly done so for innumerable Christians after them.

Only "after that" (v.17) will living Christians "be caught up" for the meeting with Christ. The interval separating the two groups will be infinitesimally small by human reckoning. Yet the dead in Christ will go first. They will be the first to share in the glory of his visit. Then the living among whom Paul still hoped to be (cf. "we") will be suddenly snatched away (*harpagēsometha*, "caught up"; cf. Acts 8:39; 2 Cor 12:2, 4; Rev 12:5). This term in Latin, *raptus*, is the source of the popular designation of this event as the "rapture." So sudden will it be that Paul likens it to a blinking of the eye (1 Cor 15:52). In this rapid sequence the living will undergo an immediate change from mortality to immortality (1 Cor 15:52, 53), after which they will be insusceptible to death.

Together with the resurrected believers, they will ascend, be enshrouded in the clouds of the sky (cf. Acts 1:9), and meet the Lord somewhere in the interspace between earth and heaven ("air," *aera*).

The nature of this "meeting" (*apantēsin*, v.17) deserves comment. Some feel that the technical force of the word obtains—i.e., a visitor would be formally met by a delegation of citizens and ceremonially escorted back into their city (Best, p. 199). On this basis, they contend that Christians go out to meet the Lord and return with him as he continues his advent to earth. Advocates of this proposal see this connotation in two other NT usages of the word (Matt 25:6; Acts 28:15, 16) (George Ladd, *The Blessed Hope* [Grand Rapids: Eerdmans, 1956], p. 91; William C. Thomas, *The Blessed Hope* [William C. Thomas, 1972], pp. 5, 6). Whether or not this is true is debatable. Even if it were true, Christ would not necessarily be escorted back to earth immediately (Gundry, pp. 104, 105). Usage of the noun in LXX as well as differing features of the present context (e.g., Christians' being snatched away rather than advancing on their own to meet the visitor) is sufficient to remove this passage from the technical Hellenistic sense of the word (Moulton, *Prolegomena*, p. 14, n. 4; Best, p. 199). A meeting in the air is pointless unless the saints continue on to heaven with the Lord who has come out to meet them (Milligan, p. 61). Tradition stemming from Jesus' parting instructions fixes the immediate destination following the meeting, as the Father's house, i.e., heaven (John 14:2, 3) (John Walvoord, *The Thessalonian Epistles* [Grand Rapids: Zondervan, 1967], p. 70).

The location is secondary, however, in light of the final outcome. To "be with the Lord forever" represents the fruition of a relationship begun at the new birth and far outweighs any other consideration of time and eternity.

18 With this word of assurance, Paul gives a basis for his converts to "encourage [*parakaleite*] each other."

Notes

13 The δε ... περι (*de ... peri*, "now about") signals a new subject (cf. 4:9; 5:1). The difference between the present participle κοιμωμένων (*koimōmenōn*, "sleeping") and the aorist κοιμη-θέντας (*koimēthentas*, "having slept," vv.14, 15) is probably the perspective represented in

each statement. The former pictures "those falling asleep from time to time," while the latter looks back from the vantage point of the *parousia* when all Christian death will be a thing of the past (Hiebert, pp. 188, 193).

14 Ἀνέστη (*anestē*, "rose again") is used by Paul only here, in v.16, and in Eph 5:14 for rising from the dead. He customarily uses some form of ἐγείρω (*egeirō*, "to rise") though his favorite noun for "resurrection" is ἀνάστασις (*anastasis*).

Διὰ τοῦ Ἰησοῦ (*dia tou Iēsou*, "in" or "through Jesus") poses a syntactical question. Whether it connects with "will bring" or with "those who sleep" is the crux of the issue. Since the former possibility entails a tautologous "God will bring through Jesus with him" and since the symmetry of the two clauses is best maintained by the latter ("Jesus died" with "those who sleep through Jesus" and Jesus "rose" with "will bring with Him"), the latter connection is preferred (Lightfoot, p. 64; Hendriksen, p. 112). "Sleeping through [or in] Jesus" signifies what death has become to the Christian because of Jesus' death and resurrection. It assumes the temporary character of sleep.

17 "With" is from ἅμα σύν (*hama syn*, "together with"). Whether to understand ἅμα (*hama*) as depicting local coherence ("together") or temporal correspondence ("at the same time") is a matter to be resolved. Most helpful in reaching a conclusion is an understanding of ἔπειτα (*epeita*, "then"; NIV, "after that"). Together with πρῶτον (*prōton*, "first," v.16), this particle indicates a temporal sequence, the living being caught up after the dead have been raised. For *hama* to have the sense of "at the same time" would make the sentence self-contradictory. Hence, local coherence, "together with," best represents the meaning of *hama syn*.

---

2. *The day of the Lord* (5:1–11)

a. *The coming of the day*

5:1, 2

> ¹Now, brothers, about times and dates we do not need to write to you, ²for you know very well that the day of the Lord will come like a thief in the night.

1 With the perplexity about the dead in Christ resolved, Paul turns to a new subject (cf. *peri de*, "now about") yet not one completely distinct from the previous one. It is wrong to say that the two are so different as to be in contrast (Ryrie, "The Church and the Tribulation: A Review," BS, April-June, 1974, p. 75; Ellicott, p. 67). But it is equally wrong to see this as a simple continuation of the same subject (W.C. Thomas, p. 7). The proper interpretation recognizes a shift in thought, but not without some connection with the foregoing (Walvoord, p. 81; Gundry, p. 105). The direct and affectionate address "brothers" marks the new discussion as an addition prompted by Timothy's report of the Thessalonians' situation. The nonarrival of the *parousia* had created another perplexity for them (Best, p. 203).

Despite their ignorance about the dead in Christ (4:13), they had received prior instruction regarding other eschatological matters. "We do not need to write to you" is Paul's attestation to this fact. "Times and dates" (*tōn chronōn kai tōn kairōn*) are well-known words describing the end times from two perspectives. The former conceives more of elapsed time and hence a particular date or dates when predictions will be fulfilled. The latter word, while including some reference to extent of time, gives more attention to the character or quality of a given period, i.e., what signs will accompany the consummating events. The two words together have this same eschatological connotation in Acts 1:7; 3:19–21. The latter word very frequently refers to this future period (Dan 9:27, LXX; Mark 13:33; Luke 21:8, 24; Eph 1:10; 1 Tim 6:15; Titus 1:3; Heb 9:10; Rev 1:3; 11:18; 22:10) (Ellicott, p. 67; Milligan, p. 63; Lightfoot, pp. 70, 71). During his first visit Paul had effectively communicated the basic features of precise times and accompanying circumstances of future events.

2 For this reason he could say to the Thessalonians, "You know very well" the features of the day of the Lord. "Very well" translates *akribōs*, a word of precision. Paul is not sarcastically alluding to their own claim, but conceding that their previous learning on this subject had been adequate, definite, and specific, ultimately including even pertinent teachings of Christ (Matt 24:43; Luke 12:39) (Lightfoot, p. 71; Ellicott, p. 68).

The focus is on "the day of the Lord." A theme for extensive biblical attention, this "day" has multiple characteristics. It is so associated with the ultimate overthrow of God's enemies (Isa 2:12) that *hēmera* ("day") sometimes means "judgment" (1 Cor 4:3). It will be a day of national deliverance for Israel and a day of salvation (1 Thess 5:9), but it will also be a day when God's wrath puts extended pressure on his enemies (Isa 3:16–24; 13:9–11; Jer 30:7; Ezek 38–39; Amos 5:18, 19; Zeph 1:14–18; 1 Thess 1:10; 2:16; 5:9). By using "day of the Lord" terminology to describe the great tribulation, Christ includes the tribulation within the day of the Lord (cf. Matt 24:21 with Jer 30:7; Dan 12:1; Joel 2:2). This time of trial at the outset of the earthly day of the Lord will thus not be brief, but comparable to a woman's labor before giving birth to a child (Isa 13:8; 26:17–19; 66:7ff.; Jer 30:7, 8; Micah 4:9, 10; Matt 24:8; 1 Thess 5:3) (Pentecost, *Things to Come* [Findlay, Ohio: Dunham, 1958], p. 230; McClain, *The Greatness of the Kingdom* [Grand Rapids: Zondervan, 1959], pp. 186–191). Growing human agony will be climaxed by Messiah's second coming to earth, a coming that will terminate this earthly turmoil through direct judgment. He cannot personally appear on earth, however, until this preliminary period has run its course. Armageddon and the series of tribulation visitations prior to it are inseparable from each other (Rev 6–19). If Christ's triumphant return to earth (Rev 19:11–21) is part of the day of the Lord, as all admit, so special divine dealings preparatory to it must also be part of it. God's eschatological wrath is a unit. It is quite arbitrary to hypothesize two kinds of future wrath, one prior to the day of the Lord and another within it (cf. Gundry, pp. 46, 54).

But this earthly wrath does not pertain to those in Christ (v.9). Their meeting with Christ will be "in the air" and separate from God's dealing with those on earth. The only way to hold that this meeting with Christ in the air is an imminent prospect is to see it as simultaneous with the beginning of the divine judgment against earth. Only if the rapture coincides with the beginning of the day of the Lord can both be imminent and the salvation of those in Christ coincide with the coming of wrath to the rest (v.9) (Walvoord, p. 81).

Were either the rapture or the day of the Lord to precede the other, one or the other would cease to be an imminent prospect to which the "thief in the night" and related expressions (1:10; 4:15, 17) are inappropriate. That both are any-moment possibilities is why Paul can talk about these two in successive paragraphs. This is how the Lord's personal coming as well as the "day's" coming can be compared to a thief (2 Peter 3:4, 10; Rev 3:3, 11; 16:15). *Erchetai* ("will come") is a vivid futuristic present (cf. John 14:3) to portray the day as already on its way with an arrival anticipated any time (cf. 1:10). "In the night" is a detail of the simile not given in other NT usages. It simply names the usual time for thievery, i.e., under cover of darkness. Such unexpectedness will mark the tribulation's inauguration.

The Thessalonians were now instructed about these matters, though later they were to be deceived regarding them (2 Thess 2:1, 2). Yet even with their present knowledge they had difficulty in applying the truths in a practical way while waiting for the day. So Paul seeks to alleviate this difficulty.

Notes

2 The anarthrous ἡμέρα κυρίου (hēmera kyriou, "day of the Lord") may be understood as a proper title, since it is already anarthrous in LXX usage. Absence of the articles may also be traced to a Semitic source, the construct state (Moule, An Idiom Book of NT Greek, p. 117). More probably, however, it is explainable by a qualitative emphasis: "a day of such character that belongs to the Lord" (Milligan, p. 64).

b. Unbelievers and the day

5:3

[3]While people are saying, "Peace and safety," destruction will come on them suddenly, as labor pains on a pregnant woman, and they will not escape.

3 The surprise beginning of the day of the Lord has a twofold impact. For those who are not in Christ and therefore unprepared, the consequences are far from cheerful. "People," "them," and "they" are identified only when v.4 contrasts them with the "brothers" who are the addressees. The "nonbrothers" compose an unbelieving world against whom the devastation of the coming day will be unleashed. Just as disaster overtakes the unsuspecting householder when set upon by a robber, so catastrophe will overcome the living who are spiritual outsiders.

They will be priding themselves on their secure life styles. "Peace" characterizes their inward repose, while "safety" reveals their freedom from outward interference (Ellicott, p. 69; Frame, p. 181). Yet at the moment that tranquility seemingly reaches its peak, "destruction will come on them suddenly." "Destruction" means utter and hopeless ruin, a loss of everything worthwhile (Milligan, p. 65; Frame, p. 182), causing the victims to despair of life itself (Rev 9:6). Without being totally annihilated, they are assigned to wrath and denied the privileges of salvation (v.9).

Comparing the beginning of this period with a period of labor pains just before childbirth makes vivid the unexpectedness with which the former comes (cf. Isa 13:8, 9; Jer 4:31; Hos 13:13; Mic 4:9). Pain is certainly involved in both (Isa 66:7) as are certainty and nearness, but "suddenly" points most prominently to the absence of any forewarning. Tribulation will suddenly become worldwide, rendering it impossible for non-Christians to escape.

Notes

3 Evidence for exchange of material between Paul and Luke sometime during their long association is prominent here as it is in several other passages (cf. 1 Cor 11:23–26 with Luke 22:19, 20;

1 Cor 15:5 with Luke 24:34; 1 Tim 5:18 with Luke 10:7) (Lightfoot, p. 72). Luke 21:34, 36 contains a number of verbal similarities to the present verse: cf. ἐπιστῇ (epistē "come on") with ἐφίσταται (ephistatai, "comes on"), αἰφνίδιος (aiphnidios, "suddenly") in both, ἡ ἡμέρα (hē hēmera, "the day") with ἡμέρα (hēmera, "day," v.2), ἐκφυγεῖν (ekphugein, "to escape") with ἐκφύγωσιν (ekphugōsin, "will escape"). A pronounced eschatological emphasis is also in both, though Luke uses the thought more in relation to the preparation of God's people. The ultimate source of the words was undoubtedly Jesus himself.

---

c. Believers and the day

5:4-11

> ⁴But you, brothers, are not in darkness so that this day should surprise you like a thief.
> ⁵You are all sons of the light and sons of the day. We do not belong to the night or to the darkness. ⁶So then, let us not be like others who are asleep, but let us be alert and self-controlled. ⁷For those who sleep, sleep at night, and those who get drunk, get drunk at night.
> ⁸But since we belong to the day, let us be self-controlled, putting on faith and love as a breastplate, and the hope of salvation as a helmet.
> ⁹For God did not appoint us to suffer wrath but to receive salvation through our Lord Jesus Christ.
> ¹⁰He died for us so that, whether we are awake or asleep, we may live together with him. ¹¹Therefore, encourage one another and build each other up, just as in fact you are doing.

4 In contrast to the non-Christians referred to in v.3 as "them" and "they," and in v.6 as "others," are the believers in Thessalonica whom Paul affectionately calls "brothers." Continuing the figure of night (v.2), "darkness" refers to the realm of wickedness and the darkened understanding and ignorance of impending doom that go with it (Ellicott, p. 70; Frame, p. 183). Such symbolical language occurs quite widely in nonbiblical and biblical writings (Best, p. 209; Conzelmann, TDNT, 7:428, 429, 431–433, 441–445; cf. Deut 28:29; Job 19:8; 22:10, 11; 30:26; Ps 11:2; 74:20; 82:5; Isa 42:6, 7; Jer 13:16; Matt 10:27; John 3:19; 8:12; Rom 13:12; 2 Cor 4:6; Eph 4:18; 5:8, 11; 1 John 1:5, 6). In reassuring his converts, Paul declares without qualification that those in Christ belong to a realm different from that of the world.

Growing out of this assertion that believers will not participate in darkness is the promise of their non-participation in "the day" of the Lord. It will not overtake them by surprise—"like a thief" overtakes his victim. As v.5 explains, their position in Christ guarantees their deliverance from this.

5 Paul's assertion, "you are all sons of the light and sons of the day," rules out dwelling in darkness. "All" brings reassurance that none are excluded. The fainthearted may take heart as may those others who have been confused about the *parousia* (cf. 4:11, 12; 5:14) (Frame, p. 184).

To reinforce his point, Paul returns to the negative side. Putting light and day in inverse order, he excludes himself along with all Christians from the night of moral insensitivity (cf. "sons of the light" ... "darkness"; "sons of the day" ... "night"). By a casual change from "you" to "we" he takes his place with his readers in accepting the exhortation of v.6. This dulls the edge of what would otherwise be a sharp rebuke (Frame, p. 185).

"The day" has no reference to the eschatological day of the Lord, as the anarthrous construction attests, but is used metaphorically in association with spiritual light (Lightfoot, p. 73). Verse 5 guarantees the readers' participation in a spiritual environment entirely different from that of non-Christians.

6 This provides a solid basis ("so then," *ara oun*) for the ethical behavior Paul now urges on the Thessalonians. It is a life style free from moral laxity. *Katheudōmen* ("let us not sleep") represents the ethical insensitivity that besets people of the other realm ("like others," *hoi loipoi;* cf. 4:13). While it is impossible for the day of the Lord to catch Christians unprepared, it is possible for them to adopt the same life style as those who will be caught unawares. Paul urges his readers not to let this happen.

Conduct in keeping with "the light" and "the day" also includes alertness. Inattention to spiritual priorities is utterly out of keeping for those who will not be subject to the coming day of wrath. Though the Thessalonians were, if anything, overly watchful to the point of neglecting other Christian responsibilities (4:11, 12; 2 Thess 3:6–15), they were not to cease watching altogether.

Apparently self-control was a great need. *Nēphō* ("to be self-controlled") is found with *grēgoreō* ("to be alert," "to watch") in a noneschatological context in 1 Peter 5:8. Its usage in 1 Peter 1:13 and 4:7 is eschatological. *Nēphō* denotes sobriety. To counteract what might become a state of wild alarm or panic, Paul urges self-control as a balance for vagaries arising from distorted views of the *parousia.* Undue eschatological excitement was a serious problem; spiritual sobriety was the cure.

7 To explain his exhortation in v.6, Paul appeals to everyday experience. Sleep and drunkenness are most often associated with the night. So he illustrates his figurative use of "sleep" in v.6 by referring to the normal habit of sleep and uses "drunkenness" to point up his reference to sobriety.

8 Here Paul resumes his exhortation but drops for the moment the need for alertness, speaking only of sobriety as a countermeasure against "spiritual" drunkenness. The idea of belonging to the realm of "spiritual" daylight goes back to vv.4, 5 and becomes the motivation for self-controlled action. So Paul goes on to describe "self-control" in figurative language drawn from Isaiah 59:17 (cf. Eph 6:14–17). Though the breastplate and helmet were Roman military apparel, lexical similarity to the Isaiah passage points to the OT as the probable source for the reference to them here.

The relation of this soldierly figure of speech to sobriety has been a puzzle. Frame suggests soberness as a prerequisite to effective vigilance by a sentry on duty (Frame, p. 187). Yet vigilance is covered in the earlier word on alertness. Obviously, intoxication prevents effective duty as a sentry, and this thought may supply the answer. To be armed against wild excitement with its disregard of normal Christian responsibilities requires soberness. Paul had earlier spoken of the need for calmness (4:11, 12). The Thessalonians had already made significant progress in faith and love (1:3; 3:6), but additional improvement was still needed (3:10; 4:1, 10). So the breastplate of faith and love could furnish protection from the problems mentioned in 5:14. To these Paul added the indispensable helmet of the hope of salvation (cf. 1:10). These three (faith, love, and hope) strengthened them for their present trials (1:3) and doubts (5:14). The Thessalonians could confidently anticipate a future deliverance not to be enjoyed by those in darkness (v.3), but assured to those in the realm of light (vv.4, 5). Self-control consists of balancing future expectations with present obligations. The well-equipped soldier wears both a breastplate and a helmet.

9 Paul now summarizes the reason for this guaranteed salvation. Negatively, "God did not appoint us to suffer wrath." Without question, this wrath is future and specific, being identified with the messianic era just prior to his reappearance (1:10; 2:16) and with the sudden destruction mentioned in v.3. "Appoint" (*etheto*) is used regularly for God's sovereign determination of events (Milligan, p. 69). When God vents his anger against earth dwellers (Rev 6:16, 17), the body of Christ will be in heaven as the result of the series of happenings outlined in 4:14–17 (cf. 3:13). This is God's purpose.

The positive side of this purpose is that believers will "receive salvation through our Lord Jesus Christ." "Receive" represents the noun *peripoiēsin* that some have translated actively as "gaining," "winning," or "acquiring" (Hiebert, p. 223; Hendriksen, p. 128; Best, p. 217) and others have interpreted passively as "possession" or "adoption" (Lightfoot, p. 76). The former meaning injects human effort into procuring future salvation and emphasizes alert activity. Yet the thought of "acquiring one's own slavation" conflicts with God's unconditional appointment of believers to salvation. Furthermore, the incompatibility of the word's usual active meaning of "preservation" (or "preserve") with future salvation is obvious. And in view of the cognate verb *peripoieō* with its technical connotation of divine action in God's procuring a people for himself, taking *peripoiēsin* passively becomes more plausible. Also the antithetical *orgēn* ("wrath") clearly implies divine activity. As Christians have been elected (1:4), they have also been adopted. For them to be possessed by God as his very own is synonymous with the future salvation to come "through our Lord Jesus Christ." In this divine operation, human diligence is not a factor. Therefore, in the certainty of this provision the Thessalonians could find relief from the frantic activity and panic that had been disturbing their tranquil anticipation of the future.

10 This verse is noteworthy. Here for the first time in all Paul's writings, he states the specific means by which Jesus Christ procures our salvation: "He died for us." In four key Epistles (Rom, 1 and 2 Cor, Gal), Paul laid prime emphasis on this about five years later. But only here in the Thessalonian letters does he mention the death of Christ, though it had undoubtedly been presented as the basis of all his teaching about salvation (cf. Acts 17:2, 3). Though the purpose of the letters does not call for an extended discussion of the death of Christ, here it is important in establishing the definite historical basis of our salvation. His death was "for us" or "on our behalf"—i.e., it was the sole condition in procuring as God's peculiar possession a people destined for salvation when the rest of the world is plunged into the wrath of the future day.

So sufficient is Christ's death that it brings assurance of future life with all obstacles removed. In fact, this was the very reason he died. It is conceivable, though highly improbable, that "awake" and "asleep" actually refer to physical conditions (cf. Luke 17:34). *Katheudō* ("asleep," NIV) has this literal sense in v.7.

A more plausible suggestion takes "awake or asleep" as metaphorical terms for the living and the dead. This is consistent with Paul's discussion in 4:13–18 and matches Jesus' use of *katheudō* ("sleep") in raising Jairus' daughter (Matt 9:24). Yet this use of *katheudō* is rare. Only with difficulty can one explain its substitution for the metaphorical *koimaō* ("sleep") of the previous section (4:13, 14, 15). Furthermore, *gregoreō* ("to be awake") is never used metaphorically for physical life in the Greek Bible (Milligan,

p. 70) or in any literature (Oepke, TDNT, 2:338–339). Paul's word for "to live" is *zaō* (4:15, 17). To assign this metaphorical sense to "awake" or "asleep" is not probable because it makes v.10 a needless repetition of what is already proved in 4:13–18.

An explanation that is exegetically preferable and of less difficulty takes *grēgorōmen* ("we are awake") and *katheudōmen* ("we are asleep") in an ethical sense as in v.6. Since future salvation has been so fully provided by Christ's finished work, it cannot be cancelled by lack of readiness. Moral preparedness or unpreparedness does not affect the issue one way or the other. Though at first this suggestion seems to nullify Paul's earlier exhortation to alertness (v.6), it must be acknowledged that this meaning for *grēgoreō* is well established in other places besides the present paragraph (Matt 24:42; 25:13; Mark 13:35, 37; Rev 3:3; 16:15) (Hogg and Vine, p. 172; Oepke, TDNT, 2:338). This conclusion also recognizes the established meaning of *katheudō* in the present context and accords with the strong case for the secure position of the believers (5:4, 5, 9).

There still remains, however, a serious obstacle to this ethical meaning of "awake or asleep," namely its seeming nullification of the exhortation of vv.6–8. Yet this is a problem only if these exhortations are understood as relating just to watchfulness. We have not, however, found this to be the case. The Thessalonians were already watchful and Paul warns them against extremes of overreaction. "Self-control" or "soberness" (vv.6, 8) serve as a complementary emphasis. Paul seeks to restore a proper balance between future anticipations and present obligations. In helping the Thessalonians, therefore, he had to calm their fears by convincing them of their participation in the *parousia* regardless of their degree of watchfulness. Every contingency has been met through the work done at Calvary by God himself. Christians need not fear missing the Lord's return, because they are "sons of the light and sons of the day" (vv.4, 5). Their enjoyment of the future resurrection life in union with Christ is certain.

11 With such a guarantee, the Thessalonians are now equipped to "encourage one another and build each other up." As in 4:18, *parakaleite* ("encourage") has more a consolatory than a hortatory meaning. Here is an unconditional pledge to strengthen even the weakest in faith. It can also build up another Christian. *Oikodomeite* ("build . . . up") was later to become one of Paul's favorite ways of writing about growth in the church (Eph 2:20–22; 4:12). An intellectual grasp of the provisions Paul has been describing leads to individual as well as collective growth of the body of Christ. Paul is quick to acknowledge progress along this line: "just as in fact you are doing." Yet he also looks forward to even greater attainments (cf. 4:1).

Notes

4 In v.4 *ἵνα* (*hina*) has one of its rarer uses—i.e., it expresses result rather than purpose, since the *hina* clause cannot be a purpose of their not being left in darkness (Milligan, p. 76; Lightfoot, p. 73; Frame, p. 183).

The accusative pl. reading of κλέπτας (*kleptas*, "thieves") rather than the nominative sing. κλέπτης (*kleptēs*, "thief"), while finding some respectable MS support, cannot be accepted because that external support is not as substantial as for the other reading and because of the harsh reversal of the figure of v.2 whereby the thief becomes the one startled by the arrival of daylight (v.4) rather than the one causing the surprise (v.2). Possibly the form *kleptas* arose as a scribe unintentionally copied the ending of the preceding ὑμᾶς (*humas*).

5 The two uses of υἱοί (huioi, "sons") are figurative and stem from a Semitic idiom denoting individuals with a quality of what is denoted by the genitive of descriptions that follow (Robertson, RHG, p. 496; Turner, p. 207; Blass-Debrunner, p. 89). Though not repeated with νυκτός (nyktos, "of night") and σκότους (skotous, "of darkness") and ἡμέρας (hēmeras, "of the day") (v.8), the force of huioi should probably be understood (Blass-Debrunner, p. 89).

7 A difference in meaning between μεθυσκόμενοι (methuskomenoi, "those who get drunk") and μεθύουσιν (methuousin, "are drunk"; NIV "get drunk") is denied by some (Best, p. 212), but it is probably wiser to allow the former an inceptive force, "get drunk," and the latter a progressive meaning, "are drunk," so as to maintain careful distinctions between synonyms (BAG, p. 500; Hiebert, p. 220).

8 The aorist participle ἐνδυσάμενοι (endusamenoi, "putting on") is simultaneous with the present νήφωμεν (nēphōmen, "let us be self-controlled"), because the antecedent relationship does not yield good sense. This combination gives the aorist an ingressive force, while the present subjunctive carries the idea of continuation after the initial act: "let us take up the armor and continue to wear it" (Best, p. 215).

9 The greatest problem in taking περιποίησιν (peripoiēsin, "obtainment"; NIV, "receive") passively is the genitive σωτηρίας (sotērias, "of salvation") associated with it (Auberlen and Riggenback, p. 85). When the noun is taken actively, the genitive is one of object, but the solution is not quite so obvious with the passive sense of "possession." In light of other considerations discussed above, however, and in light of the reasonable sense derived from a genitive of apposition, the passive sense is the better conclusion.

10 The reading ὑπέρ (hyper, "on behalf of"; NIV, "for") rather than περί (peri, "concerning") is preferable. The idea of benefit is more specific this way. Peri has too narrow MS support geographically to be taken as a serious possibility, even though the few MSS that do support it are impressive.

The adverb ἅμα (hama, "together") should be understood in the same local sense as in 4:17. It is a reinforcement of σύν (sun, "with") to emphasize union with Christ.

11 While generally equivalent to ἀλλήλους (allēlous, "one another"), εἰς τὸν ἕνα (heis ton hena, "each other") has a stronger individualizing effect. The total body is edified only as each member of it experiences growth.

C. Exhortation Regarding Ecclesiastical Needs (5:12–22)

1. Responsibilities to the leaders

5:12, 13

> 12Now we ask you, brothers, to respect those who work hard among you, who are over you in the Lord and who admonish you. 13Hold them in the highest regard in love because of their work. Live in peace with each other.

12,13 No more effective way of carrying out mutual edification (v.11) can be found than Paul's closing exhortations for improvement within the assembly (vv.12–22). Heading the list are the exhortations regarding the proper attitude toward leaders (vv.12, 13). They are introduced as a request from a friend ("we ask," erōtōmen, v.12; cf. 4:1). The request includes "respect" (eidenai, v.12) and "hold[ing] them in highest regard" (hēgeisthai, v.13), both of which represent rare verb nuances. The former verb (eidenai) directs respect toward the leaders who function in three areas: the first more general and the last two definitive of the first. "Those who work hard among you" is reminiscent of Paul and his colleagues with their unselfish toiling to support themselves while sharing the gospel with the Thessalonians (2:9). It is appropriate for those who follow them in leadership to do the same. Thus they become local exmples of how love works hard (1:3) in contrast to the problem group within the church that was doing practically nothing (4:11) (Frame, p. 193).

Paul points to two of the many areas where the hard work of the leaders was evident: "who are over you in the Lord who admonish you." The participle *proistamenous* ("who are over you") probably stipulates what is already implied by the existence of such a request as this: the presence of some form of church government in this early assembly. It was the responsibility of these leaders to "stand over" the rest of the assembly in the Lord. A secondary sense of "care for" (*proistēmi*) is also involved here and in the other uses of the verb (Rom 12:8; 1 Tim 3:4, 5, 12; 5:17) because ruling in a Christian way entails sincere interest in the welfare of those who are ruled (cf. Matt 20:26–28; 1 Peter 5:2, 3). Yet the element of "caring for" cannot erode the authority of the office and the need to "respect" the office (Reicke, TDNT, 6:701, 702). Anarchy is always wrong, particularly among Christians. If any tendency to it existed in Thessalonica, it must be rooted out. Where believers are united with Christ, respectful submission to Christian leaders is service to the Lord. The leaders were charged with guiding the congregation, and their decisions were binding (cf. Heb 13:17). It is also notable that this authority was not vested in one person. Such singular authority belonged only to an apostle (Denney, pp. 204–207; Lightfoot, p. 79).

A second phase of the leaders' hard work was "admonishing" the rest of the assembly. Admonishing is correction administered either by word or deed. It implies blame on the part of the one admonished. Naturally, it arouses resentment, since discipline is never pleasant. Still the apostle presents admonition as necessary for the congregation and requires respect for those who exercise it.

The group whose functions are thus described quite probably correspond to the elders (*presbyteroi*) and overseers (*episkopoi*), whose qualifications are described in more detail later in the pastoral Epistles (1 Tim 3:1–2; 5:17; Titus 1:5). Such leadership existed in local congregations from the earliest days of the Christian church (Acts 11:30; 14:23).

Another part of Paul's "request" regarding leadership is that leaders to be held "in highest regard in love" (v.13). Here is another unusual verbal nuance. *Hēgeisthai* here connotes "esteem" or "hold in high regard" rather than its more usual meaning of "consider." The context requires a specialized sense (Milligan, p. 72), though the more neutral meaning is possible: "consider them worthy of being loved" (Ellicott, p. 76; Olshausen, p. 452). This latter, however, injects without warrant the thought of worthiness. The exhortation is to hold these leaders in esteem "beyond all measure" (*hyperekperissōs*). No reservations are allowable. Rulers in the local assembly must be held "in the highest regard" (NIV) and given wholehearted support, and this in a spirit of "love." A suitable reason for this high appreciation is "their work" (v.13).

Concluding the brief exhortation about leadership is a general command for leaders as well as for those they lead: "Live in peace with each other." That Paul included such a command shows that relations were not all they could have been. Perhaps there was trouble between the idle and those who were admonishing them. But no matter who was to blame, there had to be peaceful relations. Leaders were to guard against abusing their authority; idlers were not to disregard those over them in the Lord.

Notes

12 The three participles represent three functions of the same group, not three distinct functioning groups. Grammatically this is shown by the single article τούς (*tous*, "the") governing all three and unifying them into a single concept.

2. Responsibilities to all

5:14, 15

14And we urge you, brothers, warn those who are idle, encourage the timid, help the weak, be patient with everyone. 15Make sure that nobody pays back wrong for wrong, but always try to be kind to each other and to everyone else.

14 A new and stonger set of brief commands begins with "And we urge you, brothers." "We urge" is more authoritative than Paul's previous "we ask" (5:12; cf. 4:1). Coupled with this stronger word are the imperative verbs in vv.14, 15 instead of the volitionally weaker infinitives in vv.12, 13.

Some early church fathers, beginning with Chrysostom, saw these strong directives as addressed to the leaders, thus counterbalancing those just given to the rest of the people (Best, p. 228). Such a distinction, however, finds more difference between the leaders and the led than is justified at this point in church history (Hogg and Vine, p. 181). It also overly restricts "brothers," which must broadly designate the whole Christian community. Furthermore, Romans 12:14–17, a section similar to 1 Thessalonians 5:15, is directed to the whole Roman church, not just to its leaders.

"Warn those who are idle" translates the same Greek word as "admonish" in v.12 (*noutheteite*). Christians in general, not just a limited few, are responsible for corrective measures. The entire local body copes with practical situations by advising an errant brother. The only ones excused from the obligation to warn are those in need of warning, in this case described as "those who are idle." *Ataktous* ("idle") describes those who are disorderly in conduct, but since disorderly conduct is so intertwined with idleness, the latter meaning very quickly associated itself with the word (cf. 2 Thess 3:6, 7). A certain amount of unbecoming behavior had already appeared in the Thessalonian church (4:11, 12).

"Encourage the timid" concerns a different need. Words of comfort (*paramutheisthe*, the word translated "comfort" in 2:12) to the "timid" or "fainthearted" are also needed. In the light of what Paul wrote in chapter 4, those who needed comfort were both troubled over their friends who had died in Christ (4:13) and confused about what the *parousia* held for themselves (5:1–11). Within this letter Paul has given ample information for removing these misgivings.

"Help the weak" almost certainly relates to moral and spiritual debility. Whether it was weakness in shrinking from persecution (3:3–5), yielding to temptations to immorality (4:3–8), or some other kind of weakness cannot be precisely determined. It may well have been weakness in exercising full Christian liberty in doubtful matters as was the case in other churches that included people from a pagan background (Rom 14:1–15:6; 1 Cor 8–10). Whatever it was, however, the strong in faith were responsible to support those who were weak.

Summing up the previous three commands is a fourth general one: "Be patient with everyone." *Makrothumeite* ("be patient") is sometimes translated "be long-suffering." It pictures the even-tempered response of one who is slow to anger. Dealing with the idle, the timid, and the weak requires this special disposition because they so often refuse to respond immediately to constructive counsel. Yet these are not the only ones requiring patient treatment. All Christians ("everyone") at one time or another provoke dissatisfaction through thoughtless or even intentionally hurtful acts. They too need patient treatment. The same patience is required toward non-Christians, but reference to them is not specific until v.15.

15 When tempers run short, the whole group (*horate*, pl.) has the responsibility for seeing that no member "pays back wrong for wrong." The natural tendency to retaliate and inflict injury for a wrong suffered must be strongly resisted, no matter what the injury. Apparently the Christian stand against retaliation crystalized very early, no doubt being formulated from principles established by Jesus in his Sermon on the Mount (Matt 5:38-42). Jesus refuted a false scribal inference drawn from Exodus 21:23, 24 (cf. Lev 24:19, 20; Deut 19:21). "An eye for an eye, and a tooth for a tooth" was originally intended to restrain people from going beyond equal retaliation in punishment for social wrongs against the community. The scribes had distorted the commandment's purpose by using it to justify personal revenge. What had been given as restrictive law had through human traditions been transformed into a permissive rule. In speaking out against this tradition, Jesus emphatically set the tone for his followers in forbidding personal revenge altogether.

That this lesson took firm hold is evidenced not only in the present verse, but also in Romans (12:17-21), where Paul treats the subject in more detail. Peter also shows the influence of this teaching (1 Peter 2:19-23; 3:9). Nonretaliation for personal wrongs is perhaps the best evidence of personal Christian maturity.

In v.15 Paul gives a constructive alternative to retaliation: "Always try to be kind to each other and to everyone else." *Diōkete* ("pursue"; NIV, "try") is immeasurably more than halfhearted effort. Eager expenditure of all one's energies is none too much in seeking *to agathon* ("the good"; NIV, "to be kind"). In place of wrong, injury, or harm dictated by a vengeful spirit, Christians must diligently endeavor to produce what is intrinsically beneficial to others, whether other Christians ("each other") or unbelievers ("everyone else"). The seriousness of the abuse suffered is no issue. Some Thessalonians doubtless had been victims of unjustified harsh treatment, but regardless of this, a positive Christian response is the only suitable recourse. The welfare of the offender must be the prime objective.

3. Responsibilities to oneself

5:16-18

> [16]Be joyful always; [17]pray continually; [18]give thanks in all circumstances, for this is God's will for you in Christ Jesus.

16 Compliance with the social regulations of vv.12-15 is impossible apart from personal communion with God. So Paul turns to the believer's inner life. In the exhortation "Be joyful always" he voices a theme that is characteristic of the NT writings. While this probably goes back to the teaching of Jesus in the Sermon on the Mount (Matt 5:10-12),

it recurs both in the historic (Acts 5:41; 16:25) and epistolary writings (e.g., Phil 1:18; 4:4). The uniqueness of Christian joy lies in its emergence under the most adverse circumstances. Paul states the paradox succinctly in 2 Corinthians 6:10: "sorrowful, yet always rejoicing" (cf. 2 Cor 12:10). The Thessalonian Christians had already suffered with joy (1 Thess 1:6) as had Paul himself (3:9). The challenge is for this joyful outlook to become constant ("always"). From a human perspective they had every reason not to be joyful—persecution from outsiders and friction among themselves. Yet in Christ they are to be more and more joyful.

17 Intimately related to constant joy is incessant prayer—the only way to cultivate a joyful attitude in times of trial. Uninterrupted communication with God keeps temporal and spiritual values in balance. *Adialeiptōs* ("continually"; cf. Rom 1:9; 1 Thess 1:2, 3; 2:13) does not mean some sort of nonstop praying. Rather, it implies constantly recurring prayer, growing out of a settled attitude of dependence on God. Whether words are uttered or not, lifting the heart to God while one is occupied with miscellaneous duties is the vital thing. Verbalized prayer will be spontaneous and will punctuate one's daily schedule as it did Paul's writings (3:11-13; 2 Thess 2:16, 17).

18 A final member of this triplet for personal development is "Give thanks in all circumstances." No combination of happenings can be termed "bad" for a Christian because of God's constant superintendence (Rom 8:28). We need to recognize that seeming aggravations are but a temporary part of a larger plan for our spiritual well-being. Out of this perspective we can always discern a cause for thanks. In fact, failure to do this is a symptom of unbelief (Rom 1:21).

"For this is God's will for you in Christ Jesus" justifies all three brief commands. Rejoicing, praying, and giving thanks do not exhaust God's will but are vital parts of it. "In Christ Jesus" is a significant qualification of God's will because only here can inner motives be touched. Paul's earlier rule, the Mosiac law, was strong on outward conformity, but was helpless to deal with human thoughts. It could not dictate an inner attitude even though it was a perfect expression of God's will (Best, p. 236). In union with Christ, together with an accompanying inward transformation (2 Cor 5:17), however, compliance with God's standards can extend to motives. These three commands penetrate the innermost recesses of human personality—the spring from which all outward obedience flows. If the source is contaminated, fulfillment of God's will in outward matters is impossible. Such is the note sounded by the Lord Jesus in his own teaching (Matt 5-7). The true victories in life are won by Christians who are joyful, prayerful, and thankful.

4. Responsibilities to public worship

5:19-22

19Do not put out the Spirit's fire; 20do not treat prophecies with contempt. 21Test everything. Hold on to the good. 22Avoid every kind of evil.

19 At this point Paul shifts from the personal life to communal worship (vv. 19-22). "Do not put out the Spirit's fire" alludes to the Holy Spirit as a burning presence (cf. 2 Tim 1:6). In particular, this is his impartation of specialized capabilities for ministry to others in the body of Christ. In his discussions of spiritual gifts elsewhere (Rom 12:6-8; 1 Cor 12:8-10, 28-30; Eph 4:11) Paul distinguishes eighteen such special abilities. Only nine

of them, however, involve speaking publicly (apostleship, prophecy, discerning of spirits, kinds of tongues, interpretation of tongues, evangelism, teaching, pastor-teaching, and exhorting). Since apostleship in the narrower sense was not present in Thessalonica, it, along with the nonspeaking gifts, could not have been the one in question here. When Paul commands, "Stop putting out the Spirit's fire," as v.19 might literally be translated, he advocates the cessation of something already being practiced. It is possible that other gifts in addition to prophecy (cf. v.20) had been abused, with the result that the more sober-minded leadership had overreacted and prohibited Spirit manifestations altogether. In 1 Corinthians 14, Paul dealt with the wrong use of tongues. But the need in Thessalonica was apparently different. Rather than allowing the error to continue as the Corinthians had done, the leadership in Thessalonica had completely repressed some gifts, with a resulting loss of spiritual benefit. Paul forbids such repression. The proper course is to allow gifted ones to share in a decent and orderly fashion what the Spirit can do through them for edification of the body of Christ (1 Cor 14:12, 26, 40). Control is necessary, but overcontrol is detrimental. So it is the responsibility of leadership and the whole community to find the right balance.

20 From Paul's next prohibition, "Do not treat prophecies with contempt," it appears that the Christians at Thessalonica like those at Corinth (1 Cor 14:1) had underrated the gift of prophecy. The directive may literally be translated "Stop treating prophecies with contempt." These were separate utterances of those who in their prophetic office proclaimed the will and command of God as well as predicted the future (Acts 11:28). Benefits from these utterances could build up a local church (1 Cor 14:3).

Apparently, however, certain "idle" brothers (v.14; cf. 4:11, 12) had misused this gift by falsifying data regarding the Lord's return. This had soured the remainder of the flock against prophecy in general. Their tendency now was not to listen to any more prophetic messages, but to discount them in view of counterfeit utterances they had heard. Once again Paul warns against overreaction and urges the church to give prophecies their proper place in edifying its members (cf. v.11).

21 To balance the two prohibitions, Paul stipulates that all charismatic manifestations be tested with a view to accepting what is valid and disallowing what is not (vv.21, 22). "Everything" is subject to the limitation of vv.19, 20, i.e., the exercise of spiritual gifts. The mere claim to inspiration was not a sufficient guarantee, because inspirations were known at times to come from below (1 Cor 12:2) as well as from above (Lightfoot, p. 84). Some have found in these words of Paul an allusion to a saying of Jesus preserved by a number of church fathers, including Clement of Alexandria and Origen. Origen wrote, "Be ye approved money changers" (*ginesthe trapezitai dokimoi*). To this Clement adds a thought about money changers "who reject much, but retain the good" (Jeremias, *Unknown Sayings of Jesus*, pp. 89–93). Followers were thus figuratively warned against accepting false prophets. Paul probably knew this saying, but the absence of "money changers" from 1 Thessalonians 5:21, 22 probably indicates that he did not have this quotation specifically in mind.

The nature of the test is not specified, but suggestions are forthcoming from related passages. In 1 John 4:1ff., as well as probably 1 Corinthians 12:3, the test is theological in nature, having to do with a proper view of Jesus as the Christ and Lord. In 1 Corinthians 12:10 and 14:29 discernment is a specific spiritual function in combination with the gift of prophecy. It consists of an ability to discern whether another prophetic spokesman has given a genuinely inspired utterance. But perhaps these two tests are too specialized for the present context, and preference should be given a more general criterion of whether a positive contribuion to the body's edification and mutual love has been made.

Testing like this will identify some spiritual activities as attractive and conducive to a growing love and to Christian power (5:11; 1 Cor 13; 14:3–5, 12, 26; so Frame, p. 207). These are genuine gifts and should be clung to tenaciously. In a very similar discussion about five years later for "hold on to the good" (*to kalon katechete,*) Paul substituted "cling to what is good" (*kollōmenoi tō agathō,* Rom 12:9). Both speak of determined tenacity to retain the beneficial. This church had been remiss (19, 20). "Good" in Thessalonians describes what is outwardly attractive and therefore beneficial and in Romans what is inherently good and therefore bound to be beneficial also.

22 Allowance must also be made for professed spiritual manifestations that do not contribute but rather detract from the development of the local body. Paul designates this category by *pantos eidous ponērou* ("every kind of evil"). The expression lends itself to varying interpretations. *Eidous* ("kind"), in keeping with its predominant NT meaning (Luke 3:22; 9:29; John 5:37; 2 Cor 5:7) may denote "appearance." Or in accord with the obvious antithesis between this and v.21, it may mean "kind" or "species." The latter meaning (as in NIV) is preferable because spiritual gifts could hardly with any credibility assume the "appearance of evil," but they could be a "species of evil" falsely attributed to the Holy Spirit.

Ponērou ("of evil") likewise presents two options: if it is taken as an adjective qualifying *eidous,* the phrase is "evil kind," or taken as a substantive, a practical equivalent of the noun *ponērias,* the phrase is "kind of evil." Though the anarthrous adjective in Paul is more frequently adjectival in force, the nature of the present contrast with *to kalon* (v. 21) resolves this particular issue in favor of the substantival use adopted by NIV.

Paul very clearly intends an antithesis with v.21 here. "Hold fast" (*katechete,* v.21) to the good, but "hold yourselves free from" (*apechesthe;* NIV, "avoid," v.22) every kind of evil that tries to parade as a genuine representation of the Spirit (Hiebert, p. 249). Only then can maximum benefit for the body of Christ in local worship be achieved.

Notes:

21 A contrast is indicated by an adversative δέ (*de,* "but," untranslated in above text). The conjunction is genuine, the progress of development being such as to demand a connective at that point (Lightfoot, p. 84). Several worthy MSS including ℵ and A omit it, but evidence for its inclusion (B D 33) is quite substantial. The omission may have arisen by the conjunction's being assimilated with the initial letter of the following word δοκιμάζετε (*dokimazete,* "test") (Metzger, *A Textual Commentary on the Greek NT,* p. 633).

V. Conclusion (5:23–28)

A. Petition for the Thessalonians

5:23, 24

23May God himself, the God of peace, sanctify you through and through. May your whole spirit, soul and body be kept blameless at the coming of our Lord Jesus Christ. 24The one who calls you is faithful and he will do it.

23 Having concluded his assorted suggestions for practical improvement, Paul looks to God to grant these objectives in the light of the Lord's return (cf. 3:12, 13). Sexual purity (4:3–8), brotherly love (4:9, 10), personal independence (4:11, 12), understanding the *parousia* (4:13–5:11), respect for leaders, love for other people, rejoicing, prayer, thankfulness, and concern for public worship (vv.12–22) are possible only through God. "I have simply told you all these things to do," Paul is saying, "but God alone has power to make your efforts a success."

Paul addresses God as the giver "of peace" (cf. 1 Cor 14:33), who has provided for a harmonious relationship between himself and man through Christ's death. At this point, following exhortations that imply at least a trace of disharmony (4:6, 10–12; 5:12–22), he invokes God's intervention as peacemaker.

Throughout the Epistle Paul has been concerned with sanctification (3:13; 4:3, 4, 7, 8). Now he prays that God will sanctify (separate to himself) the readers of the Epistle "through and through." *Holoteleis* ("through and through") speaks of the ultimate maturity of Christian character. It presents the qualitative side of spiritual advance in its final perfection. Toward this goal sanctification is directed.

The quantitative objective of the prayer is in *holoklēron* ("whole"; cf. James 1:4, where similar adjectives describe qualitative and quantitative spiritual development). Wholeness pertains to three parts of the human make-up, "spirit, soul and body." Paul petitions that this wholeness may be "kept" or "preserved" and that it may be "blameless at the coming of our Lord Jesus Christ."

The question arises as to how Paul conceives of man in the words "spirit, soul and body." Among the various explanations of this expression are these four:

1. Paul intends no systematic dissection of human personality. Instead, he uses a loose rhetorical expression emphasizing the totality of personality and reinforcing "through and through" and "whole" (H.W. Robinson, *The Christian Doctrine of Man* [Edinburgh: T. and T. Clark, 1926], pp. 108–109). This view leans heavily on comparable expressions in Deuteronomy 6:5; Mark 12:30; and Luke 10:27 (e.g., "with all your heart, with all your soul, with all your mind and with all your strength," Mark 12:30). What it fails to explain, however, is why Paul did not use this already well-known formula for completeness, if that is what he meant. It also cannot explain why he included man's material part ("body"), which the alleged analogous passages do not include. It is contrary to Paul's acknowledged careful use of words to attribute such a rhetorical device to him (Ellicott, p. 84; Hiebert, p. 252).

2. Another explanation makes "spirit" and "soul" interchangeable and sees each of them as referring to man's immaterial substance. "Body" then completes the picture by referring to man's material part: "your whole spirit (i.e., soul) and body." This sees man as dichotomous. Two terms for the same immaterial substance simply view it according to its two functions, relationship to God and relationship to the lower realm of sensations, affections, desires, etc. (Strong, *Systematic Theology*, p. 483). Defense of this approach lies in the way Paul parallels *pneuma* ("spirit") with *psychē* ("soul") in Philippians 1:27 and speaks at times of man's make-up as bipartite (2 Cor 7:1). Also, body and soul (or spirit) together sometimes describe the whole man (Matt 10:28; 1 Cor 5:3; 3 John 2) (Strong, p. 483). The weakness in the above arguments is evident, however, because Paul sometimes parallels *pneuma* with *sarx* ("flesh," "body"), with which it cannot be identical (2 Cor 2:13; 7:5, 13). Clear-cut distinctions between *psychē* and *pneuma* indicate they cannot be used interchangeably (Cremer, *Theological Lexicon of New Testament Greek*, pp. 504–505). In addition, it is doubtful whether Paul would pray for man's

functional capabilities, as this view holds, rather than two substantial parts of man's make-up.

3. Others try to escape a threefold division by dividing the last sentence of v.23 either into two independent parts (Hendriksen, p. 150) or else by joining "may your whole spirit" with the first part of the verse (Stempvort, cited by Best, p. 243). The former alternative requires inserting words that are not in v.23b, while the latter is unnecessarily complicated and causes prohibitive grammatical difficulties (Best, p. 243). To fill out the sense of either of these explanations, words must also be omitted.

4. That Paul saw man as a threefold substance in this verse has been generally recognized since the early fathers. The symmetrical arrangement of three nouns with their articles and their connection by means of two "ands" (*kai*) renders this the most natural explanation. This becomes a "distinct enunciation of three component parts of the nature of man" (Ellicott, p. 84). That Paul elsewhere does not make such a distinction (Best, pp. 242–244; Hendriksen, pp. 146–147) is no argument against trichotomy. It is always possible that Paul has been misunderstood elsewhere. It is also conceivable that he did not endeavor to make specific distinctions in other letters as he does here. That Paul possibly depends on liturgical formulation and attaches no special meaning to these separate terms (Dibelius, cited by Best, p. 244) is also inconclusive speculation. To object that this interpretation reads in the trichotomy of secular psychology (Schweizer, TDNT, 6:435) neglects Paul's occasional acceptance of portions of secular philosophy that were valid. He simply incorporated them into a divinely inspired framework (Ellicott, p. 84). A trichotomous understanding of 5:23 has so much to commend it that other interpretations cannot compete without summoning arguments from elsewhere. The difference between the material part ("body") and the immaterial parts ("spirit" and "soul") is obvious. Paul's pronounced distinction between *psychikos* ("natural"; NIV, "without the spirit") and *pneumatikos* ("spiritual") (1 Cor 2:14, 15; 15:44), his differentiation of *pneuma* ("spirit") and *egō* ("self") or *nous* ("mind"), parts of *psychē* ("soul") (Rom 7:17–23; 1 Cor 14:14), and other writers' distinguishing of *pneuma* and *psychē* (James 3:15; Jude 19) argue heavily for a substantial, not just a functional, difference between the two immaterial parts (Hiebert, p. 252; Schweizer, TDNT, 6:436; Lightfoot, p. 88).

The spirit (*pneuma*) is the part that enables man to perceive the divine. Through this component he can know and communicate with God. This higher element, though damaged through the fall of Adam, is sufficiently intact to provide each individual a consciousness of God. The soul (*psychē*) is the sphere of man's will and emotions. Here is his true center of personality. It gives him a self-consciousness that relates to the physical world through the body and to God through the spirit. This analysis of man had been Paul's training in the OT and no impressive evidence has surfaced to eradicate such a picture here (Milligan, p. 78; Olshausen, p. 457). Yet, it must be confessed, much unresolved mystery remains regarding the interrelationships between man's different parts, including the body. How one affects the other is fully understood only by him who is the Creator.

For such a composite creature Paul therefore prays, seeking an unblamable wholeness in the presence "of our Lord Jesus Christ" (23; cf. 2:19; 3:13).

24 To Paul, utterance of a prayer was not the end, but only the means to it. One who asks God for something can anticipate the fulfillment of his request because of God's character: "The one who calls you is faithful." He who issues an effectual call can be absolutely relied on to carry out his call, including among other things the sanctification and preservation prayed for in v.23. Faithfulness is the characteristic of God that determines that he will do the very thing Paul has prayed for. In his pretemporal selection of the Thessalonian church (1:4; 2:12), God had already determined to do so in his own counsels. This, however, did not render prayer for them superfluous, as human effort and application also have their place in carrying out the purposes of God.

Notes:

23 All three nouns of v.23 are governed by ὁλόκληρον (holoklēron, "entire") even though it agrees in gender with the first. The Greek adjective usually agrees with the nearest member of a compound expression. Strictly speaking, this adjective probably should not be understood attributively as in the tr. "your whole spirit, soul and body." Taking it as a predicate adjective is more faithful to the anarthrous form: "May your spirit and soul and body be preserved entire" (ASV). The singular number is no problem since it may view man as unity (cf. 3:11) or else the number, like the gender, may be determined by the nearest member of the compound expression.

The question of how to relate the adverb ἀμέμπτως (amemptōs, "blameless") is also pertinent. To let it describe the manner of keeping (τερέθειε, "may be kept") is not convincing. In all likelihood it supplements the sense of ὁλόκληρον (holokleron, "entire"): "blamelessly whole" or "whole, beyond reach of complaint."

B. Reciprocation by the Thessalonians

5:25–27

25Brothers, pray for us. 26Greet all the brothers with a holy kiss. 27I charge you before the Lord to have this letter read to all the brothers.

25 Following his prayer, Paul offers his readers opportunity to reciprocate along three lines. First, he requests prayer for himself and his fellow missionaries.

The scope of "brothers" presents two possibilities. On the one hand, because the phrase "all the brothers" of vv.26, 27 seemingly limits the addressees to church leaders, the tendency could be to limit v.25 accordingly. Yet how strict a distinction is made between leaders and followers in vv.26, 27, as well as in the rest of the letter? Certainly vv.12, 13 address the congregation at large and even tend to exclude leadership. In each case where "brothers" is found earlier in the Epistle, the whole church is included. Hence, Paul probably follows his customary policy of requesting prayer from the total body, not just from a limited few (Rom 16:16; 1 Cor 16:20; 2 Cor 13:12).

Paul depended on his converts' spiritual support (Rom 15:30; Eph 6:19; Phil 1:19; Col 4:3; 2 Thess 3:1; Philem 22). So now he asks for a continuing place in their prayers (v.17), similar to the place they have been given in his (23, 24). Good textual support indicates that "also" should be added at the end of v.25, the thought being to pray for the Pauline group in addition to others for whom they prayed.

26 A second closing request is for all the brothers to be greeted with a holy kiss. Paul's usual "one another" (Rom 16:16; 1 Cor 16:20; 2 Cor 13:12; cf. 1 Peter 5:14) is replaced

this time by an expression that may imply that the request is addressed to leaders only. This need not distinguish leaders from the rest of the assembly, however, as the Epistle will eventually find its way to all (v.27). In the meantime those receiving it first were to greet the rest (Moffatt, p. 43). The symbol of greeting was "a holy kiss" (v.26). This was not a kiss of respect as was used in ancient times to honor men of authority. Neither was it cultic as though copied from an ancient mystery religion. It most closely parallels the use of a kiss among members of the same family as a token of their close relationship. Christians have come into the family of God, which knows even closer ties than those of any human family (Matt 12:46–50). It was quite appropriate that a symbolic greeting be adopted. It was to be "holy" (hagiō), i.e., such as is becoming to saints (hagiois, 3:13). This may have been the custom of men kissing men and women kissing women so as to forestall any suspicion of impropriety. A Jewish synagogue practice, it could easily have found its way into early Christian assemblies.

27 The third parting word is more than just a request. The formula "I charge you before the Lord" shows an unusual concern on Paul's part regarding the possibility of his letter's not being read. Invoking an oath and switching to the first person singular indicate his urgency. He may have feared that the contents of the letter might be limited to those interested in a particular issue, e.g., those who had fallen asleep in Christ (4:13–18) (Ellicott, p. 86). Perhaps he was aware that some were already at work attributing wrong teaching to his name and authority (2 Thess 2:2) (Hogg and Vine, p. 216; Lightfoot, p. 91). Or he could have feared a breakdown in communications between the church's leadership and some of the communicants within the church (4:11, 12; 5:12, 13) (Frame, p. 217). Very probably Paul sensed the far-reaching import of the teaching of the Epistle and its binding authority as part of a canon of Scripture (1 Cor 14:37). Whatever the case, this charge has implications of divine punishment for failure to comply. The first recipients of the letter, probably the church leaders, were bound under oath "to have this letter read to all the brothers."

Obviously it was to be read aloud, in line with the classical meaning of anaginōskō ("read"). Under restrictions of limited educational privilege, not all participants in Christian circles were able to read for themselves. The further limitation of insufficient copies and expense of writing materials prohibited distribution to all. The only solution was to give the Epistle a place in public worship alongside the OT Scripture, the consequence of which would eventually be ecclesiastical recognition of its authority as an inspired book.

Notes

25 The reading of καί (kai, "also") is probably to be accepted. External attestation favors it slightly. It is doubtful that Colossians 4:3 could have prompted its inclusion, but it is possible that there was a scribal omission in some MSS when its reference to 5:17 was overlooked (Metzger, *Textual Commentary*, p. 633).

27 The double accusative ὑμᾶς τὸν κύριον (humas ton kurion, "you [before] the Lord") following ἐνορκίζω (enorkizō, "I charge") names the persons bound by the adjuration ("you") and the one to whom accountability is due ("the Lord"). Necessity for two objects stems from the causative nature of enorkizō; "I cause you to swear by the Lord" hence becomes "I adjure you by the Lord" (BDF, pars. 149, 155.7).

The aorist of ἀναγνωσθῆναι (anagnōsthēnai, "to have ... read") cannot be pressed into restricting Paul's meaning to one public reading. A constative aorist easily provides for regular reading as a standard practice. This latter was the sense understood by early Christianity.

The textual suggestion that "all the brothers" should be "all the holy brothers" rests basically upon TR authority. Coupled with the weakness of this external support is the internal improbability that so significant a term as ἁγίοις (hagiois, "holy") could have been dropped by copyists (Metzger, Textual Commentary, pp. 633, 634).

C. Benediction

5:28

28The grace of our Lord Jesus Christ be with you.

28 This customary benediction was probably added in Paul's own handwriting (cf. 2 Thess 3:17, 18). His distinctive farewell was always built around his favorite concept, grace, which replaced the usual epistolary farewell (cf. Acts 15:29). This trait is distinctive in his Epistles whether the benediction be longer (2 Cor 13:13 [13:14 in KJV, NASB, and others]) or shorter (Col 4:18; 1 Tim 6:21; 2 Tim 4:22; Titus 3:15). The primacy of grace resulting from the saving work of "our Lord Jesus Christ" was a constant theme as the apostle sought the welfare of those he served (cf. 1:1).

Notes

---

28 The absence of ἀμήν (amēn, "amen") from reliable representatives of both Alexandrian and Western text types indicates that it was probably added when the book was used in liturgical settings (Metzger, Textual Commentary, p. 634). It was habitual to close the portion read with "Amen," signifying accord with the content.

Subscripts found in various textual sources locate the writing of the Epistle either in Athens or Corinth. The former possibility must be a scribal inaccuracy drawn from a misunderstanding of 1 Thess 3:1. Historical data in Acts 17–18 determine that Corinth is the place of origin (cf. Introduction, p. 233).

---

2 THESSALONIANS

Robert L. Thomas

2 THESSALONIANS

Introduction

1. Background

Paul's interest in his Thessalonian converts did not terminate with the dispatch of the first Epistle. His ministry was one of continual discipling of those he had won to Christ. This second letter was written only slightly later than 1 Thessalonians.

The background of 2 Thessalonians is therefore the same as that of 1 Thessalonians (see Introduction, pp. 229–231) with only slight additions. While he was still in Corinth, Paul received further word about this church's condition. Through what channel the report came is not known, but its content was sufficiently important to prompt him to write 2 Thessalonians.

2. Unity

The division of 2 Thessalonians into two letters (1:1–12 + 3:6–16 and 2:13, 14 + 2:1–12 + 2:15–3:5 + 3:17, 18) has been proposed, but it has not received substantial support. As with 1 Thessalonians, this theory is built largely on the presence of two thanksgivings (1:3ff.; 2:13f.) and two prayers (3:16, 18). The proposal of the division of 2 Thessalonians rests on an assumption that Paul never deviated from a stereotyped literary pattern. But this has never been proved. Even if it were true, the proposals for what that pattern is can be used against the theories they allegedly support. (Best, pp. 45–50). No manuscript authority for questioning the unity of 2 Thessalonians has ever been found. We may therefore safely conclude that it has been preserved in its original form.

3. Authorship and Canonicity

The external evidence for the Pauline authorship of 2 Thessalonians is stronger than for 1 Thessalonians. Possible references to it are found in the Didache and Ignatius, and Polycarp has two passages that are almost assuredly from the Epistle. Justin Martyr also clearly refers to it. In addition, the witnesses cited for 1 Thessalonians (cf. p. 232) add their support to the Pauline authorship of 2 Thessalonians and an early recognition of its canonicity (Milligan, pp. lxxvi–lxxvii).

Yet various objections to Pauline authorship have been offered on internal grounds:

1. The one objection most widely used finds in 2 Thessalonians an eschatology different from that of 1 Thessalonians, one that represents a Christian perspective that arose after the destruction of Jerusalem in A.D. 70 (Marxen, p. 42; Reginald H. Fuller, *A Critical Introduction to the New Testament* [London: Gerald Duckworth, 1966], p. 57; Norman Perrin, *The New Testament, An Introduction* [New York: Harcourt Brace Jovanovich, 1974], p. 120). The principal difference cited is emphasis on premonitory signs of the *parousia* in 2 Thessalonians in contrast to 1 Thessalonians' presentation of the event as something that may come at any moment. The notes below, however, explain in detail why this disagreement is not present. A right understanding of the several phases of the *parousia* and of the meaning of 2 Thessalonians 2:3, shows the harmony between the two Epistles. The apostasy and the man of lawlessness (2, 2:3) come after the initial phase of the *parousia* when Christ comes for his own, so there is no disagreement. Differing circumstances at the two writings called for emphases on different aspects of end-time events in the two Epistles.

2. Paul's authorship of 2 Thessalonians is also questioned because of its different view of the last judgment. A reversal of fates, with the persecutors receiving tribulation and the persecuted relief (2 Thess 1:5ff.), is not paralleled in Paul's acknowledged writings (Fuller, p. 58). This kind of thinking is alleged to belong to a generation later than Paul's (Rev 16:5–7; 19:2) (Perrin, p. 120). This objection sterotypes Paul's thinking unreasonably to the point of prohibiting him from expressing his eschatology in added dimensions. Far from belonging to a later generation, vengeance in connection with the Lord's return is traceable to Jesus himself (Luke 21:22) and to the OT (Isa 66:15). Paul simply developed it in 2 Thessalonians more than elsewhere. Furthermore, end-time tribulation and judgment for earth's inhabitants along with relief to Jesus' followers has its part in Jesus' teaching also (Matt 24:15–22; 25:31–46). In fact, Paul elsewhere understands the same twofold judgment of the two groups (Rom 2:5–10). Second Thessalonians is therefore in agreement with Pauline perspectives and fits quite well into the Pauline canon.

3. Another objection is that it is post-Pauline to assign divine attributes and functions to Christ (2 Thess 2:16; 3:5 with 1 Thess 3:11–13) (Fuller, p. 58). This difference in the prayers of the two Epistles reveals that 2 Thessalonians could not have been written during Paul's lifetime (Perrin, p. 120). To affirm, however, that Paul never believed in the deity of Christ is precarious. Even 1 Thessalonians sees him as a source of divine grace (1:1; 5:28), as one to whom prayer is properly addressed (3:11, 12), and, in addition, one to whom future accountability must be given (2:19). These are divine prerogatives that can be ignored only by a determined predisposition to the contrary. Both 1 and 2 Thessalonians rest staunchly upon a high view of Christ's person.

Other objections to the Pauline authorship of 2 Thessalonians include its difference in tone from 1 Thessalonians; its greater use of the OT, indicating Jewish rather than Gentile readers; and similarities to 1 Thessalonians so pronounced as to make the second Epistle unnecessary (Guthrie, pp. 572, 573). The harsher tone is adequately accounted for if Paul is dealing with a worsening situation in the second letter. Increased use of the OT is easily explainable for Gentile Christians who quite soon after conversion became conversant with it. Similarities to 1 Thessalonians are not so numerous as to make 2 Thessalonians a mere carbon copy. There are also differences. The combination of similarities and differences is such as to render Pauline authorship quite reasonable (ibid.).

None of these arguments based on internal considerations is sufficient to overthrow the Epistle's self-claims and the strongly attested traditional view of Paul's authorship.

4. Date

If one accepts the accuracy of the Acts account, 2 Thessalonians must have been written during Paul's stay in Corinth because Paul, Silas, and Timothy are not known to have been together after that. The conditions are still generally the same as those represented in 1 Thessalonians. First Thessalonians must have come earlier because its autobiographical portions leave no room for correspondence between Paul's departure from the city and the Epistle itself (Marxen, p. 41).

Some efforts to prove 2 Thessalonians earlier than 1 Thessalonians have been made: (1) In 2 Thessalonians trials are said to be at their height, whereas in 1 Thessalonians they are past (T.W. Manson, *Studies in the Gospels and Epistles* [Manchester: University of Manchester, 1962], p. 269). Yet 1 Thessalonians 3:4 is easily understood to indicate trials as present in that Epistle too. (2) In 2 Thessalonians internal difficulties (3:6–15) are a new development, but in 1 Thessalonians they are already well known (4:11, 12; 5:14) (Manson, p. 272). These phenomena, however, can be explained differently. The situation had become more aggravated in 2 Thessalonians, necessitating extended discussion. In 1 Thessalonians only a passing mention was required for a problem that had not yet become serious. (3) Three didactic sections of 1 Thessalonians, each introduced by *peri de* ("now about") correspond to questions raised by 2 Thessalonians (1 Thess 4:9–12 with 2 Thess 3:12; 1 Thess 4:13–18 with 2 Thess 2:1–12; 1 Thess 5:1–11 with 2 Thess 2:1–12) (Manson, pp. 274–277). While interesting, these correspondences may be just as easily explained by postulating the traditional order for the Epistles.

If efforts to prove 2 Thessalonians earlier fail, a date shortly after 1 Thessalonians is most probable for the writing of 2 Thessalonians, perhaps late in the summer of A.D. 50.

5. Place of Origin and Destination

Like 1 Thessalonians, this second Epistle also originated at Corinth. As far as is known, Silas and Timothy were not together with Paul at any later time (cf. Acts 18:5; 2 Thess 1:1). Berea and Philippi have been suggested as possible destinations of this letter. The former is considered plausible because of the favorable reception the Jews gave Paul and his companions in that city and the larger place of the OT in 2 Thessalonians. The suggestion of Philippi is supported by references in Polycarp, who seemingly names it as the destination of several passages in 2 Thessalonians (Best, pp. 40, 41). The difference in OT usage between 1 and 2 Thessalonians has already been accounted for without assigning a different destination (see Authorship and Canonicity). Polycarp's reference to Philippi probably arose through confusion of one Pauline Epistle with another; he was thoroughly familiar with Paul's writings and quoted from memory. Other passages imply that he knew of only one Philippian Epistle and that was certainly the same as the one currently known by that title (ibid.).

6. Occasion

Second Thessalonians was apparently prompted by three main developments: (1) Persecution of the Christians had grown worse and was leaving victims at the point of despair. (2) A pseudo-Pauline letter and other false representations were on the point of convincing believers that the end time was already present because of their increased suffering. (3) The nearness of Christ's return had been misused as a basis for shirking vocational responsibilities even more than at the time of 1 Thessalonians. This problem had become quite severe.

7. Purpose

To meet the needs that occasioned the Epistle Paul pursued three broad purposes: (1) He provided an incentive for the Thessalonians to persevere a little longer by describing the reward and retribution issuing from the future judgment of God (1:3–10). (2) He clarified prominent events belonging to the day of the Lord to prove the falsity of claims that the day had already arrived (2:1–12). (3) He issued detailed instructions covering disciplinary steps the church was to take in correcting those who refused to work (3:6–15).

8. Theological Values

(Cf. Introduction to 1 Thessalonians, pp. 233–234.)

9. Bibliography

(See Bibliography for 1 Thessalonians, pp. 234–235.)

10. Outline

    I. Salutation (1:1, 2)

    II. Assurance of Repayment at God's Righteous Judgment (1:3–12)

       A. Thanksgiving for Present Perseverance (1:3–10)

          1. Healthy development (1:3–5a)

          2. Righteous judgment (1:5b–10)

             a. Categorization of participants (1:5b–7a)

             b. Circumstances of fulfillment (1:7b)

             c. Consideration of repayment (1:8–10)

                1) Alienation (1:8, 9)

                2) Glorification (1:10)

       B. Prayer for Future Acceptance (1:11, 12)

    III. Assurance of Noninvolvement in the Day of the Lord (2:1–17)

       A. The False Claim (2:1, 2)

       B. The True Condition (2:3–12)

          1. Defiance—yet to come (2:3, 4)

          2. Delay—presently in effect (2:5–7)

          3. Deception and destruction—after the delay (2:8–10)

          4. Delusion and divine judgment—because of present recalcitrance (2:11, 12)

       C. The Truth's Continuance (2:13–17)

          1. Thanks for divine deliverance (2:13, 14)

          2. Call to doctrinal adherence (2:15)

          3. Prayer for practical compliance (2:16, 17)

    IV. Encouragement to Gainful Employment for the Present (3:1–15)

       A. Prayerful Preparation for Encounter (3:1–5)

          1. Prayer for Paul (3:1, 2)

          2. Prayer for the people (3:3–5)

       B. Proper Solution for Idleness (3:6–15)

          1. Previous instruction and example (3:6–10)

          2. Renewed instruction (3:11, 12)

          3. Corrective separation (3:13–15)

    V. Conclusion (3:16–18)

       A. Prayer for God's Peace and Presence (3:16)

       B. Personalized Benediction (3:17, 18)

Text and Exposition

I. Salutation

1:1, 2

> [1]Paul, Silas and Timothy, to the church of the Thessalonians, who are in God our Father and the Lord Jesus Christ: [2]Grace and peace to you from God the Father and the Lord Jesus Christ.

1,2 After a period of probably several months, new reports from Thessalonica reached Paul while he and his missionary party were still in Corinth. These reports were such as to lead him to write a second Epistle. Conditions reflected in 2 Thessalonians are similar to those in the first letter, though in some ways problems had become worse. In this second letter he sent to the Thessalonian church Paul provides solutions for a new set of circumstances.

The salutation is identical with that of the first letter (cf. exposition of 1 Thess 1:1) except for two additions. The first is "our" in the expression "God our Father" (v.1). This relates the fatherhood of God to Christians rather than to Jesus. (However, see note below.) The latter aspect of God's fatherhood is in view elsewhere (2 Cor 1:3; Eph 1:3; 1 Peter 1:3).

The second addition is the phrase "from God the Father and the Lord Jesus Christ" (v.2). Comparable phrases identifying the sources of "grace and peace" occur in all other Pauline superscriptions except 1 Thessalonians 1:1. The words make explicit what is already implicit—viz., that God is ultimately the only source of grace and peace. Two persons of the Godhead are specified: the Father and the Son. To Paul, Jesus was Deity in the fullest sense. This is the only justification for placing his name beside the Father's as co-author of the unmerited favor and harmonious relationship pronounced in this greeting.

Notes

2 There is textual evidence for reading "from God our Father," **ℵ** and A from the Alexandrian text-type being in support of including the possessive pronoun "our." Since this is the Pauline pattern wherever this source phrase is used, however, how could the pronoun ἡμῶν (*hēmōn*, "our") ever have been omitted by substantial authorities B (Alexandrian) and D (Western)? Copyists would hardly have omitted it in light of its presence in 1:1 and other Pauline salutations. Yet they may easily have been influenced to add it to bring the expression into line with practice elsewhere. Therefore, it probably was not present in the autograph.

II. Assurance of Repayment at God's Righteous Judgment (1:3–12)

A. *Thanksgiving for Present Perseverance* (1:3–10)

1. *Healthy development*

1:3–5a

> [3]We ought always to thank God for you, brothers, and rightly so, because your faith is growing more and more, and the love every one of you has for each other is increasing.
> [4]Therefore, among God's churches we boast about your perseverance and faith in all the persecutions and trials you are enduring.
> [5]All this is evidence that God's judgment is right. . . .

3 As is his practice in every Epistle but Galatians, Paul begins his remarks by thanking God for the spiritual progress of those he is writing to. Here his appreciation is marked by a feature found nowhere else except later in this same Epistle—he was obligated to express gratitude for what God had done in their lives. "We ought" appears only here and in 2:13 in connection with his thanksgiving and gives a glimpse into how Paul conceived of his duty to God. This unusual reference to responsibility, thought by some to be prompted by the readers' remarkable progress or by a special need among them (Lenski, p. 376; Hiebert, p. 279), should be limited to a special personal duty to God (Rom 1:14; 1 Cor 9:16, 17), because the Greek verb (*opheilō*, "ought"), implies an exclusive personal responsibility. "And rightly so" later in the verse refers to the readers' sterling performance amid persecutions (Milligan, p. 86; Lünemann, p. 184). Paul never ceased feeling a compulsion to give gratitude to God for what Christ had done. His post-conversion service was invested as a partial repayment for the personal debt he incurred when God gave him salvation.

"And rightly so" supplies a second reason for thanksgiving. "Just as it is fitting," the literal meaning, is not intended to limit the thankfulness (contra Lenski, p. 376), but stipulates the nature of response that caused appreciation (Best, pp. 249, 250). Paul habitually gave credit where credit was due. The conduct of his readers "under fire" was so commendable that he could not refrain from doing so again.

So great is Paul's excitement over their progress that he gives some details: "because your faith is growing more and more, and the love every one of you has for each other is increasing." Faith and love comprehend the total Christian walk (cf. 1 Cor 16:13, 14; 2 Cor 8:7; Gal 5:6; Eph 1:15; 3:17; 6:23; 1 Thess 3:6). The absence of "hope" from this combination is not overly significant. It does not hint at a lack of hope (Morris, NIC, p. 195; Hiebert, p. 281). Nor is it to be concluded that "hope" is represented in the "perseverance" of v.4. Paul rather uses two qualities instead of three (cf. 1 Thess 1:3) to designate Christian virtue and progress.

"Faith," an area commended in the first Epistle (1:3), was one where improvement was needed. The apostle's earlier prayer (1 Thess 3:10) had in view a return visit to strengthen the believers in this respect. Apparently, however, their faith had grown during his absence. They also needed to grow in "love," a quality he had already commended them for (1 Thess 1:3, 4:9, 10). For this too, Paul had prayed (1 Thess 3:12). It is no wonder, then, to find him rejoicing over their growth in faith and love.

4 In further reference to this radical improvement Paul says, "among God's churches we boast about your perseverance and faith." "We ourselves" would better translate the emphasis of the Greek text. But why this stress on the missionaries ("we ourselves")? Was Paul intimating that those who establish a church normally do not brag about that church (Morris, NIC, pp. 195, 196)? Or was he simply pointing to their own boasting in addition to that by others (Lenski, p. 379)? He more probably meant to contrast the missionaries' boasting with the Thessalonians' self-evaluation, since the Greek text places the intensive first person (*autous hēmas*, "we ourselves") in juxtaposition with the second person (*hymin*, "you"). At least some of these Christians felt inferior because of failures (1 Thess 5:14) and so were not inclined to boast. Paul speaks to this discouragement when he says, "As far as we are concerned your progress has been tremendous, so much so that we boast about it to other churches." The churches to which Paul had boasted were probably more widespread than in the vicinity of Corinth (contra Henry Alford, *The Greek Testament*, 3:285; Milligan, p. 87). Churches everywhere had heard this report, either through letter or through personal contact with those visiting Paul in Corinth. This did not necessarily include every single church, of course, but represents a relatively widespread dissemination of the news (cf. 1 Thess 1:8) (Hogg and Vine, p. 222; Hendriksen, p. 156).

The boasting pertains to "your perseverance and faith in all the persecutions and trials you are enduring." "Perseverance" is the attitude that accepts trying circumstances without retarding progress (cf. comment on "endurance" in 1 Thess 1:3). Accompanying the perseverance of the Thessalonians was their "faith" or, perhaps better, their "faithfulness." While "faith" is the common meaning of *pistis* in Paul's writings (Morris, NIC, p. 196), the present context justifies the less frequent sense of "faithfulness" or "fidelity," which Paul also makes use of (Rom 3:3; Gal 5:22; Titus 2:10) (Lünemann, p. 188). Their tenacious loyalty to Christ in spite of fierce adversity is what Paul finds so remarkable. "Persecutions" (*diōgmois*) are sufferings incurred because of faith in Christ, while "trials" (*thlipsesin*) are troubles of any kind. The believers were "enduring" (*anechesthe*) these—but only for the time being; in God's plan such conditions were not to be permanent.

5 Instead of beginning a new paragraph, "all this is evidence that God's judgment is right" should probably be read with the end of v.4. The subject of Paul's boasting—i.e., their perseverance and faithfulness—is proof positive of God's righteous judgment. That he gives strength enough to face all the persecutions and trials victoriously shows that his "judgment is right" (Hendriksen, p. 155).

Withstanding *present* pressures demonstrates the rightness of God's *future* judgment. Some have seen present judgment in this reference because *endeixis* ("sign," "proof"), a cognate of *endeigma* ("evidence"), usually speaks of something already in force and because Peter views present suffering as a phase of God's judgment (1 Peter 4:17) (Auberlen and Riggenbach, p. 115; Olshausen, *Biblical Commentary*, 7:463). Yet subsequent descriptions (vv.6–10) relate so integrally to future accountability with the accompanying thought of reward for sufferers and retaliation against offenders that an understanding of present judgment is practically impossible (Hiebert, p. 285; Moffatt, EGT, 4:45; Lightfoot, p. 100). Quite clearly Paul uses a corresponding term (*dikaiokrisias*, "righteous judgment") in Romans 2:5 with this future sense (Frame, p. 226). The fact is that righteous judgment in 1:5a sets the tone for five and one-half verses about what is to come. The persecuted must understand clearly its twofold nature.

Notes

3   The use of ὀφείλω (opheilō, "ought") rather than δεῖ (dei, "it is necessary") probably shows that Paul's feeling of obligation at this point is unrelated to the Thessalonians' response. That he would use the same word again in 2:13, where the behavior of the Thessalonians is only remotely in view, increases the likelihood that here he is thinking strictly of his own debt to God.

To take the καθώς (kathōs, "as") clause (lit., "as it is fitting") as purely comparative implies a Pauline reluctance to "go all out" in his thanksgiving for them. The causal sense of kathōs is well established (Rom 1:28; 1 Cor 1:6; 5:7; Eph 1:4; Phil 1:7) (Robertson, RHG, p. 968; BDF, p. 236). It is much better when the comparison is allowed to take a causal flavor. From the standpoint of the Thessalonians' receptivity, it was incumbent upon Paul to express gratitude to God.

4   An additional reason for giving αὐτοὺς ἡμᾶς (autous hēmas, "we ourselves") a sense contrasted to ὑμῖν (hymin, "you") comes from 1 Thess 4:9 where the emphatic αὐτοί ... ὑμεῖς (autoi ... hymeis, "you ... yourselves") is antithetic to a supplied ἡμᾶς (hēmas, "us") with the infinitive γράφειν (graphein, "to write") (Frame, p. 223). This reflects a possible Pauline pattern of placing first and second person pronouns in such proximity for sake of contrast. In other cases where the intensive pronoun is used with the first person, it implies contrast (Rom 7:25; 9:3; 15:14; 2 Cor 10:1; 12:13) (Best, p. 251).

Used only here in the NT, ἐγκαυχᾶσθαι (enkauchasthai, "boast") governs two ἐν (en, "in") phrases, the former one specifying the object of boasting and the latter the place of boasting.

The association of πίστεως (pisteōs, "faith") with ὑπομονῆς (hypomonēs, "perseverance"), διωγμοῖς (diōgmois, "persecutions"), θλίψεσιν (thlipsesin, "trials") and ἀνέχεσθε (anechesthe, "you are enduring") argues strongly for allowing its exceptional meaning of "faithfulness." Paul boasts about tangible perseverance. To have pisteōs refer to intangible faith does not furnish a suitable parallel. It must be the visible fruit of faith—faithfulness. Paul's habitual use of πιστός (pistos) for "faithful" lends further support to the choice of "faithfulness" instead of "faith" (1 Cor 1:9; 10:13; 2 Cor 1:8; 1 Thess 5:24; 2 Thess 3:3; 2 Tim 2:13) (Lünemann, p. 188).

5a The syntactical arrangement of ἔνδειγμα ... τοῦ θεοῦ (endeigma ... tou theou, "evidence that God's judgment is right") is difficult to decipher with assurance. Probably the best evidence favors taking ἔνδειγμα (endeigma, "evidence") as accusative in apposition with the whole idea behind ὑπομονῆς (hypomonēs, "perseverance") and πίστεως (pisteōs, "faith," "faithfulness," v.4). The difference in case is explained by Paul's consolidation of the whole expression introduced by the genitives of v.4 into a single concept (Lightfoot, p. 100). The case of endeigma is accusative, in agreement with a precedent in classical literature (Milligan, pp. 87, 88) and elsewhere in Paul (Rom 12:1).

---

2. Righteous judgment (1:5b–10)

a. Categorization of participants

1:5b–7a

5. . . and as a result you will be counted worthy of the kingdom of God, for which you are suffering. 6God is just: He will pay back trouble to those who trouble you 7and give relief to you who are troubled, and to us as well. . . .

5b–7a The remainder of this section (vv.5b–10) expands on what God's future righteous judgment is. Paul first describes what it will mean to victims of present persecution (v.5b). He then points out the fate of persecutors (v.6), following this with a second look at what will happen to the persecuted (v.7a).

5b Future reckoning assures a future recognition of the worthiness of those suffering for the sake of the kingdom of God. This recognition will be God's pronouncement of fitness. It will not be self-earned but a gracious divine impartation resulting from the decision to believe in the Lord Jesus (1:3, 10; 2:13; 1 Thess 1:8), who himself earned the believer's forgiveness of sins and eternal life by dying a sacrificial death (1 Thess 5:10). The worthiness of the Thessalonian believers had already been established before persecutions came. Their firm stand in the face of persecutions (v.4) confirmed their relationship to God and was a pledge that their worthiness will be openly declared by God himself. Believers in Thessalonica were not the only ones suffering this kind of treatment. "For which you *also* [*kai*, v.5, untranslated in text above] are suffering" reminds the readers of something they already knew well—an experience they had in common with Paul, Silas, Timothy, and others (Acts 17:5; 1 Thess 2:2; cf. 2 Thess 3:2). With opposition behind them, all who are Christ's at his *parousia* will be welcomed into the messianic kingdom on the ground of their God-given worthiness.

6 On the other hand, it is well known how God will pay back those responsible for troubling Christians. They will be repaid proportionately for the suffering they have caused God's people. This is only right ("just") in God's eyes and is the reason this future judgment is called "righteous" (NIV, "right," v.5). In return, the antagonists will receive "trouble" (*thlipsin*), a term not further defined at this point. In v.9 another expression, "everlasting destruction," adds insight into these consequences. *Thlipsin* is a word often translated "tribulation." It is the present lot of Christians to undergo tribulation (v.4; 1 Thess 3:4). For the rest of the world, however, tribulation will be future and far greater in intensity (Matt 24:21; cf. Rev 3:10). In his first Epistle to this church, Paul described this period in relation to its source—viz., God's wrath (1:10; 2:16; 5:9). But here he speaks of it from the standpoint of circumstances that engulf the victims. After the period of tribulation has passed, these troublers will be denied entrance into the messianic kingdom that has welcomed the faithful followers of Christ (v.5; Matt 25:41, 46).

7a The other side of God's justice is full bestowal of rest on those who have been "persecuted" ("troubled"), a reward awaiting Paul and his co-workers also ("and to us as well"). This will be the relief from tension and suffering that is the portion of all who become Christ's disciples. Their rest and bliss in the future state (cf. Acts 3:19, 20; Rev 14:13) are guaranteed by the justice of God. A sublime anticipation thus helps suffering Christians to maintain unwavering perseverance and faithfulness (cf. v.4).

Participants in God's righteous judgment fall into these two classes: For one, the future holds the most severe threat. Though their domination is tolerated for the present, when the proper time comes, the roles will be reversed. The second class, though under the heel of the other for the moment, will become the overcomers who will enjoy all privileges in God's kingdom.

Notes

5b Here εἰς τό (*eis to*, "for the,"; NIV, "as a result") cannot introduce a purpose clause as it commonly does, because future judgment can hardly have as its objective the accomplishment of the believer's worthiness. Being counted worthy might be considered a result of God's judgment, but *eis to* introducing a result clause normally must modify a verb and this clause modifies a noun (κρίσεως, *kriseōs*, "judgment"). The most probable solution is to assign *eis to* a substantival function expanding the meaning and implications of τῆς δικαίας κρίσεως (*tēs dikaias kriseōs*, "righteous judgment," v.5a). The same function is performed by *eis to* infinitive combinations in 1 Thess 2:12; 4:9 (Milligan, p. 26; Moulton, *Prolegomena*, p. 219). Details about judgment in subsequent verses (e.g., δίκαιον, *dikaion*, "just," v.6) confirm this conclusion.

It is conceivable that the καί (*kai*, "also") views present suffering as a companion of future glory (Acts 14:22; Rom 8:17; 2 Cor 1:7; Phil 3:10; 2 Tim 2:12) (Lightfoot, p. 101; Ellicott, p. 98). Yet this contrast has already been made in vv.4, 5a and grouping the Pauline missionary staff with the Thessalonian sufferers has more point in v.5b (cf. μεθ' ἡμῶν, *meth' hēmōn*, "with us," v.7) (Best, p. 256). Paul's trying experiences at Corinth were very much the same as earlier (Acts 18:6, 12, 13) (Frame, p. 227).

---

b. *Circumstances of fulfillment*

1:7b

7... This will happen when the Lord Jesus is revealed from heaven in blazing fire with his powerful angels.

7b "When the Lord Jesus is revealed" (lit., "at the revelation of the Lord Jesus") identifies the time of God's righteous judgment. This second advent will occasion a "paying back" (v.6) of both the troublers and the troubled.

As defined by these Epistles, the objects of Christ's revelation are twofold. On the one hand, he will appear to those who are in Christ. It will be an appearance that means rest (1:7a) when he comes "from heaven" (cf. 1 Thess 4:16) to meet the dead and living in Christ in the air (1 Thess 4:17) and gather them to himself (2 Thess 2:1). This begins their unending fellowship with him (1 Thess 4:17; 5:10) and participation in his glory (2 Thess 1:10, 12). Paul hoped to be alive at this time ("and to us as well;" cf. "we who are still alive, who are left," 1 Thess 4:15, 17).

The other group on whom God's righteous judgment and the revelation of the Lord Jesus will make their impact are "those who trouble you" (v.6). The consequences for these will be prolonged and painful. Christ will not be unveiled personally to them at first, but will begin by subjecting earth's rebels to a period of intense "trouble." The human misery of those days is and will be without parallel in the annals of history (Dan 12:1; Mark 13:19). It will grow into a dominant factor during the time of "the rebellion and the man of lawlessness" (2:3). As the period runs its course, it will witness the abomination of desolation (2:4; cf. Dan 9:27; 11:31, 36; 12:11; Matt 24:15) and the Satanic deception of an unbelieving world (2:9, 10). All this is the initial phase of God's vengeance ("he will punish," v.8; lit., "rendering vengeance,") against a world that persists in rebellion (cf. Luke 21:22; Rev 6:10; 19:2).

As the period draws to its close, the Lord Jesus will be revealed personally to culminate this vengeance with "everlasting destruction" and exclusion from the Lord's presence and glory (v.9). Paul's concept of what the future holds for the lost is bleak. It is a day of wrath and revelation of the righteous judgment of God (Rom 2:5; 1 Thess 1:10; 2:16; 5:9) just before the revelation of Christ's glory in the world (Oepke, TDNT, 3:583).

Afflicted Christians, on the other hand, are offered the brightest anticipation. They look forward to the Lord Jesus' revelation from heaven and not to increased trouble and intensified persecution from the man of lawlessness (2:3, 4). Their incentive to persevere is the prospect of immediate rest "when the Lord Jesus is revealed." They will not be present for the apostasy (2:3), the rule of the lawless one (2:3, 4) or his "counterfeit miracles, signs and wonders" (2:9), because their promised rest in heaven will have begun by then. This is a marked contrast to their persecutors' fate. With a hope like this there is ample reason to continue in faithfulness to the Lord.

The "blazing fire" of his coming recalls the glory of OT theophanies (Exod 3:2; 19:18; 24:17; Deut 5:4; Ps 18:12; Isa 30:27–30; Dan 7:9, 10). It will be a revelation of glory in which the saints will share (1:10, 12). The Lord Jesus will be accompanied by "his powerful angels" (lit., "angels of his power"), who will draw on his power for their part in the revelation.

Many have chosen to limit *apokalypsei* ("revelation," "appearance") to a single event, identifying it with Christ's return to earth at the close of the tribulation. The role of "his powerful angels" in the revelation favors this understanding in the light of Matthew 24:30, 31; 25:31. It is more persuasive, however, to explain *apokalypsei* as a complex of events, including various phases of end-time happenings. The present context associates the word with Christ's coming for his own as well as his coming to deal with opponents. Since the primary thrust of vv.5–10 is to encourage suffering Christians, the meaning of *apokalypsei* for them should receive the emphasis. God's dealings with the rest of the world are included only to enhance the "relief" experienced by believers at the righteous judgment of God.

Notes

7b Δυνάμεως (*dynameōs*, "of power"; NIV, "powerful") is best understood as an objective genitive modified by αὐτοῦ (*autou*, "his"), giving the meaning "the angels of his power." The tr. "his powerful angels" treats *dynameōs* as a descriptive genitive, which makes the position of *autou* awkward (Lightfoot, p. 102; Milligan, p. 89). This rendering, moreover, unnecessarily reduces the prominence of "power" in a setting where it deserves emphasis.

If πυρὶ φλογός (*pyri phlogos*, "blazing fire") referred strictly to a purifying effect, it would find its most natural connection with v.8 rather than v.7. The more positive understanding of it as picturing glory is better, necessitating its attachment to the previous clause. Besides, to begin a participial clause with a prepositional phrase is quite rare.

c. *Consideration of repayment* (1:8–10)

1) *Alienation*

1:8, 9

> 8He will punish those who do not know God and do not obey the gospel of our Lord Jesus. 9They will be punished with everlasting destruction and shut out from the presence of the Lord and from the majesty of his power....

8 Two types of repayment to be meted out at the righteous judgment of God deserve consideration in light of the Christian's present trouble. One is toward the troublers

(vv.8, 9) and the other toward the troubled (v.10). "He will punish" is literally "rendering vengeance." The word stem for vengeance is the same as that for "right" (v.5) and "just (v.6). It has no overtones of selfish vindictiveness or revenge, but proceeds from the justice of God to accomplish appropriate punishment for criminal offenses.

Recipients of God's avenging judgment will be in two groups: "those who do not know God and [those who] do not obey the gospel of our Lord Jesus." Those coming from a Gentile background constitute the former class. They are "without God in the world" (Eph 2:12; cf. Gal 4:8; 1 Thess 4:5), being estranged from him (Rom 1:18–32). The comparable use of the expression in Jeremiah 10:25 makes the Gentile identification even more convincing. That the immediate context does nothing to prepare for separate allusions to Gentiles and Jews (Morris, p. 204) is not sufficient reason for rejecting evidence in favor of distinguishing the two groups. It is appropriate for Gentile persecutors at Thessalonica to be singled out in both Epistles (1 Thess 2:14) because of this church's history (Acts 17:5). Gentiles without any background in OT teaching about God are nonetheless culpable for their persecution of Christians.

The other group, those who do not obey the gospel of our Lord Jesus, are well-versed in OT Scriptures because of their Jewish backgrounds. Here Paul uses an apt description of unbelieving Jews, found also in Romans 10:16, where the same terminology again designates Abraham's physical descendants (cf. Rom 10:3). These are the persecutors against whom such strong feelings were evident in his first Epistle (1 Thess 2:14–16). That Jews are occasionally called those who do not know God (John 8:54, 55) and Gentiles are called those who are disobedient to God (Rom 11:30) (Morris, p. 204) is interesting but not adequate to erase the clear impression that Paul in the present verse makes an ethnic distinction. Jews, like Gentiles, had been adamant in their opposition to Christians in Thessalonica and its vicinity (Acts 17:5, 13). Because of this, when the wrath of God makes itself felt at the revelation of the Lord Jesus, both classes of humanity will face dreaded agonies.

9 The most sobering experience of all will culminate God's righteous judgment against his enemies: "They will be punished with everlasting destruction"; literally, "they will pay the penalty, everlasting destruction." A price must be paid in return for the suffering inflicted on God's people and that price is none other than "everlasting destruction." *Olethros* ("destruction") does not refer to annihilation, which cannot be "everlasting" (Hendriksen, p. 160). The word in LXX and NT usages never has this meaning but rather turns on the thought of separation from God and loss of everything worthwhile in life (Schneider, TDNT, 5:169; Morris, p. 205). Just as endless life belongs to Christians, endless destruction belongs to those opposed to Christ (Matt 25:41, 46).

The consequences of permanent separation from God come out forcibly in the phrase "from the presence of the Lord" (cf. Isa 2:10, LXX). Banishment from the Lord's presence is what Jesus taught about punishment (Matt 7:23; 8:12; 22:13; 25:30; Luke 13:27). Words cannot adequately express the misery of this condition. On the other hand, those in Christ can anticipate the very opposite: "we will be with the Lord forever" (1 Thess 4:17).

Some have questioned whether the parallel phrase, "from the majesty of his power," can likewise signify separation (Olshausen, p. 467). If "majesty" (lit., "glory") be visible manifestations proceeding from his power (lit., "strength"), there is no problem in understanding how this expression also describes the anguish of separation. Instead of enjoying that glory or majesty, an uncrossable gulf will preclude access for those destined to everlasting punishment (cf. Luke 16:24–26).

Notes

8 A repeated article before μὴ ὑπακούουσιν (mē hypakouousin, "not obeying") is in itself substantial indication that two distinct classes are intended. Other passages where two articles appear with expressions designating the same group are for one reason or another not parallel to this construction (cf. 1:10; Rom 4:12). Also, synonymous parallelism in poetic writings is not the same as this usage (cf. Ps 35:11). These are two distinct classes who make up the larger group of "those who trouble you" (v.6).

9 It is possible to assign a causal meaning to ἀπό (apo, "from"; cf. Matt 13:44; Luke 12:57), but this is a relatively infrequent NT meaning (Frame, p. 235) and presents a thought repetitious of vv.7, 8 (Lünemann, p. 195). To see the two phrases as sources from which eternal destruction proceeds is also possible (Olshausen, p. 467), since comparable meanings of the preposition are found in Acts 3:20 and 1 Thess 1:8 (Hogg and Vine, p. 234). But this explanation also goes over the same ground as vv.7, 8 (Hiebert, p. 292). The spatial sense of apo is normal and therefore preferable in the present verse (cf. Acts 5:41; Rev 12:14; 20:11) (Best, p. 263). Distance from eternal blessedness is most potent in describing eternal punishment.

As compared with δύναμις (dynamis), ἰσχύς (ischys) stresses power or ability in action. Its word group emphasizes utilization of capacity, whereas the dynamis group is more a subjective ability, not necessarily actualized. Here it is the Lord's "power" exerted, not just potential (Marvin R. Vincent, The Epistles to the Philippians and to Philemon [ICC], p. 145; Grundmann, TDNT, 3:397).

2) Glorification

1:10

> [10]on the day he comes to be glorified in his holy people and to be marveled at among all those who have believed. This includes you, because you believed our testimony to you.

10 Thankfully, another side of God's repayment remains, that of glorification. "On the day he comes" further defines "when the Lord Jesus is revealed" (v.7). Literally, it is composed of two distinct parts: "when he comes" and "in that day." The latter of these is placed emphatically at the very end of v.10 in the Gr. text. "That day" is a frequent OT designation for the day of the Lord (cf. Isa 2:11, 17). In the present verse it solemnly emphasizes a time coincident with "when he comes" as it does repeatedly in the NT (Mark 13:32; 14:25; Luke 21:34; 2 Tim 1:12, 18; 4:8) (Milligan, p. 92). Earlier Paul has disclosed how the day of the Lord will encompass in its initial stage a period of wrath and tribulation. The tribulation will be climaxed when Jesus Christ returns personally to judge and to inaugurate his reign on earth. In v.10, however, Paul has in view an event at the very beginning of the day and before the wrath—the meeting of Christ with his saints in the air (1 Thess 4:17; 2 Thess 1:7a; 2:1). This is the moment of reward for those who have faithfully persevered in all their persecutions and trials (v.4).

The substance of their reward will be participation in the glory and marvel of the Lord's return. In a unique sense he is the glory and the object of wonder, but he purposes to share these "in [the midst of] his holy people and ... among all those who have believed." Psalm 89:7 is the source of the phrase "in his holy people." It speaks of "a God greatly feared in the council of the holy ones." Here is a glorified assembly. Christ's glorification belongs to Christians also. Along with the mutual experience of wonder "among all those who have believed," the fact that we will be glorified constitutes more than sufficient incentive to endure life's present trials (cf. Rom 8:17, 18; 9:23).

"Those who have believed" becomes very personal as Paul adds "because you believed our testimony to you." These words remind the troubled readers that they themselves will participate in the glory and amazement of that day—i.e., "because at a decisive moment you personally appropriated the gospel to yourselves, you can live with the sustaining hope and certainty of knowing you are included." Enjoyment of the future glory of Christ's coming is the leading idea of the chapter (Lightfoot, p. 105) and a prime incentive for faithfulness.

Notes

10 Whether ἐν (en, "in") stipulates cause (Best, p. 264; Frame, p. 237) or sphere (Lünemann, p. 196; Robertson, Word Pictures, 4:44) in its first two occurrences is debated. A causal force is an established possibility in Paul and the rest of the NT (Turner, Syntax, p. 253). The causal usage is thought by some to be required in the parallel case of v.12. Yet this draws attention away from the Lord by attributing the glory of the occasion to "his holy people." The more usual locative force of the preposition allows the saints participation in the glory but recognizes Christ as its focal point.

An issue revolves about τοῖς ἁγίοις (tois hagiois, "holy people") similar to the one with τῶν ἁγίων (tōn hagiōn, "holy ones") in 1 Thess 3:13. Here as there, these are redeemed people, not angels. Contextual emphasis on persecuted believers, as well as the use of ἀγγέλων (aggelōn) for angels in v.7, makes this even clearer.

The aorist τοῖς πιστεύσασιν (tois pisteusasin, "those who have believed") has been understood by some as written from the standpoint of Christ's return when belief will be past (Ellicott, p. 102). But it is better to explain the aorist in terms of the precise moment when faith in "our testimony" was initiated. This conclusion is dictated by the ἐπιστεύθη (episteuthē, "you believed") immediately following and by the same verb's aorist usage elsewhere in Paul (1 Cor 15:2, 11; 2 Cor 4:13) (Lightfoot, p. 104; Milligan, p. 92; Best, p. 266).

The textual variant of ἐπιστώθη (epistōthē, "you were persuaded") instead of ἐπιστεύθη (episteuthē, "you believed") has external evidence too slight to merit serious consideration. It probably arose through failure to notice the ὅτι (hoti, "because") clause's proper connection with the rest of the verse.

Lenski chooses to connect the final ἐν (en, "in" ["in that day"]) phrase of v.10 with μαρτύριον (martyrion, "testimony") rather than to allow it to resume the ὅταν (hotan, "whenever") earlier in the verse. "In connection with," a meaning for en required by this view, is so rare that it is better to follow the more usual temporal meaning. The eschatological force of "that day" requires the phrase to resume and solemnly repeat the anticipation of "when he comes."

B. *Prayer for Future Acceptance*

1:11, 12

> ¹¹With this in mind, we constantly pray for you, that our God may count you worthy of his calling, and that by his power he may fulfill every good purpose of yours and every act prompted by your faith. ¹²We pray this so that the name of our Lord Jesus may be glorified in you, and you in him, according to the grace of our God and the Lord Jesus Christ.

11 Not content with the certainty of coming glorification, Paul now prays for its realization. Human minds wrestle with the problem of praying for something already fixed in the unalterable purpose of God. Yet has not Paul already done this in these Epistles (1 Thess 3:12, 13; 5:23)? Is it not God's pleasure for saints to cooperate with his ongoing program? (Phil 2:12, 13). For example, the NT closes on the note of John's prayer for the already certain return of the Lord Jesus (Rev 22:20).

The purpose of Paul's prayer is "that our God may count you worthy of his calling." This probably corresponds to their worthiness for the kingdom mentioned in v.5. No uncertainty of ultimate acceptance is implied in the prayer. Uncertainty would undercut, not build, assurance for the fainthearted. Though the worthiness of the Thessalonian believers was confirmed (v.5), certainty in the security of God's purposes does not diminish the need to keep on praying. Ultimate salvation rests on the sure foundation of God's faithfulness (1 Thess 5:24), but until its actual accomplishment, Paul continues praying for it (Hogg and Vine, p. 237).

"His calling" is usually regarded by Paul as a past decree (Rom 11:29; 1 Cor 1:26) (Milligan, p. 93; Best, p. 268). To construe it like this here could imply the possibility of falling away from it (Lünemann, p. 198; Frame, p. 239). Yet such cannot happen to those already assured of a future worthiness (v.5) based solely on the grace of God (v.12). It is reassuring to know that God's call is made effective quite apart from human merit (cf. Gal 1:13–15). Instead of limiting the call to what happened before the foundation of the world, the present emphasis on Christ's return (v.10) and the eschatological kingdom of God (v.5) argues for extending the scope of "calling" to include its future outworking at God's righteous judgment (v.5).

Paul's other prayer objective is for God to "fulfill every good purpose [lit., 'every resolve for goodness'] of yours and every act prompted by your faith." "Goodness" is part of the fruit of the Spirit (Gal 5:22). Paul prays for the kind of desire that produces goodness—i.e., the active quality that constantly pursues what is right and beneficial for others. "Every act prompted by your faith" is what he had witnessed in them previously (cf. "work produced by faith," 1 Thess 1:3). What they had already attained was important, but room for growth was still there (cf. 1 Thess 3:10; 4:1). Realization of these objectives can come only "by his power," i.e., that of him the prayer is addressed to.

12 Here Paul states the purpose of his prayer—the glorification of Christ in the believers and they in him (cf. Isa 66:5). This is an intermediate step toward the final recognition of the Lord's own worthiness and majesty and the saints' participation in these things with him. "Name" is a reference to the dignity, majesty, and power of the Lord's revealed character.

Several have chosen to understand "in you ... in him" causally: "because of you ... because of him" (Frame, p. 241; Best, pp. 271, 272); i.e., glory comes to the Lord because of the saved and to the saved because of the Lord. It is unnecessary to resort to this rare meaning of en ("in"), however. The more common locative meaning allows us to see this as the "en of mystic indwelling" (Robertson, RHG, pp. 587, 588). A technical expression initiated by Jesus (John 15:4; 17:21), this was taken up by Paul and developed more completely (Rom 6:11, 23; 1 Cor 1:5; 2 Cor 13:4; et al.). The thought is that of reciprocity resting on the union of the Lord with his people. They are to share the future moment of glorification together—as a unit.

Elsewhere Paul shows a continuing zeal to exclude merit from the salvation process (cf. Rom 4:16; 11:5, 6; Eph 2:5, 8); so here also grace is the source of everything (Lightfoot, p. 107). Grace is from both Father and Son as in the salutation. We pray for such things as these and our prayers are answered in harmony with the working of God's grace.

Notes

11 The antecedent of ὅ (ho, "which"; NIV, "this") is not immediately apparent. Some identify it as the entirety of vv.5–10. Future glorification of the Lord in his saints (v.10) is another possibility because of proximity, but this is only a subordinate part of the very involved sentence in vv.3–10. The most probable antecedent is worthiness for the kingdom mentioned in v.5. All intervening material is a digression and development of this thought. Confirmation of this choice is found in the way καταξιωθῆναι (kataxiōthēnai, "be counted worthy," v.5) is picked up by ἀξιώσῃ (axiōsē, "may count ... worthy," v.11) (Hogg and Vine, p. 237).

The presence of the first καί (kai, "and," "also") of v.11 (untranslated in NIV here) deserves clarification. "We also constantly pray" is sometimes understood as contrasting hope and expectation (v.10) with the prayer of this verse (Ellicott, p. 103). Morris says it joins the apostle's prayers with those of the Thessalonians (Morris, p. 209). Still others see it as connecting prayer with the earlier thanksgiving (v.3), boasting (v.4), testimony (v.10), or some combination of these (Hiebert, p. 295; Frame, p. 238). A further viewpoint accords with NIV in attributing no significance at all to the kai (Best, pp. 267, 268). Its position before προσευχόμεθα (proseuchometha, "we pray") probably indicates a new activity, something done along with the thanksgiving of v.3. Thus, εὐχαριστεῖν ὀφείλομεν (eucharistein opheilomen, "we ought to thank," v.3) and proseuchometha ("we pray," v.11) are the controlling grammatical features of vv. 3–12.

Some have preferred to give ἀξιώσῃ (axiōsē, "may count worthy") the meaning "make worthy" (Foerster, TDNT, 1:380; BAG, pp. 77, 78). Whether this meaning is lexically demonstrable may be questioned, however, especially in NT usage (Ellicott, pp. 103, 104; Lightfoot, p. 105). Giving καταξιωθῆναι (kataxiōthēnai, "to be counted worthy") a judicial sense in v.5 probably indicates that the same should be done for axiōsē in v.11. This agrees with the verb's predominant meaning of "esteem worthy" in the NT (1 Tim 5:17; Heb 3:3; 10:29) (Hogg and Vine, p. 237; Frame, p. 240; Milligan, p. 93).

"Every good purpose" takes ἀγαθωσύνης (agathōsynēs, "of goodness") as a genitive of description. Factors favoring such an interpretation are minimal. Agathōsunēs, a very meaningful and prominent noun, is robbed of its fulness by being construed as a subordinate adjective, "good." Εὐδοκίαν (eudokian) has the force of "resolve" (Hendriksen, p. 163) and unless agathōsynēs is seen as an objective genitive, the goal of the resolve is left undefined. "Resolve for goodness" therefore makes better sense (Best, p. 270).

12 The definiteness of the second κυρίου (kyriou, "Lord") diminishes the probability that τοῦ (tou, "of the") governs it as well as the preceding θεοῦ (theou, "God"). In other words, Paul names the Father as well as the Son. This is not a case to use the grammatical principle of one article governing two nouns connected by καί (kai, "and") to demonstrate the deity of Christ as is Titus 2:13 or 2 Peter 1:1 (Robertson, RHG, p. 786).

III. Assurance of Noninvolvement in the Day of the Lord (2:1–17)

A. The False Claim

2:1, 2

¹Concerning the coming of our Lord Jesus Christ and our being gathered to him, we ask you, brothers, ²not to become easily unsettled or alarmed by some prophecy, report or letter supposed to have come from us, saying that the day of the Lord has already come.

1,2 The hortatory words "we ask you, brothers" are identical in the Greek with "now we ask you, brothers" of 1 Thessalonians 5:12. This formula provides a transition from what Paul has been saying about the day of the Lord to an acute problem related to it.

The problem has to do with the events he has just described. It is "concerning" or "on behalf of" the Lord's coming and the saints' gathering to him that Paul now writes. In the interest of truth about this vital hope, we must set down accurately certain features of "the day of the Lord" as a corrective to what some were falsely claiming.

He must explain what he means by "the coming of our Lord Jesus Christ and our being gathered to him" or else the solution to the problem cannot be grasped. *Episynagōgēs* ("being gathered") defines what part of the *parousias* ("coming") Paul has in mind. This is the great event he has described more fully in 1 Thessalonians 4:14–17—i.e., the gathering of those in Christ to meet him in the air en route to the Father in heaven. This begins the day of the Lord. What relationship this happening bears to the tribulation phase of the day of the Lord so frequently mentioned in these Epistles is important. Some limit the *parousia* to a single event and insist that it comes after the tribulation (Morris, pp. 151, 152; Gundry, pp. 113, 114). It is hardly possible, though, to explain the variety of relationships belonging to *parousia* in these Epistles if it is understood only as a single event. Even the meaning of the word suggests a longer duration.

Another problem is encountered if the *parousia* that initiates the day of the Lord is considered only the single event of Christ's return to earth following the tribulation. If Paul had given oral or written instruction to this effect, the false claim that the day of the Lord was already present could hardly have alarmed these Christians. According to this scheme, the day of the Lord could not begin without Christ's personal reappearance. His continued absence was obvious to all.

Yet the claim *was* made and accepted to the extent that the church was troubled. This implies Paul had not taught that a one-phase *parousia* after the period of wrath will begin the day of the Lord. He had told them that the coming of the Lord to gather his saints into heaven would initiate both the tribulation and the day of the Lord. They were promised immediate "rest" (1:7) and glorification with Christ (1:10), not increased persecution.

The false instruction had, however, denied them an imminent "rest." They would first have to undergo the severe persecution of the tribulation and possibly even suffer martyrdom before Christ's coming, according to these misrepresentations. They were even told that their current suffering indicated the arrival of the expected tribulation. Second Thessalonians 2:3, 4, 8–12 speaks of this future period in terms quite similar to those of Revelation 13 and 17. The man of lawlessness has a number of affinities with the beasts of Revelation, enough to show that the two books describe the same period (R.H. Charles, *Eschatology* [New York: Schocken Books, 1963], p. 441n). Though 2 Thessalonians does not specifically mention the beast's war with the saints and their martyrdom, Revelation 13:7, 10 declares it explicitly. If this is a possibility for the church, why did Paul at no point teach this kind of anticipation? The answer must lie in the removal of Christians (including the Thessalonian believers) from earth before this persecution. It is another group of God's people, following the church's translation, who must face the terror of this archenemy.

Despite their "persecutions and trials" (1:4) these Thessalonian Christians were not living in the day of the Lord as they had been erroneously told. A right understanding of "being gathered to him" reveals that they could not be so enmeshed, because for them Christ's *parousia* will antedate the awful period to come. In fact, their "being gathered to him" will be the event that signals the day's beginning.

As their friend and brother, Paul respectfully requests (*erōtōmen*, "we ask," v.1; cf. 1 Thess 4:1) them not to become "unsettled or alarmed" (v.2). This might easily happen if they were led to believe that somehow the glorious coming had passed them by. "Unsettled" means "to be shaken from your sensibleness [lit., mind]." Distorted teaching had alarmed them. Paul cautioned them against hastily (*tacheōs*, "easily" [NIV]) adopting something other than the instruction he had previously given them (cf. v.15). Teaching that seemed to have come from Paul had reached them through various avenues. One was the spiritual gift of prophecy or something related to it (lit., "spirit," v.2). There were prophets in this church (cf. 1 Thess 5:19, 20) and *pneuma* ("spirit") is a name for this gift and others (cf. 1 Cor 14:12). Whatever the specific medium, the teaching was represented as having Paul's authority.

Another avenue for the false teaching was the spoken word ("report," *logou*). Though this did not claim the direct inspiration of prophecy, it too was based on an allegedly Pauline foundation. The same basis was claimed for a third medium of communication ("letter"). Someone had apparently misrepresented Paul's views in an epistle bearing his name, a mistake he intends to rectify in any future correspondence (cf. 3:17, 18). It is not clear whether the readers had been misguided through one or all three channels, but in any case Paul denounces them all.

The false teaching consisted in the claim "The day of the Lord has already come [Gr., 'is present']" (v.2). *Enestēken* ("is present") does not denote imminence, but actual presence. These readers who knew about the day (1 Thess 5:2) knew that its earlier phase would be a time of heightened persecution for the saints. Their suffering had already been so severe that someone tried to convince them that the period was already in progress, even though the Lord had not yet come to gather them to heaven (Auberlen and Riggenbach, p. 126; Moffatt, EGT, 4:47; Hogg and Vine, p. 245; Morris, p. 217; Hiebert, p. 304). They knew of the time of trouble and the Lord's return to culminate it (1:7–9). They had been led to believe, however, that his coming for them would spare them the anguish of that hour (1 Thess 5:9). But here were people telling them, with Paul's apparent backing, that such a deliverance was not to be.

Therefore they were in great need of an authentic word from Paul assuring them that they had understood him correctly in his first Epistle. They needed to know that the *parousia* (coming) of Christ for his church would mark the beginning of the future day of trouble and consequently that the day had not yet arrived. To accomplish this, Paul proceeds to describe features, obviously not yet present, that will characterize the day's early stages.

Notes

1 The choice of ὑπέρ (*hyper*, "on behalf of") rather than περί (*peri*, "concerning") implies that Paul was speaking "in the best interests of" the παρουσία (*parousia*, "coming"). *Hyper* adds the idea of advocacy not found in *peri* (Ellicott, p. 106; Lightfoot, p. 108).

Arguments favoring the review that a posttribulational rapture is implied in this verse refer to a cognate verb of ἐπισυναγωγῆς, (*episynagōgēs*, "being gathered") that is used for a gathering of the elect following the tribulation in Matt 24:29–31 and to the noun itself along with its cognate verb in LXX to describe the regathering of dispersed Jews to Palestine after the tribulation (cf. Isa 52:12) (Best, p. 274). But these are not sufficient to overthrow the inability of advocates of posttribulationism to show a satisfactory relationship between believers' being gathered to Christ at the *parousia* and the presence of the day of the Lord (v.2). In vv.1, 2 the gathering must be the event that signals the opening of the day. If that day opens with the tribulation, as it obviously will (cf. discussion of 5:2), the gathering must come at the beginning of the tribulation.

2 Ἐνέστηκεν (*enestēken*, "is present") in all its other NT uses marks something as already present (Rom 8:38; 1 Cor 3:22; 7:26; cf. Gal. 1:4; 1 Tim 3:1; Heb 9:9). The present tense is thus the word's acknowledged meaning (Frame, pp. 248, 249).

B. *The True Condition* (2:3–12)

1. *Defiance (yet to come)*

2:3, 4

> ³Don't let anyone deceive you in any way, for that day will not come until the rebellion occurs and the man of lawlessness is revealed, the man doomed to destruction. ⁴He opposes and exalts himself over everything that is called God or is worshiped, and even sets himself up in God's temple, proclaiming himself to be God.

3 Paul supplements his request in v.1 with a prohibition: "Don't let anyone deceive you in any way." Apparently those who willfully and maliciously troubled the Thessalonian believers had done this by deceiving anyone who would listen to them regarding the day of the Lord. Paul warns his readers not to be taken in by these speculations, whether through "prophecy, report or letter" (v.2) or "in any way." Paul does not say what moved these promoters of error. Perhaps a misunderstanding of grace led them to teach that Christians must earn their part in the *parousia* by persevering through severe suffering. Whatever it was, Paul is determined to prove that his readers were not in the day of the Lord.

His proof of the day's nonpresence consists of citing two phenomena that had not yet occurred. The text does not explicitly say whether these will come before the day of the Lord or immediately after it begins, because the Greek sentence is not complete, but it presupposes something to be added from the previous verse; i.e., "that day will not come" (NIV) or "that day is not present" (cf. note). Grammatically similar constructions elsewhere (Matt 12:29; Mark 3:27; John 7:51; Rom 15:24) show these two happenings are conceived of as within the day of the Lord, not prior to it. The day of the Lord had not yet arrived because these two conspicuous phenomena that will dominate the day's opening phase had not yet happened.

Some wonder how the failure of these two to arrive can be a proof of the nonarrival of the day. The answer lies in understanding Paul's reference to these phenomena as his way of identifying the very earliest stage of this eschatological period. The readers had not missed the rapture (1 Thess 4:15–17) and were not in the day of the Lord (v.2) because these two clear indicators of the day's presence had not yet appeared (cf. Introduction to 1 Thess, pp. 233–234).

Let us put it this way. Suppose the government of some country should announce, "In the near future on a date known only to us, Christianity will be suppressed. To mark the official beginning of this policy, on the appointed day the largest church in the country will be demolished and its pastor required to renounce Christianity publicly. Thereafter, all who admit they are Christians will be placed in jeopardy of imprisonment." At that time a foreigner might arrive in that country, having heard nothing more than that

Christianity would be cruelly suppressed. He would doubtless find some Christians already experiencing certain hardships and, in his ignorance of the timing of the actual beginning of the policy of suppression, might assume that it was already in effect. A citizen who knew the details of the policy would have to tell him, "The period of suppression of Christianity is not yet present, because the largest church in the country has not yet been demolished and its pastor has not yet renounced Christianity publicly."

So far there is no logical problem. But some who have problems with the pretribulational view of the rapture ask, "How can the nonarrival of two events ('the rebellion' and the revealing of 'the man of lawlessness,' v.3) that initiate the day of the Lord, a period that will come after the believers have been raptured—how can the nonarrival of these events prove to the confused Thessalonian believers (who are to be raptured and thus will not be in the day of the Lord) that they are not actually in that day?" The answer still is that the absence of the phenomena demonstrates the nonpresence of the day of the Lord. Obviously, had "the rebellion" and the revealing of "the man of lawlessness" already taken place when Paul was writing this letter, then the teaching of the priority of the rapture to "the day of the Lord" would have been called into question. But here in 2 Thessalonians 2 Paul is not discussing the timing of the rapture. He is simply reassuring his readers that "the day of the Lord" had not come. Nor does he at any place in this context (2 Thess 2:1–12) tell his readers that they will at some future time "see" the two initial phenomena of "the day of the Lord." Had he said that, there would indeed be a problem. But he did not speak of the Thessalonians' actually seeing the phenomena. He simply stressed the present nonarrival of the phenomena.

To sum up, let us return to the analogy of the newcomer to the country facing the suppression of Christianity. Suppose now that, arriving after the initial announcement, he is a short-term visitor due to leave before the official beginning of the anti-Christian policy. The answer to his confusion about being in the country with the policy already in effect would be corrected by his realizing that the largest church would have to be destroyed and its pastor publicly renounce Christianity before suppression of Christianity began. And this would be a valid answer, even though he would not be present when these things took place.

The troubled at Thessalonica could take heart in knowing they had not missed the gathering of those in Christ at the *parousia* (v.1). Their present persecutions were not identifiable with those to be inflicted by the man of lawlessness on a later group of saints after the eschatological day begins.

A closer look at the two phenomena accompanying the day of the Lord illuminates the characteristics of that day. "The rebellion" represents *apostasia*, from which the English word *apostasy* comes. Usage in LXX and elsewhere in the NT gives this word a religious connotation (Josh 22:22; 2 Chron 29:19; 33:19; Jer 2:19; Acts 21:21). It points to a deliberate abandonment of a former professed position. Attempts to identify the apostasy Paul is speaking of here with some past or present movement are futile because of its contextual association with the Lord Jesus' second advent (v.1). An illustration of this kind of apostasy was that of faithless Jews just before the Maccabean uprising (Dan 8:23ff.; 11:36f.) (Hendriksen, p. 169). A similar defection of professing Christians is elsewhere anticipated (Matt 24:11, 12, 24; 1 Tim 4:1ff.; 2 Tim 3:1–5; 4:3, 4; 2 Peter 2:1–22; 3:3–6; Jude 17, 18). After the catching away of those in Christ (1 Thess 4:17), all who are truly in him will be gone. Conditions will be ripe for people, especially those who call themselves Christian but are not really such, to turn their backs on God in what they do as well as in what they already have in thought. Then their insincerity will demonstrate itself outwardly. This worldwide anti-God movement will be so universal as to earn for itself a special designation: "*the* apostasy"—i.e., the climax of the increasing apostate tendencies evident before the rapture of the church.

Following and in conjunction with the apostasy will come the unveiling of a mighty figure embodying everything opposed to God. His whereabouts before his unveiling are not given. He will be alive for years before his unveiling, but his dramatic public presentation will occur after the rebellion begins.

Paul characterizes him in three ways. First, as "the man of lawlessness," he is the epitome of opposition to the laws of God. Satan so indwells and operates through him that his main delight will be in breaking God's righteous laws. Second, he is called "the man doomed to destruction"—literally, "the son of perdition." The Hebrew idiom "son of" indicates character or destiny. He belongs to a class so destined. The same expression describes Judas Iscariot (John 17:12), another member of this class. It does not, however, identify this later "son of perdition" with Judas.

4 Third, this individual "opposes and exalts himself over everything that is called God or is worshiped." His direct and determined opposition to the true God will be a leading feature of the continuing apostasy. It will be especially marked by removal of the symbolic articles from the Jerusalem temple. The man of lawlessness will occupy the holy precincts in order to accept and even demand worship that is due God alone. This evidently is a Jewish temple to be rebuilt in Jerusalem in the future. Dependence of these words on Daniel 9:26, 27; 11:31, 36, 37; 12:11 (cf. Matt 24:15; Mark 13:14) demands such a reference. There is no impressive evidence for understanding *naon* ("temple") in a nonliteral sense. The well-known "abomination that causes desolation" is sometimes regarded as a person and sometimes as an act of desecration by that person (Mark 13:14) (Hubbard, *Wycliffe Bible Commentary*, p. 1364). The act of desecration to which this verse looks will transpire half-way through the seventieth prophetic week of Daniel 9:24–27, when the covenant made earlier with the Jewish people is broken. This will mark the climax of this lawless one's career. Historically, a foreshadowing of this blasphemous intrusion happened when Antiochus Epiphanes desecrated the temple in Jerusalem just before the Maccabean revolt.

The lawless man's identity has been studied by many throughout the Christian era. Some deny that he is a historical person. They write off the terminology as detached from history and mythically oriented like the Jewish apocalyptic writings by which Paul was strongly influenced (Best, p. 289; J. Julius Scott, "Paul and Late-Jewish Eschatology—A Case Study, 1 Thessalonians 4:13–18 and 2 Thessalonians 2:1–12," JETS, (Summer, 1972), (15:139–141). But closer scrutiny of the parallels between late-Jewish eschatology and Paul's words reveals more by way of difference than similarity (Scott, pp. 141, 142).

The relationship of this apocalyptic portion of 2 Thessalonians to Christ's *parousia* (coming) confirms the impression that Paul must be referring to a single historical personage. Quests for such a person in the past and present have proved fruitless. Resemblances to Antiochus Epiphanes, Nero, Diocletian, one of the popes, and others may be admitted. But fulfillment of all details of the prophecy must await the future period of this man's prominence. It is futile to suppose that Judas Iscariot, Antiochus Epiphanes, or Nero will be brought back to life to fill this role. "The man of lawlessness" will be a new historical figure whom Satan will energize to do his will in the world. As "man of God" in the OT regularly designates a divine prophet, the present "man of lawlessness" designates a false prophet, probably to be identified with the second beast of Revelation

13 (Rev 13:11ff.; 16:13; 19:20; 20:10) (Best, pp. 283, 284, 288). His primary function will be to preside over the religious apostasy in cooperation with the beast out of the sea (Rev 13:1ff.), who leads political opposition to God. As God's chief opponent in Jerusalem whose background is probably Jewish (cf. Dan 11:36, 37), the lawless one will give religious leadership to complement the dominance of his associate over governments of the world's nations.

The presence of such an apostasy and counterfeit god will not escape international observation. The nonpresence of these things when Paul wrote proves his thesis regarding the nonarrival of the day of the Lord.

Notes

3 The preference of most English translations for a future tense apodosis in v.3 is probably explained by the frequency of that tense with conditional clauses with ἐάν (ean, "if"; with μὴ [mē, "not"] = "if not," "unless"; NIV, "until"). Circumstances here justify a present tense in the apodosis, however, the carry-over thought from ἐνέστηκεν (enestēken, "is present") (v.2) being a prime consideration (cf. Robertson, RHG, p. 1019). Other NT combinations of ἐάν ... πρῶτον (ean ... prōton, "if ... first") (Matt 12:29; Mark 3:27; John 7:51; Rom 15:24) reveal preference elsewhere for a present-tense apodosis under similar circumstances. They also reveal that actions of the conditional clause are included within the scope of the apodosis. These other passages show that πρῶτον (prōton, "first") in the protasis does not indicate priority to the apodosis, but priority to another action contained in (or implied by) the protasis—i.e., the rebellion precedes the revelation of the lawless one. All this confirms what is necessitated by Paul's viewpoint throughout the rest of these Epistles: the parousia for the church and the launching of the day of the Lord can come at any moment. The apostasy and the revelation of the man of lawlessness are not necessary preludes to them, but follow the church's gathering to Christ and lie within the day of the Lord.

Whether to read ἀνομίας (anomias, "lawlessness") or ἁμαρτίας (hamartias, "sin") presents a choice between two "harder" readings. The former is harder because of its rarer use by Paul (Metzger, Textual Commentary, p. 635). It is also harder because its meaning is narrower and less certain (Best, p. 283). On the other hand, hamartias is harder because anomias in v.7 presupposes an earlier anomias (Metzger, p. 635). Better MS and versional support for reading anomias tips the weight of probability against hamartias.

4 The ἐπί (epi, "over") phrase must be read with ἀντικείμενος (antikeimenos, "opposing") as well as with ὑπεραιρόμενος (hyperairomenos, "exalting himself"). Otherwise, the direction of opposition in the former is left unstated. So a hostile sense of "against" rather than one of position ("above") is preferable for the preposition. This is an accepted meaning of the word wherever hostility is in the context (John 13:18) (Alford, The Greek Testament, 3:289; Robertson, RHG, p. 602).

Figurative meanings of ναός (naos, "temple") elsewhere, including its reference to the church (1 Cor 3:16; 2 Cor 6:16; Eph 2:21) and possible allusions to the heavenly temple where God is (Heb 8:1-4; 9:23, 24; Rev 15:5), fall short of the literal significance required by the present passage. A human being can take his seat in none of these others. The article with naon (accusative) is a further indication that the Jerusalem temple of the God of Israel is intended (Olshausen, p. 482; Lünemann, p. 211).

2. Delay (presently in effect)

2:5-7

> 5Don't you remember that when I was with you I used to tell you these things? 6And now you know what is holding him back, so that he may be revealed at the proper time. 7For the secret power of lawlessness is already at work; but the one who now holds it back will continue to do so till he is taken out of the way.

5 A note of impatience may be detected in Paul's question. If the Thessalonian believers had recalled Paul's oral teaching, disturbing elements in the newly arisen false system could have been eliminated. Paul was certain about their previous familiarity with the substance of vv.3, 4 because he had personally (sing. "I," v.5) given them this information.

6 So he can declare, "You know what is holding him back." "Now" should be connected with "what is holding him back" to indicate that "holding back" is a present phenomenon. *To katechon* ("what is holding back") is a neuter title for this restraining force. The word recurs in the masculine in v.7 where it is translated "who . . . holds it back."

Proposed identifications of *to katechon* have been multiple. Because of inability to explain the neuter-masculine combination, such suggestions as the preaching of the gospel, the Jewish state, the binding of Satan, the church, Gentile world dominion, and human government are improbable. To identify *to katechon* with a supernatural force or person hostile to God is difficult in a paragraph such as this because the restrainer is limiting Satan (vv.7-9), not cooperating with him (Best, pp. 298-301). A popular understanding since early times has been that this is a reference to the Roman Empire (neuter) and its ruler (masc.) (See George Ladd, *NT Theology* [Grand Rapids: Eerdmans, 1974], pp. 530, 560). Paul had several times benefited from the intervention of the Roman government (Acts 17:6ff.; 18:6ff.). In other writings he limits the role of human government to its dealing with wrong-doing (Rom 13:1, 3) (Milligan, p. 101). Though preferable to some other solutions, this explanation is disappointing in several ways. To predict the demise of the Roman Empire (cf. v.7) is very uncharacteristic of Paul (Frame, p. 260). Then too, the Roman emperors sometimes precipitated anti-Christian activities rather than restrained them (Auberlen and Riggenbach, p. 139; Hogg and Vine, p. 260). Elimination of this solution is sealed when we remember that the Roman Empire has long since ceased to exist, and the appearance of Christ or the lawless one has yet to take place (Hogg and Vine, p. 259).

It is evident that the restrainer, to accomplish his mission, must have supernatural power to hold back a supernatural enemy (v.9). God and the outworking of his providence is the natural answer (Ladd, *The Blessed Hope*, p.95). Reference to God is favored by the restrainer's harmony with divine purpose and a divine timetable ("at the proper time," v.6) (Hiebert, p. 313; Delling, TDNT, 3:460, 461).

Yet to say that God is the restrainer is not quite enough to explain the variation in gender. To one familiar with the Lord Jesus' Upper Room Discourse, as Paul undoubtedly was, fluctuation between neuter and masculine recalls how the Holy Spirit is spoken of. Either gender is appropriate, depending on whether the speaker (or writer) thinks of natural agreement (masc. because of the Spirit's personality) or grammatical (neuter because of the noun *pneuma;* see John 14:26; 15:26; 16:13, 14) (Robertson, RHG, pp. 208, 209). This identification of the restrainer with deep roots in church history (Alford, 3:57, 58) is most appealing. The special presence of the Spirit as the indweller of saints will terminate abruptly at the *parousia* as it began abruptly at Pentecost. Once the body of Christ has been caught away to heaven, the Spirit's ministry will revert back to what he did for believers during the OT period (Ryrie, p. 113). His function of restraining evil through the body of Christ (John 16:7–11; 1 John 4:4) will cease similarly to the way he terminated his striving in the days of Noah (Gen 6:3). At that point the reins will be removed from lawlessness and the Satanically inspired rebellion will begin. It appears that *to katechon* ("what is holding back") was well known at Thessalonica as a title for the Holy Spirit on whom the readers had come to depend in their personal attempts to combat lawlessness (1 Thess 1:6; 4:8; 5:19; 2 Thess 2:13).

God has a "proper time" for the lawless one's revelation just as he does for the revelation of the Lord Jesus from heaven (1:7). No one knows that time, since it is part of the future day of the Lord (1 Thess 5:2; 2 Thess 2:2, 3). Until the gathering of saints (2:1), the Spirit will continue his restraining work.

7 Further clarification ("for") is in order. The "secret power [or, mystery] of lawlessness" was already evident in such things as their own persecutions (1:4), but lawlessness will be open when the rebellion arrives and the lawless one is unveiled (2:3, 8). The secrecy and limitation is attributable to "the one who now holds it back." Upon his removal, the rebellion will break out.

Notes

6 It is necessary to take νῦν (*nun*, "now") temporally and connect it with "what is holding him back" to balance off the ἐν τῷ αὐτοῦ καιρῷ (*en tō autou kairō*, "at the proper time") in the last part of the same verse. A temporal *nun* connected with οἴδατε (*oidate*, "you know") and answering to ἔτι (*eti*, "when") of v.5 does not render a satisfactory sense (Lightfoot, p. 114; Moffatt, EGT, 4:49). An inferential *nun* can also be excluded because of conflict with another conjunction, καί (*kai*, "and") at the beginning of v.6.

"Hold back" or "restrain" is the more plausible choice for the meaning of κατέχω (*katechō*) because the atmosphere of conflict pervades the passage. "Hold fast" and "hold sway," though legitimate for the verb elsewhere, cannot satisfy the obvious antagonism in the present discussion.

Other suggestions as to the identity of τὸ κατέχον (*to katechon*, "what is holding . . . back") include Michael, Elijah, the apostles, the saints in Jerusalem before its destruction, the Mosaic law, Paul, and Seneca. Some feel it fruitless to attempt identification, either because we are too far removed from the original situation (Morris, pp. 226, 227) or because the whole passage is so apocalyptic that it defies identification of single individuals within it (Best, p. 301). All the above positions either have very slight foundations or else shy away from an issue where exegetical data can be brought to bear. That the ongoing conflict between God and Satan lies behind specific naming of the restrainer and the man of lawlessness is quite clear. Varying forms and stages of the Spirit's ministry among men adequately explain how God in the person of the Spirit can be removed; i.e., the Spirit terminates a form of God's special presence.

7 Since μόνον (*monon*, "only"; NIV, "but") pertains to a limitation of "the secret power of lawlessness," the better choice is to connect it with ἕως (*heōs*, "till") to indicate the terminal point of restraint: "only until the one who now holds it back is taken out of the way." Ὁ κατέχων ἄρτι (*ho katechōn arti*, "the one who now holds . . . back") stands prior to the *heōs*, separating it from *monon*, to give the words an appropriate emphasis in the clause (Auberlen and Riggenbach, p. 129; Frame, pp. 264, 265).

3. Deception and destruction (after the delay)

2:8-10

> [8]And then the lawless one will be revealed, whom the Lord Jesus will overthrow with the breath of his mouth and destroy by the splendor of his coming. [9]The coming of the lawless one will be in accordance with the work of Satan displayed in all kinds of counterfeit miracles, signs and wonders, [10]and in every sort of evil that deceives those who are perishing. They perish because they refused to love the truth and so be saved.

8-10 Departure of the restrainer is the cue for the revelation (v.8) and coming (v.9) of the lawless one. His revelation, already mentioned in v.3 in conjunction with the rebellion and in v.6 as being delayed until the proper time by the restrainer's presence, is of Satanic origin, though admittedly it can happen only by God's permission. Satan's present efforts to effect unhindered lawlessness are frustrated by divine restraint (v.7), but through cessation of the Spirit's indwelling ministry to the body of Christ, his lawless one will be granted a future interval to do his worst.

8 After this time has elapsed, the Lord Jesus will personally come to earth to slay (*anelei*, "overthrow," NIV) the lawless one "with the breath of his mouth" and abolish (*katargēsei*, "destroy," NIV) him "by the splendor of his coming." By putting the lawless one to death, the Lord will also bring to a stop his program of deceiving the world. "The breath of his mouth" could be a figurative reference to a word spoken by Christ, but a literal sense is quite satisfactory. The breath of God is a fierce weapon according to the OT (Exod 15:8; 2 Sam 22:16; Job 4:9; Ps 33:6; Isa 30:27, 28) (Milligan, p. 103; Best, p. 303). "The splendor of his coming" is his other means of conquest. Probably "the appearance of his coming" does more justice to *epiphaneia*, since in the Pastoral Epistles it is practically equivalent to *parousia* as a name for his coming (1 Tim 6:14; 2 Tim 1:10; 4:1, 8; Titus 2:13). This "appearance" phase of the *parousia* differs from the "gathering" phase (v.1). It concludes and climaxes the tribulation instead of beginning it. The visible presence of the Lord Jesus in the world will put an immediate stop to an accelerated diabolical program.

9,10a That Satan is the root of the lawless one's deception is explicit in a further elaboration. *Energeian* ("work") in the NT is reserved for supernatural activities. A superhuman person will utilize the supernatural means of "miracles, signs and wonders." These remarkable phenomena, which in the past have been used so effectively in laying a foundation for the church (Acts 2:22, 43; 4:30; 5:12; 6:8; 7:36; 14:3; 15:12; Rom 15:19; 2 Cor 12:12; Heb 2:4), will be redirected to purposes of deceit. They will not be "counterfeit" (see text) but genuine supernatural feats to produce false impressions, deluding people to the point of accepting the lie as truth (cf. v.11). The motivation of the lawless one is to deceive. "Every sort of evil that deceives" is literally "every deceit of unrighteousness"—i.e., every sort of deceit that unrighteousness produces. It is the nature of unrighteousness to palm itself off as righteousness (Hiebert, p. 317). "Those who are perishing" will be particularly vulnerable to trickery. Not only will they confuse unrighteousness with righteousness; they will also attribute deity to this lawless one (v.4).

10b Their blindness will be self-imposed because of a prior refusal to "love the truth and so be saved." They lack a positive committal to the gospel. This is just as blamable as indifference or even antagonism toward the truth. The right choice could have brought them salvation and deliverance from the lawless one's devices, but they elected not to receive God's salvation.

Notes

8 Alexandrian and Western witnesses—including uncials, versions, and fathers—provide support for reading Ἰησοῦς (*Iēsous*, "Jesus"). This support is stronger than that of the authorities omitting this human name of the Lord. Thus, "the Lord Jesus" is the correct translation.

External evidence supporting ἀνελεῖ (*anelei*, "will remove," "will destroy"; NIV, "will overthrow") is also quite impressive. The other readings ἀνέλοι (*aneloi*, "consumed," "destroyed"), ἀναλοῖ (*analoi*, "consumes," "destroys"), and ἀναλώσει (*analōsei*, "will consume," "will destroy"), though quite interesting, cannot muster sufficient MS authority for their inclusion (Metzger, *Textual Commentary*, p. 636).

Paul's preoccupation with the glory of Christ's return (1:7, 9, 10) supports the rendering of ἐπιφανείᾳ (*epiphaneia*) by "splendor." Still, the redundancy that would result in Titus 2:13 where it is used in combination with δόξα (*doksa*, "brightness") more probably excludes the notion of "brightness" from the word. It merely describes the visibility of his *parousia* (coming). The glory of it is frequently described elsewhere.

9 The time perspective of this verse is set by the future tenses of v.8. Ἐστιν (*estin*, "is"), though a present tense, has the *parousia* as its point of reference. Ψεύδους (*pseudous*) is probably not a genitive of description, "counterfeit," telling the intrinsic quality of the miracles (contra Lenski, p. 426). Emphasis on deceit and "the lie" in the next two verses shows these to be miracles "leading to a lie" (Ellicott, p. 116). A genitive of the object is therefore preferable.

10 "Every sort of evil that deceives those who are perishing" properly makes ἀδικίας (*adikias*, "of unrighteousness"; NIV, "of evil") a genitive of the subject (or ablative of source). This is deceit wrought by or proceeding from unrighteousness (Hendriksen, p. 185; Best, p. 307). This supplies the best contextual sense and is normal with a genitive following ἀπάτη (*apatē*, "deceit") (Mark 4:19; Heb 3:13) (Frame, p. 270).

Refusal "to love the truth" is not quite the same as refusing the truth. Loving the truth is a very positive dedication to the gospel. One can refuse to love the truth without refusing the truth. This positive commitment furnishes a suitable opposite to εὐδοκήσαντες τῇ ἀδικίᾳ (*eudokēsantes tē adikia*, "having delighted in unrighteousness," v.12), which is a commitment at the other extreme (Lightfoot, p. 117; Best, p. 308).

4. Delusion and divine judgment (*because of present recalcitrance*)

2:11, 12

> [11]For this reason God sends them a powerful delusion so that they will believe the lie [12] and so that all will be condemned who have not believed the truth but have delighted in wickedness.

11 By covering again the same ground in vv.11, 12 as in vv.9, 10, Paul reemphasizes the fate of rejectors of the truth and adds more information about them. Already he has shown Satan's part in getting them to believe lies and bewildering them with deceitful measures and he has shown their refusal to love the truth. Because they deliberately reject God, he himself will send "them a powerful delusion so that they will believe the lie." This "working of error" will be supernatural in character (*energeian*, cf. v.9) so as to prove irresistible to rebellious humanity. "Powerful delusion" is another way of referring to the lie (v.9) and deceit (v.10) already predicted. God will create false belief to make them "believe the lie." This is their only alternative because they have refused to love the truth (v.10). They will be completely defenseless against the false claims of the lawless one (v.4) and his perversion of the true gospel. The Satanic promise that deceived Eve (Gen 3:5) will find its ultimate fulfillment in the end-time master of deceit (Auberlen and Riggenbach, p. 132). They will mistake someone else and his lying promises for God and his truth.

12 The ultimate consequences for them will be condemnation. Failing to appropriate the truth of the gospel, they willingly choose wickedness instead. They cannot blame circumstances. Retrospect will show their own wrongly directed personal delight to be the cause of God's adverse judgment against them (cf. 1:9). What an incentive this powerful passage is for non-Christians to turn to God before the rebellion and delusion arrive.

Notes

---

11 The present tense of πέμπει (*pempei*, "sends") has a future significance because the point of reference is the coming period of the lawless one's activity. After his future revelation (v.8), the rest of the paragraph takes on this as-if-present perspective (cf. ἐστὶν [*estin*, "is" v.9]) (Best, p. 304).

Ἐνεργείαν (*energeian*, "working"; NIV, "powerful") is a supernatural operation as in v.9, but this time traceable to God rather than Satan. The genitive πλάνης (*planēs*, "of error"; NIV, "delusion") immediately following is objective, "a working that enhances and develops error," as evidenced in the εἰς τό (*eis to*, "so that") clause.

C. The Truth's Continuance (2:13–17)

1. Thanks for divine deliverance

2:13, 14

> 13But we ought always to thank God for you, brothers loved by the Lord, because from the beginning God chose you to be saved through the sanctifying work of the Spirit and through belief in the truth. 14He called you to this through our gospel, that you might share in the glory of our Lord Jesus Christ.

13 Paul is thankful that God chose some to believe the truth and to be delivered from delusion and from divine judgment. He and his co-workers can rejoice in looking forward to salvation for themselves and their converts, an anticipation drastically different from the outlook for those awaiting perdition (cf. v.10). The salvation viewed from its human side in 1:3ff. is now seen as an undertaking of God.

For Paul to address these "brothers" as those "loved by the Lord" (cf. 1 Thess 1:4) is appropriate, because God chose them to be saved. "From the beginning" refers to their pretemporal election (cf. 1 Thess 1:4). Paul usually places God's prior choice of men to salvation (v.13) alongside their historical call (v.14; cf. Rom 8:30) (Hendriksen, p. 188). This salvation is what will elude those who refuse to love the truth (v.10). It entails present benefits and also future deliverance from the doom that will befall the lost at Christ's return (cf. 1:6, 8, 9; 2:8–12). God's choice operates in the realm of belief in the truth and of the Spirit's sanctifying work. The role of the Spirit in sanctification looms large for Paul (Rom 15:16; 1 Cor 6:11, 12; 1 Thess 4:7, 8) as it does for Peter (1 Peter 1:2) (Best, pp. 314, 315). The sphere of God's choice of believers for salvation is also marked by its faith-in-truth emphasis. Belief in the truth is the means of the beginning and continuing relationships of salvation (cf. vv.10–12).

14 God has fulfilled his foreordained purpose by calling the chosen to this salvation "through our gospel." The good news of divine truth conveyed through Paul's preaching was the means through which God called these Thessalonian converts at a particular point in time. What God purposed in eternity was carried out in history that the future might bring them a share "in the glory of our Lord Jesus Christ." God's design was to make them adopted ones who participate in Christ's glory at the *parousia* (coming) (cf. 1:10, 12). As God's purchased possessions, they will be granted this matchless privilege. They do not earn it or in any other way acquire it for themselves. It is accomplished solely by God, as is all else referred to in this context (vv. 13, 14).

Notes

---

13 The choice between the variants ἀπαρχήν (*aparchēn*, "firstfruits") and ἀπ' ἀρχῆς (*ap' archēs*, "from the beginning") is difficult. The latter has a slight edge in external support, being found in both Western and Alexandrian text-types. It is a hard reading because of the absence of the phrase from Paul's other writings. On the other hand, *aparchēn* is extremely difficult, because without an explanatory genitive, it renders no satisfactory sense in the verse (Best, p. 313). "Firstfruits" points to a larger group, but no group can be found among which these believers were first. Hence, *ap' archēs* has been chosen as the correct reading.

A locative instead of an instrumental force has been chosen for ἐν (*en*, "in") because the clause names an act in eternity past. To render the preposition by "through" (NIV) unduly anticipates the historical call of v.14. The means of their call is expressed in the διά (*dia*, "through") phrase v.14, while the ἐν (*en*, "in") phrase of v.13 indicates the spiritual state in which God chose them to salvation (Ellicott, p. 220).

14 Whether to take περιποίησιν (*peripoiēsin*, "acquisition"; NIV, "share") actively (Hendriksen, p. 128; Hiebert, p. 223) or passively (Lightfoot, p. 76) recalls the discussion of 1 Thess 5:9. An active sense in a setting that so strongly emphasizes God's part in the total salvation process is inappropriate, to say the least. More congruity is obtained by omitting the element of personal attainment that the active meaning of *peripoiēsin* would convey. Human responsibility comes in v.15, but vv.13, 14 are devoted to what God has done. The meaning of "acquired possession" is therefore preferred over "acquiring" for *peripoiēsin*. This necessitates taking δόξης, (*doxēs*, "of glory") as a genitive of apposition.

---

2. Call to doctrinal adherence

2:15

> [15]So then, brothers, stand firm and hold to the teachings we passed on to you, whether by word of mouth or by letter.

15 "So then" turns the discussion to a practical responsibility derived from God's elective purpose (vv.13, 14). Against a background of such an imminent world crisis as described in vv.1–10, the beneficiaries of God's saving work cannot afford to lapse into lethargy, but must respond with loyal steadfastness ("stand firm") and keep a firm hold on the traditions ("teachings") taught them by Paul and his associates. A continuing stability and firm grasp on basic Christian doctrines would have alleviated the instability and alarm that prompted the writing of this Epistle (cf. v.2). They had received instructions about ethical matters (1 Thess 4:1, 2; 2 Thess 3:6), but the particular data needed at this point is doctrinal, as shown by Paul's reference to "our gospel" in v.14 (cf. 1 Cor 15:3–5) (Best, p. 317). Paul himself had been a recipient of Christian traditions subsequent to his conversion. Through divine revelation he had originated other traditions (1 Thess 4:15). These he had passed on to his converts both "by word of mouth" and "by letter" in his previous contacts with them. In light of their inclusion in God's saving purpose (vv.13, 14), he commands them to remain unmovable and cling tenaciously to these doctrines.

3. Prayer for practical compliance

2:16, 17

> [16]May our Lord Jesus Christ himself and God our Father, who loved us and by his grace gave us eternal encouragement and good hope, [17]encourage and strengthen you in every good deed and word.

16,17 The prayer that closes chapter two is in slight contrast (de, v.16, untranslated in NIV) to the appeal of v.15. Paul and his co-workers cannot in themselves make the appeal effective. Only God himself, who initially chose them, (vv.13, 14) can do that. Addressing his prayer to the first two persons of the Trinity, Paul names the Son before the Father (contra 1 Thess 3:11), probably in line with the Son's worthiness of equal honor with the Father and his special prominence in the chapter's emphasis on future salvation and glory. Yet the two persons are one God as shown by several structural features in vv.16, 17: (1) The pronoun autos ("himself," v.16) is singular and probably should be understood as emphasizing both persons—"our Lord Jesus Christ and God our Father himself" (cf. 1 Thess 3:11). (2) "Loved us and . . . gave us" (v.16) represents two singular participles whose actions are applicable to both the Son and the Father. The singular number is explained by Paul's conception of the two persons as one God. (3) "Encourage and strengthen" (v.17) are likewise singular in number though they express the action of a compound subject. This grammatical feature is attributable to the oneness of essence among the persons of the Godhead (cf. John 10:30). Paul conceived of Jesus Christ as God in the same full sense as he conceived of God the Father. No other explanation of this unusual combination of grammatical features is satisfying.

Reminding himself and his readers of why God has every reason to answer this prayer, Paul notes that the Son and the Father "loved us" and graciously "gave us eternal encouragement and good hope." Evidence of this can be seen in the incarnation and death of Jesus Christ, which are so often referred to in terms of God's loving and giving (John 3:16; Rom 5:5, 8; 8:35, 37; Gal 2:20; 1 John 4:10). Because of God's love displayed in Christ, the present readers had a source of unending encouragement to offset their persecutions and accompanying doubts.

Paul prays that the encouragement provided in the crucifixion and resurrection of

Christ may be appropriated inwardly—literally, "encourage your hearts"—as a motivation for giving them strength for "every good deed and word." Disquiet regarding the coming of the Lord (v.2) was the need to be met. As God undertakes their cause, they can "stand firm and hold to the teachings" (v.15).

Notes

---

16 To put the emphasis of αὐτός (*autos*, "himself") on the Son alone (and on the Father alone in 1 Thess 3:11) presents an unbalanced picture, as though Paul expected one person to answer one prayer and another to answer the other. The best way to solve this imbalance is to take the pronoun as extending to both persons in each case (cf. note on 1 Thess 3:11).

Galatians 1:1 presents a comparable situation of a singular participle following "Jesus Christ and God the Father," when the participle goes only with the latter of the two persons. Yet it is questionable whether Galatians 1:1 is parallel, since the participial expression "who raised him from the dead" cannot logically modify "Jesus Christ." The same is not true here. Both the Son and the Father have loved (Rom 8:35–39). Both the Son and the Father have given (Rom 8:32; Gal 2:20). In light of the stress in this verse on the unity of the Godhead, it is more plausible to refer the participles to both Persons (Frame, p. 286; Hiebert, p. 327).

IV. Encouragement to Gainful Employment (3:1–15)

A. *Prayerful Preparation for Encounter (3:1–5)*

1. *Prayer for Paul*

3:1, 2

> ¹Finally, brothers, pray for us that the message of the Lord may spread rapidly and be honored, just as it was with you. ²And pray that we may be delivered from wicked and evil men, for not everyone has faith.

1 Eschatological matters were Paul's main concern in writing 2 Thessalonians. "Finally" indicates that these have in the main been dealt with. Yet an important and related matter needs to be discussed before the letter ends. Before discussing it, Paul makes one of his typical requests for prayer (cf. Rom 15:30, 31; Eph 6:18, 19; Col 4:3; 1 Thess 5:25; Philem 22). "Spread rapidly" (*trechē*) relates to the idea of running. Paul also desired that the gospel be "honored." This speaks of triumph. As more people receive the good news, victories are won and God is glorified. "Spread rapidly and be honored" does not apply to isolated victories or a single great triumph but to a continuing progress—viz., the word is to "keep on running and keep on being honored." "Just as it was with you" recalls the amazing success of the message in Thessalonica (cf. 1 Thess 1:5, 6, 8; 2:13). Paul wanted this repeated in other communities where he would preach Christ.

2 Again, Paul asked prayer for deliverance "from wicked and evil men." "Wicked" labels them as capable of outrageous and harmful acts against others. "Evil" speaks of persons not only themselves thoroughly corrupted but intent on corrupting others and drawing them into their own slide toward perdition. Who were they? Suggestions have ranged from heretics like Hymenaeus and Alexander (1 Tim 1:20) (Chrysostom) to hypocrites and false brothers more generally (Zwingli, cited by Auberlen and Riggenbach, p. 150). It has also been suggested that they were unbelievers, both Jewish and Gentile, since both Paul and his readers had encounters with each group (Acts 16:19-24; 1 Thess 2:15; 2 Thess 1:8) (Best, p. 326). A more pointed identification, however, ties these "wicked and evil men" to unbelieving Jews in Corinth where Paul was encountering opposition as he wrote (Acts 18:5, 6, 12, 13). This is confirmed by the definiteness of the expression (definite article tōn) and by the use of an aorist tense of the verb "may be delivered," suggesting one particular act of deliverance (Hendriksen, p. 195; Best, p. 325). As Paul wrote this second Epistle, he was facing a severe crisis in Corinth.

Evil men exist because "not everyone has faith." This understatement effectively highlights the large number of those who have not responded to the gospel by believing in Christ. That the persecutors had had the opportunity to believe but had rejected it accounts for their vicious reaction against the message and those who preached it.

Notes

1 A καί (kai, "and," "also," "even"), untranslated here in NIV, adds a thought to the last clause: "just as it also was with you"—i.e., Thessalonica was not the only place where the word had received a good response (Ellicott, p. 124).
2 The suggestion that "faith" in this verse has the sense of the body of Christian teaching, i.e., "the faith" (Morris, p. 246), finds support in the ordinary usage of ἡ πίστις (hē pistis, "the faith") in the NT (Lightfoot, p. 125). Yet the present context does not criticize noncompliance with orthodox doctrine, but unwillingness to embrace Jesus' messiahship in a personal way. So here the better understanding of "faith" is its subjective sense of "trust" (Hiebert, p. 332; Best, p. 326).

---

2. Prayer for the people

3:3-5

3But the Lord is faithful, and he will strengthen and protect you from the evil one. 4We have confidence in the Lord that you are doing and will continue to do the things we command. 5May the Lord direct your hearts into God's love and Christ's perseverance.

3 In contrast with the widespread lack of faith among men (v.2) is the faithfulness of the Lord Jesus. He can be relied on to "strengthen [2:17] and protect" Christians "from the evil one." Here is assurance of inner security and an outward protection from the author of evil whose activity is so prominent in these letters (1 Thess 2:18; 3:5; 2 Thess 2:9). Phylaxei ("protect") is often used of military protection against a violent assault. Jesus' faithfulness provides a defense against even the touch of the enemy (cf. 1 John 5:18).

4 The faithfulness of the Lord is supplemented by the faithfulness of his people. So Paul can add, "We have confidence in the Lord that you are doing and will continue to do the things we commanded." This rendering does not translate the phrase eph' hymas ("about you" or "concerning you") after the clause "we have confidence." Paul has

confidence in Christian people. In them union with Christ counteracts the weakness of human nature. Paul and his co-workers could rely on the Thessalonian believers to do what they had been taught (cf. 1 Thess 4:2). By this favorable opinion, he paves the way for further instruction (cf. 3:6–15).

5 Paul realizes that the Lord's help is indispensable. That he has complimented them (v.4) does not imply that they are self-sufficient. Therefore he requests the Lord to direct them into a fuller appreciation of God's love for them and Christ's perseverance on their behalf. To comply with Paul's command to discipline the idle (vv.6–15) will be difficult. So the strongest possible motivation—recollection of God's love and Christ's endurance of suffering—will undergird the discipline of idle believers.

Notes

3 "The evil one" takes τοῦ πονήρου (tou ponērou) as masc., a reference to Satan. Though neuter adjectives appear in Rom 12:9 and 1 Thess 5:22, the masc. form of this word outnumbers the neuter by four to one in the NT (Lightfoot, pp. 125–127), strongly favoring the masc. in these Epistles where the devil is prominent (1 Thess 2:18; 3:5; 2 Thess 2:9).
4 Paul's confidence about the Thessalonians ἐφ᾽ ὑμᾶς (eph᾽ hymas, "about you") regarded them as "in the Lord" and so he was protected from the disappointment due to fickle human nature (Best, pp. 328, 329). An ἐπί (epi, "about") phrase is often construed as the object of πείθω (peithō, "to be confident") (Matt 27:43, 2 Cor 2:3) (Frame, pp. 295, 296).
5 "Love toward God" and "patient waiting for Christ" have sometimes been advocated as translations of τὴν ἀγάπην τοῦ θεοῦ (tēn agapēn tou theou) and τὴν ὑπομονὴν τοῦ Χριστοῦ (tēn hypomonēn tou Christou) (Alford, 3:295; Hiebert, p. 336). This takes the genitives as objective. Contextually this is acceptable, but it is unlikely because Paul usually refers to our human love for God by the verb ἀγαπάω (agapaō, "to love") and because ὑπομονή (hypomonē) in its other uses by Paul never has the sense of "patient waiting." He generally uses the genitive with ἀγάπη (agapē, "love") subjectively, and this satisfies the present sentence quite well. Also, the frequent teaching of a suffering Messiah and his perseverance (Heb 12:1–3; 1 Peter 2:21) argues for a subjective genitive in τοῦ Χριστοῦ (tou Christou, "of Christ") (Milligan, p. 112; Hendriksen, p. 198).

B. *Proper Solution for Idleness* (3:6–15)

1. *Previous instruction and example*

3:6–10

6In the name of the Lord Jesus Christ, we command you, brothers, to keep away from every brother who is idle and does not live according to the teaching you received from us. 7For you yourselves know how you ought to follow our example. We were not idle when we were with you, 8nor did we eat anyone's food without paying for it. On the contrary, we worked night and day, laboring and toiling so that we would not be a burden to any of you. 9We did this, not because we do not have the right to such help, but in order to make ourselves a model for you to follow. 10For even when we were with you, we gave you this rule: "If a man will not work, he shall not eat."

6 Now Paul comes to his command regarding the idle. That he invokes "the name of the Lord Jesus Christ" shows the urgency of the command. Every brother who remains idle is to be denied the privilege of associating with his fellow Christians. "Idle" translates a word meaning "disorderly" (cf. 1 Thess 5:14). The disorder defined by the remainder of the paragraph is loafing, being remiss in daily work and conduct. This is contrary to the "teaching" ("tradition") that Paul had given them earlier (cf. 1 Thess 4:11, 12; 5:14). No excuse could justify such misconduct. Paul therefore advocates the drastic discipline of keeping away from the "idle."

7–9 Paul himself was not idle. His readers could verify this claim ("you yourselves know," v.7; cf. 1 Thess 2:1; 3:3; 4:2; 5:2). In imitating Paul, they would be imitating the Lord himself (1 Thess 1:6) because Paul's life was so carefully patterned after his Lord's. He did not loaf at Thessalonica (v.7b), nor depend on others to supply him with free food (v.8a). He supported himself in spite of much fatigue ("laboring," v.8) and many obstacles ("toiling," v.8; cf. 1 Thess 2:9) in order to relieve the new Christians in Thessalonica of the burden of maintaining him.

Paul did not have to exert himself so tirelessly. As an apostle, he had "the right to such help" (v.9; cf. 1 Cor 9:4ff.; 1 Thess 2:7) from his converts. He decided, however, to forego this privilege and leave an example for them to imitate.

10 Paul reinforced his example by this definite command. From a very early time denying food to the lazy was a traditional form of discipline in the church. (Note Genesis 3:19.)

Notes

6 Παρελάβοσαν (*parelabosan*, "they received") is preferred over παρελάβετε (*parelabete*, "you received') because of its stronger external support. It is also the harder reading because of the change from the second to third person and is therefore the reading that best explains the origin of the alternative readings (Metzger, *Textual Commentary*, p. 367).

8 "Eat anyone's food" is literally "eat bread from anyone." "Eat bread" is a Semitic idiom for eating any kind of food. It should probably not be broadened to include one's total living (contra Morris, p. 253; Hiebert, p. 342). Paul claims nothing regarding his living accommodations with Jason (Acts 17:7) beyond payment for his own meals. What the apostle did for housing is not stated here.

2. Renewed instruction

3:11, 12

> [11]We hear that some among you are idle. They are not busy; they are busybodies. [12]In the name of the Lord Jesus Christ, we command and urge such people to settle down and earn the bread they eat.

11,12 Here the previously given rule (v.10) is repeated because of reports that the problem of loafing had recurred. People who came from Thessalonica to Corinth had reported this. Some of their number had stopped working, even since receiving the corrective of 1 Thessalonians 4:11, 12 and 5:14. They were using the extra time to interfere in other people's affairs. *Periergazomenous* ("they are busybodies," v.11) graphically shows them to be meddling in the lives of others.

"In the Lord Jesus Christ" (cf. note on v.12) Paul commanded such people to settle down and earn the bread they eat (v.12). He uses the common union of believers with Christ as ground for his appeal. He might well have addressed the idle ones pejoratively as "you loafers," but instead he tactfully refers to them as "such people," doubtless hoping to lead them back to earning their own food. Thus, order would replace the disruption caused by their idleness and meddling. The tense of the verb implies that they were to work steadily, not occasionally or spasmodically.

Notes

11 Ἀκούω (*akouō*) is one of the special verbs that take on a perfective force in the present (cf. Luke 9:9) (BDF, par. 322). This is the probable force here. Paul had recently heard about the problem, so he proceeds to deal with it.

12 "In the name of the Lord Jesus Christ" appears to be identical with a comparable phrase in v.6, but this is not so. The literal rendering in v.12 is "in the Lord Jesus Christ." Hence the emphasis in this verse is not on authority as in v.6, but on union with Christ: "by virtue of our union with the Lord Jesus Christ we as fellow members of Christ command and urge such people . . ." (cf. Hendriksen, p. 203). This sets a tone of gentleness for v.12. Had Paul wanted to convey authority, he would have reused the formula "in the name of" (Best, p. 341).

3. *Corrective separation*

3:13–15

> ¹³And as for you, brothers, never tire of doing what is right.
> ¹⁴If anyone does not obey our instruction in this letter, take special note of him. Do not associate with him, in order that he may feel ashamed. ¹⁵Yet do not regard him as an enemy, but warn him as a brother.

13–15 Paul now describes how the Thessalonian Christians should deal with loafers who disobey his instructions. First, they are urged to keep on doing right. *Enkakēsēte* ("tire") implies the possibility of their losing heart in struggling with their idle brothers. Exemplary conduct serves as a constant reprimand to wrongdoers and is an incentive for them to turn from their delinquency. Included in "doing what is right" is generosity toward those in need. Yet to keep on supporting those who have nothing because they refuse to work is wrong (v.10).

So the Thessalonians should deal firmly yet charitably with the mistakes of their brothers. Anyone refusing to comply with the work ethic set out in this letter was not to be associated with, so that he might be ashamed of his behavior. He was not to be expelled from the church like the sinning brother referred to in 1 Corinthians 5. In Corinth the offense was so flagrant as to bring disrepute on the whole church. In Thessalonica, however, the lapse was not yet so aggravated as to bring the reproach of the pagans on the church. Here the erring brother was allowed to continue in the meetings, but probably was denied participation in such things as the love feast and the

Lord's Supper. Certainly he was not to be given food, because this would make the community appear to condone his offense. *Mē synamignysthai* ("do not associate") implies "let there be no intimate association [with him]" (Frame, p. 309).

To sum up, the recalcitrant idler was not to be treated as an enemy cut off from all contacts, but was allowed to continue in a brotherly status. So lines of communication were kept open for continued warnings about his behavior.

Notes

13 Καλοποιοῦντες (*kalopoiountes*, "doing what is right") has been taken to mean "doing good" to others (Best, pp. 341, 342). This is the meaning in Gal 6:9, with the sense of giving financial help, but it is difficult so to understand v.13. Here Paul's emphasis is the very opposite—viz., that of disciplining loafers by witholding food from them. So it is a better choice to render the participle more generally as "acting correctly" or "doing what is right" (Milligan, p. 116; Hiebert, p. 348).

14,15 The meaning of "do not associate with him" can hardly be pressed to include formal excommunication. Συναναμίγνυσθαι (*synanamignysthai*) is not a word for official action. A limited social ostracism is much more in order (Hendriksen, p. 306). If this discipline proves unsuccessful, however, formal excommunication might follow (cf. Matt 18:17; 1 Cor 5:11). Continued treatment of the offenders as "brothers" indicates they were not to be denied fellowship altogether.

V. Conclusion (3:16-18)

A. *Prayer for God's Peace and Presence*

3:16

> [16]Now may the Lord of peace himself give you peace at all times and in every way. The Lord be with all of you.

16 "Now" (or perhaps more accurately "but") once again marks a transition from command and exhortation to prayer. The prayer recognizes that ultimately God alone can bring about compliance with what Paul has asked of his readers. "Yet without the Lord's help all your efforts will be in vain" is the thought behind this petition. "The Lord of peace" alone can make harmony among believers a reality. While this is, first and foremost, peace with God, it provides the ground for believers' peace with one another (Eph 2:14-18; cf. 1 Thess 5:23). "At all times" asks that there be no break in the flow of Christ's peace (cf. John 14:27; 16:33; Col 3:15); "in every way" asks that the prevalence of peace continue no matter what the outward circumstances. "The Lord be with all of you" requests what was previously guaranteed for Christians. His promise never to leave or forsake his own provides the assurances of this (Heb 13:5). Here is an instance of the cooperation of prayer in fulfilling what God's purpose predetermines (cf. 1:11, 12).

B. *Personalized Benediction*

3:17, 18

> [17]I, Paul, write this greeting in my own hand, which is the distinguishing mark in all my letters. This is how I write.
> [18]The grace of our Lord Jesus Christ be with all of you.

17,18 Paul was dictating to an amanuensis up to 3:17 (cf. Rom 16:22; 1 Cor 16:21; Col 4:18). At this point he took the pen into his own hand to add a closing greeting. Though he undoubtedly did this quite frequently, he has called attention to it only here, in 1 Corinthians 16:21, and in Colossians 4:18. The greeting in his own hand, "which is the distinguishing mark" in all his letters (v.17), includes also the benediction of v.18. Apparently Paul followed this practice consistently, expecting churches where he had served to recall his distinctive handwriting. It was particularly needed in this Epistle as a deterrent against any future attempt to forge a letter in his name (cf. 2:2). The practice was customary in ancient times (Frame, p. 312). When Paul says "in all my letters" (v.17), he does not mean just the letters previous to this, for he was also to follow this procedure later. Neither is the expression to be limited only to books found in the NT, because he is known to have written other Epistles besides these (cf. 1 Cor 5:9). The handwriting furnished a key by which his Thessalonian readers could recognize a spurious Epistle bearing his name.

Even when Paul did not call attention to it, a closing benediction came in his own hand. "The grace of our Lord Jesus Christ be with all of you" or a near equivalent is found at the close of all Paul's writings. In the autographa (the original MSS) they were all in Paul's handwriting, though most of his Epistles may have been written through amanuenses. The present benediction agrees verbatim with that of 1 Thessalonians 5:28 except for the "all" added here. Significantly, no one was excluded from Paul's good wishes toward this church, not even those he had rebuked at various points.

Notes

17,18 That Paul here inaugurates the policy of a self-written greeting because of the problem of 2:2 (Alford, 3:298, 299) cannot be substantiated, since only two of his remaining ten Epistles (1 Cor; Col) have this kind of greeting (Lünemann, p. 254). That it was a policy to follow only in his future Thessalonian correspondence (Eadie, *A Commentary on the Greek Text of the Epistles of Paul to the Thessalonians* [London: Macmillan, 1877], p. 323) would require a future tense of εἰμί (*eimi*, "to be") rather than the present tense ἐστίν (*estin*, "is") (3:17). It apparently was a widespread custom in ancient letter writing for the author to do this at the close of the letter. In the present instance there was a particular occasion for calling attention to it—viz., to guard Christians from being misled in the future as they had been in the past (cf. 2:2).

1 TIMOTHY
Ralph Earle

1 TIMOTHY

Introduction 1 and 2 Timothy

First Timothy, Titus, and Second Timothy—probably written in that order and commonly called the pastoral Epistles—form a rather closely knit unity. They are somewhat distinct from Paul's other ten Epistles and share common problems of authorship and date. It is logical, then, to treat them together in a single introductory article. For a fuller treatment of Titus, however, see the Introduction to that Epistle.

1. Authorship

The four Gospels and Acts are all anonymous. In connection with these, we are faced with the question of authorship, but not of genuineness. But since all three pastoral Epistles begin with Paul's name, the matter of authorship involves the crucial problem of whether or not they are genuine. We must therefore investigate this subject at some length.

Four arguments commonly raised against the Pauline authorship of the pastoral Epistles need to be answered.

1) *Historical.* The events in the pastoral Epistles do not fit into the account in Acts. Nowhere in Acts do we read about Paul preaching in Crete and leaving Titus there (Titus 1:5). Nor does his leaving Timothy at Ephesus fit into the Acts account. On these points all scholars agree.

But was Paul put to death at the end of his Roman imprisonment described in the closing verses of Acts? This is assumed by many scholars, and so they say that Paul could not have written these epistles.

The answer is that Paul was released from his first Roman imprisonment and made further journeys, during which he wrote First Timothy and Titus. It was during a later imprisonment that he wrote Second Timothy.

There is considerable evidence for this position. Clement of Rome (A.D. 95) says that

Paul went "to the extreme limit of the west."[1] For a man living in Rome, this would mean Spain. The Muratorian Canon (c. A.D. 200) says that the apostle "departed for Spain." Paul had written to the Romans that he planned to go past them to that country (Rom 15:24, 28). Here we have the statement that he carried out this purpose, and this would have to be after his first Roman imprisonment—as any careful reading of Acts will show.

The most definite statement comes from Eusebius. He writes:

> Paul is said, after having defended himself, to have set forth again upon the ministry of preaching, and to have entered the city [Rome] a second time, and to have ended his life by martyrdom. Whilst then a prisoner, he wrote the Second Epistle to Timothy, in which he both mentions his first defence, and his impending death.[2]

2) *Ecclesiastical.* In the pastoral Epistles we read about bishops, elders (presbyters), and deacons. It is claimed by scholars that this shows a more advanced church organization than existed during the lifetime of Paul.

But a careful reading of Titus 1:5–9 shows that "elders" and "bishops" are terms used interchangeably. And in Philippians 1:1 Paul addresses the "bishops and deacons" in the church at Philippi.

Very different is the situation in the Epistles of Ignatius (c. A.D. 115). Here each local church has one bishop, several presbyters and several deacons. The evidence is clear that the pastoral Epistles reflect the type of church organization known to Paul, rather than the type Ignatius was familiar with. Thus, a second-century date for the Pastorals, as held by many today, seems unrealistic.

3) *Doctrinal.* A third argument against Pauline authorship is the claim that the doctrinal emphases of the Pastorals are different from those in Paul's previous Epistles, especially the recurring use of the expression "sound doctrine" (2 Tim 4:3; Titus 1:9; 2:1). Kümmel makes much of this. But he admits that "the Jewish-Christian Gnostic heresy which the Pastorals combat is . . . quite conceivable in the lifetime of Paul."[3] He also states, "The Pauline origin of the Pastorals was not challenged from the time of their recognition as canonical writings toward the end of the second century till the beginning of the nineteenth century."[4]

Paul opposes Gnostic ideas in his Epistle to the Colossians. The error of the nineteenth century critics was their belief that these did not exist until the second century. Today it is generally acknowledged that Gnostic ideas had already penetrated Judaism before the advent of Christianity. But that there is no evidence of a pre-Christian Gnostic system has been fully demonstrated by Edwin M. Yamauchi in his recent scholarly study, *Pre-Christian Gnosticism.*[5]

4) *Linguistic.* The most serious argument against the genuineness of the pastoral Epistles is their difference in style and vocabulary from Paul's earlier writings. This is the main point stressed today by negative critics.

Harrison found 175 words used nowhere else in the NT and 130 non-Pauline words

---

[1] Clement 5.
[2] *Ecclesiastical History* (A.D. 326) 2:22.
[3] Feine-Behm-Kümmel, *Introduction to the New Testament* (Abingdon, 1966), p. 267.
[4] Ibid., p. 261.
[5] Grand Rapids: Eerdmans, 1973.

shared by other NT writers. Working with a word-per-page method, he found an abrupt, sharp rise in new words in the Pastorals. So he concluded that Paul could not have written these later Epistles.[6]

These statistics have carried great weight with many twentieth century scholars. Guthrie answers: "But numerical calculations cannot with the limited data available from Paul's letters take into account differences of subject-matter, differences of circumstances and differences of addressees, all of which may be responsible for new words."[7] Cambridge statistician Yule declared that samples of about ten thousand words are necessary as a basis for valid statistical study.[8] This, of course, we do not have in the case of the Pastorals. Bruce M. Metzger asserts that Harrison's use of the statistical method has proved to be unsound.[9]

In recent years several scholars have been suggesting that Luke was the amanuensis (secretary) who actually composed the pastoral Epistles for Paul. Moule writes, "My suggestion is, then, that Luke wrote all three Pastoral epistles. But he wrote them during Paul's lifetime, and, in part but only in part, at Paul's dictation."[10] The careful student can discover a considerable number of significant Greek words that occur in both Luke-Acts and the Pastorals but nowhere else in the NT. It appears that amanuenses were sometimes given considerable liberty in writing manuscripts, and we know that Paul was in the habit of using amanuenses for the actual writing of his Epistles (Rom 16:22).

In his volume on the pastoral Epistles (in ICC, 1924), Walter Lock comes out emphatically for the genuineness of these letters. He notes that there are many points of contact between the Pastorals and Paul's farewell address to the Ephesian elders (Acts 20:17–38): "The evidence of Church writers is the same as for the other letters of St. Paul." He also declared that the doctrinal background is essentially Pauline.[11] Moreover, Lock and Guthrie point out the Lucan language in the Pastorals.[12]

Perhaps more significant is the fact that J.N.D. Kelly of Oxford, in his 1963 volume in "Harper's New Testament Commentaries," gives adequate answers to all the negative arguments we have noted. After a careful reappraisal of the whole situation, he concludes that the evidence "tips the scales perceptibly ... in favour of the traditional theory of authorship."[13] W.J. Lowstuter wrote in the *Abingdon Bible Commentary* (p. 1276) that, taken altogether, the evidence is favorable to the Pauline authorship.

2. Date

The date of Paul's first Roman imprisonment was perhaps A.D. 59–61. (Some say 60–62, others 61–63 or 62–64.) The early church unanimously testifies that Paul was put to death by Emperor Nero, who committed suicide in June of A.D. 68. Since Paul asked Timothy to come to him "before winter" (2 Tim 4:21), it is obvious that the second

---

[6]P.N. Harrison, *The Problem of the Pastoral Epistles* (London: Oxford University Press, 1921).

[7]Donald Guthrie, *New Testament Introduction: The Pauline Epistles* (Chicago: InterVarsity, 1961), p. 221.

[8]G.U. Yule, *The Statistical Study of Literary Vocabulary* (Cambridge, 1944).

[9]Expt, 70:91–94.

[10]C.F.D. Moule, "The Problem of the Pastoral Epistles: A Reappraisal," in *Bulletin of John Rylands Library,* vol. 47 (March, 1965), p. 434.

[11]p. xxv.

[12]Ibid., p. xxix; Guthrie, *New Testament Introduction,* p. 235.

[13]p. 34.

Epistle to Timothy was written not later than A.D. 67. It may have been as early as 65. This means that 1 Timothy and Titus were probably written between 62 and 66. If we assume omitted details in the Acts account, earlier dates might be possible.

3. Place of Origin

First Timothy 1:3 seems to indicate that Paul was in Macedonia when he wrote that Epistle. Second Timothy was written from prison in Rome, shortly before the apostle's death. We have no clear indication as to where the Epistle to Titus was written.

4. Destination

Titus was on the island of Crete when Paul wrote to him (Titus 1:5). Timothy was at Ephesus when the apostle wrote him the first Epistle (1 Tim 1:3). Presumably he was still there when Paul wrote the second Epistle.

5. Purpose

These Epistles are called "pastoral" because they are addressed to pastors of churches to outline their pastoral duties. These responsibilities were twofold: to defend sound doctrine and maintain sound discipline. This double emphasis is especially obvious in the Epistle to Titus, but it appears in all three letters.

To be more specific, Paul says he had urged Timothy to "stay on in Ephesus so that you may command certain men not to teach false doctrines any longer" (1 Tim 1:3). The apostle also deals with numerous problems that would arise in the church and gives advice as to how they should be handled.

The occasion and purpose of 2 Timothy are stated more fully. Paul is in prison at Rome, awaiting his expected execution. He longs to see his "son" Timothy (1:4). He is getting cold in the dungeon and urges Timothy to come before winter (4:21) and bring the warm coat Paul left at Troas, and his books and parchments (4:13). He wants to study.

6. Summary of 1 and 2 Timothy

Paul begins his First Epistle to Timothy by warning him against false teachers, who seem to have been Judaizers (1:3–11). He thanks "Christ Jesus our Lord" for his amazing grace to him, "the worst of sinners" (1:12–20). Chapter 2 is taken up with instructions for public worship, chapter 3 with the qualifications of the overseers and deacons in the church. In Chapter 4 Paul gives personal instructions to Timothy, again warning him against false teachers (vv.1–5) and admonishing him to maintain sound doctrine and sound discipline (vv.6–16). Chapter 5 deals mainly with the place of widows in the church (vv.3–16) and the treatment of elders (vv.17–20). Chapter 6 has instructions for slaves (vv.1, 2) and more warnings against false teachers (vv.3–5) and the love of money (vv.6–10). After a personal charge to Timothy (vv.11–16), Paul gives special instructions to the rich (vv.17–19).

The second Epistle is much more personal, written near the close of Paul's life. He talks more directly to Timothy than in the first letter, urging him to maintain the spiritual glow (1:1–7) and to be a faithful partner of his in suffering for the gospel (1:8–2:13). Again the apostle warns against the false teachers (2:14–19) and urges Timothy to be a noble servant of Christ (2:20–26). The third chapter contains a description of conditions in the last days (vv.1–9). Then the aged apostle gives his final charge to his son in the faith (3:10–4:5) and his own testimony (4:6–8). The Epistle closes with personal remarks about the current situation (4:9–18) and the final greetings (4:19–21) and benediction (4:22).

Because these two letters were written primarily to an individual whom Paul loved dearly, they provide us with some valuable insights into his life and character. Yet, through his associate Timothy, Paul is speaking to the entire church at Ephesus, and indeed to the whole church of Jesus Christ today.

7. Theological Values

There is a strong OT background here. It is reflected in the use of the phrase "God our Savior," which occurs five times in the Pastorals (1 Tim 1:1; 2:3; Titus 1:3; 2:10; 3:4) and nowhere else in Paul's Epistles. It is found in Jude 25, and a similar expression, "God my Savior," occurs in a hymn that is full of OT language (Luke 1:47). But we also find in the Pastorals the typically Pauline emphasis on "our Savior, Christ Jesus" (2 Tim 1:10), "Christ Jesus our Savior" (Titus 1:4), and "Jesus Christ our Savior" (Titus 3:6). Also the significant Pauline expression "in Christ" occurs seven times in 2 Timothy and twice in 1 Timothy.

Furthermore, the fact that salvation is through God's grace rather than our own good works is clearly asserted (2 Tim 1:9; Titus 3:5). Closely allied to this is the teaching that eternal life comes by faith in Jesus Christ (1 Tim 1:16).

More precisely than anywhere else it is stated: "For there is one God and one mediator between God and men, the man Christ Jesus" (1 Tim 2:5). It is also declared that this Mediator gave himself "as a ransom for all men" (v.6). Here the doctrine of the atonement comes through clearly. By his coming, Christ "has destroyed death and has brought life and immortality to light through the gospel" (2 Tim 1:10).

The divine inspiration of the Scriptures is stated in the Pastorals more forcefully than anywhere else in the NT. We read, "All Scripture is God-breathed and is useful for teaching, rebuking, correcting and training in doing what is right" (2 Tim 3:16).

The pastoral Epistles are primarily practical rather than theological. The emphasis lies rather on the defense of doctrine than on its explication or elaboration. The distinctively doctrinal passages comprise only a small part of the whole; Timothy and Titus had already been instructed.

8. Canonicity

Guthrie states that the external attestation for the Pastorals—the testimony of the early church fathers—"is as strong as that for most of the other Epistles of Paul, with the exception of I Corinthians and Romans."[14] The pastoral Epistles were known and used by Polycarp, Justin Martyr, and Irenaeus—all of the second century.

---

[14]Guthrie, *New Testament Introduction*, p. 199.

The one negative note is found in the heretic Marcion (c. A.D. 140), but then he rejected the whole Bible except ten Pauline Epistles and a mutilated copy of Luke's Gospel.

The first "orthodox" NT canon was the so-called Muratorian Fragment (c. 170–200), the opening part of which is broken off. After mentioning Paul's letters to seven different churches, it says, "But he wrote one letter to Philemon, and one to Titus, and two to Timothy from affection and love." From this time until the rise of negative criticism in the nineteenth century, there seems to have been no question about the acceptance of the pastoral Epistles as Pauline and as a part of the inspired NT Scriptures.

9. Special Problems

In most of Paul's Epistles he is apparently concerned about the work of the Judaizers in hindering the progress of the gospel. The mention of "myths and endless genealogies" (1 Tim 1:4) may refer to Judaistic or Gnostic emphases, or both. But when Paul says that the troublemakers want to be "teachers of the law" (v.7), he is evidently talking about Judaizers. (See also Titus 1:14.)

There also seems to be a combination of Gnosticism and Judaism in those who "forbid people to marry, and order them to abstain from certain foods" (4:3). The first of these prohibitions arose from a false asceticism, based on the Gnostic idea that all matter is evil.

Another troublesome topic concerned who should be enrolled as widows. Paul deals with this at some length and gives specific instructions about their qualifications (1 Tim 5:3–16).

10. Bibliography for Pastoral Epistles

Alford, Henry. *The Greek Testament.* 4 vols. Revised by E.F. Harrison. Chicago: Moody, 1958 (1861).

Barclay, William. *The Letters to Timothy, Titus and Philemon.* Philadelphia: Westminster, 1960.

Barrett, C.K. *The Pastoral Epistles.* Oxford: Clarendon, 1963.

Bernard, J.H. *The Pastoral Epistles.* Cambridge: Cambridge University Press, 1899.

Easton, B.S. *The Pastoral Epistles.* New York: Scribner's, 1947.

Erdman, Charles R. *The Pastoral Epistles of Paul.* Philadelphia: Westminster, 1923.

Fairbairn, Patrick. *Commentary on the Pastoral Epistles.* Grand Rapids: Zondervan, 1956 reprint, (1874).

Falconer, Robert. *The Pastoral Epistles.* Oxford: Clarendon, 1937.

Feine, Paul, and Behm, Johannes. *Introduction to the New Testament.* Completely reedited by W.G. Kümmel. Translated by A.J. Mattill. Nashville: Abingdon, 1966.

Guthrie, Donald. *The Pastoral Epistles.* Grand Rapids: Eerdmans, 1957.

Harrison, Everett F. *Introduction to the New Testament.* Grand Rapids: Eerdmans, 1964.

Hayes, D.A. *Paul and His Epistles.* New York: Methodist Book Concern, 1915.

Hendriksen, William. *New Testament Commentary: Pastoral Epistles.* Grand Rapids: Baker, 1957.

Hiebert, D. Edmond. *An Introduction to the Pauline Epistles.* Chicago: Moody, 1954.

Kelly, J.N.D. *A Commentary on the Pastoral Epistles.* New York: Harper & Row, 1963.

Lenski, R.C.H. *Interpretation of St. Paul's Epistles to the Colossians, to the Thessalonians, to Timothy, to Titus and to Philemon.* Columbus, Ohio: Wartburg, 1937.

Lock, Walter. *A Critical and Exegetical Commentary on the Pastoral Epistles.* Edinburgh: T. & T. Clark, 1924. On the Greek text.

Lowstuter, W.J. "The Pastoral Epistles." *Abingdon Bible Commentary*. Nashville: Abingdon, 1929.

Scott, E.F. *The Pastoral Epistles*. New York: Harper and Brothers, n.d. (1936).

Simpson, E.K. *The Pastoral Epistles*. Grand Rapids: Eerdmans, 1954.

Vine, W.E. *An Expository Dictionary of New Testament Words*. 4 vols. Westwood, N.J.: Revell, 1940.

Zahn, Theodor. *Introduction to the New Testament*, vol. 2. Grand Rapids: Kregel, 1953 reprint, 1909.

11. Outline of 1 Timothy

Text and Exposition

I. Salutation

1:1, 2

> ¹Paul, an apostle of Christ Jesus by the command of God our Savior and of Christ Jesus our hope,
> ²To Timothy my true son in the faith:
> Grace, mercy and peace from God the Father and Christ Jesus our Lord.

1 In keeping with the custom of that day, every one of Paul's thirteen Epistles begins with his name (*Paulos*). Born a Roman citizen (Acts 22:27, 28), he had been given the Latin name "Paulus" in addition to his Jewish name Saul. At the beginning of his Gentile mission the apostle adopted the habit of using his Roman (Latin) name (Acts 13:9), and this is what we find in all his letters.

In all but four of his Epistles—Philippians, 1 and 2 Thessalonians, and Philemon—Paul identifies himself as "an apostle." The Greek *apostolos* literally means "one sent on a mission." This was the title that Jesus gave to his first twelve disciples (Luke 6:13). After the death of Judas Iscariot, Matthias was elected to take his place (Acts 1:23–26). Later the term was extended to take in Paul and Barnabas (Acts 14:14), the first two missionaries to the Gentile world. Paul uses it at the beginning of his Epistles to underscore the fact that he is writing with apostolic authority.

He was "an apostle of Christ Jesus." That is, Christ had commissioned and sent him as a missionary. It was not by his own choice but "by the command of God . . . and of Christ Jesus." Paul was very conscious of his divine call to the apostolic ministry. He had evidently expected to be a Jewish rabbi, but God had other plans for his life. Only the firm assurance of this could have carried him through all his hardships.

Some have asked why Paul mentioned his apostolic authority in writing to his two faithful colleagues. He understandably omitted this item in his letters to the loving, loyal churches at Thessalonica and Philippi and in his brief personal note to Philemon. But why does he include it in his Epistles to Timothy and Titus?

The answer seems to be that the apostle intended these letters to be read to the local church congregations. He knew that both his recipients were being challenged by false teachers and he wanted to strengthen the hands of these two pastors.

The expression "God our Savior" occurs five times in the Pastorals and nowhere else in Paul's Epistles. Besides this passage, it is found in 2:3 and in Titus 1:3; 2:10; 3:4. Elsewhere in the NT we find it only in Jude 25. A similar phrase, "God my Savior, occurs in Luke 1:47, in a hymn that is characterized largely by OT language. We have already noted in the Introduction the view held by a number of scholars that Luke acted as Paul's amanuensis in the writing of the pastoral Epistles. If so, he may have had some influence on the apostle's language at this point. It may be, too, that Nero's claim to the title "Savior of the world" caused Paul to assert emphatically that the only real Savior is God, the Supreme Being.

Another unique feature is the designation of Christ as "our hope," although Paul elsewhere calls him "the hope of glory" (Col 1:27). In the early second century, Ignatius borrowed the phrase, speaking of "Jesus Christ our hope" (*Epistle to the Trallians*, ch. 2). He is our only hope.

2 The Epistle is addressed to Timothy (*Timotheos*), "my true son in the faith." Elsewhere Paul refers to him as "my son whom I love, who is faithful in the Lord" (1 Cor 4:17) and says, "Timothy has proved himself, because as a son with his father he has served with me in the work of the gospel" (Phil 2:22).

The word *true* (*gnēsios*) means "genuine, true-born." Perhaps the thrust here is two-fold: Timothy was a true believer and he was also a genuine convert of Paul's ministry.

We first meet Timothy in Acts 16:1-3. There we are told that on Paul's second missionary journey he found at Lystra a young disciple named Timothy, the son of a Jewish Christian mother and a Greek father. Paul was so impressed with the young man that he asked him to join the missionary party. It seems clear that Timothy had been converted under Paul's preaching at Lystra on the first missionary journey (about A.D. 47). He had matured so well as a Christian that only two years later (A.D. 49) he was ready to become an apprentice to the great apostle. He became one of Paul's most trusted helpers, so that the apostle could write, "I have no one else like him, who takes a genuine interest in your welfare" (Phil 2:20). The life of Timothy is a constant challenge to every young Christian to imitate his devotion and faithfulness.

After the name of the writer (v.1) and the recipient (v.2a) comes the greeting (v.2b). In all ten of Paul's previous Epistles the greeting is twofold—"grace and peace." Here and in 2 Timothy it is "grace, mercy and peace." These all come to us "from God the Father and Christ Jesus our Lord."

Two things may have suggested the addition of "mercy" (which is not found in the best Greek text of Titus 1:2). One would be Timothy's frail health (see 5:23). As a loving father, the apostle wishes mercy for his son. The other would be the difficulties that Timothy was encountering at Ephesus. He was in need of God's mercy and help.

"Grace" (*charis*) is a favorite word with Paul, occurring nearly one hundred times in his Epistles. First meaning "gracefulness" and then "graciousness," it is used in the NT for the "divine favor" that God bestows freely on all who will believe.

"Peace" has always been the typical greeting of the East. It is one of God's best gifts to men. In a world of war and hate this term becomes particularly significant. In Christ we have peace of heart and mind.

Notes

1 The word ἀπόστολος (*apostolos*) occurs eight times in the Gospels (six of those in Luke), thirty times in Acts, thirty-two times in Paul's Epistles (including five in the Pastorals) and eight times in the rest of the NT. In most cases it refers either to Paul or to the Twelve.

Twice in this verse we have the name "Christ Jesus." In the earlier Epistles of Paul, as in the Epistles of James, Peter, John, and Jude, the order is more frequently "Jesus Christ," which may be interpreted as meaning "Jesus the Messiah." But in Paul's later Epistles "Christ Jesus" becomes the dominant expression, particularly in the Pastorals. The emphasis here is more on the title ("Christ" means "Anointed One") than on the personal name.

Surprisingly, σωτήρ (*sōtēr*, "Savior") is found only twenty-four times in the NT ("salvation" 44 times). Of these, ten are in the pastoral Epistles and five in 2 Peter. Apparently the term came into prominent use in the later period, perhaps because of its false use by Nero (see Exposition), under whom both Peter and Paul were executed.

2 Aside from 1 Tim 1:2 and Titus 1:4, γνήσιος (*gnēsios*, "true," "genuine") is found only twice in the NT (2 Cor 8:8; Phil 4:3). But it is found frequently in the papyri in the sense of "genuine." It "becomes an epithet of affectionate appreciation" (MM, p. 129). That is its use here.

The addition of "mercy" has been cited as evidence against the Pauline authorship of the

Pastorals. But Simpson cogently observes: "A copyist would have surely avoided such a deviation from precedent" (p. 26).

We are apt to think of ἔλεος (*eleos*, "mercy"), as indicating God's attitude toward the sinner in bringing him to a place of repentance and forgiveness. But the word has broader connotations. In LXX it is used to tr. the Heb. term that means "lovingkindness" or "steadfast love." This is probably the full import here.

II. Timothy's Task at Ephesus (1:3–11)

1. *Suppression of False Teachers*

1:3–7

> ³As I urged you when I went into Macedonia, stay there in Ephesus so that you may command certain men not to teach false doctrines any longer ⁴nor to devote themselves to myths and endless genealogies. These promote controversies rather than God's work—which is by faith. ⁵The goal of this command is love, which comes from a pure heart, a good conscience and a sincere faith. ⁶Some have wandered away from these and turned to meaningless talk. ⁷They want to be teachers of the law, but they do not know what they are talking about or what they so confidently affirm.

3 When Paul went into Macedonia—at exactly what time we do not know—he urged Timothy to "stay [*prosmenō*, 'remain still'] there in Ephesus." As noted in the Introduction, it appears that Paul was released from his first Roman imprisonment of two years, recorded at the close of Acts, and that he made another visit to Ephesus. There he discovered some conditions that needed extended attention. So he left Timothy as pastor of this important church.

3b, 4a What was the problem that concerned Paul? We find the answer here in the purpose for which Timothy was to remain: "that you may command certain men not to teach false doctrines any longer nor to devote themselves to myths and endless genealogies." The church has always had false teachers—they appeared on the scene in the very first generation, within thirty-five years of the church's birth at Pentecost (A.D. 30–65).

What was the nature of these "false doctrines"? What is meant by "myths and endless genealogies" (*genealogiai*)?

There are two possible answers. In the first place, the reference could be to the vagaries of Gnosticism, with its endless genealogies of aeons between God and man. But v.7 suggests that these were Jewish teachers, who were caught up in the mythological treatment of OT genealogies. Titus 1:14 speaks of "Jewish myths." There is abundant evidence that both these features were found in the Judaism of that day, especially in its apocalyptic literature.

4b Paul declares that such teachings "promote controversies rather than God's work—which is by faith." The word translated "work" is *oikonomian*, which literally means "stewardship" but is often rendered "dispensation." Simpson aptly remarks, "The divine dispensation of truth does not beget fable-spinning but faith.... By faith we stand, not by weaving webs of whimsical fancies" (p. 28).

5 The "goal" or "end" (*telos*) of "this command"—literally, "the command"—"is love." It may be seriously questioned whether the translation limiting it to "this command" is fully justified. We would agree with Walter Lock when he comments: "Primarily, the charge which Timothy has to give . . . but the last [preceding] words . . . have carried the mind on to the whole scheme of salvation, and perhaps extend the meaning more widely—the end of all Christian moral preaching, the whole moral charge which is given to God's stewards" (p. 10). That is, the highest goal of true religion is love—*agapē*, the unselfish love of full loyalty to God and boundless goodwill to our fellowmen. This must be our ultimate goal in life.

This love comes "from a pure heart, a good conscience and a sincere faith." Our hearts must be cleansed from self-centeredness if we are going to obey the first and second commandments enunciated by Jesus (Matt 22:37–40). Then we must maintain a good conscience if love is to function properly. And all this is based on "sincere" (literally, "unhypocritical") faith. All love comes from God and it comes to us only as we are united to him by faith.

6 Unfortunately, some at Ephesus had missed the mark (*astochēsantes*) and had turned to "meaningless talk" (*mataiologian*, "empty chatter"—only here in the NT). They were doing much talking, but saying nothing of value. Simpson calls them "wordmongers."

7 Paul scores these would-be teachers of the Law rather heavily. His verdict: "They do not know what they are talking about or what they so confidently affirm." Their self-confidence was empty pretense. Simpson comments, "These whipper-snappers have an exchequer of words, but no fund of insight" (p. 29). They were what Philo called "syllable-squabblers."

8 Having identified the false teachers at Ephesus as self-appointed teachers of the Law, the apostle now points out the purpose of the Law. He says that "the law"—probably here meaning the Mosaic law—"is good if a man uses it properly." Here the KJV rendering preserves the play on words in the Greek—"law" (*nomos*) . . . "lawfully" (*nomimōs*).

Notes

3 "To teach false doctrines" is all one word in Greek, ἑτεροδιδασκαλεῖν (*heterodidaskalein*, lit., "to teach differently"), found only here and in 6:3, and never found outside of Christian writings. Paul may well have coined the term as a contrast to the claim of these false leaders that they were νομοδιδάσκαλοι (*nomodidaskaloi*, "teachers of the law," v.7). Actually they were teaching something "different" (*heteros*).

4 Our word *myth* comes directly from the Greek μῦθος (*mythos*). At first this meant simply a story or narrative. But finally it became equivalent to the Latin *fabula*, "a fable" or "fiction."

"Controversies" translates ἐκζητήσεις (*ekzētēseis*, only here in NT and found only in Christian writings). It means "useless speculations" (BAG).

"Godly edifying" (KJV) is based on an inferior reading, οἰκοδομίαν (*oikodomian*, "act of building"), rather than οἰκονομίαν (*oikonomian*, "administration").

5 "Conscience" comes from the Latin—*cum*, "with," and *scio*, "know." So it literally means "a knowing together"—the exact meaning of the Gr. word here, συνείδησις (*syneidēsis*). Among the Greeks it meant "self-consciousness," which was primarily an intellectual matter. It was the Jews, along with the Stoics, who introduced a moral content into the term, so that "consciousness" became "conscience."

2. The Purpose of the Law

1:8-11

> 8We know that the law is good if a man uses it properly. 9We also know that law is made not for good men, but for lawbreakers and rebels, the ungodly and sinful, the unholy and irreligious; for those who kill their fathers or mothers, for murderers, 10for adulterers and perverts, for slave traders and liars and perjurers —and for whatever else is contrary to the sound doctrine 11that conforms to the glorious gospel of the blessed God, which he entrusted to me.

9a "Law" in this verse is without the definite article and so probably refers to law in general. The apostle indicates that the purpose of law is not to police good men but bad men. In other words, we need law for the punishment of criminals and the protection of society. He says that law is not appointed "for good men"—literally, "for a righteous person." Rather, it is intended to deal with those who are unrighteous.

The list that follows is typically Pauline (cf. Rom 1:24–32). It starts with more general terms, in three pairs: "lawbreakers and rebels, the ungodly and sinful, the unholy and irreligious." These represent attitudes or states of mind. "Lawbreakers" is literally "lawless"—that is, those who ignore the law. The Greek word translated "rebels" literally means "not subject to rule," and so "insubordinate." The word for "ungodly" means one who is deliberately guilty of "irreverence." The adjective "irreligious" means "profane" (KJV) in the sense of having no sense of the sacred—a common sin of secular society.

9b,10a "For those who kill their fathers . . . mothers" translates only two words in Greek (*patrolōais . . . mētrolōais*). The two terms (found only here in the NT) are constructed, respectively, of the words for "father" and "mother" with the verb meaning "to smite." So J.H. Bernard writes, "The rendering of A.V. and R.V. 'murderers of fathers' is, no doubt, legitimate, but it is not the sin of *murder*, but of *dishonouring parents*, which is here uppermost in the writer's thought, and the wider translation is justified by the usage of the words elsewhere. For this extreme and outrageous violation of the Fifth Commandment the punishment of death was provided in the Mosaic law (Ex. xxi.15)" (p. 27). The fact that "murderers" immediately follows perhaps lends some support to "smiters of fathers and smiters of mothers" as the correct translation here. This is favored by Alford, Fairbairn, Simpson, and others.

Paul goes on to say that law is made for adulterers and "perverts." The last term is *arsenokoitais*, which means "male homosexuals." The word occurs only once elsewhere in the NT, in 1 Corinthians 6:9, where it is stated that "homosexual offenders" will not inherit the kingdom of God. Despite its condonation by some church leaders today, homosexuality is categorically condemned in both the OT and NT. It is the peculiar sin for which God destroyed Sodom and Gomorrah. It is widely recognized as one of the causes for the downfall of the Roman Empire, and its rapid increase today in Europe and North America poses a threat to the future of Western civilization.

"Slave traders" is *andrapodistais*, which may be translated "kidnapers." The Jewish rabbis specifically applied the eighth commandment, "Thou shalt not steal," to kidnaping—a crime that has greatly increased in the last few years. Philo, a Jew of the first century, makes this interesting observation: "The kidnaper too is a kind of thief who steals the best of all the things that exist on the earth" (*Spec. leg.* 4:13).

We have noted that "smiters of fathers" refers to the fifth commandment. The terms that follow relate to the sixth, seventh, eighth, and ninth commandments. So these items cover most of the second table of the Decalogue.

10b,11 Lest he miss any other important item, Paul adds, "And for whatever else is contrary to the sound doctrine that conforms to the glorious gospel of the blessed God, which he entrusted to me." The one Greek word for "is contrary to" literally means "lies opposite," and so "opposes" or "resists."

"Sound" is one of the key words of the pastoral Epistles. Here it is the verb *hygiainō* (from which comes "hygienic"), which occurs eight times in the Pastorals and only four times elsewhere in the NT. (The adjective *hygiēs* is found in Titus 2:8). The verb means "*be in good health, be healthy* or *sound*" (BAG, p. 839). Both words are used with reference to physical health in the Gospels. But the ethical, metaphorical usage here is widely paralleled in Greek literature.

Does "sound" mean "healthy" or "healthful"—that is, conducive to good health? A.T. Robertson supports the latter, as do Patrick Fairbairn and J.H. Bernard. But Lock says that it does not mean "wholesome" (p. 12), although this is the translation in Wey and NEB.

Perhaps this is a false antithesis. It may be a question not of either/or but of both/and. E.F. Scott points out that this phrase, "sound doctrine," fits in with its previous context (vv.3-10) and its following context (v.10). He writes, "As contrasted with all morbid types of belief, the gospel is healthy. . . . Law is a sort of medicine, only to be applied where the moral nature is diseased; Christian teaching is a healthy food for healthy people, a means of joy, freedom, larger activity" (p. 10).

"That conforms to the glorious gospel of the blessed God" is literally "according to the gospel of the glory of the blessed God." Fairbairn felicitously observes, "The gospel of God's glory is the gospel which peculiarly displays His glory—unfolds this to the view of men by showing the moral character and perfections of God exhibited as they are nowhere else in the person and work of Christ" (p. 90).

Paul declares that this gospel was "entrusted to me." Again and again he makes this assertion (see 1 Cor 9:17; Gal 2:7; 1 Thess 2:4). It amazed him that God should have placed such trust in him—the one who had formerly opposed the gospel and persecuted the church (cf. vv.12-14). The last clause of this paragraph is therefore a fitting introduction to the next section, in which he thanks God for choosing him.

Notes

9 "Murderers" translates the compound ἀνδροφόνοις (*androphonois*, lit., "men-killers." It is found only here in NT.
10 The question as to whether ἀνδραποδισταῖς (*andrapodistais*)—only here in NT—should be tr. "slave traders" or "kidnapers" is difficult to decide. Hendriksen comments that "it clearly refers primarily to 'slave-dealers' (the word ἀνδράποδον means slave) and then, by extension, to all 'men-stealers' or 'kidnapers' " (p. 69).

Διδασκαλία (*didaskalia*, "teaching") is used (in the NT) only by Paul, except in a quotation from Isa 29:13 (Matt 15:9; Mark 7:7). It occurs fifteen times in the Pastorals and four times in his other Epistles. Originally it meant the act of teaching, and then a body of doctrine. It is evidently used in the latter sense here.

III. Thanksgiving to God (1:12-17)

1. God's Abundant Grace

1:12-14

> [12]I thank Christ Jesus our Lord, who has given me strength, that he considered me faithful, appointing me to his service. [13]Even though I was once a blasphemer and a persecutor and a violent man, I was shown mercy because I acted in ignorance and unbelief. [14]The grace of our Lord was poured out on me abundantly, along with the faith and love that are in Christ Jesus.

12 Usually the thanksgiving in Paul's Epistles follows the salutation. But in this case the apostle has inserted between them a statement of his purpose in leaving Timothy at Ephesus. Now we find the familiar expression of thanks. In previous Epistles it was usually to God; here it is to "Christ Jesus our Lord." The lordship of Jesus finds increasing emphasis in Paul's later Epistles.

It is Christ who has "given me strength" (*endynamōsanti me*). This could be translated, "who has empowered me." This was because the Lord "considered" or "counted" (KJV) him faithful, "appointing me to his service." The last word is *diakonia*, which basically means "service" but is also used in a somewhat technical sense in the NT. Probably "putting me into the ministry" (KJV) is also a satisfactory translation.

13 Formerly Paul had been "a blasphemer." This probably means that in his opposition to the new movement he cursed the name of Jesus. Now he realized that this was blasphemy, because Jesus was divine.

Paul was also "a persecutor." This fact is documented abundantly in Acts 8:3; 9:1, 2, 4, 5; 22:4, 5; 26:9-11; Galatians 1:13. In his zeal to protect Judaism, the young Saul believed that he must destroy Christianity.

Still worse, he was "a violent man." This is one word, *hybristēn*. This term, found only here and in Romans 1:20, is much stronger than "injurious" (KJV). It refers to insolence and violence (cf. Acts 8:3).

Paul is fond of trilogies, and this is another example. Lock summarizes it this way: "A triad (as so often in St. Paul) with perhaps an ascending scale rising from words to acts of authorized persecution and of illegal violence" (pp. 14, 15).

In spite of this, he was "shown mercy" because he "acted in ignorance and unbelief." Paul was sincere in believing he was serving God in acting this way. When brought before the Sanhedrin in Jerusalem, he had testified, "I have fulfilled my duty to God in all good conscience to this day" (Acts 23:1). This apparently included his pre-Christian life.

14 It was more than mercy that Paul received from God. He declares, "The grace of our Lord was poured out on me abundantly, along with the faith and love that are in Christ Jesus." This is another of the apostle's great trilogies. "Grace" provided his salvation, "faith" appropriated it, and "love" applied it.

Notes

---

14 "Was poured out on me abundantly" translates one word in Gr.: ὑπερεπλεόνασε (*hyperepleonase*, "exceedingly abounded"). Paul is fond of compounds with ὑπέρ (*hyper*, "above"). This one is found only here in the NT. Bunyan found here his title for *Grace Abounding to the Chief of Sinners.*

---

2. The Worst of Sinners

1:15–17

15Here is a trustworthy saying that deserves full acceptance: Christ Jesus came into the world to save sinners—of whom I am the worst. 16But for that very reason I was shown mercy so that in me, the worst of sinners, Christ Jesus might display his unlimited patience as an example for those who would believe on him and receive eternal life. 17Now to the King eternal, immortal, invisible, the only God, be honor and glory for ever and ever. Amen.

15,16 "Here is a trustworthy saying" is literally "faithful the word" (*pistos ho logos*). This formula is found only in the pastoral Epistles (see 3:1; 2 Tim 2:11; Titus 3:8). Here and in 4:9 we find the added words: "that deserves full acceptance." The repeated formula is always attached to a maxim (relating either to doctrine or practice) on which full reliance can be placed. The saying here is "Christ Jesus came into the world to save sinners." This is the Good News, the heart of the gospel.

Paul felt that of all sinners he was "the worst"—literally, "first" or "chief." This was because he had persecuted Christ's followers so vigorously. As far as morality was concerned, young Saul had been a strict Pharisee, living a life that was blameless before the Law. But in his case as chief sinner, Christ's "unlimited patience" had been displayed as an example to all who would believe in Jesus and thus receive eternal life. Paul's life was a powerful demonstration of divine grace.

17 This verse is typical of Paul's habit of breaking out spontaneously into praise. We find briefer doxologies at 6:16 and 2 Timothy 4:18, as well as extended ones in Romans 11:36; 16:27; Galatians 1:5; Ephesians 3:21 and Philippians 4:20.

Notes

---

15 The term πιστός (*pistos*, "faithful" or "trustworthy") is found eleven times in 1 Tim and three times each in 2 Tim and Titus—a total of seventeen times in the Pastorals. It is obviously a key word in these three Epistles.

17 "King eternal" is lit. "King of the ages," a phrase found in Tobit 13:6, 10.

IV. Timothy's Responsibility

1:18–20

> 18Timothy, my son, I give you this instruction in keeping with the prophecies once made about you, so that by following them you may fight the good fight, 19holding on to faith and a good conscience. Some have rejected these and so have shipwrecked their faith. 20Among them are Hymenaeus and Alexander, whom I have handed over to Satan to be taught not to blaspheme.

18,19 "Instruction" is the same word, *parangelia*, that is translated "command" in v.5. It means "instruction, charge, command." The aged apostle is giving his son in the faith a solemn charge "in keeping with the prophecies once made about you"—perhaps at the time of Timothy's ordination or of his induction into missionary work. "Once made" is *proagousas*, "leading to" or "going before." So the phrase has sometimes been translated, "according to the prophecies leading me toward you," or "predictions leading up to you." They seem to have been prophetic utterances that pointed Timothy's way into the ministry. Because of these he was to "fight the good fight [lit., 'war the good warfare'] holding on to faith and a good conscience." Paul was much concerned that he and his colleagues should have a good conscience always. Some have rejected this "and so have shipwrecked their faith."

20 Paul names two who have been shipwrecked: Hymenaeus and Alexander. The former is mentioned again as a heretical teacher in 2 Timothy 2:17. Two Alexanders are spoken of in connection with Ephesus. The first was a Jew (Acts 19:34). The second is "Alexander the metalworker," who did Paul a great deal of harm (2 Tim 4:14). He may be the one intended here.

The apostle had handed these two ringleaders "over to Satan to be taught not to blaspheme." The language here is similar to that found in 1 Corinthians 5:5, where it seems to indicate excommunication from the church. The purpose was to jolt the offender into repentance, induced by the fearful thought of being turned over to Satan's control. Bernard observes, "It is certainly a *disciplinary* or *remedial* and not a merely *punitive* penalty in both cases" (p. 36).

V. Worship and Conduct (2:1–3:16)

1. *Prayer*

2:1–7

> 1I urge, then, first of all, that requests, prayers, intercession and thanksgiving be made for everyone—2for kings and all those in authority, that we may live peaceful and quiet lives in all godliness and holiness. 3This is good, and pleases God our Savior, 4who wants all men to be saved and to come to a knowledge of the truth. 5For there is one God and one mediator between God and men, the man Christ Jesus, 6who gave himself as a ransom for all men—the testimony given in its proper time. 7And for this purpose I was appointed a herald and an apostle—I am telling the truth, I am not lying—and a teacher of the true faith to the Gentiles.

1 Chapter 2 of 1 Timothy consists of instructions for public worship. The apostle was concerned that divine worship should be carried on in Ephesus most effectively and helpfully.

So he says, "I urge." The verb used here (*parakaleō*) may be translated "beseech" or "exhort." It indicates the urgency of Paul's admonition.

"First of all" probably emphasizes primacy in importance rather than in time (Guthrie). The most essential part of public worship is prayer.

In the NT we find seven different Greek nouns used for prayer. Four of them occur in this verse.

The first is *deēseis*, which is found nineteen times. Translated here as "requests" (KJV, "supplications"), it basically carries the idea of desire or need. All true prayer begins in a sense of need and involves a deep desire, although it should never stop there. God wants us to bring our "requests" to him, and he always has a listening ear.

The second word is *proseuchē*. It is the most general word for prayer, occurring thirty-seven times. Regularly translated as "prayer," it always signifies praying to God. It is used for both private and public prayers. The context suggests that here Paul had the latter in mind, although the former is certainly not excluded.

The third word, *enteuxis*, is found in the NT only in 1 Timothy (here and in 4:5). Translated here as "intercession," it seems to be used there in a more general way for prayer. The Greek word was used in the sense of "conversation" and then of "petition." Perhaps it suggests the idea that prayer should be a conversation with God.

Trench (p. 190) says that it implies "free familiar prayer, such as boldly draws near to God." Origen, the greatest Bible scholar of the early church, taught that the fundamental idea of *enteuxis* was boldness of access to God's presence.

This, again, is one aspect of successful, satisfying prayer. We must come to God with full confidence and enter into close communion with him in a conversational atmosphere if we wish to experience depth and richness in our prayer life. And only he who really communes with God in private can edify others in his public prayers.

The fourth word is *eucharistia*, from which we get "eucharist." The Lord's Supper, or Holy Communion, should always be a time of "thanksgiving." And "giving of thanks" (KJV) should be a part of all our praying. Thanking God for what he has done for us in the past strengthens our faith to believe that he will meet our needs in the future. Trench observes that this is the one aspect of prayer that will continue throughout eternity, where it will be "larger, deeper, fuller than here" (p. 191), because there the redeemed will know how much they owe their Lord.

2 Prayers of these varied types are to be made "for everyone" (v.1), but especially "for kings and all those in authority." The term *basileus* ("king") was applied in that day to the emperor at Rome, as well as to lesser rulers. When it is remembered that the Roman emperor when Paul wrote this Epistle was the cruel monster Nero—who later put Paul and Peter to death—it will be realized that we should pray for our present rulers, no matter how unreasonable they may seem to be. Prayer for "all those in authority" in various levels of government should have a regular place in all public worship.

The purpose of this is very logical and significant: "that we may live peaceful and quiet lives in all godliness and honesty." The fact that we are permitted to assemble peaceably for public worship is dependent on our rights under law—law as upheld and enforced by our legislators, administrators, and judicial leaders. We ought to pray for them, and also thank God for them.

The Greek adjective translated "peaceful" occurs only here in the NT. It means "quiet, tranquil." The basic idea is that of "restfulness unmarred by disturbance" (Vine, p. 34). The word for "quiet" (only here and in 1 Peter 3:4) "suggests the stillness that accompanied restfulness, in contrast to noisy commotion and merely bustling activity" (ibid.). Marvin Vincent says of these two terms: "*Ēremos* denotes quiet arising from the absence of outward disturbance; *hēsychios* tranquility arising from within" (Vincent, 4:217).

131

The word for "godliness" basically means "piety" or "reverence." The man who is irreverent is living an ungodly life.

"Holiness" is more accurate than "honesty" (KJV), which reflects an archaic sense no longer associated with that term. The Greek word *semnotēs* suggests "reverence, dignity, seriousness, respectfulness, holiness, probity" (BAG). Elsewhere in the NT it occurs only in 3:4 ("respect") and Titus 2:7 ("seriousness"). It is one of a considerable list of terms found only in the pastoral Epistles.

3,4 Such a life is "good"—*kalos* also means "beautiful, excellent"—and pleasing (acceptable) to God our Savior (cf. 1:1). He "wants all men to be saved and to come to a knowledge of the truth." This statement is in accord with John 3:16 and with the declaration in 2 Corinthians 5:14, 15 that Christ died for all. Salvation has been provided for all, but only those who accept it are saved. Vine writes, "Salvation is universal in its scope but conditional in its effect" (p. 35).

"Knowledge" (*epignōsis*) may also be translated "recognition." The compound noun means "precise and correct knowledge" (Thayer). "Knowledge of the truth" is both the root and fruit of salvation. Paul here sounds a frequent note of the Pastorals—true knowledge saves from error.

5 This is one of the most significant verses of the NT. It declares first of all that "there is one God." This is a primary affirmation in the OT, in opposition to the many polytheisms of that day. Monotheism is the basic premise of both Judaism and Christianity.

But then comes a difference. For Christianity goes on to assert that "there is one mediator between God and men, the man Christ Jesus."

The Greek word for "mediator," *mesitēs*, occurs only once in LXX (Gr. tr. of the OT). Job was frustrated by the fact that God was not a man with whom he could converse. In despair he concluded, "Neither is there any daysman [*mesitēs*] betwixt us, that might lay his hand upon us both" (Job 9:33). Christ is the answer to this ancient cry for help.

The basic meaning of *mesitēs* is "one who intervenes between two, either in order to make or restore peace and friendship, or to form a compact, or for ratifying a covenant." Thayer goes on to say that Christ is called the mediator between God and men "since he interposed by his death and restored the harmony between God and man which human sin had broken" (*Lexicon*, p. 401).

To be of any use, a bridge across a chasm or river must be anchored on both sides. Christ has closed the gap between deity and humanity. He has crossed the grand canyon, so deep and wide, between heaven and earth. He has bridged the chasm that separated man from God. With one foot planted in eternity, he planted the other in time. He who was the eternal Son of God became the Son of Man. And across this bridge, the man Christ Jesus, we can come into the very presence of God, knowing that we are accepted because we have a Mediator.

6 This Christ "gave himself as a ransom for all men." The word for "ransom," *antilytron*, occurs only here in the NT. It means "what is given in exchange for another as the price of his redemption" (Thayer). In the first century the simple word *lytron* was used for the ransom price paid to free a slave. So Christ paid the ransom to free us from the slavery of sin. Because of this we are rightfully his possession.

Jesus gave his life as a ransom "for all men." The Greek word translated "for" means "on behalf of." Christ died on behalf of all people, but only those who accept his sacrifice are actually set free from the shackles of sin.

This message of the redemptive death of Christ was the distinctive apostolic witness—

"the testimony given in its proper time." The last phrase is literally "in its own appointed times." Christ's sacrifice for sin took place at God's appointed hour. The Twentieth Century New Testament translates the whole clause: "This is the fact to which we are to bear our testimony, as opportunities present themselves."

7 For the purpose of giving this witness, Paul was "appointed"—literally, "placed, set"—"a herald and an apostle." The term *kēryx* ("herald") was used for "*a messenger* vested with public authority, who conveyed the official messages of kings, magistrates, princes, military commanders, or who gave a public summons or demand, and performed various other duties" (Thayer, p. 346). In the NT it signifies "God's ambassador, and the herald or proclaimer of the divine word" (ibid.). So the "preacher" (KJV) is one who makes a public proclamation for the King of kings. He is not to air his own opinions or debate other people's ideas but proclaim the Word of God. What a glorious privilege and what an awesome responsibility! No wonder Paul says "*I* [emphatic *egō* in Gr.] was appointed." Perhaps he is thinking "even I"—the one who blasphemed Christ and persecuted the church (see 1:12-14).

The word *apostle* (*apostolos*) has been discussed in connection with 1:1. It is almost equivalent to "missionary," which comes from the Latin. But probably it means here Christ's authoritative representative as a leader of the church.

Paul adds, "I am telling the truth, I am not lying." This implies that some of the church members at Ephesus were challenging his apostolic authority, as had happened at Corinth (2 Cor 10:10).

Paul was not only a herald and an apostle but also "a teacher of the true faith to the Gentiles." This was his special assignment from the Lord (Acts 9:15). Though he was "a Hebrew of the Hebrews" (Phil 3:5) and brought up a strict Pharisee, he had been born in Tarsus, one of the three main centers of Greek learning (after Athens and Alexandria), and was therefore suited to this assignment. The Christian leaders at Jerusalem agreed that he should evangelize the Gentiles (Gal 2:9).

Notes

3 We have already observed in connection with 1:1 that the use of "God our Savior" may point toward Luke as being the one who actually composed the pastoral Epistles under Paul's supervision. In this verse we find an additional item possibly pointing in the same direction. "Pleases God our Savior" is literally "acceptable"—ἀπόδεκτος (*apodektos*), only here and in 5:4—"in the presence of" (ἐνώπιον, enōpion) "God our Savior." The preposition *enōpion* is found twenty-two times in Luke's Gospel and fifteen times in Acts (not at all in Matthew or Mark and only once in John). Elsewhere it occurs very infrequently except in Revelation, where it is used thirty-six times. Martin McNamara shows that "in the presence of God" is a phrase that was adopted in the Aramaic Targums of the OT (*Targum and Testament* [Eerdmans, 1972], pp. 93–97).

6 Of ἀντίλυτρον (*antilytron*) Vine writes, "The word *antilutron*, a ransom, denotes an equivalent (or adequate) ransom price (from *anti*, corresponding to, and *lutron*, a ransom, from *luō*, to loose ...). The prefix *anti* expresses that the ransom is equivalent in value to that which is procured by it. It indicates the vicarious nature of the expiatory sacrifice of Christ in His death" (p. 39).

Walter Lock (p. 28) suggests that the "testimony" may include "the whole chain of witnesses," that is, "(a) The law and the prophets pointing to it, cf. Ro 3²¹.... (b) The witness of the Lord Himself in His Life (cf. 6¹³ and John 18³⁷).... (c) The witness which the writer and all future teachers have to give, cf. 1 Co 1⁶, 2 Th 1¹⁰."

2. Men

2:8

> 8I want men everywhere to lift up holy hands in prayer, without anger or disputing.

Getting back specifically to the matter of public worship, the apostle wants "men everywhere to lift up holy hands in prayer, without anger or disputing." The last word is translated "doubting" in KJV, a meaning that was adopted by several of the early church fathers. But the context seems to favor "disputing," a sense that the Greek word *dialogismos* clearly has in Romans 14:1 and Philippians 2:14.

Lifting up one's hands in prayer is often mentioned in the OT (e.g., 1 Kings 8:22; Pss 141:2; 143:6). It is a natural gesture, indicating earnest desire. The word "holy" is not the more common *hagios* but *hosios*, which means "devout, pious, pleasing to God" (BAG).

Lock says of the expression "lifting up holy hands" that it "combines the idea of moral purity . . . with that of consecration" (p. 30). We cannot pray effectively unless our lives are clean and committed.

Concerning "anger," Jeremy Taylor many years ago observed, "Anger is a perfect alienation of the mind from prayer" (quoted by Bernard, p. 44). And Bernard says about "disputing": "In our prayers we leave our differences behind us" (ibid.).

Notes

KJV has "will" in vv.4, 8; NIV, "want." But in the Gr. the former uses θέλω (*thelō*), while the latter uses βούλομαι (*boulomai*). Thayer writes: "As respects the distinction between βούλομαι and θέλω, the former seems to designate the will which follows deliberation, the latter the will which proceeds from inclination" (p. 286). But Cremer says: "Both words are, upon the whole, used synonymously" (p. 143). (So BAG, p. 145).

3. Women

2:9–15

> 9I also want women to dress modestly, with decency and propriety, not with braided hair or gold or pearls or expensive clothes, 10but with good deeds, appropriate for women who profess to worship God.
> 11A woman should learn in quietness and full submission. 12I do not permit a woman to teach or to have authority over a man; she must be silent. 13For Adam was formed first, then Eve. 14And Adam was not the one deceived; it was the woman who was deceived and became a sinner. 15But women will be kept safe through childbirth, if they continue in faith, love and holiness with propriety.

9,10 The first clause of v.8 reads literally: "I desire therefore the men to pray in every place." In v.9 Paul says, "Likewise also women." The use of the definite article with men and not with women may suggest that the apostle was laying down the pattern that public worship should be conducted by the men. Now he proceeds to tell how women should conduct themselves in church services.

First, they are to "dress modestly." This is a compact translation that represents the thought correctly. In the Greek there is a play on words: *kosmein heautas . . . en katastolē kosmiō.* The verb *kosmeō* (cf. the English word "cosmetic") means first "put in order" and then "adorn, decorate" (BAG). The adjective *kosmios* (in NT only here and in 3:2) means "orderly, decent, modest" (A-S, p. 255). *Katastolē* (only here in the NT) is "attire," though it sometimes had the wider sense of outward appearance or deportment. The full expression signifies: "adorn themselves in modest clothes." This is a much needed admonition today.

The word for "decency" is *aidōs* (only here in the NT). The translation "shame-facedness" (KJV) is both inaccurate—as every scholar agrees—and unfortunate. Paul is not urging women to go around looking ashamed of themselves, with faces averted or veiled. Bernard says that the Greek word "signifies that modesty which shrinks from overstepping the limits of womanly reserve" (p. 45). This should apply to both dress and deportment, although the rest of the verse suggests that the primary reference here is to one's clothing (as indicated in NIV).

Women are also to dress with "propriety." The Greek word (*sōphrosynē*) means "soundness of mind, good sense" (A-S). It could be translated "sound judgment," or as we might say today, "good judgment." Vine makes the timely observation: "What the apostle had in view in the present passage was the snare of the extreme forms of current fashions" (p. 43).

"Braided hair" is one word in Greek—*plegma*, which means something woven or braided. But clearly "hair" is understood. This is shown by a comparison with 1 Peter 3:3, where "hair" is expressed in the Greek. These two passages are very similar, a coincidence that is all the more striking since there was probably no collusion between the authors.

The Christian woman is not to adorn herself with "gold or pearls or expensive clothes" so as to draw attention to herself. At worst, this is what the prostitutes did. At best, it shows pride and self-centeredness, both of which are contrary to the spirit of Christ. Such dress is especially unbecoming in church.

Rather, Christian women are to adorn themselves "with good deeds, appropriate for women who profess to worship God." The Greek literally says "through good deeds." That is the way we express our faith. This thought is more dominant in the pastoral Epistles (occurring a dozen times) than in Paul's earlier letters—perhaps because the need for such emphasis became more apparent.

11,12 The teaching of these two verses is similar to that found in 1 Corinthians 14:33–35. There Paul tells the women that they are not allowed to talk out loud in the public services; here he says that they are to "learn in quietness and full submission." Titus 2:5 suggests that he means a wife is to be submissive to her husband. But it may well have the wider application of "submission to constituted authority, i.e., the officials and regulations of the Church" (Ramsay, quoted in Lock, p. 32).

The attitude of the Greeks toward women's place in society was not altogether uniform. Plato gave them practical equality with men. But Aristotle thought their activities should be severely limited, and his views generally prevailed. Plutarch (*Moral Essays,* p. 785) sounds much the same note as Paul does here.

The expression "full submission" needs to be treated intelligently. Vine offers this helpful comment: "The injunction is not directed towards a surrender of mind and conscience, or the abandonment of the duty of private judgment; the phrase 'with all subjection' is a warning against the usurpation of authority, as, e.g., in the next verse" (p. 45).

135

Specifically Paul says, "I do not permit a woman to teach or to have authority over a man." Some have even said that the apostle's prohibition excludes women from teaching Sunday school classes. But he is talking about the public assemblies of the church. Paul speaks appreciatively of the fact that Timothy himself had been taught the right way by his godly mother and grandmother (2 Tim 1:5; 3:15). The apostle also writes to Titus that the older women are to train the younger (Titus 2:3, 4). Women have always carried the major responsibility for teaching small children, in both home and church school. And what could we have done without them!

The word *silent* translates *en hēsychia*, exactly the same phrase that is rendered "in quietness" in v.11. Quietness is an important Christian virtue. Paul was especially opposed to confusion in the public services of the church (1 Cor 14:33).

13,14 The apostle adds that the wife's role of submission to her husband is inherent in creation. Adam was created first, and then Eve.

The story is told in Genesis 2:21–23. The Lord God made Eve from a rib taken from Adam. Matthew Henry pointed out beautifully the implication of this description: "The woman ... was not made out of his head to rule over him, nor out of his feet to be trampled upon by him, but out of his side to be equal with him ... and near his heart to be beloved" (*Commentary*, 1:20). This expresses perfectly the ideal of a happy married life. The husband who has this concept will usually find his wife eager to please him.

Paul makes one further point. It was the woman who was deceived by Satan and who disobeyed God (cf. Gen 3:1–6). Since she was so easily deceived, she should not be trusted as a teacher.

15 This verse is obviously a difficult one to explain. Thousands of godly women have *not* been "kept safe through childbirth."

The passage literally reads, "But she will be saved through the childbirth, if they continue in faith. ..." The verb *sōzō* ("save") is used in the NT for both physical healing (mostly in the Gospels) and spiritual salvation (mostly in the Epistles). Perhaps it carries both connotations here. The wife may find both physical health and a higher spiritual state through the experience of bearing and rearing children. "They" probably means "women" (so NIV), though it could possibly refer to the husband and wife.

Three interpretations of this verse have been suggested. The first emphasizes the use of the definite article with "childbirth" and suggests that the reference is to the birth of Christ, through whom salvation has come to the world. Lock, Ellicott, and some other good modern commentators favor this meaning, but Bernard dismisses it almost with scorn: "The interpretation must be counted among those pious and ingenious flights of fancy, which so often mislead the commentator on Holy Scripture" (pp. 49, 50).

A second interpretation is closely related to this. It connects the statement here with Genesis 3:15. The seed of the woman would crush the serpent's head and bring salvation to mankind.

The third interpretation is suggested by Vine. He writes, "By means of begetting children and so fulfilling the design appointed for her through acceptance of motherhood ... she would be saved from becoming a prey to the social evils of the time and would take her part in the maintenance of the testimony of the local church" (p. 47). This fits best with the context and the main emphasis of this Epistle.

Notes

9 Of σωφροσύνη (sōphrosynē, "propriety"), found in the NT only three times (here, v.15, and Acts 26:25), Trench writes, "It is that habitual inner self-government, with its constant rein on all the passions and desires, which would hinder the temptation to this from arising, or at all events from arising in such strength as should overbear the checks and barriers which aidōs opposed to it" (p. 72).

The word πλέγμα (plegma, "braided") is found only here (in the NT). But a cognate term is used with τριχῶν (trichōn, "hair") in 1 Peter 3:3.

12 "To have authority over" is αὐθεντεῖν (authentein, only here in the NT). It comes from αὐθέντης (authentēs, "one who acts on his own authority").

13 "Formed" is the Greek verb πλάσσω (plassō, only here and in Rom 9:20). It signifies to form or mold. The cognate adjective πλαστός (plastos) gives us our word "plastic"—something molded.

4. Overseers

3:1-7

> ¹Here is a trustworthy saying: If anyone sets his heart on being an overseer, he desires a noble task. ²Now the overseer must be above reproach, the husband of but one wife, temperate, self-controlled, respectable, hospitable, able to teach, ³not given to much wine, not violent but gentle, not quarrelsome, not a lover of money. ⁴He must manage his own family well and see that his children obey him with proper respect. ⁵(If anyone does not know how to manage his own family, how can he take care of God's church?) ⁶He must not be a recent convert, or he may become conceited and fall under the same judgment as the devil. ⁷He must also have a good reputation with outsiders, so that he will not fall into disgrace and into the devil's trap.

This paragraph gives the qualifications for overseers in the church. The requirements are spelled out specifically. For a list similar to that of vv.2-7, see Titus 1:6-9.

1 "Sets his heart on" may well be translated "aspires to" (oregetai). "Being an overseer" is one word, episkopē. It comes from episkopeō, which literally means "look upon," and so "oversee, care for." So the concrete noun episkopos (v.2) means "overseer" and the abstract noun episkopē (v.1) means "office of overseer" (cf. KJV, "the office of a bishop"). The word is used in this sense in one other passage in the NT (Acts 1:20).

The apostle says that one who aspires to the position of overseer in the church "desires a noble task"—and, we might add, a place of heavy responsibility. One needs to be sure that such a desire is not an expression of carnal pride, but that rather it reflects a deep consecration to the work of the church.

2 As we have just noted, episkopos means "overseer." It is translated that way in KJV in Acts 20:28. Elsewhere in the NT it is rendered "bishop" (Phil 1:1; 1 Tim 3:2; Titus 1:7; 1 Peter 2:25). Our word episcopal, of course, comes from it. But Titus 1:6, 7 seems to suggest that "elder" (presbyteros) and "bishop" (episkopos) were the same person. An even more definite proof of this is found in Acts 20. In v.17 we read that Paul sent for the "elders" (presbyterous) of the church at Ephesus. But in v.28 he calls them "overseers" (episkopous). So there were several bishop-elders in each local church. That suggests something far different from the diocesan "bishop" in the ecclesiastical struc-

ture of our day. So it seems best to translate *episkopos* as "overseer" rather than "bishop."

Since the subject of ecclesiastical organization bulks larger in the pastoral Epistles than anywhere else in the NT (see Introduction), it has called for rather extended treatment. Philippians 1:1 mentions the "overseers" (*episkopoi;* KJV, "bishops") and "deacons" (*diakonoi*) in the church at Philippi. The fact that "elders" are not mentioned gives added support to the evidence of the Pastorals that the same leaders in each local congregation were called both elders and overseers.

Now we come to the specific qualifications of an "overseer." Fifteen are listed in vv.2-7. The first is that he must be "above reproach." This is one word in the Greek, the double compound *anepilēmptos* (only here and in 5:7; 6:14). Literally it means "not to be laid hold of." N.J.D. White says it describes "one against whom it is impossible to bring any charge of wrong doing such as could stand impartial examination" (EGT, 4:111). Because it stands at the head of the list, Lock suggests that it means: "Not liable to criticism as he would be if he failed in any of these qualities" (p. 36).

The second qualification is that he must be "the husband of but one wife." The same was required of deacons (v.12). Some have interpreted this as meaning "married only once." By the end of the second century this interpretation was being promulgated, under the influence of an asceticism that led to clerical celibacy in the Roman Catholic Church. Bernard defends this view emphatically. He writes of the phrase here: "It excludes from ecclesiastical position those who have been married more than once" (p. 52). But most commentators agree that it means monogamy—only one wife at one time—and that the overseer must be completely faithful to his wife.

The third qualification is "temperate." The word *nēphalios* in classical Greek meant "not mixed with wine." In later writers it came to have the broader sense of "temperate" or "sober." One of a considerable number of words found only in the pastoral Epistles, it occurs again in v.11 and in Titus 2:2.

The fourth qualification is "self-controlled." *Sōphronos* (in the NT only here and in Titus 1:8; 2:2, 5) means "of sound mind." So it carried the sense of "self-controlled" or "sober-minded."

Fifth in the list is "respectable." This is the same word, *kosmios,* that is translated "modestly"—literally, "with modesty" in 2:9. "Of good behaviour" (KJV) is obviously a rather free rendering. The basic meaning of the word is "orderly." But Greek writers used it in the sense of "respectable" or "honorable." That fits well here.

The sixth qualification is "hospitable." The word *philoxenos* (found again in Titus 1:8; 1 Peter 4:9) literally means "loving strangers." Christians traveling in the first century avoided the public inns with their pagan atmosphere and food that had already been offered to idols (cf. 1 Cor 8). So they would seek out a Christian home in which to stop for the night. A valuable by-product was that believers from widely scattered areas would get to know each other, thus cementing lines of fellowship. So hospitality was an important Christian virtue in that day. Even in our modern hotel-motel age it can have its place.

The seventh item is "able to teach" (*didaktikos,* "didactic," only here and in 2 Tim 2:24). Vine makes this helpful comment: "Not merely a readiness to teach is implied, but the spiritual power to do so as the outcome of prayerful meditation in the Word of God and the practical application of its truth to oneself" (p. 51).

3 The eighth qualification for an overseer is that he must not be "given to much wine." The last four words represent one word in Greek, *paroinos* (literally, "beside wine"), "lingering with the cup." It is one of several terms found only here and in the parallel

list in Titus (1:7). Aristotle's use of this and related words suggests that it meant "tipsy" or "rowdy." It is a sad commentary on the culture of that day that such a warning would have to be given concerning church overseers.

Ninth on the list is "not violent"—literally, "not a striker" (*mē plēktēn*, only here and in Titus 1:7). The person who is given to wine is apt to become involved in drunken brawls.

This verse has four negative items and one positive one, "gentle" (*epieikēs*, five times in the NT). This is the word that Matthew Arnold translated "sweet reasonableness." E.K. Simpson says: "*Epieikēs* defies exact translation ... *Gracious, kindly, forbearing, considerate, magnanimous, genial,* all approximate to its idea" (p. 51).

The eleventh item is "not quarrelsome" (*amachos*, only here and in Titus 3:2). The word literally means "abstaining from fighting" or "noncombatant." Here it is used in the metaphorical sense of "not contentious." A contentious leader is a sad feature in any church.

Number twelve is "not a lover of money"—all one word in the Greek, *aphilargyros* (only here and in Heb 13:5). The love of money (cf. 6:10) is one of the greatest dangers confronting every Christian worker. One who finds that he can make big money in part-time secular work is apt to be diverted from an effective ministry.

4,5 Verses two and three list a dozen qualifications for overseers (most of them a single adjective in Greek). Now we come to three more that are stated at greater length. The first of these covers two verses. The overseer of the church must be one who can "manage his own family well." His children must be obedient and respectful. This implies that the overseer would normally be a married man.

In v.5 Paul makes the logical point, in the form of a question, that if one cannot "manage" (KJV, "rule") his own house, he should not be expected to take proper care of God's church. It is an argument from the lesser to the greater, and the case is clear and incontrovertible. (In this passage "church" clearly means a local congregation.)

6 The overseer must not be "a recent convert" (KJV, "a novice"). The Greek word (only here in the NT) is *neophytos* ("neophyte") an adjective that literally means "newly planted." Here it is used metaphorically, as a substantive, for a new convert.

The reason for this prohibition is spelled out in the rest of the verse. There is danger that such a person might "become conceited." This is the verb *typhoō* (only here and in 6:4; 2 Tim 3:4). It comes from *typhos*, "smoke," and so literally means to "wrap in smoke." But in the NT it is always used metaphorically in the passive in the sense of being "puffed up" with pride.

When this happens, the person will "fall under the same judgment as the devil." We believe that only God is uncreated and so it is he who created all life. But we also know (Gen 1) that God pronounced "good" all that he created. It follows, then, that Satan was created by God as a good creature. It is generally assumed that Satan is a fallen archangel, and that the cause of his fall was pride. All proud people are subject to the same judgment as he.

7 The fifteenth and last qualification of an overseer that is given here is that he must "have a good reputation with outsiders"—literally, "a good testimony from those outside." When a leader in the church has a bad reputation in the community, it often brings irreparable damage to the local congregation and indeed to the entire cause of Christ.

A church leader must have a good reputation "so that he will not fall into disgrace and into the devil's trap"—literally, "the snare of the devil." This could be taken as the snare in which the devil was caught, that is, pride. But most commentators feel that it means the snare or trap which the devil lays for unsuspecting Christians. This is clearly the meaning in 2 Timothy 2:26—"escape from the trap of the devil, who has taken them captive to do his will."

Paul's careful concern for the right choice of leaders in the church, and the extensive qualifications listed here, should serve as guidelines for those who are charged with the responsibility of such selection today. Attention at this point could save much grief.

Notes

1 The familiar formula "Here is a trustworthy saying" (cf. 1:15) was applied by Chrysostom and others—both ancient and modern—to the end of the previous chapter. But probably NIV is correct in indicating that it applies to what follows (the last part of v.1).
2 For "the husband of but one wife"—lit., "a husband of one wife"—Lock lists no fewer than five distinct interpretations: a bishop must (1) be a married man; (2) not be a polygamist; (3) be a faithful husband, having no mistress or concubine; (4) not divorce one wife and marry another; (5) not marry a second time after the wife's death. He properly rejects the first and last, but supports the other three. The word *but* is added before "one wife" in NIV apparently to avoid the possibility of taking the passage as condemning all second marriages, but it may be doubted whether it succeeds in doing this.
3 The thoughtful reader who compares the KJV rendering of this verse with NIV or NASB will wonder at the wide divergence. The reason is that KJV is based on TR, a Greek text derived from a few late MSS of the Middle Ages, while modern translations are from the Textus Criticus, which is formed from the earliest Gr. MSS that come from the third, fourth, and succeeding centuries.
4,5 "Family" is literally "house," (*oikos*), as in KJV. But here, as in many other places, it clearly means "household." In those days it often included a man's servants, as well as his wife and children.
4 For the meaning of σεμνότης (*semnotēs*, "respect"), see the comments on 2:2.
6,7 Bernard (pp. 56, 57) takes "the devil"—τοῦ διαβόλου (*tou diabolou*, "the slanderer")—as referring to a human accuser or slanderer, who passes judgment on the overseer or catches him in a trap. But παγὶς τοῦ διαβόλου (*pagis tou diabolou*) in 2 Tim 2:26 clearly refers to the "snare of the devil" and should be taken that way here.

5. Deacons

3:8–13

8Deacons, likewise, are to be men worthy of respect, sincere, not indulging in much wine, and not pursuing dishonest gain. 9They must keep hold of the deep truths of the faith with a clear conscience. 10They must first be tested; and then if there is nothing against them, let them serve as deacons.

11In the same way, their wives are to be women worthy of respect, not malicious talkers but temperate and trustworthy in everything.

12A deacon must be the husband of but one wife and must manage his children and his household well. 13Those who have served well gain an excellent standing and great assurance in their faith in Christ Jesus.

In vv.1–7 we find the qualifications for the overseers of the church. Here in vv.8–13 are the qualifications for deacons.

8 The word *deacon* comes from the Greek *diakonos*. The simple meaning of this word is "servant," and it is used that way many times in the Gospels. Specifically, it was used by Josephus and other writers of that period for those who wait on tables.

This leads us to chapter 6 of Acts. The apostles as overseers of the church in Jerusalem did not have time to take care of the material needs of the poorer members, such as the widows. They said, "It would not be right for us to neglect the ministry of the word of God in order to wait on tables" (Acts 6:2, where the verb *diakoneō* is used). So the church chose seven men to assume this responsibility, while the apostles gave their attention to public "prayer and the ministry of the word" (v.4). Although the term *deacon* is not used in this connection, it would seem that these men were the forerunners of the deacons in the church.

The term is first used in a technical sense in Philippians 1:1. That Epistle is addressed to "all the saints in Christ Jesus at Philippi, together with the overseers and deacons"—those in charge of the spiritual life of the church and those who supervised its material affairs. This distinction of two groups with differing functions is prominent in the pastoral Epistles.

Paul says that the deacons, like the overseers, are to be men "worthy of respect." This is one word in Greek, the adjective *semnos* (cf. the noun *semnotēs* in 2:2 and 3:4). Vine says of this term: "No English word exactly conveys the meaning of *semnos*, which combines the thoughts both of gravity and dignity," or, as Moule points out, "both of seriousness of purpose and self-respect in conduct" (p. 55).

In the second place, the deacons are to be "sincere"—literally, "not double-tongued." The adjective *dilogos* (only here in the NT) has the idea of saying something twice, with the bad connotation of saying one thing to one person and something else to another. Bunyan typically speaks in *Pilgrim's Progress* of "the parson of our parish, Mr. Two-Tongues." Metaphorically, the word means "insincere," and "not insincere" becomes "sincere."

The third qualification is "not indulging in much wine." This is a longer and stronger expression than that found in v.3 in relation to the overseers.

Item number four is "not pursuing dishonest gain" (*mē aischrokerdeis*, only here and in Titus 1:7). The adjective is compounded of *aischros* ("base, shameful") and *kerdos* ("gain") and so means "fond of dishonest gain."

9 KJV gives a literal rendering of this verse: "Holding the mystery of the faith in a pure conscience." The word *mystērion* was used in that day for a secret that was unknown to the masses but disclosed to the initiated. In the NT it signifies the secret of salvation through Jesus Christ, which is revealed by the Holy Spirit to all who will believe. Today the word *mystery* implies knowledge withheld; in the Bible it indicates truth revealed. That is the reason for the change in translation.

Probably "the faith" is to be taken in an objective sense, referring to the truths of the Christian religion, rather than as subjective, having to do with one's personal faith in Christ.

This Epistle has a strong emphasis on a pure conscience as well as a pure faith. We have already had the expression "a good conscience" twice (1:5, 19). Vine writes, "A pure conscience is that which has been cleansed by the blood of Christ, Heb. 10:22, and is exercised to avoid offence towards God and men, Acts 24:16" (p. 56).

10 Deacons "must first be tested" (KJV, "proved"). The verb *dokimazō* has three stages: (1) test, (2) prove by testing; (3) approve as the result of testing. Perhaps all three are in mind here. Before men were accepted as deacons they had to prove themselves before the community. Then they could serve as deacons, "if there is nothing against them"— literally, "being not called in" (*anenklētos*, "not called to account," and so, "irreproachable").

11 In the Greek language the same word, *gynē*, is used for "woman" and "wife." Since this single word is found here for "their wives," there are three possible interpretations as to what group Paul is talking about.

NIV follows KJV in assuming that these women were the wives of the deacons. The main argument against this is that the word for "their" is missing in the Greek. Yet Vine feels that this meaning is "probable."

Some have suggested that he is speaking of women in general. But the context of vv.8–12 would seem to rule this out.

White argues strongly that the reference is to deaconesses, of whom Phoebe (Rom 16:1) is an example (EGT, 4:115, 116). He would take these as a separate group of church officials. The same view is maintained by Bernard (pp. 58, 59) and Lock (pp. 40, 41). We know that there were deaconesses in the church in later centuries; but whether there was such an order in the first century is debatable.

Hendriksen takes somewhat of a mediating position. He writes,

> They are a group by themselves, not just the wives of the deacons nor *all* the women who belong to the church. . . . On the other hand, the fact that no special and separate paragraph is used in describing their necessary qualifications, but that these are simply wedged in between the stipulated requirements for deacons, with equal clarity indicates that these women are not to be regarded as constituting a third order in the church, the office of 'deaconesses,' on a par with and endowed with authority equal to that of deacons (pp. 132, 133).

In spite of this weight of scholarly opinion, we are still inclined to favor the idea that the reference is to "their wives." Paul talks about the qualifications of the deacons in vv.8–10 and again in vv.12, 13. It would seem natural to assume that he is talking about their wives in v.11.

He says that these women—whoever they are—must, "in the same way" as the deacons, be "worthy of respect." This is the same adjective (*semna*, fem.) as in v.8 (masc.).

They are also not to be "malicious talkers." This is one word in Greek, the adjective *diabolos*, which means "slanderous, accusing falsely." It can well be translated here as "slanderous." But most versions take it as a substantive (e.g., "slanderers," KJV). This note was a needed warning in the early church, and is still needed today.

For a discussion of "temperate," see the comments on v.2. It was necessary that the wives as well as the husbands have this virtue.

"Trustworthy in everything" is a comprehensive requirement. Church workers must not be lax in taking care of their assigned duties.

12 Now Paul returns to the specific qualifications of deacons. He says that the deacon, like the overseer (v.2), must be the husband of one wife. He must also "manage his children and his household well" (cf. v.4). The Greek word for "household" (*oikos*) is the same as that translated "family" in v.4.

13 Those who serve well in their assigned duties in the church are gaining (present

tense) for themselves (*heautois*) "an excellent standing" (KJV, "a good degree"). The noun *bathmos* (only here in the NT) literally means "a step," and so metaphorically "standing" or "rank." Some think this suggests promotion to a higher rank (e.g., overseer). Others think it means great respect in the eyes of the church. Still others would relate it to good standing in God's sight. Probably the best interpretation is a combination of the last two.

"Great assurance" in relation to men or in relation to God? Again, why not both? Often a both/and interpretation is more reasonable than an either/or, and is certainly more fruitful. Christian workers should have "an excellent standing and great assurance" in relation to both God and their fellowmen.

Notes

---

8 William Barclay (*More New Testament Words* [New York: Harper, 1958], pp. 144, 145) writes, "*Semnos* is the word which describes the man who carries himself towards other men with a combination of dignified independence and kindly consideration. . . . The Christian should be *semnos*; he should ever display in his life the majesty of Christian living."

11 *Diabolos*, usually with the definite article, is tr. "devil" some thirty-five times in the NT. Only here (and possibly in vv.6, 7; see comments there) and in 2 Tim 3:3 and Titus 2:3 is it used of human beings as slanderers. Judas is called "a devil" in John 6:70.

13 The noun παρρησία (*parrēsia*) first meant "freedom or plainness of speech." Then it came to be used more generally for "courage, confidence, boldness." BAG tr. it here as "joyousness" or "confidence" toward God that is the result or accompaniment of faith (p. 636).

---

6. The Mystery of Godliness

3:14-16

14Although I hope to come to you soon, I am writing you these instructions so that, 15if I am delayed, you will know how people ought to conduct themselves in God's household which is the church of the living God, the pillar and foundation of the truth. 16Beyond all question, the mystery of godliness is great:

> He appeared in a body,
>   was vindicated by the Spirit,
> was seen by angels,
>   was preached among the nations,
> was believed on in the world,
>   was taken up in glory.

14,15 Paul was hoping to visit Timothy soon. But just in case he was delayed, he was writing to his young associate so that Timothy might know "how people ought to conduct themselves in God's household." The KJV rendering "how thou oughtest to behave thyself" is out of keeping with the context. The apostle is laying down rules for church members and their leaders. This is a summary of what we find in chapters 2, 3.

"The house of God" (KJV) might well be taken by readers as meaning a church building; so "God's household" is a more adequate translation. This is "the church of the living God." The language of v.5 suggests that the primary reference is to the local congregation, although the general church of Jesus Christ may also be in view.

This church is "the pillar and the foundation of the truth." The idea of "pillar" is that of support, which is further strengthened by "foundation" or mainstay (*hedraiōma*, only here in the NT). Taken together, these two terms emphasize the certainty and firmness of "the truth" that is revealed in God's Word. The meaning of this clause is well expressed by Lock: "Each local Church has it in its power to support and strengthen the truth by its witness to the faith and by the lives of its members" (p. 44).

16 "Beyond all question" (KJV, "without controversy") is *homologoumenōs*, "confessedly." Found only here in the NT, it may be translated "by common agreement" or "by common profession." The "mystery of godliness" is "the revealed secret of true religion, the mystery of Christianity, the Person of Christ" (Lock, p. 44). It is particularly the incarnate Christ who is revealed here in the striking credal statement that follows.

In KJV the first word of the creed is "God" (*theos*). But the oldest Greek MSS have *hos*, "he who" as the subject of "appeared." The verb (*phaneroō*) means, in the active voice, "make visible, clear, manifest, or known." The eternal Son of God, existing as pure spirit, was made visible, was manifested, in his incarnation. "Incarnation" is from the Latin and literally means "in flesh," which is exactly what the Greek has here (*en sarki*).

In the second place, Christ "was vindicated by the Spirit"; "the Redeemer's profound claims are vindicated on the basis of His Deity" (Simpson, p. 61). Christ's miracles, climaxing in his resurrection, were demonstrations of his deity, sure evidences that he was the sinless Son of God. (The word *vindicated* is *edikaiōthē*, usually tr. "justified.")

The third line of this credal hymn reads, "was seen by angels." This may refer to the fact that during his earthly ministry angels watched over him (Matt 4:11; Luke 22:43).

The fourth statement is that he "was preached among the nations." The Greek *ethnesin* literally means "nations" but is often translated "Gentiles" (KJV), as distinct from Jews. This preaching among the Gentiles took place, of course, after Christ's death. It will be noted that what was preached was not a theory or even a creed, but a Person. Paul declared, "We preach Christ" (1 Cor 1:23).

In the fifth place, he "was believed on in the world" (*kosmos*). This follows closely from the previous line, for the true preaching of Christ produces faith in him on the part of many hearers.

The last statement is that he "was taken up in glory." The same verb (*analambanō*) is used of Christ's ascension in Acts 1:2. This was the climax of his earthly ministry. Preaching Christ means preaching his life, death, resurrection, and ascension as the glorified Lord.

Notes

16 In the earliest Gr. MSS of the NT "God" is usually written in abbreviated form. Instead of θεός (*theos*) we find ΘC. This could easily be confused with the relative pronoun OC, meaning "who." Most scholars agree that the pronoun is more probably the original reading. But the meaning is much the same, as the antecedent could well be "God" (v.15). Even if it is taken as "Christ Jesus" (v.13), his deity is clearly implied here.

VI. Special Instructions to Timothy (4:1-16)

1. *False Ascetism*

4:1-5

¹The Spirit clearly says that in later times some will abandon the faith and follow deceiving spirits and things taught by demons. ²Such teachings come through hypocritical liars, whose consciences have been seared as with a hot iron. ³They forbid people to marry and order them to abstain from certain foods, which God created to be received with thanksgiving by those who believe and who know the truth. ⁴For everything God created is good, and nothing is to be rejected if it is received with thanksgiving, ⁵because it is consecrated by the word of God and prayer.

1 This chapter consists of special instructions given to Timothy on various subjects. Verses 1-5 discuss the matter of ascetic teachings.

The Holy Spirit says "clearly"—*rhētōs* means "expressly" or "explicitly"—that in later times some people will "abandon" the faith. The verb means "to withdraw." For this passage BAG gives "fall away, become apostate."

Instead of being led by the Holy Spirit, these apostates give their attention to deceiving spirits and the teaching of "demons." Since this last word occurs only here in the pastoral Epistles, we might pause to look at it. KJV has "devils," and British scholars still use this term (cf. NEB). But in the Greek there is a clear distinction between *daimonion* ("demon," often in the pl.) and *diabolos* ("devil," regularly in the sing.). The NT clearly teaches that there are many "demons" but only one "devil." The plural of *diabolos* occurs only in the Pastorals (1 Tim 3:11; 2 Tim 3:3; Titus 2:3), where it is used for human "slanderers."

The expression "in later times" is not as strong as the phrase "in the last days" (2 Tim 3:1). The conditions that Paul is discussing here evidently took place during his lifetime.

2 The apostle uses strong language in describing the teachers of the false doctrines he is about to mention. He declares that they are "hypocritical liars" (*en hypocrisei pseudologōn*, "speaking falsely in hypocrisy"). This implies that they know better. They have deliberately forsaken the faith. They are men whose consciences "have been seared as with a hot iron"—all one word in Greek: *kekaustēriasmenōn*, "branded with a red-hot iron." They have been "seared in their own conscience," so that they have become unfeeling about their willful wrongdoings. Some commentators, however, feel that the meaning is that they have been branded as sinners, as the slaves of Satan.

3 Paul mentions two of their false teachings: "They forbid people to marry and order them to abstain from certain foods." This ascetic emphasis crept into the church in the first century and was widely felt in the second century, under the influence of Gnosticism. The Gnostics taught that all matter is evil; only spirit is good. So all physical pleasure is sin. Holiness was identified with asceticism. This was the error that the Jewish sect of the Essenes had made, and it cropped up early in Christianity.

What these false teachers forgot is that marriage "is ordained by God," as we are reminded at weddings. God clearly established marriage as the normal thing in human society. Those who commend celibacy as being more holy or religious are promoting the heresy of Gnosticism, not the teaching of the NT. Paul uses powerful language (v.2) to describe those who forbid people to marry—as some still do.

The idea of abstaining from certain foods goes back, of course, to the Mosaic law. But Christ has freed us from the Law (Gal 5:1-6). We are no longer under its restrictions regarding certain kinds of food, "which God created to be received with thanksgiving by those who believe and who know the truth." Only those "whose faith is weak" avoid eating meat and restrict themselves to a vegetable diet (Rom 14:1, 2). In spite of this, some still advocate and practice vegetarianism in the name of Christianity. Paul deals much more severely with this heresy in 1 Timothy than he did in Romans. Evidently the false teaching of asceticism was spreading in the church and the apostle struck out forcefully against it as a negation of our freedom in Christ—which is true Christianity.

4,5 The simple fact is that "everything God created is good." This is an echo of the first chapter of Genesis, where the statement "God saw that it was good" occurs no fewer than five times (vv.10, 12, 18, 21, 25). It is true that vegetarianism may have prevailed before the flood (cf. Gen 2:9, 16), but God clearly told Noah that animals could be eaten as food, as well as vegetables and grains (Gen 9:3).

Paul declares that "nothing is to be rejected [*apoblēton,* 'thrown away,' only here in NT] if it is received with thanksgiving." This perhaps underscores the importance of "offering thanks" always before we eat, and this is reinforced by v.5: "because it is consecrated by the word of God and prayer." The Greek for "consecrated" is *hagiazetai,* "made holy." Lock writes, "It becomes holy to the eater; not that it was unclean in itself, but that his scruples or thanklessness might make it so to him" (p. 48). "The word of God" may suggest the use of Scripture phrases when saying grace at the table. White thinks it may also mean "a scriptural prayer; a prayer in harmony with God's revealed truth" (EGT, 4:122).

2. Superiority of the Spiritual

4:6-10

> 6If you point these things out to the brothers, you will be a good minister of Christ Jesus, brought up in the truths of the faith and of the good teaching that you have followed. 7Have nothing to do with godless myths and old wives' tales; rather, train yourself to be godly. 8For physical training is of some value, but godliness has value for all things, holding promise for both the present life and the life to come.
>
> 9This is a trustworthy saying that deserves full acceptance 10(and for this we labor and strive), that we have put our hope in the living God, who is the Savior of all men, and especially of those who believe.

6 Paul tells Timothy that if he calls the attention of "the brothers" (believers) to these truths, he will be a good "minister" (*diakonos,* "servant," but probably carrying here the modern technical connotation of "minister"). To be "a good minister of Christ Jesus" should be the aim of every pastor today.

Timothy had been "brought up [*entrephomenos,* 'trained up' or 'nurtured,' only here in the NT] in the truths [*logois,* lit., 'words'] of the faith." His earliest training was in Judaism, but he had been converted as a young man to Christianity. He had "followed" its teachings. The Greek verb *parakoloutheō* comes from *akoloutheō,* "follow," and *para,* "beside." So it suggests that he had "closely followed" the teachings of the new religion.

7,8 "Godless myths and old wives' tales" is literally "profane and old-womanish myths." The second adjective, *graōdēs* (only here in the NT) means "characteristic of old women." The reference is to "tall tales" such as elderly women love to tell children. That is the way Paul describes the Jewish legends of his day (cf. Titus 1:14).

Instead of giving himself to these, Timothy is admonished: "Train yourself to be godly." The word for "train" (KJV, "exercise") is *gymnaze.* "Physical training" (KJV, "bodily exercise") rather clearly refers to athletic discipline. Some think that in view of the earlier verses ascetic discipline may also be included. But would the apostle assign any worth to it? The Greek word for "training" is *gymnasia,* from which we get "gymnasium."

Paul concedes that physical training "is of some value." KJV says "profiteth little," which is probably too derogatory. The Greek *pros oligon* could be translated "for a little time"—that is, for this life. "For all things" would then suggest "for all time," or forever. Literally, the passage says that bodily gymnastics are beneficial (*ōphelimos,* "useful, profitable") "for a little." This certainly does not mean that physical exercise is of no value. But spiritual exercise is far more important, for it has value for eternity—"holding promise for both the present life and the life to come."

9,10 Again we find the formula, "This is a trustworthy saying that deserves full acceptance" (cf. 1:15). The consensus of commentators is that this refers to the preceding statement (v.8). The NIV rendering follows the punctuation of UBS, which connects v.9 with v.10. This is the interpretation of NEB, which puts a colon at the end of v.9 and begins v.10 with a quotation mark. But even NEB follows most of the other versions in translating *hoti* ("that," after parenthesis in NIV) as "because." The NIV treatment of the first clause of v.10 (making it parenthetical) is unique. But this is perhaps logical if we connect v.9 with v.10.

"Labor" and "strive" are both strong terms in the Greek. The first verb (*kopiaō*) means "grow weary" and so in the NT "work with effort, toil." The second (*agōnizō,* "agonize") was used for competing in an athletic contest. So it meant "struggle" or "strive." Just as athletes exert what seems to be their last ounce of energy to win a race, so Paul was giving the ministry all he had.

God is "the Savior of all men, and especially of those who believe." This statement has provoked much discussion. In what sense is he the Savior of all men? To interpret this in terms of universal salvation would be contrary to the whole tenor of Scripture.

Hendriksen explains at considerable length how God is the Savior of all people in the general sense of watching over them and delivering them. But it seems best to adopt the more familiar interpretation that God is potentially the Savior of all men, because of Calvary, but actually the Savior of those who believe.

Notes

6 The best Gr. text, based on the earliest MSS, has "Christ Jesus" rather than "Jesus Christ." The order of these two words is much confused in the MSS, due in part to the custom of abbreviating them, using only the first and last letters. In the Gr. the last letters are the same and the first letters look more alike than in English.

9 For the last clause of this verse Hendriksen prefers, "as it holds promise of life both for the present and for the future" (p. 152).

10 "Suffer reproach" (KJV) has very little MS support in the Gr. It translates ὀνειδιζόμεθα (*oneidizometha*). But ἀγωνιζόμεθα (*agōnizometha,* "strive") is clearly the correct reading.

3. Pastoral Duties

4:11-16

> [11]Command and teach these things. [12]Don't let anyone look down on you because you are young, but set an example for the believers in speech, in life, in love, in faith and in purity. [13]Until I come, devote yourself to the public reading of Scripture, to preaching and to teaching. [14]Do not neglect your gift, which was given you through a prophetic message when the body of elders laid their hands on you.
> [15]Be diligent in these matters; give yourself wholly to them, so that everyone may see your progress. [16]Watch your life and doctrine closely. Persevere in them, because if you do, you will save both yourself and your hearers.

11 "Command" and "teach" are both in the present tense of continuous action. Timothy is to keep on doing these two things. He is to exercise his authority as pastor.

12 Timothy was urged to conduct himself in such a way that no one would look down in a condescending way on his youthfulness. The word for "youth" (KJV) is *neotēs*, "used of grown-up military age, extending to the 40th year" (Lock, p. 52). Timothy was probably about thirty years old at this time.

On the positive side, he was to be "an example." The word *typos* (cf. "type") meant "a figure, image" and then ethically "an example, pattern." Timothy was to present the proper image of the Christian and he was to be a pattern for other believers to follow. This is an awesome responsibility that one accepts on entering the ministry.

He was to be an example in "speech" (*logos*, "word"), in "life" (*anastrophē*, "manner of living," not "conversation," KJV), and in "love" (*agapē*), "faith" (*pistis*), and "purity" (*hagneia*, only here and in 5:2). These are all vital constituents of Christian living. Carelessness in any one of these areas can spell failure and even disaster.

13 Until Paul came, Timothy was to devote himself "to the public reading of Scripture." The Greek simply says "to the reading," but the NIV rendering is undoubtedly correct. The early church followed the example of the Jewish synagogue in publicly reading the Scriptures at every service.

He was also to give himself to "preaching" (*paraklēsis*, lit., "exhortation"). This is an important part of every pastor's duties. He must not only read the Word of God to his people but also exhort them to obey it.

The third important function of the pastoral ministry is "teaching" (*didaskalia*). The people need instruction in Christian living, and the pastor should give it to them.

14 Paul has some more advice to give his younger colleague: "Do not neglect your gift" (*charismatos*). The term *charisma* occurs sixteen times in Paul's Epistles and only once elsewhere in the NT (1 Peter 4:10). It comes from the root *charis*, "grace," and so means "*a gift of grace, a free gift*, especially of extraordinary operations of the Spirit in the apostolic church but including all spiritual graces and endowments" (A-S, pp. 479, 480).

The verb *ameleō*, "neglect," is not used elsewhere by Paul. It literally means to be careless about something. Bernard rightly observes: "To neglect God's gifts, whether of nature or of grace, is a sin" (p. 72).

This gift was "given you through a prophetic message"—literally, "through prophecy" (*prophēteia*)—when "the body of elders"—one word in Greek, *presbyterion*—"laid their hands on you." We are not told when or where this happened. Lock thinks that this ceremony took place at Ephesus when Paul left Timothy there (p. 54). We find similar references in 1:18 and 2 Timothy 1:6.

15 "Be diligent" is *meleta*. The verb *meletaō* comes from *meletē*, "care." So it literally means "care for." It was used frequently by Greek writers of that period in the sense of "practice, cultivate, take pains with," and that is the meaning assigned to it in this passage by BAG. But it can also mean "think about, meditate upon" (cf. KJV), as it does in the only other place where it occurs in the NT, in a quotation from LXX (Acts 4:25; NIV, "plot"). Bernard prefers the translation "ponder these things" for our passage (p. 73).

There is a play on words here in the Greek that does not come through in English. In v.14 Paul says, "Do not neglect" (*amelei*, *melō* with *a*-negative). In v.15 he says, "Be diligent" (*meleta*). What he is saying is "Don't be careless about your gift, but be careful about your pastoral duties."

"Give yourself wholly to them" (also in KJV) is literally, "Be in these things" (*toutois isthi*). NASB puts it well: "Be *absorbed* in them." But NIV represents the thought accurately.

The purpose of this was that everybody might see Timothy's "progress." The term *prokopē* (only here and in Phil 1:12, 25) was "a favourite word in Stoic writers of a pupil's progress in philosophy" (Lock, p. 54). Timothy was to make progress in his own spiritual life and in his effectiveness in the ministry.

16 "Watch your life and doctrine closely." This is a good way of representing the Greek, which says, "Give attention to yourself and to the teaching." The first thing that every Christian worker must watch is himself, not only his outward life but also his inner thoughts and feelings. No matter how straight a person may be in his doctrine or how effective he may be in his teaching, if there is a flaw in his inner or outer life, it will ruin him. This is where many ministers have failed tragically. While he is watching over others, the pastor must keep an eye on himself.

"Persevere" is *epimene*, which literally means "stay" or "remain" and then figuratively (as here), "continue, persist in, persevere." Paul is saying to Timothy, "Stay right in there; keep on doing the things I have called your attention to."

By so doing, the pastor will save both himself and his hearers. For a soul-winner to save others and lose his own soul is an unmitigated tragedy. For one to save his own soul and have his hearers lost is no less tragic. We must give attention to both.

VII. Special Groups in the Church (5:1–6:2)

1. The Older and the Younger

5:1, 2

> [1]Do not rebuke an older man harshly, but exhort him as if he were your father. Treat younger men as brothers, [2]older women as mothers, and younger women as sisters, with absolute purity.

1 "Do not rebuke an older man harshly." The reason for adding the modifier "harshly" to "rebuke" (KJV) is that the verb *epiplēssō* (only here in the NT) literally means "strike at." Older men are to be treated with gentleness and kindness.

"Older man" is better than "elder" (KJV), since the latter term has a technical use in the pastoral Epistles for an overseer in the church. That "older man" is the correct meaning is shown by the parallel in v.2: "older women."

"Exhort" and "intreat" (KJV) are both correct translations of *parakaleō*, which also means "encourage." Goodspeed puts it well: "But appeal to him as to a father."

The "younger men" are to be treated as brothers. Grammatically, the verb *exhort* carries through to the end of v.2.

As a young man, Timothy was to treat the "older women" as mothers. Even today in that part of the world an elderly woman is greeted as "mother." Fortunate is the young pastor who has godly "mothers in Israel" in his congregation.

In relation to "younger women," a needed caution is added. They are to be treated as sisters—because the Christians are all one family in the Lord—but "with absolute purity." The pastor who does not heed this warning will soon be in trouble. BAG translates "with all propriety."

2. Widows

5:3-16

> 3Give proper recognition to widows who are left all alone. 4But if a widow has children or grandchildren, these should learn first of all to put their religion into practice by caring for their own family and so repaying their parents and grandparents, for this is pleasing to God. 5The widow who is all alone puts her hope in God and continues night and day to pray and to ask God for help. 6But the widow who lives for pleasure is dead even while she lives. 7Give the people these instructions, too, so that no one may be open to blame. 8If anyone does not provide for his relatives, and especially for his immediate family, he has denied the faith and is worse than an unbeliever.
>
> 9No widow may be put on the list of widows unless she is over sixty, has been faithful to her husband, 10and is well-known for her good deeds, such as bringing up children, showing hospitality, washing the feet of the saints, helping those in trouble and devoting herself to all kinds of good deeds.
>
> 11As for younger widows, do not put them on such a list. For when their sensual desires overcome their dedication to Christ, they want to marry. 12Thus they bring judgment on themselves, because they have broken their first pledge. 13Besides, they get into the habit of being idle and going about from house to house. And not only do they become idlers, but also gossips and busybodies, saying things they ought not to. 14So I counsel younger widows to marry, to have children, to manage their homes and to give the enemy no opportunity for slander. 15Some have in fact already turned away to follow Satan.
>
> 16If any woman who is a believer has widows in her family, she should help them and not let the church be burdened with them, so that the church can help those widows who are really in need.

3 "Give proper recognition to" is explicatory of "honour" (KJV). The verb *timaō* comes from the noun *timē*, which means first "price" or "value" and then "honor" or "reverence." In view of the following context, it could possibly mean "give proper compensation to" widows in real need. "Who are left all alone" is literally "who are really [*ontos*] widows." Goodspeed catches the thought: "Look after widows who are really dependent."

4 The case is different with widows who have children or "grandchildren" (*ekgona*, only here in the NT). In explanation of "nephews" in KJV, the *Oxford English Dictionary* (7:91) notes that in the seventeenth century (when KJV appeared) the term *nephew*

was commonly used for a grandson, though that meaning is now obsolete. Paul is saying here that if a widow has children or grandchildren, they are to take care of her.

"To put their religion into practice by caring for their own family" is literally "to show piety toward [*eusebein*] one's own household." This would be shown especially by "repaying"—literally, "to give" (*apodidonai*) "recompenses" (*amoibas*, only here in the NT)—to their "parents and grandparents" (*progonois*). This word (only here and in 2 Tim 1:3) may mean either parents or ancestors (literally, "born before")—hence the dual translation in the NIV. BAG translates the whole clause, "make a return to those who brought them up." This is "pleasing" (or, "acceptable") to God.

The Jewish synagogues gave careful attention to the care of their widows, and the early church followed that custom (Acts 6:1). This was due to the fact that in the culture of those days a widow could not ordinarily find any employment and so would need financial support. Today, with insurance income, social security, and job opportunities, the situation is very different. But each church should still see that no widow in its congregation is left destitute. Christian love demands this, and it is especially appropriate in view of the NT concept that all believers are one in Christ, fellow members of the family of God. We should care for each other.

5 This verse gives the characteristics of a true Christian widow. She is first identified as "the widow who is all alone"—literally, "the one who is a real widow and left all alone" (*memonōmenē*, perfect passive participle of *monoō*, "leave alone," only here in the NT). This means that she is childless.

Such a woman puts her hope in God, for she has no earthly hopes. So she "continues night and day to pray and ask God for help"—literally, "continues in her supplications and her prayers night and day." One is reminded of the widow Anna, who was eighty-four years old. We are told that "she never left the temple but worshiped night and day, fasting and praying" (Luke 2:37).

6 In contrast with that picture is this statement: "But the widow who lives for pleasure is dead even while she lives." The expression "lives for pleasure" is one word in Greek, the verb *spatalaō*. It means to live luxuriously or self-indulgently. White comments, "The modern term *fast*, in which the notion of prodigality and wastefulness is more prominent than that of sensual indulgence, exactly expresses the significance of this word" (EGT, 4:129).

7 Timothy is to "give the people these instructions." *Tauta parangelle* can have the stronger meaning, "command these things," but perhaps NIV is best. The purpose of the instruction is "that no one may be open to blame"—literally, "that they may be irreproachable" (*anepilēmptoi*).

8 Paul speaks strongly on this matter of caring for the needy. He declares that if anyone does not "provide for" (*pronoeō* lit., "think of beforehand," and so "take thought for") his own (relatives) and especially those of his own family, "he has denied the faith and is worse than an unbeliever." White observes, "The Christian who falls below the best heathen standard of family affection is the more blameworthy, since he has, what the heathen has not, the supreme example of love in Jesus Christ" (EGT, 4:129).

9,10 Having defined who a real widow is—one bereft of all relatives to take care of her—Paul now restricts the matter further. He gives instructions that no widow under sixty years of age should be "put on the list" (*katalegō*, only here in the NT, "enrolled"). It seems evident that an official list of widows was kept by each church and that only these received material support.

The further stipulation is made that she must have "been faithful to her husband"— literally, the "wife of one man." This is exactly the same sort of expression as is found in the qualifications for overseers (3:2) and deacons (3:12). As we noted there, only scholars with strong ascetic or ecclesiastical bias insist that this means "only once married." Verse 14 shows that widows were not forbidden to remarry.

To qualify for enrollment, a widow must also be well known for her good deeds. Several of these are spelled out. The first is "bringing up children"—one word in Greek, the verb *teknotropheō* (only here in the NT). This would most naturally refer to her own children but could include the care of orphans. The second is "showing hospitality." This is also one word in Greek, *xenodocheō* (only here in the NT)—literally, "welcome strangers" (cf. *philoxenos* in 3:2). The third item is "washing the feet of the saints." This was an important courtesy whenever guests entered a house. So this function belonged to that culture.

The verse closes with two more general duties: "helping those in trouble and devoting herself to all kinds of good deeds" (lit., "to every good deed"). This is the kind of a life that the widows were expected to live if they were going to be supported by the church. They were to be helpers, not troublemakers.

11,12 Regarding the widows under sixty years of age, Paul says, "Do not put them on such a list." This is all one word in Greek—*paraitou*, "refuse" or "reject." He goes on to tell why: they are overwhelmed by their feelings and want to marry. "Their sensual desires overcome their dedication" is all one word in Greek, *katastrēniasōsi* (only here in the NT). The verb means "become wanton against." Lock says it here suggests that they "grow physically restless and so restive against the limitations of Christian widowhood" (p. 60). In a similar vein, Bernard comments, "The metaphor is that of a young animal trying to free itself from the yoke, and becoming restive through its fulness of life" (p. 82).

If they do marry, they incur "judgment" (*krima*), or "condemnation" (but not "damnation," KJV). This is because they have "broken" (*ēthetēsan*, "disregarded" or "set aside") their first "pledge" (*pistis*, which may indicate "solemn promise" or "oath"). Lock thinks this means "the original impulse of faith which led her to join the widows; or more exactly 'the first troth' or 'promise of allegiance' made when she joined " (ibid.). It would seem that they promised to be devoted only to Christ.

13 Another risk with younger widows is that "they get into the habit of being"—one word, *manthanousi*, "learn" (to be)—"idle" or inactive. Instead of working, they go from house to house as "gossips"—the adjective *phlyaroi* (only here in the NT), "gossipy, foolish." In their visits to homes they pick up private matters and spread them abroad. This is always a snare to those who go from home to home or church to church.

"Busybodies" is the adjective *periergoi*, "paying attention to things that do not concern one, meddlesome" (BAG). The related verb, *periergazomai*, occurs in 1 Thessalonians 3:11.

As gossips and busybodies, these younger widows were "saying things they ought not to." This always happens when people talk too much. The consequences of this meddling in other people's business can be tragic.

14 In view of these dangers, Paul writes, "So I counsel [*boulomai*] younger widows"—"widows" is not in the Greek but probably is implied by the context—"to marry, to have children [*teknogonein*], to manage their homes" (*oikodespotein*). These last two compound verbs are found only here in the NT. Paul is dealing with new situations and he employs new terms.

The reason for the injunction to marry is that these younger women may "give the enemy no opportunity for slander." The word for "enemy" means "the adversary" (*antikeimenō*), one who opposes. It is generally agreed that the reference here is to a human adversary, not to Satan (who is mentioned in the next verse), although some think it may mean the devil (BAG).

The word for "slander" is *loidoria* (only here and 1 Peter 3:9). It is a strong term meaning "abuse" or "railing." Paul fears that the unfortunate conduct of younger widows might bring serious reproach on the church.

15 He goes on to say that some of them have already turned away to follow "Satan." This is a Hebrew word taken over into Greek and English. Since its literal meaning is "the adversary," it may be that the "enemy" (adversary) of the previous verse is Satan.

16 "Woman who is a believer" is one word in Greek, *pistē*, the feminine of the adjective *pistos*, "believing." "In her family" is not in the Greek, but of course is implied. The woman believer who has widows dependent on her (cf. NASB) "should help them and not let the church be burdened with them." This will free the church to help "those widows who are all alone—literally, "those who are really widows" (cf. v.3).

Notes

7 The adjective ἀνεπίλημπτοι (*anepilēmptoi*, "without blame") is found only in 1 Tim (see 3:2; 6:14). It is compounded of *a*-negative and the verb ἐπιλαμβάνω (*epilambanō*, "lay hold of"). It suggests that there should be nothing in the Christian's life that anyone can seize upon for censure.

8 Τὴν πίστιν (*tēn pistin*, "the faith") is used here in an objective sense, as elsewhere in the Pastorals, for Christianity or the body of Christian doctrine. This fact has been cited as an argument against Pauline authorship. But Paul uses this expression in the same way in his prison Epistles (Eph 4:5; Phil 1:27; Col 2:7).

16 KJV "man or woman" is based on the reading πιστὸς ἢ πιστή (*pistos ē pistē*, "believer [masc.] or believer [fem.]"), found in the late Gr. MSS. Most textual critics prefer the shorter reading πιστή (*pistē*, "believer" [fem.], ℵA,C,), although the translators of NEB chose the longer reading, on the internal argument that this charge would not be laid on women alone (R.V.G. Tasker, *The Greek New Testament*, p. 441).

3. Elders

5:17-25

17The elders who direct the affairs of the church well are worthy of double honor, especially those whose work is preaching and teaching. **18**For the Scripture says, "Do not muzzle the ox while it is treading out the grain," and "The worker deserves his wages." **19**Do not entertain an accusation against an elder unless it is brought by two or three witnesses. ²⁰Those who sin are to be rebuked publicly, so that the others may take warning.

²¹I charge you, in the sight of God and Christ Jesus and the elect angels, to keep these instructions without partiality, and to do nothing out of favoritism.

²²Do not be hasty in the laying on of hands, and do not share in the sins of others. Keep yourself pure.

²³Stop drinking only water, and use a little wine because of your stomach and your frequent illnesses.

²⁴The sins of some men are obvious, reaching the place of judgment ahead of them; the sins of others trail behind them. ²⁵In the same way, good deeds are obvious, and even those that are not cannot be hidden.

17 In 5:1 *presbyteros* is clearly used in its literal sense of "older man." Here it is just as clearly used in its technical sense of "elder."

"Direct the affairs of the church" is literally "preside over" or "rule" (*proestōtes*). It was the responsibility of these earliest church officials (cf. Acts 14:23) to supervise the work of the local congregation.

Those who performed their functions well were worthy of "double honor." Since the word for "honor" (*timē*) was used in the sense of a price paid for something, it has been suggested that here it might be translated "honorarium" (BAG). But that raises the problem of "double"—double what was paid to the widows, or double what the other elders received? The NEB has: "reckoned worthy of a double stipend." Williams softens it a bit perhaps by translating it "considered as deserving twice the salary they get." Bernard's suggestion is helpful: "*Double* honour, i.e. *ample* provision, must be ensured for them; *diplē* is not to be taken as equivalent to 'double of the sum paid to widows,' or in any similiar way, but without any definite numerical reference" (p. 85). Perhaps we should allow both "honor" and "honorarium," as Paul may have intended both.

Highest honor is to be given to "those whose work is preaching and teaching"—literally, "those laboring in word and teaching." Some have found here a distinction between ruling elders and teaching elders. But this is doubtful. Probably it means that some elders gave themselves to preaching and teaching in addition to their regular duties. Such was the case with Stephen and Philip as deacons (Acts 6–8).

18 This verse, as well as the preceding discussion of support for widows (vv.3–16), suggests definitely that the "double honor" for elders was to be a financial remuneration. Quoting Deuteronomy 25:4 (as he does in 1 Cor 9:9) and Luke 10:7, Paul makes the point that the workman should receive compensation.

As usual, Paul quotes the OT as "Scripture." But does the introductory formula, "For the Scripture says," apply also to the second quotation? Bernard and others think not. But White (EGT, 4:135) seems to favor it, and Lock allows the possibility that this may be "the earliest instance of the Lord's words being quoted as "Scripture' " (p. 63).

19,20 Paul sounds a salutary warning: "Do not entertain [*paradechou*, 'receive, admit'] an accusation [*katēgorian*, tr. 'charge' in Titus 1:6] against an elder unless it is brought by two or three witnesses." The last part of this verse is almost a quotation from Deuteronomy 19:15 (cf. Deut 17:6). An accusation concerning an individual was not to be admitted as a charge against him unless it was supported by two or three witnesses. Paul appealed to this same principle in 2 Corinthians 13:1. Any accusation brought before him by the church at Corinth would have to be "established by the testimony of two or three witnesses."

The context suggests that "those who sin" (v.20)—literally, "are sinning" (present participle)—refers to presbyters. Such offenders Timothy is to rebuke "publicly"—literally, "before all" (enōpion pantōn). Does this mean before the whole church or only before the other elders? The next clause seems to favor the latter: "so that the others"— hoi loipoi, "the rest"—"may take warning"—literally, "may have fear" (phobon echōsi). "The rest" would normally be the other presbyters.

21 "Charge" is "solemnly charge" (diamartyromai, an intensive compound). The mention of "elect angels" is typical of Paul (cf. 3:16; 1 Cor 4:9).

Timothy is solemnly charged to keep these instructions without "partiality" (prokrimatos, "pre-judging, prejudice," only here in the NT). He is to do nothing out of "favoritism" (prosklisin, "inclination"). The verb prosklinō was used in the sense of to "make the scale incline one way or another." Timothy was not to permit his personal prejudices to tip the scales of justice.

22 What is meant by "the laying on of hands"? Lock and White feel that the context favors the idea of laying hands of reconciliation on repentant fallen elders when they are received back into the communion of the church. Eusebius (4th century) says of heretics who repented: "The ancient custom prevailed with regard to such that they should receive only the laying on of hands with prayers" (Ecclesiastical History, vii.2). Martin Dibelius and Hans Conzelmann adopt this interpretation in their volume on the pastoral Epistles in the new "Hermeneia" series.

On the other hand, J.N.D. Kelly in the "Harper's New Testament Commentaries" says, "The command *Don't be in a hurry to lay hands on anyone* almost certainly refers to ordination" (p. 127). This is the view of exegetes such as Chrysostom and Theophylact. Theodoret (5th century) wrote, "For one ought first to inquire into the life of him on whom hands are to be laid (or who is ordained), and so to invoke on him the grace of the Spirit" (quoted in Fairbairn, p. 223). Most recent versions and commentaries favor the interpretation that this passage prohibits hasty ordination. That fits in well with the main discussion of this chapter. And the laying on of hands in these epistles seems to be regularly associated with ordination (cf. 4:14; 2 Tim 1:7).

But what about "Do not share in the sins of others"? If Timothy ordained an elder, he thereby became in a measure a surety for this person's character and thus was implicated in any sins the man might commit. So the young superintendent is warned, "Keep yourself pure"—primarily by being cautious about ordaining candidates. Of course, the more general application to the whole of life may well be intended also.

23 Apparently for medicinal purposes, Timothy is told not to restrict himself to drinking water but to "use a little wine because of your stomach [Greek stomachon] and your frequent illnesses." The word for wine (oinos) is sometimes used in LXX for "must," or unfermented grape juice (Thayer, p. 442). Furthermore, it is generally agreed that the wine of Jesus' day was usually rather weak and, especially among the Jews, often diluted with water. Moreover, safe drinking water was not always readily available in those eastern countries.

24,25 The sins of some men are "obvious." The adjective prodēlos literally means "evident beforehand" (cf. KJV) and so "clearly evident." These sins precede a man to judgment. The less obvious sins of others "trail behind them"—but finally catch up! Similarly, good deeds are "obvious" (v.25, same Greek word), "and even those that are not cannot be hidden."

What does this have to do with avoiding hasty ordination? Apparently the sense is that some men's sins are so evident that there is no question about rejecting them as candidates. Their sins precede them to judgment—first Timothy's judgment and finally divine judgment. The sins of others do not show up so soon but careful investigation will discover them.

In the same way, the good deeds of qualified candidates will be easily seen. Those that seem less obvious will still appear on further search; they cannot be hidden.

4. Slaves

6:1, 2

> [1]All who are under the yoke of slavery should consider their masters worthy of full respect, so that God's name and our teaching may not be slandered. [2]Those who have believing masters are not to show less respect for them because they are brothers. Instead, they are to serve them even better, because those who benefit from their service are believers, and dear to them. These are the things you are to teach and urge on them.

1 The word for "servants" (KJV) is *douloi*, which is correctly rendered "slaves." This is further emphasized by the phrase "under yoke" (*hypo zygon*). Putting it together, we have "all who are under the yoke of slavery."

It is claimed that half the population of the Roman Empire in the first century was composed of slaves. Several times in the NT we read of the conversion and baptism of entire households (e.g., Acts 16:15; 1 Cor 1:16). So there were many Christian slaves at that time. They were admonished to "consider their masters worthy of full respect [literally, 'all honor,' *pasēs timēs*] so that God's name and our teaching may not be slandered." Paul was always concerned that the conduct of Christians should be such as to bring glory to God and not reproach on his name and on the gospel.

2 Not all Christian slaves had "believing masters." But those who did were not "to show less respect for them"—all one word in Greek, *kataphroneitōsan*, "think down on, despise." Instead, they were to serve them even better, realizing that they were benefiting their brothers in Christ. This would give added incentive to their service. The masters were "dear to them" (*agapētoi*, "beloved").

Notes

1,2 The word used here for "masters" of slaves is not the usual one in the NT, κύριος (*kyrios*, "master," "lord"), which occurs about 750 times and refers to masters of slaves at least seven times (e.g., Eph 6:5, 9; Col 3:22; 4:1). Here it is δεσπότης (*despotēs*), which occurs only ten times in the NT. It is used five times for masters of slaves (1 Tim 6:1, 2; 2 Tim 2:21; Titus 2:9; 1 Peter 2:18). Otherwise it is used as a title for God or for Christ. Both words are very common in LXX, sometimes together (e.g., Gen 15:2, 8, "Lord God"), and Philo held them to be syononymous.

Should βλασφημῆται (*blasphēmētai*) be translated "slandered" or "blasphemed" (KJV)? The word means the former when directed toward man and the latter when directed toward God. Part of the problem is ἡ διδασκαλία (*hē didaskalia*), which literally means "the teaching." This can be taken as referring either to "our teaching" (NIV) or "*his* doctrine" (KJV). This is the problem of the ambiguity of the definite article in Greek. It could go either way.

Is "because they are brothers" nonrestrictive (KJV, ASV) or restrictive (RSV, NAB, JB, NEB, NASB)? The latter, making the relationship the possible cause of a lack of showing respect, seems to give the better sense.

In the last part of v.2 we cannot be certain whether πιστοί (pistoi) should be tr. "faithful" (KJV) or "believers" (NIV). Since it is the same word that is tr. "believing" (KJV, NIV) in the first part of the verse, the latter is preferable.

NIV ends this paragraph with "These are the things you are to teach and urge [παρακάλει, parakalei, 'exhort'] on them." (The last two words are not in the Gr.) UBS places this with the next paragraph. This arrangement is followed by RSV and NEB, making it a general command, rather than one directed particularly to slaves. Either way makes good sense.

VIII. The Danger of the Love of Money

6:3-10

3If anyone teaches false doctrines and does not agree to the sound instruction of our Lord Jesus Christ and to godly teaching, 4he is conceited and understands nothing. He has an unhealthy interest in controversies and arguments that result in envy, quarreling, malicious talk, evil suspicions 5and constant friction between men of corrupt mind, who have been robbed of the truth and who think that godliness is a means to financial gain.

6But godliness with contentment is great gain. 7For we brought nothing into the world, and we can take nothing out of it. 8But if we have food and clothing, we will be content with that. 9People who want to get rich fall into temptation and a trap and into many foolish and harmful desires that plunge men into ruin and destruction. 10For the love of money is a root of all kinds of evil. Some people, eager for money, have wandered from the faith and pierced themselves with many griefs.

3-5 "Teaches false doctrines" (KJV, "teach otherwise") is heterodidaskalei (cf. 1:3, the only other place where it occurs in the NT). "Agree to" is proserchetai, "come to." Elsewhere in the NT this verb always describes the movement of a body to a place. But in later Greek it came to be used for the assent or consent of the mind. "Sound" is a participle of the verb hygiainō, "be healthy," found (in the NT) only in the Pastorals in a metaphorical sense (cf. 1:10). "Instruction" is literally "words" (logois). But logos can be translated many ways.

Having defined the false teacher in v.3, Paul goes on to describe him in vv.4, 5. Bluntly he declares that such a person "is conceited and understands nothing." The word for "is conceited" (KJV, "proud") is tetyphōtai, the perfect passive (indicating a fixed state or condition) of typhoomai (cf. 3:6), "puffed up."

Although he understands nothing, the false teacher "has an unhealthy interest"—one word, nosōn (only here in the NT), "being sick" (mentally), "having a morbid craving for" (BAG)—"in controversies and arguments." The first of these two nouns is zētēseis. It basically means "investigation," and so in the pastoral Epistles (cf. 2 Tim 2:23; Titus 3:9) the investigation of religious and theological problems. But the context suggests that here it indicates "debates" or "disputes." "Arguments" is logomachias (only here in the NT), "word-battles," or disputes about words. White observes, "The heretic spoken of is a theorist merely; he wastes time in academic disputes; he does not take into account things as they actually are" (EGT, 4:141). A morbid craving for controversies and arguments is not the sign of good health, either psychologically or spiritually. Even well-intentioned theological discussions sometimes have a tendency to degenerate into mere word-battles or exercises in semantics.

"That result in" is literally "out of which come" (*ex hōn ginetai*). Five things are mentioned as the result of the disputes and arguments. The first two are "envy" and "quarreling" (*eris*, "strife"). These two also occur together in Romans 1:29 and Galatians 5:21. Envy always produces quarreling and strife.

"Malicious talk" is *blasphēmiai* (pl.). When directed against God, it means "blasphemy," but when directed against men, as here, it means "abusive speech" or "slander." "Evil suspicions" is *hyponoiai ponērai*. The first of these words (only here in the NT) means "surmisings." The combination could also be "evil conjectures" or "false suspicions" (BAG).

The fifth result is spelled out at considerable length, comprising all of v.5. "Constant friction" is *diaparatribai* (only here in the NT). It means "mutual irritations" or "incessant wranglings," and so "constant friction." This is found in the relations between "men of corrupt minds" (*diephtharmenōn anthrōpōn ton noun*). The compound form of this verb and the fact that it is a perfect passive participle suggest that it means "thoroughly corrupted or depraved." These men "have been robbed of the truth." This expresses well the force of the verb. White says that *apostereō* "conveys the notion of a person being deprived of a thing to which he has a right. . . . The truth was once theirs; they have disinherited themselves. The A.V., *destitute of*, does not assume that they ever had it" (EGT, 4:142). These men think that godliness is "a means to financial gain"—all one word in Greek, *porismos* (only here and v.6). It literally means "a procuring," and so "a means of gain."

6 Although "godliness," or "piety," should never be used as a means to secure financial gain, it is nevertheless true that "godliness with contentment is great gain." The word for "contentment" (*autarkeia*) was used in classical Greek in a philosophical sense for "a perfect condition of life, in which no aid or support is needed" (Thayer). In the only other passage in the NT where this word occurs (2 Cor 9:8) it is used objectively for "a sufficiency of the necessities of life." But here it is used subjectively for "a mind contented with its lot," and so "contentment" (EGT, 4:142). The closest parallel passage in thought is Philippians 4:11, where the adjective *autarkēs* is employed. Contentment is one of the greatest assets of life.

7,8 The reason we should be content is that "we brought nothing into the world, and we can take nothing out of it." That is, "nothing the world can give is any addition to the man himself" (White, EGT, 4:143).

So if we have food and clothing, we should be content with these things. The words for "food" (*diatrophas*) and "clothing" (*skepasmata*) are both plural and are found only here in the NT. The ordinary word for food in the NT is *trophē*. But the compound occurs in the literature of that time. The term *skepasma* comes from *skepazō*, the verb meaning "to cover." So it could mean both clothing and shelter. But Josephus uses it clearly in the sense of clothing alone (*Antiq.*, xv.9.2).

9 Those who "want," or are determined (*boulomenoi*), to be rich fall into temptation and "a trap" (*pagis*, "trap" or "snare") and into many desires that are "foolish" ("senseless") and "harmful." The adjective *blaberos* (only here in the NT) comes from the verb *blaptō*, which means "hurt" or "injure," and so this means "hurtful" or "injurious." "Plunge" is *bythizousi*, "plunge into the deep" (*bythos*), as a sinking ship in the sea (cf. Luke 5:7, the only other place where this verb occurs in the NT). Wrong desires plunge men into "ruin" (*olethron*) and "destruction" (*apōleian*). Both words mean "destruction," but the

second is somewhat stronger. Thayer says that it is used in particular for "the destruction which consists in the loss of eternal life," and so means "eternal misery" or "perdition" (cf. KJV). Lock observes, "The combination (found here only) is emphatic, 'loss for time and eternity' " (p. 69).

10 The first part of this verse is often quoted—though sometimes misquoted as "Money is the root of all evil." Rather, it is "the love of money" (*philargyria*) that is "a root" of "all kinds of evil"—literally, "all the evils." (The Greek has no definite article before "root.")

"Eager" is the present participle of the verb *orego* (cf. 3:1)—always "reaching after, grasping at" money. This is the curse of too much of modern living. Some Christians, unfortunately, have been trapped in this way. They have "wandered" (*apeplanethesan*, "been led astray," only here and Mark 13:22) from the faith. In straying from the straight path, they have been caught in the thorn bushes and have "pierced themselves with many griefs" (*odynais*, only here and Rom 9:2). Another translation is: "They have pierced themselves to the heart with many pangs" (BAG).

Some have questioned the validity of the first part of this verse. But this proverbial statement echoes what had already been said by both Greek and Jewish writers. Fairbairn gives this helpful interpretation: "The sentiment is, that there is no kind of evil to which the love of money may not lead men, when once it fairly takes hold of them" (p. 239).

Notes

5 "Supposing that gain is godliness" (KJV) is not a correct translation. The noun εὐσέβειαν (*eusebeian*, "godliness") has the definite article, whereas πορισμόν (*porismon*, "gain") does not. The rule in Gr. grammar is that in such cases the noun that has the article is the subject.

The last clause of this verse in KJV is not found in the early Gr. MSS. It is almost certain that it was added by a later scribe, perhaps because he felt that it was needed to complete the grammatical sense of this very long sentence.

7 UBS has ὅτι (*hoti*, "because") at the beginning of the second clause. Though this reading is found in some of the very earliest MSS, it is given only a "C" rating because does not seem to fit. This is one of the unsolved problems of textual criticism.

8 Bernard says that ἀρκεσθησόμεθα (*arkesthesometha*, "we will be content") is "not imperatival, but future, with a slightly *authoritative* sense" (p. 96).

IX. Paul's Charge to Timothy

6:11-16

11But you, man of God, flee from all this, and pursue righteousness, godliness, faith, love, endurance and gentleness. 12Fight the good fight of the faith. Take hold of the eternal life to which you were called when you made your good confession in the presence of many witnesses. 13In the sight of God, who gives life to everything, and of Christ Jesus, who while testifying before Pontius Pilate made the good confession, I charge you 14to keep this commandment without spot or blame until the appearing of our Lord Jesus Christ, 15which God will bring about in his own time—God, the blessed and only Ruler, the King of kings and Lord of lords, 16who alone is immortal and who lives in unapproachable light, whom no one has seen or can see. To him be honor and might forever. Amen.

11 Paul begins by saying, "But you"—the "you" is emphatic (placed first) in the Greek. Then he addresses Timothy as "man of God." This is a common designation for prophets in the OT (e.g., 1 Sam 9:6; 1 Kings 12:22; 13:1). There has been considerable discussion as to whether it carries that connotation here or is used as a general title for all Christians. The only other place in the NT where it occurs is in 2 Timothy 3:17. Even there it is not absolutely clear whether it is used in a particular or general sense. J.N.D. Kelly says of the expression: "It connotes one who is in God's service, represents God and speaks in his name, and admirably fits one who is a pastor" (p. 139). That seems to be a reasonable interpretation.

"Pursue" (*diōke*) means "keep on pursuing," make these things your lifelong pursuit. Then Paul names six Christian virtues. Only the last two are different from KJV. We have already noted that *hypomonē* means "endurance," not "patience." *Praupathia* (only here in the NT) may equally well be translated "meekness" (KJV) or "gentleness."

12 "Fight the good fight" is *agōnizou ton kalon agōna*, "agonize the good agony." The related verb and noun come from the verb *agō*, which means "lead" or "bring." From this was derived the noun that we have here, *agōn*. It meant first "a gathering," especially for "games" (the sports events in the various Greek cities). Then it was used for the athletic competitions themselves. Similarly, the verb *agōnizō* meant "to enter a contest; contend in the gymnastic games"; and then more universally, "to contend with adversaries, fight" (Thayer). In the NT both words are used to describe the struggles of the Christian life. The background of the words suggests exerting every ounce of energy to win. Paul uses this same combination of words again in 2 Timothy 4:7.

Timothy is told to take hold of the eternal life to which he was called "when you made your good confession"—literally, "and professed the good profession" or "confessed the good confession" (*hōmologēsas tēn kalēn homologian*). But the repetition of a cognate noun after the verb is an ancient custom that is not idiomatic today. BAG suggests for this passage "made the good profession of faith." Probably the reference is to Timothy's confession of faith in Christ at the time of his baptism, when "many witnesses" were no doubt present.

13,14 Typically, Paul appeals to God, who "gives life to" (*zōogonountos*, "preserves alive") everything, and to Christ Jesus, "who while testifying before Pontius Pilate made the good confession." It is in their sight that he solemnly charges Timothy to keep "this commandment," literally, "the commandment" (*tēn entolēn*), possibly broader than the immediate context here. He is to keep it "without spot" (*aspilon*, "spotless, unblemished") "or blame" (*anepilēmpton*, lit. "without reproach"; cf. 3:2).

There has been much discussion as to whether these two adjectives modify "commandment" or "you." Elsewhere in the NT they are applied to persons, but here they are more closely attached to "commandment." Perhaps the best way is to try to combine the two ideas. White comments, "If Timothy 'keeps himself unspotted' (Jas. i.27) and 'without reproach,' the *entolē*, so far as he is concerned, will be maintained flawless" (EGT, 4:147).

Timothy is to keep the commandment until the "appearing" of our Lord Jesus Christ. *Epiphaneia*, "manifestation, appearance," occurs five times in the pastoral Epistles (cf. 2 Tim 1:10; 4:1, 8; Titus 2:13) and only once elsewhere in the NT (2 Thess 2:8, "splendor"). It is found in late Greek writers and in the inscriptions of that period for a visible manifestation of an invisible deity. It is also used frequently in the LXX for manifestations of God's glory. In 2 Timothy 1:10 it refers to the first coming of Christ. Elsewhere it is used only for the Second Coming.

This is one of three words in the NT for the return of our Lord. *Apokalypsis,* "revelation" ("apocalypse"), is found eighteen times, but not in the Pastorals. The most common word (24 times) is *parousia,* "presence," which also does not occur in the pastoral Epistles.

15,16 God will "bring about" (*deixei,* "show, exhibit, display") this Second Coming "in his own time." The use of this verb in John 2:18 (see NIV there) suggests that the return of Christ will be God's final proof to the world that Jesus is the Son of God and Savior.

The word for "time" (pl. here) is *kairos,* which means a fixed or definite time. In the NT it is often used eschatologically (in a prophetic sense) for God's appointed time, especially in relation to the Second Coming and the future judgment.

The last part of v.15 and all of v.16 form a doxology, such as we often find in Paul's Epistles (cf. 1:17; 2 Tim 4:18). Much of the language is derived from the OT (see note below).

God is first described as "the blessed and only Ruler." The last word is *dynastēs* (cf. "dynasty"). Elsewhere in the NT it is found only in Luke 1:52 ("rulers") and Acts 8:27 ("important official"). BAG translates it here as "Sovereign." It indicates a "possessor of power" (Cremer, *Lexicon,* p. 221).

The next two titles, "King of kings and Lord of lords," are applied to Christ twice in Revelation (17:14; 19:16). They are used for God in the OT (Dan 4:34, LXX; cf. Deut 10:17; Ps 136:3).

God alone is "immortal"—literally, "the only one having immortality" (*athanasia,* only here and 1 Cor 15:53, 54). The Greek word comes from *a*-negative and *thanatos,* "death." So it means "not subject to death."

The idea of immortality is not clearly expressed in the OT (see note below). But the NT teaching is that God alone has inherent immortality; ours is derived from him. It is in the resurrection that the true believer receives an immortal body (1 Cor 15:53), so that the whole man, body and soul, becomes immortal.

We are next told that God lives in light "unapproachable" (*aprositon,* only here in the NT). Philo uses this adjective for Mount Sinai when it was covered with God's glory (*de Vita Mosis* iii.2). Josephus, like Paul, applies it to God (*Antiq.* iii.5.1). The declaration is added here that no person has ever seen God or can see him. This truth is stated in the OT (Exod 33:20) and repeated in the New (John 1:18).

The doxology ends with the ascription: "To him be honor and might forever. Amen." It is typical of Paul to inject a doxology in the midst of a discussion (cf. 1:17; Rom 1:25; 11:36).

Notes

15,16 For a complete list of "Apostolic Doxologies" see B.F. Westcott, *The Epistle to the Hebrews,* pp. 464, 465. William Hendriksen (pp. 205, 206) gives a number of OT parallels to each phrase of this doxology.

16 Besides ἀθανασία (*athanasia*), the idea of "immortality" is expressed in the NT by ἀφθαρσία (aphtharsia, lit., "incorruption" and ἄφθαρτος (aphthartos, "incorruptible"). The adjective ἀθάνατος (athanatos, "immortal") is not found in the NT. All four words are used in the apocryphal books of LXX, but none of them occurs in the canonical books of LXX. This concept evidently developed in the inter-testamental period.

The word κράτος (kratos, "might") is common in NT doxologies (cf. 1 Peter 4:11; 5:11; Jude 25; Rev 1:6; 5:13).

X. Closing Instructions (6:17–21)

1. Admonitions to the Wealthy

6:17–19

> 17Command those who are rich in this present world not to be arrogant nor to put their hope in wealth, which is so uncertain, but to put their hope in God, who richly provides us with everything for our enjoyment. 18Command them to do good, to be rich in good deeds, and to be generous and willing to share. 19In this way they will lay up treasure for themselves as a firm foundation for the coming age, so that they may take hold of the life that is truly life.

17 In vv.17–19 we find admonitions to the wealthy. Timothy is to command them not "to be arrogant" (hypsēlophronein, only here in the NT). This verb means "to be high-minded, proud, haughty." Bernard comments, "The pride of purse is not only vulgar, it is sinful" (p. 101). It is evident that in the wealthy city of Ephesus there were some church members who had money.

Timothy is to warn them not to put their hope in "wealth, which is so uncertain"—literally, "uncertainty" (adēlotēti, only here in the NT) "of riches" (ploutou). The uncertainty of wealth has been commented on from ancient times. It takes to itself wings and flies away (Prov 23:5). Even great fortunes have disappeared almost overnight.

One should instead put his hope in God (cf. Ps 52:7). He is the one who "richly provides us with everything for our enjoyment." The last word is apolausin (only here and Heb 11:25). This strong compound suggests that physical pleasure is in itself not sinful, but divinely ordained when sought within the structure of God's will. White rightly observes, "No good purpose is served by pretending that God did not intend us to enjoy the pleasurable sensations of physical life" (EGT, 4:149). Such an attitude comes from Gnosticism, not the NT (see 4:1–5).

18 The wealthy are to use their money "to do good" (agathoergein, only here and Acts 14:17); they are "to be rich in good deeds" (en ergois kalois). Wealth imposes a heavy responsibility on its possessor. The greater our means for doing good, the greater our obligation. What an opportunity wealthy people have for benefiting the needy!

So they are to be "generous" (eumetadotos, only here in the NT). This adjective is compounded of eu, "good, noble," and the verb metadidōmi, "give a share of." They are also to be "willing to share"—one word, the adjective koinōnikos (also only here). It comes from koinōnia, "fellowship, communion." It may therefore suggest that wealthy Christians should share their hearts as well as their money. This combination is what pleases God and imparts a double blessing to the recipient. Bernard comments, "A kind heart as well as a generous hand is demanded of the rich" (p. 102). Paul rejoiced that the generous Macedonians first gave themselves (2 Cor 8:1–5). It is easier to give money than to give ourselves, but love requires both.

19 By following these instructions the well-to-do will "lay up treasure" (*apothēsaurizon-tas*, only here in NT) "as a firm" (*kalon*, "good") "foundation for the coming age." This is in line with Jesus' teaching in Matthew 6:19–21: "Do not store up (*thēsaurizete*) for yourselves treasures (*thēsaurous*) on earth.... But store up for yourselves treasures in heaven.... For where your treasure (*thēsauros*) is, there your heart will be also." In contrast to the uncertainty of earthly riches (v.17) will be the "firm foundation" (v.19) of treasure laid up in heaven.

The purpose of this is that they may take hold of "the life that is truly life"—literally, "the truly life" (*tēs ontōs zōēs*). In place of *ontōs* ("really, truly") the late, medieval MSS have *aiōnou*, "eternal" (cf. KJV). We have already found *ontōs* used in connection with widows (5:3, 5, 16). There is no question but that it is the correct reading here.

2. Admonition to Timothy

6:20,21a

> 20Timothy, guard what has been entrusted to your care. Turn away from godless chatter and the opposition of what is falsely called knowledge, 21which some have professed and in so doing have wandered from the faith.

20 Paul concludes with a personal admonition to Timothy: "Guard what has been entrusted to your care" (*tēn parathēkēn phylaxon*, lit., "guard the deposit"). The noun *parathēkēn*—literally, "what is placed beside," and so a "deposit" or "trust"—occurs elsewhere in the NT only in 2 Timothy 1:12, 14. Here the context suggests that it means the sound doctrine that had been entrusted to Timothy. Simpson comments, "The deposit he is to guard can be nothing else than 'the revelation of Jesus Christ' in all its fulness" (p. 92).

Timothy is to turn away from "godless chatter" (*bebēlous kenophōnias*).The first word, an adjective, means "unhallowed, profane." The second, a noun, (only here and 2 Tim 2:16), compounded of *kenos*, means "empty" and *phōneō*, "talk aloud." So it means "empty talk, babbling." This is how Paul characterizes what the false teachers were saying.

"Opposition" is *antitheseis* (only here in the NT; cf. "antithesis"). The noun literally means "a placing over against," and so the plural here signifies "contrasts." It is true that the term in Paul's day commonly meant "opposition." But Lock is probably right in thinking that there the term (pl.) means "rival theses, sets of antitheses." These could have been "the Gnostic contrasts between the O.T. and the New, which found their fullest expression in Marcion's 'Antitheses' " or, "more probably" the arguments of Jews (p. 76). This is what Hort indicates when he suggests that it means "the endless contrasts of decisions, founded on endless distinctions, which played so large a part in the casuistry of the Scribes as interpreters of the Law" (*Judaistic Christianity*, p. 140).

The "opposition" consisted of "what is falsely called knowledge." "Falsely called" is the compound adjective *pseudōnymos* (cf. "pseudonymous"), found only here in the NT. It means "under a false name." "Knowledge" is *gnōsis*. We have already seen that several times in this Epistle Paul is combating the false teachings of Gnosticism—those who professed a superior *gnōsis* and believed that salvation comes to those who have this secret, intellectual treasure. But, as noted above, Paul may be here warning against the teachings of both Gnostics and Judaizers.

21 This is the kind of false gospel that some have "professed" (*epangellomenoi*, cf. 2:10).

In doing so they "have wandered" (aorist of *astocheō*, "miss the mark"), have deviated from the faith.

3. *Farewell*

6:21b

Grace be with you.

The closing benediction is "Grace be with thee" (KJV) in the late MSS. But most of the early MSS have "Grace be with you" (pl.). This would include the church along with Timothy.

2 TIMOTHY

Ralph Earle

Outline

Note: For introduction to 2 Timothy, see pp. 341–347.

Text and Exposition

I. Salutation

1:1, 2

> ¹Paul, an apostle of Christ Jesus by the will of God, according to the promise of life that is in Christ Jesus,
>
> ²To Timothy, my dear son:
>
> Grace, mercy and peace from God the Father and Christ Jesus our Lord.

This salutation is very similar to the one found at the beginning of 1 Timothy. There Paul identifies himself as "an apostle of Christ Jesus by the command of God," here as "an apostle . . . by the will of God." In this second Epistle he adds, "According to the promise of life that is in Christ Jesus." All spiritual life comes to us only "in Christ." And the more fully and consciously we live in him, the richer that life becomes.

In the first Epistle Paul greeted Timothy as "my true son in the faith." Here it is "my dear (agapētos, "beloved") son." Paul had a warm affection for his young convert and colleague. The greeting (v.2b) is exactly the same as that in 1 Timothy (see comments there). Everything we have comes to us from God through Christ.

Notes

1 Paul begins five of his Epistles (cf. 1 Cor 1:1; 2 Cor 1:1; Eph 1:1; Col 1:1) with this identification: "Paul, an apostle of Christ Jesus by the will of God" (Παῦλος ἀπόστολος Χριστοῦ Ἰησοῦ διὰ θελήματος θεοῦ, Paulos apostolos Christou Iesou dia thelēmatos theou). He was God's called man.

For the expression "promise of life" (ἐπαγγελίαν ζωῆς, epangelian zōēs) see 1 Tim 4:8.

II. Thanksgiving (1:3–7)

1. Timothy's Heritage

1:3–5

> ³I thank God, whom I serve, as my forefathers did, with a clear conscience, as night and day I constantly remember you in my prayers. ⁴Recalling your tears, I long to see you, so that I may be filled with joy. ⁵I have been reminded of your sincere faith, which first lived in your grandmother Lois and in your mother Eunice, and I am persuaded, now lives in you also.

3 In his first Epistle, before stopping to thank God, Paul talked to Timothy about the urgent task that faced him at Ephesus. But here he follows his regular custom (except in Galatians) of having a thanksgiving right after the greeting. Paul was serving God "as my forefathers did." He appreciated very much his religious heritage (cf. Acts 22:3; 24:14), and so today should all those who have been brought up in a Christian environment.

The apostle served God "with a clear"—literally, "clean" or "pure" (kathara) "conscience." (For this last word, see the note on 1 Tim 1:5.) Acts 23:1 implies that he had maintained a clear conscience even in his earlier years.

"Night and day" Paul was "constantly" (*adialeipton*, "unceasingly") remembering Timothy in his prayers (cf. Rom 1:10; 1 Thess 1:2; 3:6). He must have had a large heart to carry such a loving concern for so many people. It is true that letter writers of that period sometimes mentioned that they were always remembering their correspondents. But Paul put a new Christian dimension into these epistolary conventions.

4 "Long" is a strong compound verb, *epipotheō* (only here in the Pastorals; "long for, desire"). Recalling Timothy's tears, probably at the time of their last parting, Paul had an intense longing to see his son in the faith, that he might be "filled with joy." One of the fascinating aspects of Pauline studies is the very real humanity of this man of God. Paul was a stalwart soldier, but he had a tender heart.

5 "I have been reminded" is literally "having received a reminder" (*hypomnēsin labōn*). The noun *hypomnēsis* (only here and 2 Peter 1:13; 3:1), Bernard says, "is an act of the memory prompted from without" (p. 108). J.A. Bengel wrote, "Some external occasion, or a message from Timothy, had brought his faith to Paul's remembrance" (*Gnomon of NT*, 4:291).

"Sincere" is literally "unhypocritical" (*anhypokritou*). "Grandmother" is *mammē* (only here in the NT). In classical Greek it was a child's name for its mother, like our "mama." But in later Greek it means "grandmother." "Eunice" literally means "good victory." Timothy had a godly mother and grandmother.

Notes

3 Instead of Paul's usual verb εὐχαριστέω (*eucharisteō*, "I thank"), he begins his thanksgiving here and in 1 Tim 1:12 with χάριν ἔχω (*charin echō*, lit., "I have thanks"). This more literary expression (Simpson, p. 121) may well reflect the fact that Luke, the highly educated Greek physician, was his amanuensis (cf. Luke 17:9; Heb 12:28).

"I serve" is λατρεύω (*latreuō*), not used elsewhere in the Pastorals. In the NT it is used only for serving or worshiping God, and occurs most frequently in Hebrews.

Πρόγονοι (*progonoi*) occurs elsewhere in the NT only in 1 Tim 5:4, where it refers to one's immediate parents or grandparents. Here it is used in the more remote sense of "ancestors" ("forefathers"). It is an adjective meaning "born before."

For δεήσεσιν (*deēsesin*, "prayers") see the note on 1 Tim 2:1.

Bernard thinks that "night and day," which comes at the very end of the verse in Gr., goes with "longing to see you" at the beginning (in the Gr.) of v.4. Lock agrees, but White connects it with "remember." The Gr. allows either.

2. God's Gift to Timothy

1:6, 7

> [6]For this reason I remind you to fan into flame the gift of God, which is in you through the laying on of my hands. [7]For God did not give us a spirit of timidity, but a spirit of power, of love and of self-discipline.

6 Because of his sincere faith and spiritual heritage, Timothy is urged to "fan into flame" (*anazōpyrein*, only here in the NT) "the gift (*charisma*) of God, which is in you through the laying on of my hands" (see comments on 1 Tim 4:14). This would most naturally be taken as the time of Timothy's ordination. Concerning "gift," Bernard writes, "The *charisma* is not an ordinary gift of God's grace, such as every Christian may seek and obtain according to his need; but it is the special grace received by Timothy to fit him for his ministerial functions" (p. 109). (It should be remembered that *charisma* comes from *charis*, "grace.")

General Booth, the founder of the Salvation Army, once sent this message to those under him: "The tendency of fire is to go out; watch the fire on the altar of your heart." Anyone who has tended a fireplace fire knows that it needs to be stirred up occasionally.

7 Paul is fond of making a negative statement and then following it with three positive ideas, thus giving the introduction and three points of the outline for a textual sermon (cf. Rom 14:17). Here he says that God has not given us a spirit of "timidity" (*deilia*, "cowardice," only here in the NT), but rather a spirit of "power" (*dynamis*), of "love" (*agapē*) and of "self-discipline" (*sōphronismos*, "self-control," only here in the NT). This is a significant combination. The effective Christian worker must have the power of the Holy Spirit (cf. Acts 1:8). But that power must be expressed in a loving spirit, or it may do damage. And often the deciding factor between success and failure is the matter of self-discipline.

This is one of the several passages in these two Epistles that hint at Timothy's naturally timid nature. He had been brought up by his mother and grandmother, and now Paul was taking the place of a father to him.

III. Suffering for the Gospel (1:8–18)

1. *Plea to Timothy*

1:8

> [8] So do not be ashamed to testify about our Lord, or ashamed of me his prisoner. But join with me in suffering for the gospel, by the power of God.

8 In view of the spirit that has been divinely given to Timothy (cf. v.7), he is urged not to be ashamed "to testify about our Lord." Since "do not be ashamed" is in the aorist, not present, tense, Paul is not implying that Timothy was already guilty of doing this. But apparently he felt that his young colleague needed to have his courage strengthened.

Paul also urges Timothy not to be ashamed of "me his prisoner." The aged apostle was now a prisoner of the emperor (probably Nero) and facing almost certain death. Timothy must not be so fearful as to be ashamed to visit Paul in prison.

Instead, he is told: "Join with me in suffering"—all one word, *synkakopathēson* (only here and in 2:3). It is compounded of *patheō*, "suffer"; *kakos*, "bad"; and *syn*, "together." So it means "bear evil treatment along with," "take one's share of ill-treatment" (A-S).

Notes

8 "To testify about our Lord " is τὸ μαρτύριον τοῦ κυρίου ἡμῶν (to martyrion tou kyriou hēmōn, lit., "the testimony of our Lord"). White takes tou kuriou as subjective genitive: "testimony borne by our Lord, His words, His ethical and spiritual teaching" (EGT, 4:156). Bernard, however, prefers treating it as objective genitive: "about our Lord." Lock agrees. This is almost equivalent to "the gospel" (cf. Rom 1:16).

Lock says of συγκακοπάθησον (synkakopathēson, "join ... in suffering"): "not found in earlier writers; probably coined by St. Paul, who frequently coins compounds of σύν out of his deep sense of the close 'withness' of Christians with each other and with Christ" (p. 86). (TDNT, 5:937 does not give any earlier occurrence.) A-S has twelve pages treating words beginning with σύν (syn, "with"). A large proportion of these are found only in Paul's Epistles. He believed in "togetherness"! "For the gospel" means "for the sake of the gospel," that is, because of preaching it. It is only "by the power of God" that Timothy will be able to suffer for the gospel.

2. Paul's Testimony

1:9-12

9who has saved us and called us to a holy life—not because of anything we have done but because of his own purpose and grace. This grace was given us in Christ Jesus before the beginning of time, 10but it has now been revealed through the appearing of our Savior, Christ Jesus, who has destroyed death and has brought life and immortality to light through the gospel. 11And of this gospel I was appointed a herald and an apostle and a teacher. 12That is why I am suffering as I am. Yet I am not ashamed, because I know whom I have believed, and am convinced that he is able to guard what I have entrusted to him for that day.

9 Paul says that God "saved us and called us to a holy life"—or "with a holy calling" (klēsei hagia). Lock says of this phrase: "Mainly 'with a calling to be holy' ... but with the further thought of God's holiness which we have to imitate" (p. 87). We are called to holiness (1 Thess 4:7).

The next part of this verse is as Pauline as Romans—"not because of anything we have done" (lit., "not according to our works") "but because of his own purpose and grace ... given us in Christ Jesus." This is Paul's doctrine of grace that is central to his theology.

"Before the beginning of time" is literally "before times eternal" (pro chronōn aiōn- iōn). Lock comments, "The grace of God is embodied in Christ Jesus: we only gain it through union with Him, and it was given to Him by God long before we were born" (ibid.).

10 This grace has now been "revealed" (phanerōtheisan, "manifested"). Thayer says that phaneroō means "to make manifest or visible or known what has been hidden or unknown" (p. 648). How has this grace been made known? "Through the appearing of our Savior, Jesus Christ." The word "appearing" is epiphaneia. Elsewhere in the NT (2 Thess 2:8; 1 Tim 6:14; 2 Tim 4:1, 8; Titus 2:13) it refers to Christ's second coming. But here it obviously refers to the first coming. It was at his first coming that Christ "de- stroyed death" through his own death on the cross (cf. Heb 2:14). He has also "brought life and immortality [aphtharsia, 'incorruptibility'] to light through the gospel." That is,

the preaching of the gospel has offered men life and immortality. This is the good news Christ came to bring.

11 For the proclamation of this gospel Paul was appointed "a herald and an apostle and a teacher." We find the same three functions, together with exactly the same introductory formula in Greek in 1 Timothy 2:7 (see comments there).

12 Paul's appointment as a preacher of the gospel had cost him much in "suffering" and persecution. But he was not ashamed. Why not? "Because I know whom I have believed [not just 'what I have believed'] and am convinced [same verb as 'persuaded' in v.5] that he is able to guard what I have entrusted to him for that day." For "what I have entrusted to him" (lit., "my deposit") see the comments on 1 Timothy 6:20.

What was this deposit? As Lock says, "He does not define or limit; it will include his teaching . . . his apostolic work, his converts . . . his life which has been already in God's keeping and which will remain safe there even through death" (p. 88).

Notes

11 The added phrase "of the Gentiles" in KJV is not in ℵ our oldest Gr. MS for this passage (4th century), nor A (5th century). It was probably imported here from 1 Tim 2:7.
12 Παραθήκη (paratheke, "deposit") is found only in these two verses and in 1 Tim 6:20. Lock has an excellent additional note on this (pp. 90–92). He says that it "always implies the situation of one who has to take a long journey and who deposits his money and other valuables with a friend, trusting him to restore it on his return" (p. 90). Paul was preparing for his last long journey, and he was depositing his gospel (a body of truth) with Timothy. This fits vv.13, 14. With regard to v.12 Lock has this comment: "The life which at first was God's deposit with us becomes our deposit with God" (p. 92).

3. Paul's Admonition

1:13, 14

13What you heard from me, keep as the pattern of sound teaching, with faith and love in Christ Jesus. 14Guard the good deposit that was entrusted to you—guard it with the help of the Holy Spirit who lives in us.

13 "Pattern" is hypotyposin. Elsewhere in the NT it occurs only in 1 Timothy 1:16, where it is translated "example." What Timothy had heard from Paul he was to keep as the pattern of "sound" (hygiainonton) "teaching" (logon, lit., "words"). But this was to be done "with faith and love in Christ Jesus." The only way to keep doctrine is to both live and proclaim it with faith and love.

14 Timothy was to "guard the good deposit" ("that was entrusted to you" is not in the Greek, but implied). This was evidently the gospel that Paul had entrusted to Timothy to preach and the doctrine he was to preserve. How could he do this? Only "with the help of the Holy Spirit who lives in us." It has been well said that the Holy Spirit is the great Conservator of orthodoxy. (See note on v.12 for paratheke, "deposit.")

4. Paul Deserted

1:15

> 15You know that everyone in the province of Asia has deserted me, including Phygelus and Hermogenes.

15 The term *Asia* in the NT does not mean the continent, as now, but rather the Roman province of Asia, at the west end of Asia Minor. It was made into a province by the Romans about 133 B.C. and Ephesus finally became its capital.

On his third missionary journey Paul had spent three years in Ephesus (Acts 20:31), longer than anywhere else. While he was there, the preaching of the gospel reached every part of the province (Acts 19:10). There is deep pathos, then, in this verse: "You know that everyone in the province of Asia has deserted me"—i.e., turned away from me. Paul singles out two men for special mention among the deserters, perhaps because they were well known to Timothy. But of "Phygelus and Hermogenes" we know nothing further.

When did the Christians of Asia turn away from Paul? Perhaps it was when he was arrested and taken to Rome for his second and final imprisonment. If so, one can understand the "tears" (v.4) Timothy shed at that time.

5. Paul Befriended

1:16–18

> 16May the Lord show mercy to the household of Onesiphorus, because he often refreshed me and was not ashamed of my chains. 17On the contrary, when he was in Rome, he searched hard for me until he found me. 18May the Lord grant that he will find mercy from the Lord on that day! You know very well in how many ways he helped me in Ephesus.

16–18 In contrast to the attitudes and actions of the majority was the kindness of Onesiphorus. He had lived up to his name, which means "help-bringer" (cf. Onesimus, "helpful," "useful," Philem 10, 11). Onesiphorus had often "refreshed" (*anepsyxen*, only here in the NT) Paul and had not been ashamed of the apostle's chains, as the others had been. When he went to Rome, Onesiphorus had "searched hard" for Paul until he finally found him. There were many prisoners in Rome, and it was not an easy task to locate this particular one. Paul prays that mercy may be shown to Onesiphorus "on that day"—presumably the day of judgment. Then he adds that Timothy knew very well how this faithful Christian had often helped Paul when the latter was in Ephesus.

Those must have been lonely hours for the aged apostle in prison, facing almost certain death and forsaken by his friends. It is difficult for us to understand why God's servants who have given themselves in sacrificial service to others should suffer like this at the end. But Paul knew that the glory of the next life would repay it all.

IV. Three Symbols of the Christian (2:1–7)

1. Introduction

2:1, 2

> 1You then, my son, be strong in the grace that is in Christ Jesus 2And the things you have heard me say in the presence of many witnesses entrust to reliable men who will also be qualified to teach others.

1,2 After exhorting Timothy to "be strong in the grace that is in Christ Jesus," Paul sounds his frequent note in the Pastorals about preserving and transmitting the tradition of truth (cf. 1:13, 14). "Entrust" (v.2) is *parathou*, which is related to *parathēkē* (see note on v.12). The deposit that Timothy had received from Paul he was to pass on to "reliable men who will also be qualified to teach others."

2. The Soldier

2:3, 4

³Endure hardship with us like a good soldier of Christ Jesus. ⁴No one serving as a soldier gets involved in civilian affairs—he wants to please his commanding officer.

3 "Endure hardship" is *synkakopathēson* (see comments on 1:8). One aspect of the Christian life is that it is a warfare against the forces of evil. So Timothy must be "a good soldier of Christ Jesus." Paul uses this figure especially for ministers of the gospel (Phil 2:25; Philem 2).

4 No one "serving as a soldier" (*strateuomenos*) gets involved in "civilian affairs"— literally, "the affairs" (*pragmateiais*, "business, occupations," only here in the NT) "of the [this] life." The verb "gets involved" is *empleketai* (only here and 2 Peter 2:20). In the active voice *emplekō* means "weave in, entwine." In the passive, as here, it is used metaphorically in the sense of "be involved, entangled in." The soldier has to lay aside all secular pursuits, and the Christian minister must be willing to do the same.

"His commanding officer" is literally "the one who enrolled him as a soldier" (*to stratologēsanti*, only here in the NT). When Christ has enrolled us as full-time soldiers in his army, we should seek to please him by giving ourselves to his service without distraction.

3. The Athlete

2:5

⁵Similarly, if anyone competes as an athlete, he does not receive the victor's crown unless he competes according to the rules.

5 Paul is fond of both military and athletic metaphors. The Christian, and especially the minister, must be spiritually a good soldier and a good athlete. "Competes as an athlete" is *athlē*, found (in the NT) only in this verse (twice). We have already noted a similar verb in 1 Timothy 6:12 (see comments there). The verb here is used for competing in an athletic contest in the arena.

"Receive the victor's crown" is also one word, *stephanoutai* (only here and Heb 2:7, 9). The Greek has two words for crown: *diadēma* ("diadem," Rev 12:3; 13:1; 19:12), which means a royal crown; and *stephanos*, the victor's wreath given to the winner in an athletic contest. Hence the full translation here of the verb *stephanoō*.

The winning athlete does not receive this crown unless he competes "according to the rules"—one word in the Greek, *nomimōs*, "lawfully" (only here and 1 Tim 1:8). The man who breaks the rules is disqualified.

4. The Farmer

2:6, 7

> [6]The hard-working farmer should be the first to receive a share of the crops. [7]Reflect on what I am saying, for the Lord will give you insight into all this.

6 The Christian ministry can also be compared to farming. The pastor must sow the seed and cultivate the growing plants. Paul says, "The hard-working farmer should be the first to receive a share of the crops." The emphasis here is on "hard-working" (*kopiōnta*, "toiling"). Bernard puts it well: "The main thought is that labour, discipline, striving are the portion of him who would succeed in any enterprise, be he soldier or athlete or farmer" (p. 118).

7 Paul winds up this section by saying, "Reflect on what I am saying." If Timothy does this, he will understand what it is all about. The three similes that Paul uses here—soldier, athlete, farmer—are found together in 1 Corinthians 9:6; 7:24-27. The closest parallel between these two Scriptures is in the case of the athlete, who must go into strict training if he is going to win the prize. So a Christian must have intense devotion and firm self-discipline if he is to win out for the Lord.

V. Suffering and Glory

2:8-13

> [8]Remember Jesus Christ, raised from the dead, descended from David. This is my gospel, [9]for which I am suffering even to the point of being chained like a criminal. But God's word is not chained. [10]Therefore I endure everything for the sake of the elect, that they too may obtain the salvation that is in Christ Jesus, with eternal glory.
> [11]Here is a trustworthy saying:
> If we died with him,
>   we will also live with him;
> [12]if we endure,
>   we will also reign with him.
> If we disown him,
>   he will also disown us;
> [13]if we are faithless,
>   he will remain faithful,
>   for he cannot disown himself.

8 Now Paul urges Timothy to keep on remembering (present tense) Jesus Christ. "Raised from the dead" emphasizes his deity; "descended from David," his humanity (cf. Rom 1:3, 4). It is not the dead Christ that Timothy is to contemplate, but the risen living Lord. This is Paul's gospel ("good news").

9 For preaching this gospel, Paul is suffering. The Greek literally says, "I am suffering evil . . . as an evil-doer" (*kakopathō . . . hōs kakourgos*). He was "chained like a criminal." But he rejoices that "God's word is not chained." The preacher is in prison, but the Word of God is still moving on and transforming lives.

10 Because of this, the apostle patiently endures (*hypomenō*) everything for the sake of the "elect." The adjective *eklektos* (lit., "chosen") comes from the verb *eklegō*, "choose." Thayer says that this is used "of Christians, as those whom he [God] has set apart from

174

among the irreligious multitude as dear unto himself, and whom he has rendered, through faith in Christ, citizens in the Messianic kingdom" (p. 197). The important qualification here is "through faith in Christ." E.F. Brown says: "The elect are those whom God has already chosen or those whom He will choose for admission into the Christian Church. ... It does not mean 'chosen to final salvation,' as is shown by the words which follow" (*The Pastoral Epistles*, "Westminster Commentaries," p. 67).

The whole purpose of Paul's ministry was that people might "obtain the salvation that is in Christ Jesus." The ultimate goal of this salvation is "eternal glory." But from beginning to end it is all in Christ.

11–13 For the opening formula see the comments on 1 Timothy 1:15. Some scholars think it goes with the preceding verse, but it seems more reasonable to apply it to what follows. In these three verses we find what is usually thought to be an early Christian hymn. It is in the typical form of Hebrew poetic parallelism—four "if " clauses, each followed by a balancing conclusion. The first two are positive, the other two negative.

"If we died with him" is in the aorist tense, (*synapethanomen*), indicating a crisis (EGT, 4:163). Paul spells this out in Romans 6:3–6. It is only as we die with Christ, by identification with him in his death, that we can have spiritual life in him. "We will also live with him" does not refer to our future resurrection, but to our present life in Christ. The parallel is Romans 6:8, 11. Right here and now we are to count ourselves "dead to sin but alive to God in Christ Jesus." The Pauline formula is "You have to die to live."

Then Paul goes on to say, "If we endure, we will also reign with him." The verb "endure" is in the present tense of continuous action (*hypomenomen*). It is only as we keep on enduring to the end that we will be saved in time of persecution (Matt 10:22; cf. context.).

The third proposition is negative: "If we disown him" (aorist tense, *arnēsometha*), "he will also disown us." This is a serious warning. We cannot reject Christ without being rejected ourselves.

"If we are faithless" is in the present tense (*apistoumen*), indicating a settled state of refusing to believe in Jesus and obey him. But whatever we do, "he will remain faithful, for he cannot disown himself." God's faithfulness is eternal.

Notes

12,13 It may be wondered why NIV changed the familiar "deny" to "disown." The reason is that "deny" means primarily "to declare untrue; assert the contrary of, contradict," whereas "disown" means "to refuse to acknowledge or accept as one's own" (*American Heritage Dictionary*). Thus, "disown" was more accurate when applied to persons as its object.

VI. Contrasts in the Church (2:14–26)

1. *True and False Teachers*

2:14–19

> **14**Keep reminding them of these things. Warn them before God against quarreling about words; it is of no value, and only ruins those who listen. **15**Do your best to present yourself to God as one approved, a workman who does not need to be ashamed and who correctly handles the word of truth. **16**Avoid godless chatter,

because those who indulge in it will become more and more ungodly. [17]Their teaching will spread like gangrene. Among them are Hymenaeus and Philetus, [18]who have wandered away from the truth. They say that the resurrection has already taken place, and they destroy the faith of some. [19]Nevertheless, God's solid foundation stands firm, sealed with this inscription: "The Lord knows those who are his," and, "Everyone who confesses the name of the Lord must turn away from wickedness."

14,15 In these two verses Paul challenges Timothy to be an approved workman. He is to "keep on reminding" the believers of "these things," the things about which Paul has been speaking. He is also to warn them before God against "quarreling about words"—*logomachein* (only here in the NT; cf. *logomachia*, 1 Tim 6:4). Fighting over mere words is a waste of time; "it is of no value." It only brings ruin (*katastrophē*, "catastrophe," only here in the NT) to the listeners.

"Do your best" is *spoudason*, which literaly means "make haste," and so "be zealous or eager." "Study" (KJV) is obviously too narrow a term, usually referring today to the studying of books. The true meaning is "make every effort."

"Who does not need to be ashamed" is one word, the compound adjective *anepaischynton* (only here in the NT), literally "not to be put to shame." White suggests that the combination here means "a workman who has no cause for shame when his work is being inspected" (EGT, 4:165).

"Who correctly handles" is *orthotomounta* (likewise only here in the NT)—"holding a straight course" in the word of truth. The renowned Syrian exegete Theodoret (c. 393–c. 458) applied the verb to "a plowman who drives a straight furrow." BAG says "Found elsewhere independently of the NT only in Prov 3:6; 11:5, where it is used with *hodous* and plainly means 'cut a road across country (that is forested or otherwise difficult to pass through) in a straight direction,' so that the traveler might go directly to his destination.... Then *orthotomein ton logon tēs alētheias* would perhaps mean *guide the word of truth along a straight path* (like a road that goes straight to its goal), without being turned aside by wordy debates or impious talk" (p. 584). The context suggests that Paul is warning against taking the devious paths of deceiving interpretations in teaching the Scriptures.

16–18 In these three verses the apostle describes heretical teachers. He warns Timothy to "avoid" ("shun") godless "chatter" (*kenophōnias*, "empty sounds," only here and 1 Tim 6:20). Lock paraphrases this: "But to all these irreligious and frivolous hair-splittings give a wide berth" (p. 97). For they *prokopsousin*—"will cut forward," or "advance"— "to more of ungodliness" (so the Greek). Probably "they" means the false teachers, as suggested in NIV.

Paul goes on to say that their "teaching [*logos*] will spread"—literally, "will have pasture" (*hexei nomēn*). The noun *nomē* is found (in the NT) only here and in John 10:9 ("pasture"). But Bernard notes that it "is often used by medical writers of the 'spreading' of a disease, as here" (p. 123). "Gangrene" is *gangraina* (only here in the NT), used by medical writers of that day for a sore that eats into the flesh.

Hymenaeus is probably the one mentioned in 1 Timothy 1:20. Nothing is known about Philetus. These had "wandered away [*ēstochēsan*, see 1 Tim 1:6; 6:21] from the truth." Specifically, they said that the resurrection had already taken place, and thereby they were destroying, or "subverting," the faith of some people. They were evidently explaining the resurrection in a spiritual sense, equating it with regeneration, or the new birth.

First Corinthians 15 is Paul's extended answer to this false teaching, which was propagated by some in the church at Corinth.

19 In this verse the apostle emphasizes the solid foundation of truth. He declares that in spite of the subversion, God's "solid" (*stereos*) foundation "stands firm" (*hestēken*). Lock says that the foundation is "either Christ Jesus and his Apostles (cf. 1 Cor 3:11; Eph 2:20; Rev 21:14): or, more widely, 'the Church' (cf. 1 Tim 3:15); or 'the truth,' 'the deposit' " (p. 100). Bernard favors "the church," which stands firm inspite of the waywardness of some of its members.

The foundation is "sealed with this inscription"—literally, "having this seal" (*echōn tēn sphragida tautēn*). White comments, "The one seal bears two inscriptions, two mutually complementary parts or aspects: (a) The objective fact of God's superintending knowledge of His chosen; (b) the recognition by the consciousness of each individual of the relation in which he stands to God, with its imperative call to holiness" (EGT, 4:167).

Notes

14 Καταστροφή (*katastrophē*) is found also in 2 Peter 2:6 (TR) but not in the best Gr. text.
19 The first quotation is taken from Num 16:5. The second one is not an exact quotation from the OT, but is probably also related to Korah's rebellion (cf. Num 16:26).

2. Noble and Ignoble Vessels

2:20, 21

> 20In a large house there are not only articles of gold and silver, but also of wood and clay; some are for noble purposes and some for ignoble. 21If a man cleanses himself from the latter, he will be an instrument for noble purposes, made holy, useful to the Master and prepared to do any good work.

20,21 Having drawn at some length the contrast between true and false teachers (vv.14–19), Paul now points up a second contrast—that between noble and ignoble vessels. Both will be found in the church.

"In a large house," where a wealthy man lives, "there are not only articles of gold and silver, but also of wood and clay." The word translated "articles" is *skeuē* (plural). The noun *skeuos* literally means "a vessel, jar, or dish." Plutarch (Caes. 48.7) speaks of four kinds, as here.

"Of gold" is the adjective *chrysa*, from the noun *chrysos*, "gold." One of the most eloquent preachers in the early church was a man named John who was called Chrysostom—*chrysos*, "gold," and *stōma*, "mouth"—John of the Golden Mouth. He was certainly "a vessel unto honour" (KJV).

Some less eminent articles were "of silver." But others were of "wood"—for example, wooden bowls for holding flour—or "clay" (*ostrakina*, cf. "*ostraca*," a term used in archaeology for fragments of ancient pottery).

Some of these, apparently the ones made of gold and silver, are "for noble purposes"—literally, "for honor" (*eis timēn*)—and some "for ignoble" (*eis atimian*, "for dishonor").

We find the same two expressions in Romans 9:21. In the verses that follow there we find that the former vessels are "objects of his [God's] mercy, whom he prepared in advance for glory" (v.23), whereas the latter are "objects of his wrath—prepared for destruction" (v.22). On the basis of this, as well as the context here in 2 Timothy, some scholars feel that the articles for ignoble purposes are the false teachers in the church (vv.16–18), who are destined for eternal destruction. In that case, "if a man cleanses himself from the latter" (v.21) means that Timothy must expel from the church the ignoble members.

Another interpretation is less drastic. It holds that in "a large house"—the visible church or a local congregation—there are members who are prepared for "noble purposes" and others who are fitted for more menial tasks. Both have their place and function in the church. Verse 21 would then mean that the individual who cleanses himself from "the latter" (*toutōn*, "these things," perhaps false teachings) will be "an instrument for noble purposes" (*skeuos eis timēn*). He will be "made holy" (*hēgiasmenon*, "sanctified"), "useful to the Master" (*euchrēston tō despotē*) "and prepared to do any good work."

Both of these interpretations seem valid. Since we cannot be sure which one Paul had in mind, perhaps we should make both applications.

Notes

20 Some of the early church fathers held that the "large house" was the world. But it seems much more logical to take it as being the church.

20,21 Martin Dibelius and Hans Conzelmann write, "We are not dealing with a problem of those who are less gifted, but with the seducers and the seduced. This interpretation is demanded by the context." They paraphrase v.21 like this: "Even though these vessels for disreputable use ... are present in the house, nevertheless be sure that you yourself remain a vessel for honorable use ... by cleansing yourself of these—perhaps ... the actions designated as 'disreputable'" (*The Pastoral Epistles*, "Hermeneia," p. 113).

3. The Kind and the Quarrelsome

2:22-26

22Flee the evil desires of youth, and pursue righteousness, faith, love and peace, along with those who call on the Lord out of a pure heart. 23Don't have anything to do with foolish and stupid arguments, because you know they produce quarrels. 24And the Lord's servant must not quarrel; instead, he must be kind to everyone, able to teach, not resentful. 25Those who oppose him he must gently instruct, in the hope that God will give them a change of heart leading them to a knowledge of the truth, 26and that they will come to their senses and escape from the trap of the devil, who has taken them captive to do his will.

The last of the three "contrasts in the church" is that between kind people and quarrelsome people (vv.22-26). Unfortunately, both types are in the visible, organized church.

22 Timothy was still a rather young man, probably in his early thirties, and so the aged apostle warns him: "Flee the evil desires of youth" (*neōterikas*, only here in the NT). The

verb "flee" is in the present tense of continuous action; he must keep on fleeing youthful lusts. But he must keep on pursuing (*diōke*, present imperative) the positive virtues. It is not enough to run away from wrong; we must run after what is good. To do this is the only way to escape temptations to evil (cf. Rom 12:21).

Timothy was to pursue four things: "righteousness, faith, love and peace." The first three of these are mentioned in a similar context in 1 Timothy 6:11. Although Timothy must purge the church of false teachers, he had to be careful to promote "love and peace" among the Christian believers committed to his care. "Faith" (*pistis*) may also be translated "faithfulness." Both ideas fit well here.

23 "Don't have anything to do with" is one word, *paraitou* (cf. 1 Tim 4:7). "Foolish" is the adjective *mōros* (cf. "moron"): "1. properly of the nerves, *dull, sluggish.* . . . 2. Of the mind, *dull, stupid, foolish*" (A-S, p. 299). "Stupid" is *apaideutos* (only here in the NT), "uninstructed, ignorant." "Arguments" is *zēteseis*, "questionings, debates." *Paraitou* is a strong verb: "refuse," not merely "avoid" (KJV). White gives the force of it: "Such questions will be brought before you: refuse to discuss them" (EGT, 4:168). Sometimes the wise pastor has to do this. Why? Because "they produce quarrels" (*machas*, "fights"). These tend to divide the church and so destroy it.

24 "The Lord's servant"—every Christian, but particularly the pastor of a church—must not "quarrel" (*machesthai*). Rather, he must be "kind" (*ēpios*, "gentle") to everyone, "apt to teach" (*didaktikon*, only here and 1 Tim 3:2), "not resentful" (*anexikakon*, only here in the NT). It means "bearing evil without resentment" (BAG). This is the attitude that Christians must have toward those who oppose them.

25,26 And so Paul goes on to say that the good minister must "gently instruct" ("in meekness") "those who oppose him"—*tous antidiatithemenous* (only here in the NT). He does this in the hope that God will give them "a change of heart" (*metanoia*, "repentance"), leading to "a knowledge" (*epignōsis*, "full knowledge") of the truth. He hopes that "they will come to their senses and escape" (v.26). This is all one word in the Greek: *ananēpsōsin*. The verb (*ananēphō*) literally means "return to soberness." Thayer says that this passage indicates "to be set free from the snare of the devil and to return to a sound mind ['one's sober senses']" (*Lexicon*, p. 40).

Notes

23 On this verse Bernard says, "The irrelevancy of much of the controversy then prevalent among Christians seems to have deeply impressed St. Paul; again and again he returns to this charge against the heretical teachers, that their doctrines are unprofitable and vain, and that they breed strife about questions either unimportant or insoluble" (p. 126).

26 "Who has taken them captive" is literally "having been taken captive by him" (ἐζωγρημένοι ὑπ᾽ αὐτοῦ, *ezōgrēmenoi hyp᾽ autou*). The verb *zōgreō* occurs only here and in Luke 5:10, where it means "catch alive."

"His will" is τὸ ἐκείνου θέλημα (*to ekeinou thelēma*, "the will of that one"). The change from *autou* (his) to *ekeinou* (that) leads Bernard to think it is "God's will" in rescuing them from the devil's trap. But Dibelius and Conzelmann say, "Both pronouns . . . refer to the devil" (p. 114). We agree.

179

VII. Characteristics of the Last Days (3:1-9)

1. Love of Money and Pleasure

3:1-5

> ¹But mark this: There will be terrible times in the last days. ²People will be lovers of themselves, lovers of money, boastful, proud, abusive, disobedient to their parents, ungrateful, unholy, ³without love, unforgiving, slanderous, without self-control, brutal, not lovers of the good, ⁴treacherous, rash, conceited, lovers of pleasure rather than lovers of God—⁵having a form of godliness but denying its power. Have nothing to do with them.

1 The expression "in the last days" (*en eschatais hēmerais*) comes from the OT (e.g., Isa 2:2; Mic 4:1). In Peter's quotation of Joel 2:28 on the day of Pentecost (Acts 2:17) it clearly refers to the whole messianic age, for he declared that the prophecy was being fulfilled that very day. Hendriksen insists that the phrase has that meaning here (pp. 281-283). But it seems more natural to take it as applying especially to the last days of this age, before the Second Coming, as in 2 Peter 3:3 and Jude 18. This does not at all deny that these conditions have been and will be present throughout the church age. It is simply to say that the characteristics enumerated here will be more intensive and extensive as the end approaches.

Paul declared that in the last days "there will be [*enstēsontai*, 'will be upon us'] terrible times." The adjective *chalepos* ("terrible") occurs only here and in Matthew 8:28, where it is used for the "violent" demoniacs. It means "hard to bear, troublesome, dangerous" (Thayer).

2-4 In these three verses we find a list of no fewer than eighteen vices that will characterize people in the last days. These conditions have always existed in some measure but they have become more marked in recent decades. "Lovers of themselves" is *philautoi* (only here in the NT, "selfish"). "Lovers of money" is *philargyroi* (only here and Luke 16:14, "avaricious"). The cognate noun *philargyria* ("love of money") is found in 1 Timothy 6:10.

Men will also be "boasters" (*alazones*, "imposters" or "braggarts," here and Rom 1:30). They will be "proud" (*hyperēphanoi*, lit., "showing oneself above others"). Originally used in a good sense in Greek literature for truly superior persons, this word soon took on the bad connotation that it always has in the NT: "with an overweening estimate of one's means or merits, despising others or even treating them with contempt, haughty" (Thayer, p. 641). Bernard translates these two words as "*boastful, haughty,* the former term referring specially to *words,* the latter to *thoughts*" (p. 130).

"Abusive" is *blasphēmoi* ("evil-speaking, slanderous"). And it may well be questioned whether children and young people were ever more "disobedient to their parents" than they are today.

The next four adjectives all begin with *a*-negative. *Acharistoi* (only here and Luke 6:35) is the opposite of being thankful. *Anosioi,* "unholy" (only here and 1 Tim 1:9) describes the person who has no fellowship with God and so is living a merely "secular" life. *Astorgoi* ("without love") is found elsewhere (in the NT) only in Romans 1:31, where several of these terms are included in a list of vices. It literally means "without family affection." *Aspondoi,* "unforgiving" (only here) originally indicated "without a treaty or covenant" and so "irreconcilable."

"Slanderous" is *diaboloi*. This usually occurs in the NT as a substantive with the definite article and is translated "the devil." But the adjective connotes "prone to slander" or "accusing falsely."

The next three adjectives also begin with *a*-negative. *Akrateis* (only here in the NT), " 'without self-control' . . . in the widest sense, but more particularly in regard to bodily lusts" (Bernard, p. 130). The adjective literally means "without strength." So it describes the weak man who is easily led into sin. *Anēmeroi*, "brutal" (only here in the NT) means "not tame, savage, fierce." *Aphilagathoi* ("not lovers of the good") has not been found elsewhere in Greek literature. But its meaning is clear from its composition: *a*-negative, *philos* ("lover") and *agathos* ("good").

"Treacherous" is *prodotai*, a noun meaning "traitor" or "betrayer." It is used for Judas Iscariot (Luke 6:16). "Rash" is *propeteis* (only here and Acts 19:36). Literally it meant "falling forward, headlong." Metaphorically it came to mean "hasty, rash, reckless." *Tetyphōmenoi*, "conceited," is the perfect passive participle of typhoō, found elsewhere in the NT only in 1 Timothy 3:6; 6:4 (see comments there).

"Lovers of pleasure rather than lovers of God" is a play on words: *philēdonoi* . . . *philotheoi*. Both words are found only here in the NT. They describe those who put self in the place of God as the center of their affections—a commentary on *philautoi* (v.2).

5 Yet they are religious—"having a form of godliness but denying its power" (v.5). Timothy is told to "have nothing to do" (*apotrepou*, "turn away from," only here in the NT) with such hypocrites.

2. *Depraved Living and Thinking*
3:6–9

> ⁶They are the kind who worm their way into homes and gain control over weak-willed women, who are loaded down with sins and are swayed by all kinds of evil desires, ⁷always learning but never able to acknowledge the truth. ⁸Just as Jannes and Jambres opposed Moses, so also these men oppose the truth—men of depraved minds, who, as far as the faith is concerned, are rejected. ⁹But they will not get very far because, as in the case of those men, their folly will be clear to everyone.

6,7 In the first five verses of this chapter Paul has been pointing out the characteristics of those who love money and pleasure. Now he scores them for their depraved living and thinking. He says that they "worm their way into homes." The verb is *endynō*, which means "to creep into, insinuate one's self into; to enter" (Thayer).

"Gain control over" is *aixmalōtizō* (lit., "take captive" in war), but here perhaps only "deceive" (BAG). "Weak-willed women" is one word, *gynaikaria* (only here in the NT), literally, "little women"—a contemptuous diminutive (KJV, "silly women"). These women are further described as "loaded down" or "overwhelmed," with sins—the perfect passive of the verb *sōreuō* (only here and Rom 12:20), which means "to heap on." They are also "swayed" ("led," *agomena*) "by all kinds of evil desires." Such women become an easy prey for false teachers. Verse 7 suggests that these women wanted to pose as learned people. But actually they remained in ignorance of the truth.

8,9 Jannes and Jambres are not mentioned in the OT. But there was a Jewish tradition that they were two of the Egyptian magicians who withstood Moses and Aaron. They

181

are thus mentioned in the Targum (Aramaic paraphrase) of Jonathan on Exodus 7:11. Pliny in his *Natural History* (A.D. 77) names Jannes along with Moses. It has been suggested that the names mean "the rebel" and "the opponent" (Lock, p. 107).

Paul likens the false teachers at Ephesus to these ancient magicians. He describes them as "men of depraved minds." "Depraved" is the perfect passive participle of *kataphtheirō* (only here in the NT). It means "utterly corrupted." As far as the faith is concerned, they are "rejected" (*adokimoi*, "rejected after testing"). They cannot be trusted to teach the truth. But they will not get far. As in the case of Jannes and Jambres, their "folly" (*anoia*, only here and Luke 6:11) will be clearly seen.

Notes

6 Several lexicons discuss the verb ἐνδύνω (*endynō*) under ἐνδύω (*endyō*, "dress" or "clothe"), giving "enter" as a special meaning in this one place. But BAG lists it separately as an "epic, Ionic, poetic form beside ἐνδύω, as early as Homer" (p. 263).

VIII. Persecution and Steadfastness (3:10-17)

1. All Christians Persecuted

3:10-13

¹⁰You, however, know all about my teaching, my way of life, my purpose, faith, patience, love, endurance, ¹¹persecutions, sufferings—what kinds of things happened to me in Antioch, Iconium and Lystra, the persecutions I endured. Yet the Lord rescued me from all of them. ¹²In fact, everyone who wants to live a godly life in Christ Jesus will be persecuted, ¹³while evil men and impostors will go from bad to worse, deceiving and being deceived.

10,11 The "you" is emphatic here, expressed by the pronoun *sy*. "Know all about" is the verb *parakoloutheō* (from *para*, "beside," and *akaloutheō*, "follow," and so "follow closely"). In the NT it occurs elsewhere only in Luke 1:3 ("investigated") and 1 Timothy 4:6 ("followed"). Thayer, A-S, and BAG all give for this passage: "follow as a rule" (standard of conduct), or "follow faithfully." NIV is in line with KJV ("fully known") and RSV ("observed"). Both of these basic ideas fit the context. NASB has the simple translation "followed," which can be taken either way. Verse 11 would seem to point toward the traditional interpretation (KJV, RSV, NIV).

In any case, Paul says that Timothy was familiar with the apostle's life and "teaching" (*didaskalia*). "Way of life" is *agōgē* (only here in the NT). "Purpose" (*prothesis*) is used elsewhere by Paul only for God's purposes. *Pistis* ("faith") also means "faithfulness." It may mean here Paul's loyalty to the Christian faith. "Patience" is *makrothymia*. In KJV this is usually rendered "longsuffering"—a quality Paul had to show toward his opponents. *Agapē* is the constant, steadfast "love" that God implants in our hearts. "Endurance" is *hypomonē*, which Ellicott defines as "the *brave* patience with which the Christian contends against the various hindrances, persecutions, and temptations that befall him in his conflict with the inward and outward world" (comments on 1 Thess 1:3).

In v.11 Paul adds two more things that Timothy knew about: "persecutions" (*diōgmois*, from *diōkō*, "pursue, persecute") and "sufferings" (*pathēmasin*, from *paschō*, "suffer"). These things had happened to the apostle-missionary in Pisidian Antioch, Iconium, and Lystra (Acts 13:50; 14:2, 5, 19)—cities in the Roman province of Galatia where Paul had founded churches on his first missionary journey. He was actually bombarded with stones in Lystra, and left for dead. Since Timothy was a young man in Lystra at that time and had evidently just been converted under Paul's ministry, he had poignant memories of this incident. But out of them all the Lord had delivered Paul, even reviving him from the stoning.

12,13 Paul was not alone in his sufferings. He declares that "everyone who wants [*thelontes*, 'is willing'] to live a godly life in Christ Jesus will be persecuted." Meanwhile, "evil men and imposters will go from bad to worse"—literally, "will make advance [*prokopsousin*] toward the worse." The Greek word for "impostors" is *goēs* (only here in the NT), which originally meant "a wailer, howler," and then "a juggler, enchanter"— "because incantations used to be uttered in a kind of howl"—and so finally "a deceiver, impostor" (Thayer, p. 120). BAG gives "swindler, cheat." Such men are "deceiving and being deceived." Having been deceived by false teachers, they are now deceiving others.

2. The Adequacy of Scripture

3:14–17

> 14But as for you, continue in what you have learned and have become convinced of, because you know those from whom you learned it, 15and how from infancy you have known the holy Scriptures, which are able to make you wise for salvation through faith in Christ Jesus. 16All Scripture is God-breathed and is useful for teaching, rebuking, correcting and training in righteousness, 17so that the man of God may be thoroughly equipped for every good work.

14,15 Timothy is not to be led astray by these impostors. Instead, he is to continue in what he had learned and had "become convinced of " (*epistōthēs*, only here in the NT), "have been firmly persuaded of," or "have been assured of." Why? "Because you know those from whom you learned it." Who were his teachers? His grandmother Lois and his mother Eunice (1:5), as the next clause shows: "and how from infancy you have known the holy Scriptures." Bernard comments, "It was the custom to teach Jewish children the law at a very early age, and to cause them to commit parts of it to memory" (p. 135). This was Timothy's heritage. "The holy Scriptures" is *ta hiera grammata* (lit., "the sacred writings"), an expression found in both Philo (*Life of Moses*, iii.39) and Josephus (*Antiq.* x.10.4) for the OT, which is what Timothy was taught as a child.

These OT Scriptures were able to make him "wise" in preparation "for salvation through faith in Christ Jesus." They disciplined him in obedience to God and also pointed forward to the coming Messiah, through whom salvation by faith would become available.

16 "All Scripture is God-breathed." That is exactly what the Greek says. The adjective *theopneustos* (only here in the NT) is compounded of *theos*, "God," and the verb *pneō*, "breathe." This is one of the greatest texts in the NT on the inspiration of the Bible. (The noun *theopneustia* does not occur in the NT.) Another outstanding passage is 2 Peter 1:21, which indicates something of how the divine inspiration took place. Here in 2 Timothy we have the fact simply and plainly stated; the process of inspiration is not dealt with.

This God-inspired Scripture is "useful" (*ōphelimos*, "profitable," only here and 1 Tim 4:8; Titus 3:8). Paul then notes some areas in which it is useful. "Teaching" (*didaskalia*) is the most general. "Rebuking" (*elegmos*, only here in the NT) is used for "conviction" of a sinner in LXX (Num 5:18ff.). "Correcting" (*epanorthōsin* only here) literally means "restoration to an upright position or a right state." *Paideia* ("training") comes from *pais*, ("child"). So it originally meant "the rearing of a child." Then it came to mean "training, learning, instruction." Christians need to be trained in "righteousness"—both inward and outward.

17 The purpose of all this is that "the man of God may be thoroughly equipped for every good work." "Thoroughly equipped" is the combination of an adjective and the perfect passive participle of a verb. The adjective is *artios* (only here in the NT). BAG defines it thus: "*complete, capable, proficient*=able to meet all demands" (p. 110). The verb is *exartizō* (only here and Acts 21:5), "equip, furnish." See F.E. Gaebelein, *The Christian Use of the Bible* (Chicago: Moody Press, 1946) for an extended treatment of 2 Timothy 3:16, 17.

Notes

16 This verse has no verb in the Gr. but "is" has to be inserted somewhere in English to make sense. ASV took θεόπνευστος (*theopneustos*, "God-breathed") as attached to γραφή (*graphē*, "Scripture"), and so reads, "Every scripture inspired of God *is* also profitable . . . ." Bernard (CGT) and White (EGT) both defend this translation on the twofold basis that (1) there is no evidence in the context that the inspiration of the Scriptures was being called into question and (2) the emphasis of the entire passage is on the usefulness of the Scriptures in fitting the believer for service. Bernard notes that this was the interpretation of Origen, the Vulgate and Syriac versions, Martin Luther, and also the early English translations of Wycliffe, Tyndale, Coverdale, and Cranmer (p. 137).

On the other hand, Lock (ICC) thinks it is better to take *theopneustos* as a predicate adjective: "All Scripture is inspired by God . . . and therefore useful" (p. 110). Simpson presents a convincing fourfold defense of this translation, and notes that Chrysostom interpreted it this way (p. 150).

IX. Preach the Word

4:1-5

> [1]In the presence of God and of Christ Jesus, who will judge the living and the dead, and in view of his appearing and his kingdom, I give you this charge: [2]Preach the Word; be prepared in season and out of season; correct, rebuke and encourage—with great patience and careful instruction. [3]For the time will come when men will not put up with sound doctrine. Instead, to suit their own desires, they will gather around them a great number of teachers to say what their itching ears want to hear. [4]They will turn their ears away from the truth and turn aside to myths. [5]But you, keep your head in all situations, endure hardship, do the work of an evangelist, discharge all the duties of your ministry.

1 Here Paul speaks of Christ Jesus as the one who will "judge the living and the

dead"—a clause found in all the early creeds of the church. The two classes mentioned here are reminiscent of 1 Thessalonians 4:16, 17.

"In view of his appearing and his kingdom" is what is called the accusative of adjuration. "I give you this charge" is one word in Greek—*diamartyromai* ("I adjure, I solemnly charge"). Simpson notes that "it has the weight of a legal affirmation" (p. 152). Timothy is to be governed in his thinking, not just by the present life but also by the coming judgment and the eternal kingdom of Christ.

2 The basic charge is: "Preach ['herald, proclaim'—*kēryxon*] the Word." The preacher is not to air his own opinions but to proclaim God's eternal, authoritative Word of truth. "Be prepared" is the verb *ephistēmi*, which means "be ready, be on hand." The minister has to be on duty constantly, ready for any emergency. "In season and out of season" is simply *eukairōs akairōs*. The first word occurs also in Mark 14:11, the second only here. In addition to preaching the Word, Timothy is to "correct" (*elenxon*, "convict, reprove"), "rebuke" (*epitimēson*, "censure, admonish"), and "encourage" (*parakaleson*, which also means "comfort" and "exhort"). But he is to do these things with great "patience" (*makrothymia*, "longsuffering") and careful "instruction" (*didachē*, the act of teaching). Bernard makes the sage observation: "Rebuke and exhortation must be accompanied with *teaching*, or they will be unprofitable" (p. 140). And it must all be done in patience and love.

3 Timothy is warned that the time will come when men will not "put up with [*anexontai*, 'endure' or 'listen to'] sound doctrine" (*hygiainousēs didaskalias*). As has already been noted (cf. 1 Tim 1:10), this is probably the key phrase of the pastoral Epistles. It occurs again in Titus 1:9; 2:1. Timothy's major responsibility in Ephesus was to defend and proclaim sound doctrine. He must do this constantly, since the time would come when people would not listen to the truth. Instead, "to suit their own desires"—*epithymias*, translated "evil desires" in 3:6—"they will gather around them" (*episōreusousi*, lit., "heap together," only here in the NT) teachers "to say what their itching ears want to hear" (*knēthomenoi tēn akoēn*, "itching in their ears"). These were ears "which were always pricking with an uneasy desire for what would gratify the taste of a carnal, self-willed heart" (Fairbairn, p. 385).

4 People like this will "turn away" (*apostrepsousin*, cf. 1:15) their ears from the truth and will "turn aside" (*ektrapēsontai*, see 1 Tim 1:6; 5:15; 6:20) to "myths" (*mythous*, see 1 Tim 1:4; 4:7). The carnal heart prefers senseless myths rather than solid truth.

5 "Keep your head" is *nēphe*. This verb literally meant "be sober, abstain from wine." But in the NT (cf. 1 Thess 5:6, 8; 1 Peter 1:13; 4:7; 5:8) it has the metaphorical sense of being self-controlled or self-possessed. Simpson thinks the meaning here is "Be wide-awake" (p. 154). But probably the idea of keeping one's self-control under all circumstances fits best in this passage. Timothy is again urged to "endure hardship" (*kakopathēson*, see 2:9). He is to do the work of an "evangelist" (*euangelistou*). This interesting word occurs only three times in the NT. It obviously comes from the familiar verb *euangelizō* ("announce the good news, preach the gospel"). In the two other passages (Acts 21:8; Eph 4:11) it may well refer to an itinerant preacher. But here it perhaps suggests that a pastor must also be an evangelist, pointing sinners to Christ.

The summary of Paul's solemn charge to Timothy is this: "Discharge all the duties of your ministry"—literally, "fulfill [or 'fill full'] your ministry" (*tēn diakonian sou plēro-*

phorēson). Timothy is to fulfill his "calling" (NEB) by packing his ministry to the full with the things Paul has been exhorting him to do in these two Epistles. Fairbairn says that the verb means "fill it up, perform it fully, or make it, as far as you can, a complete and effective service" (p. 389).

Notes

1 "Christ Jesus" is the correct reading, rather than "the Lord Jesus Christ" (KJV). Because these names for Jesus are abbreviated in the early Gr. MSS, there is much variation in the readings.
2 "Great" and "careful" both tr. the adjective πάσῃ (*pasē*, "all").

X. Paul's Final Testimony

4:6–8

> 6For I am already being poured out as a drink offering, and the time has come for my departure. 7I have fought the good fight, I have finished the race, I have kept the faith. 8Now there is in store for me the crown of righteousness, which the Lord, the righteous Judge, will award to me on that day—and not only to me, but also to all who have longed for his appearing.

6 In Philippians 2:17 Paul wrote, "But even if I am being poured out like a drink offering on the sacrifice. . . ." But here he says, "For I am already being poured out as a drink offering." In both passages "I am being poured out like a drink offering" is one word in the Greek: *spendomai* (not elsewhere in the NT). The picture is that of a drink offering poured on the lamb of sacrifice just before it was burned on the altar (Num 28:24).

There is both comparison and contrast in these unique passages. In both places Paul is talking about pouring out his life. But when he wrote to Philippi from his first Roman imprisonment he was expecting to be released soon and revisit that city (Phil 2:24). So he uses the word *if.* Probably he felt that things were fast winding up for him, but the time had not yet come for pouring out his blood "on the sacrifice and service" of his devoted ministry.

Now the case is different. He is nearing the end of his second, final imprisonment at Rome. He is conscious that his fate is sealed, for he adds, "And the time has come for my departure."

The word for "departure" is *analysis* (only here in the NT). It comes from the verb *analyō,* which literally meant "unloose." The noun was used for the "loosing" of a vessel from its moorings or of soldiers "breaking up" camp for departure. Paul was about ready to "strike tent" (leave his physical body) and forsake this earth for the presence of his Lord. This second Epistle has sometimes been called his "swan-song" or his valedictory.

7 There are two ways of interpreting this verse. One is to assume that we have here three figures of speech: the first military, the second athletic, the third religious (stewardship). Simpson insists strongly on this (p. 159).

But the three clauses of the verse may all be taken as related to athletics. The verb translated "fought" here is *agōnizomai.* It is true that in John 18:36 it clearly means "to fight" in a military way. But just as clearly it relates to athletics in 1 Corinthians 9:25, where it is translated "competes in the games." Though it may go either way in its other occurrences in the NT, it seems more natural to take it in the athletic sense in all of them—"make every effort" (Luke 13:24); "struggling" (Col 1:29); 'wrestling" (Col 4:12); "strive" (1 Tim 4:10); and "fight" (1 Tim 6:12). In the last of these (see the comments in loc.) we have the same expression as here ("agonize the good agony"). And there seems to be no question but that the popular use of the noun *agōn* here was for gatherings for games. In Hebrews 12:1 this noun is, of necessity, translated "race"—a race to be run.

If we accept the dominance of the athletic metaphor here, we can paraphrase the verse like this: "I have competed well in the athletic contest [of life], I have finished the race, I have kept the rules"—not "fouled out" and so been disqualified from winning. The word for "race" is *dromon* (only here and Acts 13:25; 20:24). It comes from the second aorist stem of *trechō* ("run"), and so clearly means a racecourse (cf. KJV).

8 One of the main reasons for preferring the athletic interpretation in v.7—which is favored by Bernard and Fairbairn, and allowed by Lock—is that it fits in perfectly with v.8. Paul says that a "crown" awaits him. This is not *diadēma* ("diadem"), the royal crown, but *stephanos*, the laurel wreath given to the winner of the Marathon race (cf. 1 Cor 9:25). The Lord, the righteous Judge (of the contest) was ready to "award" this prize to Paul at the end of the race, his victorious life. The same reward awaits all who run the Christian race successfully to the finish and long for "his appearing" (the Second Coming).

Notes

8 The genitive, τῆς δικαιοσύνης (*tēs diakaiosynēs*, "of righteousness"), is difficult to interpret. Bernard thinks it means "the crown appropriate to the righteous man, and belonging to righteousness" (p. 143). Lock defines it as "the crown which belongs to, which is won by righteousness; perhaps also the crown which consists in perfect eternal righteousness" (p. 115). This would be the genitive of apposition.

XI. Paul's Final Plea

4:9-13

9Do your best to come to me quickly, 10for Demas, because he loved this world, has deserted me and has gone to Thessalonica. Crescens has gone to Galatia, and Titus to Dalmatia. 11Only Luke is with me. Get Mark and bring him with you, because he is helpful to me in my ministry. 12I sent Tychicus to Ephesus. 13When you come, bring the cloak that I left with Carpus at Troas, and my scrolls, especially the parchments.

9 "Do your best" is *spoudason* ("make haste"). Paul had already said that he longed to see Timothy (1:4). Now he urges him to come speedily.

10 Verses 10–12 give the reasons for this. Paul was left almost alone. Demas, his trusted associate, had deserted him. During the apostle's first Roman imprisonment, he twice mentioned Demas as one of his fellow workers (Col 4:14; Philem 24). Some have tried to put a good construction on the reference to Demas in 2 Timothy, suggesting that he had gone on a missionary errand to Thessalonica. But Paul uses the same verb *enkataleipō* here as in v.16 ("deserted"). And we are told that Demas left "because he loved this world." He was not willing to pay the price of hardship and suffering that Paul was paying.

Crescens (mentioned only here) had gone to Galatia, and Titus to Dalmatia. The latter place was on the eastern shore of the Adriatic Sea, north of Macedonia. We are not told the reason why these two men left Paul at Rome. We would assume that they were sent by him to do missionary work, though this is not specifically stated. Incidentally, this verse also shows that Titus had completed his work in Crete (Titus 1:5) and had joined Paul at Rome.

11 "Only Luke is with me." There is pathos, "a tremulous note" (Simpson) in these words. Since Luke was alone with Paul, he was probably the one who acted as the apostle's secretary in the actual writing of this Epistle (see Introduction). Perhaps Luke's own loneliness is also reflected here.

Why did Luke stay with Paul to the end? Perhaps it was because the aged, ailing apostle needed the care of "the beloved physician" (Col 4:14, KJV) in his closing years and because Luke's deep personal devotion to Paul would lead him to stay right with him.

"Mark" had had a checkered career. We first meet him in Acts 12:12. When Peter was miraculously delivered from prison, "he went to the house of Mary the mother of John, also called Mark." Barnabas and Paul took him to Antioch (Acts 12:25) and then took him with them as "their helper" on the first missionary journey (13:5). But the young Mark "flunked out" and returned to Jerusalem (13:13). Because of this, Paul refused to take him along on the second journey (15:36–40). Later Mark matured and was with Paul in his first Roman imprisonment (Col 4:10). Now the aging apostle gives his young associate his highest accolade: "Get Mark and bring him with you, because he is helpful to me in my ministry." So John Mark is a vivid example of a young man who failed in his first assignment, but finally made good.

12 "Tychicus" was from the province of Asia and accompanied Paul on his last journey to Jerusalem (Acts 20:4). He was the bearer of the letters to the Colossians (4:7, 8) and to the Ephesians (6:21). In both places he is described as a "dear brother" and "faithful servant in the Lord." It is obvious that Paul had high regard for Tychicus.

"I sent" (*apesteila*) may well be taken as the epistolary aorist, "I am sending." If so, Tychicus was the bearer of this Epistle and was being sent by Paul to take Timothy's place as supervisor of the work at Ephesus. The apostle wanted his "dear son" (1:2) with him in the closing days of his life. We can only conjecture as to whether Timothy reached Paul before the latter's death.

13 It is evident that Timothy was not to go by ship directly to Rome from the large seaport of Ephesus, for he is requested to pick up the cloak Paul had left with Carpus at Troas. Nothing further is known about Carpus. The "cloak" was probably "a travelling cloak with long sleeves, such as would be specially desirable in cold weather" (Bernard, p. 146).

Timothy was also to bring Paul's "scrolls." The Greek is *biblia*, from which comes "Bible." *Biblion* meant "a paper, letter, written document" (A-S), and it is so used in

Matthew 19:7 and Mark 10:4. But its common use in the NT, as in the literature of that day, is for a "roll" or "scroll." These were probably made of papyrus.

Paul especially wanted his "parchments." This kind of writing material was more expensive than papyrus; *membrana* (a Latin word, only here in the NT) were scrolls or codices written on animal skins (vellum). These may have been leather scrolls of OT books. There is an interesting historical parallel to Paul's request. William Tyndale, who translated the first NT printed in English, was imprisoned in Vilvorde Castle near Brussels before his execution in 1536. In the year preceding his death he wrote to the governor, begging for warmer clothing, a woolen shirt, and above all his Hebrew Bible, grammar, and dictionary.

Notes

10 Instead of Γαλατίαν (*Galatian*, "Galatia") two old MSS (‎‎א C) have Γαλλίαν (*Gallian*, "Gaul"). But the former reading seems to be the original one. Greek writers of the first century, however, commonly used Γαλατία (*Galatia*) for Gaul (modern France), northwest of Italy. So we cannot be sure whether the reference is to Asiatic Galatia—as always elsewhere in Acts and Paul's Epistles—or to European Gaul. If it was the latter, as held by some early church fathers, the reference would show Paul's interest in the evangelization of the far west and would imply that he visited Spain between his first and second Roman imprisonments.

13 The word for "cloak" is φαιλόνης (*phailonēs*, only here in the NT). This is listed as φελόνης (*phelonēs*) in A-S, but as φαιλόνης in BAG. The latter admits, however, that φελόνης is the spelling in "the great uncials and critical editions" (p. 859).

XII. Human Opposition and Divine Support

4:14-18

14Alexander the metalworker did me a great deal of harm. The Lord will repay him for what he has done. 15You too should be on your guard against him, because he strongly opposed our message.

16At my first defense, no one came to my support, but everyone deserted me. May it not be held against them. 17But the Lord stood at my side and gave me strength, so that through me the message might be fully proclaimed and all the Gentiles might hear it. And I was delivered from the lion's mouth. 18The Lord will rescue me from every evil attack and will bring me safely to his heavenly kingdom. To him be glory for ever and ever. Amen.

14,15 We know nothing further about "Alexander." This was a common name; so there is no necessary identification with the Alexander of Acts 19:33 or 1 Timothy 1:20 (see comments there). He is called a "metalworker" (*chalkeus*, only here in the NT). Since the word comes from *chalkos*, "copper," it originally was used for a "coppersmith" (KJV), but later in a more general sense for a worker in any metal, especially iron.

We do not know when, where, or in what way Alexander did Paul "a great deal of harm." One good guess is that he had been responsible for the apostle's arrest and imprisonment.

"The Lord reward him according to his works" (KJV) sounds like an imprecatory prayer. But the oldest and best Greek text does not have *apodōē* (the optative of wishing) but the future indicative *apodōsei,* "will repay." It is not an imprecation but a prophecy.

Paul warns Timothy to be on guard against this malicious enemy who "strongly opposed our message" (*logois,* "words"). This may possibly have included not only Paul's preaching but his defense before the court, mentioned in the next verse.

16 The word for "defense" is *apolgia,* from which we get "apology." But our English word has changed its meaning in common usage. Whereas now it means "I was wrong," it originally meant a speech in defense—"I was right!" (cf. Acts 22:1). This sense of the word survives in the term "apologetics" and in the transliteration "apologia," a literary term for a defense of one's position.

What is indicated by Paul's "first defense" when no one came to his support but everyone deserted him? Eusebius (4th century) held that it was in connection with Paul's first Roman imprisonment (Acts 28:30), which resulted in his release. This accords well with the end of v.17, and Lock prefers this interpretation.

But most commentators feel that the language here is too strong for that earlier event, when in accordance with Roman custom, he may have been automatically released without trial at the end of two years. Today scholars generally agree that the reference is to the *prima actio,* the first hearing in court.

Paul's magnanimous Christian love is revealed in the last sentence of this verse: "May it not be held against them." He could and did forgive his deserters for their weakness in fearing to stand by him.

17 But he did not lack support. Triumphantly and gratefully he cries, "But the Lord stood at my side and gave me strength" (*enedynamōsen me,* "infused me with strength, empowered me, made me dynamic!"). The result was that the Gentiles in Caesar's court heard the gospel, which thereby got wider publicity in Rome. When was Paul "delivered from the lion's mouth"? If we accept the reference to his first imprisonment, the answer seems simple. But was he threatened to the extent implied by this vivid figure? The only alternative would be that his first trial had seemed to go well for him, with perhaps a temporary reprieve. The "lion" would then be Nero. But if so, it was this same emperor who later, according to the unanimous tradition of the early church, condemned him and put him to death.

18 "Rescue" and "delivered" (v.17) are from the same verb in Greek, *rhyomai.* There is a striking connection between its use here and in the Lord's Prayer: "Deliver us from the evil one" (Matt 6:13). "Attack" is literally "work" (*ergon*), but the correct thought is expressed here (see Lock, p. 119). The same can be said for "bring me safely" (*sōsei,* "will save"). The exact phrase "his heavenly kingdom" (*tēn basileian autou tēn epouranion*) is not found elsewhere in the NT, but is closely paralleled by "the kingdom of heaven," found thirty-two times in Matthew. Probably the reference here, however, is to the future kingdom in the eternal realm.

Paul is fond of breaking out into spontaneous praise now and then in his Epistles. One of his many doxologies occurs here: "To him"—the Lord; that is, Christ—"be glory for ever and ever. Amen."

Notes

17 There is no definite article with λέοντος (*leontos,* "lion"). This has led some scholars to say that the reference is not to Nero or Satan, but to some imminent deadly peril. But why not allow all three applications?

XIII. Closing Greetings, Farewell

4:19-22

19Greet Priscilla and Aquila and the household of Onesiphorus. 20Erastus stayed in Corinth, and I left Trophimus sick in Miletus. 21Do your best to get here before winter. Eubulus greets you, and so do Pudens, Linus, Claudia and all the brothers. 22The Lord be with your spirit. Grace be with you.

19 Priscilla and Aquila figured prominently in Paul's life. When Paul first arrived in Corinth—evidently short of funds and disappointed at the meager results of his ministry in Athens—he found both employment and lodging with Aquila and Priscilla. Like him, they were tentmakers (Acts 18:2, 3). When Paul left Corinth, this couple sailed across the Aegean with him to Ephesus and stayed there (Acts 18:18, 19). They performed a useful function by instructing Apollos (v.26). From there they, and the church that met in their home, sent greetings to the Christians at Corinth (1 Cor 16:19). Later we apparently find them back in Rome (Rom 16:3); Paul sent greetings to them there and referred (Rom 16:4) to an occasion when they had "risked their lives" for him. But now they are once more in Ephesus. In those days prosperous Jews traveled a great deal from city to city. In four of the six places where Priscilla and Aquila are mentioned, Priscilla's name comes first. Evidently she was the stronger character of the two. It may well be that their moves were due as much to her missionary concern as to her husband's trade.

The "household of Onesiphorus" is mentioned with great appreciation in 1:16–18 (see comments there). But we know nothing further about this devoted Christian.

20 When Paul wrote to Rome from Corinth, he sent greetings from "Erastus, who is the city's director of public works" (Rom 16:23). There was also an Erastus who, along with Timothy, was Paul's helper, at Ephesus (Acts 19:22). We have no way, of course, of knowing whether these three passages refer to the same person. Lock thinks that the Erastus mentioned here was "probably" the same as the one in Romans and "perhaps" the same as the one in Acts (p. 120). At any rate, "Erastus stayed in Corinth," possibly when Paul left there for the last time.

The apostle had "left Trophimus sick in Miletus" (near Ephesus). This man is mentioned as from the province of Asia and as one of Paul's associates in carrying the offering from the Gentile churches to the poor saints at Jerusalem (Acts 20:4). There he became the cause, unintentionally, of Paul's being mobbed and arrested (Acts 21:29).

21 Paul is beginning to feel the cold and dampness in his prison cell. So now he speaks with fresh urgency: "Do your best" (*spoudason,* cf. v.9) "to get here before winter." If not, he will suffer desperately in the cold weather.

Finally, Paul sends greetings from four members of the church at Rome—Eubulus, Pudens, Linus, Claudia—"and all the brothers." Linus is mentioned by Irenaeus (*Against*

Heresies, iii.3) as the first bishop of Rome after the death of Peter and Paul. About the others, we have no certain knowledge.

Paul pronounces a personal benediction on Timothy ("your" is singular in the Greek), before concluding comprehensively: "Grace be with you all."

Notes

19 "Priscilla" is Πρίσκα (*Priska*, "Prisca") here and elsewhere in Paul's Epistles (Rom 16:3; 1 Cor 16:19). But she is better known to us as Priscilla (Πρίσκιλλα, Priskilla) in Acts 18:2, 18, 26.

TITUS

D. Edmond Hiebert

TITUS

Introduction

As the shortest of the pastoral Epistles, Titus has often been overshadowed by the longer Epistles to Timothy. But it is rich in doctrinal and practical values and is worthy of study in its own right.

1. Authorship

The Pauline authorship of the Epistle was not questioned in the early church. Arguments against its authenticity are of modern origin. Its claim to Pauline authorship is here accepted without reserve. (See the introduction to the pastoral Epistles.)

2. Recipient

The letter is addressed to "Titus, my true son in our common faith" (1:4). The appended identification marks a close and affectionate relation between Paul and Titus. Titus 2:6, 7 implies that he was still a comparatively young man when Paul wrote to him.

Scriptural references to Titus are surprisingly rare. Although he was closely connected with Paul, Titus's name never occurs in Acts and, aside from the letter addressed to him, his name is found in only three Pauline Epistles (2 Cor 2:13; 7:6, 13, 14; 8:6, 16, 23; 12:18; Gal. 2:1, 3; 2 Tim 4:10).

Chronologically, the first mention of Titus is in Galatians 2:1–3. When Paul went from Antioch to discuss "his" gospel with the leaders in Jerusalem, he took along Titus, an uncircumcised young Greek, as a worthy specimen of the fruits of his ministry to the Gentiles. "My true son" implies that he was Paul's convert, perhaps won during the ministry in Acts 11:25, 26. At Jerusalem Paul's position that Gentile believers are not under the Mosaic law was vindicated when Titus was not compelled to be circumcised (Gal 2:3–5). Paul's selection of Titus to test this crucial issue speaks well of the spiritual vitality of his young convert.

We hear nothing further of Titus till the time of Paul's ministry at Ephesus on the third missionary journey. Perhaps Paul took him along to Ephesus from Antioch (Acts 18:22–19:1). He was an unnamed member of the group of assistants to Paul there (Acts 19:22). Second Corinthians reveals that at this time he was an esteemed and trusted co-worker with Paul. On more than one occasion Paul sent Titus to Corinth on important missions. Most probably three separate trips to Corinth were made, but the precise number of visits and the sequence of events are uncertain from 2 Corinthians.

About a year before the writing of 2 Corinthians, Paul sent Titus to Corinth to enlist Corinthian participation in the collection for the Judean saints (1 Cor 16:1–4; 2 Cor 9:2; 12:18). Apparently shortly after writing 1 Corinthians, Paul again sent Titus to Corinth to help straighten out the tangled affairs in that church and to counter the work of opponents to Paul there. Plans called for a reunion at Troas where Paul was to engage in missionary work (2 Cor 2:12, 13). The failure of Titus to return as planned caused Paul much anxiety. Terminating the inviting work at Troas, Paul went into Macedonia, hoping in this way to meet Titus sooner. Eventually Titus appeared in Macedonia with the good news that his difficult mission to Corinth had been successful (2 Cor 7:5–7). Paul rejoiced in this success and was encouraged by the personal joy of Titus at the response of the Corinthians (2 Cor 7:6, 7, 13–15). Cheered by these developments, Paul wrote the second Epistle to the Corinthians and sent it back with Titus, instructing him also to complete the collection at Corinth (2 Cor 8:6, 7, 16–22). Paul gave Titus and the two men sent with him (8:18–22) his strong recommendation (8:23, 24), assuring any critical Corinthian that Titus could be fully trusted as one motivated by Paul's own spirit (2 Cor 12:17, 18).

When Paul came to Corinth for three months (Acts 20:2), the difficulties there had been resolved and the collection completed. Titus had successfully completed another sensitive assignment. But he was no longer at Corinth when Paul wrote to the Romans, for his name does not appear among those of Paul's co-workers who sent greetings to the Roman saints (Rom 16:21–23). Nothing further is heard of Titus till the time of the pastoral Epistles.

When Paul wrote to him, Titus was working on the island of Crete. "I left you in Crete" (1:5) indicates that Paul had been with Titus in Crete. Their joint labors there apparently were of short duration, but long enough for Paul to realize the deplorable conditions of the local churches. Apparently Titus had been working there for some time when Paul wrote. He informed Titus that as soon as a replacement arrived, he was to rejoin Paul at Nicopolis (3:12), apparently the Greek city in Epirus on the Gulf of Actium, in western Greece. The request indicates that Paul was formulating further plans for Titus.

We get a last fleeting glimpse of Titus in 2 Timothy 4:10, where Paul informed Timothy that Titus had gone to Dalmatia. This implies he had been with Paul during his second Roman imprisonment. Although the reason for the trip is not given, we may assume that he went there at the call of Christian duty.

These scanty references to Titus reveal that he was a trustworthy, efficient, and valued young co-worker. He possessed a forceful personality, was resourceful, energetic, tactful, skillful in dealing with difficult situations, and effective in conciliating people.

3. Occasion

The external occasion for the letter to Titus was the trip through Crete planned by Zenas and Apollos (3:13). They conveyed the letter to Titus. The internal occasion for

196

writing was Paul's concern to strengthen the hand of Titus as his personal representative in Crete in carrying out a difficult assignment.

4. Purpose

One purpose of the letter was, as has just been stated, to encourage and strengthen Titus in the fulfillment of the commission from Paul. Because of conditions in Crete, Paul knew that Titus would face opposition (1:10, 11; 2:15; 3:10). He aimed to reinforce Titus's authority in working among the churches in Crete. The letter would serve as written authorization for this task, proof to them that he was working in accordance with Paul's own instructions. As the close associate of Paul, Titus must personally have been familiar with the exhortations and instructions contained in the letter, which set forth Paul's concerns for the Cretan churches.

The origin of the Cretan churches is unknown. They had evidently been in existence for some time when Paul visited Crete. Their condition was discouraging. They were inadequately organized, so Titus was directed to appoint morally and doctrinally qualified elders in the various churches (1:6–9). In view of the operation of false teachers (1:10–16), this was essential.

The prevailing moral conditions in the churches were far from what they might be. Naturally prone to be lax and indifferent, the Christians were adversely influenced by the prevailing low moral standards in Crete. Perhaps the gospel of the grace of God had been misinterpreted to mean that salvation was unrelated to daily conduct. Titus was urged to insist on the need for sound doctrine and a high level of moral and social conduct by the Christians (2:1–10; 3:1–3). Christian behavior must be grounded in the basic truths of the gospel (2:11–14; 3:4–8).

The letter also conveyed personal information for Titus. The instruction to join Paul at his winter quarters at Nicopolis after a replacement arrived (3:12) apprised Titus of the fact that Paul was formulating further plans for their joint labors.

5. Date

The date assigned the letter depends on the reconstruction accepted for Paul's journeys following his release from the first Roman imprisonment, as well as the dating for that imprisonment, commonly accepted as A.D. 61–63, though it may have been as early as 59–61. Since this letter makes no mention of the Neronian persecution, which apparently began in October 64, it seems best to date it between the time of Paul's release and the commencement of that persecution. The journeys to the east indicated in 1 Timothy and Titus were apparently made as soon as he was released. The letter to Titus may have been written during the fall of A.D. 63, not long after Paul left Crete.

6. Place of Origin

This can only be conjectured. The remark in 3:12 indicates that Paul had not yet reached Nicopolis. Any suggested place will depend on the reconstruction of Paul's movements following his release. A case can be made for Corinth as the place of origin.

7. Theological Value

The Epistle of Titus covers the same general ground as 1 Timothy but is more compact and less personal. Its greater part deals with ministerial duties and social relations, yet it contains no fewer than three summary passages that are theological gems (1:1–3; 2:11–14; 3:3–7). In 1 Timothy Paul stresses sound doctrine; in Titus he stresses worthy Christian conduct and insists that Christian conduct must be based on and regulated by Christian truth. Nowhere else does Paul more forcefully urge the essential connection between evangelical truth and the purest morality than in this brief letter. Here the basic truths of the gospel are displayed in the abiding glory of their saving and sanctifying appeal. The regenerating work of the Holy Spirit is the experiential basis for Christian conduct (3:3–7).

8. Text

Although the manuscript sources for this letter manifest the usual presence of variant readings, the text of Titus presents no unusual critical problems. The editors of the UBS text felt it desirable to include only four textual problems in their textual apparatus as significant for interpretation.

9. Summary

After the customary salutation (1:1–4), Paul deals first with the qualifications to be looked for in church officials (vv.5–9), then goes on to condemn the false teachers who were undermining the work in Crete (vv.10–16).

In chapter 2 Paul gives Titus advice on how to handle the situation there: he lays down rules for Christian behavior, with special reference to the aged (vv.1–3), younger people (vv.4–8), and slaves (vv.9, 10).

The closing verses (11–15) of that chapter reflect a more theological emphasis in the discussion that, continued into chapter 3, covers the implications of Christian living in the community (vv.1, 2). Then comes a reminder of the transformation wrought by the gospel through the appearance and work of the Savior (vv.4–7).

An admonitory word on good works (v.8; cf. v.14) and false teachers (vv.9–11) follows, and the brief Epistle concludes with personal messages and counsel, and with the benediction (vv.12–15).

10. Bibliography

(See Introduction to 1 Timothy, pp. 346–347.)

11. Outline

    I. Salutation (1:1–4)
        A. The Writer (1:1–3)
        B. The Reader (1:4a)
        C. The Greeting (1:4b)
    II. Concerning Elders and Errorists in Crete (1:5–16)
        A. The Appointment of Qualified Elders (1:5–9)
          1. The Duties of Titus in Crete (1:5)
          2. The Qualifications of the Elders (1:6–9)
        B. The Refutation of False Teachers (1:10–16)
          1. The picture of the false teachers (1:10–13a)
          2. The response to the situation (1:13b–14)
          3. The condemnation of the false teachers (1:15–16)
   III. Concerning the Natural Groups in the Congregations (2:1–15)
        A. The Instructions for the Different Groups (2:1–10)
          1. The instructional duty of Titus (2:1)
          2. The instruction to different age groups (2:2–6)
          3. The personal example of Titus (2:7–8)
          4. The instructions to the slaves (2:9–10)
        B. The Foundation for Godly Living (2:11–14)
          1. The manifestation of God's grace (2:11)
          2. The training by God's grace (2:12)
          3. The expectation of Christ's return (2:13)
          4. The purpose of Christ's redemption (2:14)
        C. The Restatement of the Duty of Titus (2:15)
   IV. Concerning Believers Among Men Generally (3:1–11)
        A. Their Obligations As Citizens (3:1–2)
        B. The Motives for Such Godly Conduct (3:3–8)
          1. The motive from our own past (3:3)
          2. The motive from our present salvation (3:4–7)
            a. Its manifestation (3:4)
            b. Its basis (3:5a)
            c. Its means (3:5b–6)
            d. Its results (3:7)
          3. The necessary connection between doctrine and conduct (3:8)
        C. The Reaction to Spiritual Error (3:9–11)
    V. Conclusion (3:12–15)
        A. The Concluding Instructions (3:12–14)
        B. The Personal Greetings (3:15a)
        C. The Closing Benediction (3:15b)

Text and Exposition

I. Salutation

1:1–4

> [1]Paul, a servant of God and an apostle of Jesus Christ for the faith of God's elect and the knowledge of the truth that leads to godliness— [2]a faith and knowledge resting on the hope of eternal life, which God, who does not lie, promised before the beginning of time, [3]and at his appointed season he brought his word to light through the preaching entrusted to me by the command of God our Savior,

> [4]To Titus, my true son in our common faith:

> Grace and peace from God the Father and Christ Jesus our Savior.

The salutation is remarkably long and weighty for such a brief letter. Only in the lengthy Epistle to the Romans is the salutation much longer. The paragraphing displays the usual three parts of an epistolary salutation of that day—writer, reader, greeting. Each part might be expanded according to the occasion and the writer's purpose.

A. *The Writer* (1:1–3)

1 Here, as in Romans, the length of the salutation is due to the expansion of the first part. The emphasis here on the writer and his authoritative message indicates the purpose of the letter. This solemn self-identification of the writer was not needed by Titus as Paul's devoted co-worker; it effectively stressed the authoritative commission and message of the one for whom Titus acted in Crete. This letter was written for the preservation and furtherance of that message, which was closely linked with godliness in daily life.

To his name Paul added two credentials. "A servant of God" occurs only here in Paul; elsewhere it is "servant of Jesus Christ" (Rom 1:1; Gal 1:10; Phil 1:1). It is hard to understand why an imitator would thus vary from the uniform model. The nearest parallel is James 1:1. "Servant" (*doulos*) is the common term for "slave" and its use implies Paul's acknowledged ownership by God and complete dependence on him. It denotes his personal position. It is here best rendered "servant," since "servant of God" was used of Moses (Josh 1:2) and the prophets (Jer 7:25; Amos 3:7) to denote their use by God to accomplish his will. He is nothing less than *God's* agent. (Note the five occurrences of "God" in this salutation.) Apparently this stress was needed in Crete.

"An apostle of Jesus Christ" marks Paul's official rank among God's servants. "And" (*de*) does not equate but adds an additional fact: "and further." He is Jesus Christ's "apostle," having been called, equipped, and sent forth as his authoritative messenger. "Apostle" is here used in the narrow sense to denote the apostolic office.

"For the faith of God's elect and the knowledge of the truth" further describes his apostolic office. "For" renders the preposition *kata*, the first of four occurrences in the salutation (vv.1 [twice], 3, 4). Its local meaning is "down," and with the accusative case (so in all four occurrences), it means "down along, according to, in harmony with," and marks the standard of measurement. By usage it can mean goal or purpose, "for the purpose of, to further," thus denoting that Paul's mission was to promote Christian faith and knowledge. This is the view of the above rendering which, however, cannot be given to all four occurrences. The translation "according to" which fits all four of them in the salutation, means that his apostleship is in full accord with the faith and knowledge that God's elect have received. His apostleship is not regulated by their faith (cf. Gal

200

1:11–17) but is wholly in accord with it. The Cretan Christians needed to evaluate their faith by that fact.

"God's elect" are those who have responded to God's call through the gospel. The expression embodies a true balance between the divine initiative and the human response. Although surrounded with mystery, the biblical teaching on election is for believers and is intended as a practical truth. It assures faithful, struggling believers that their salvation is all of God from beginning to end.

Christian faith is linked with "knowledge of the truth," the full apprehension of "truth," the inner realization of divine reality as revealed in the gospel. Faith is a heart response to the truth of the gospel, but it must also possess the mind. God never intended his people to remain intellectually ignorant of the truth of the gospel.

Christian truth has a moral character. It "leads to godliness" (more literally, "that is according to godliness"). Conduct must be evaluated by the demands of godliness, that reverential attitude that leads to conduct well pleasing to God. Those gripped by God's truth walk in harmony with such demands. There is an intimate connection between a vital possession of truth and genuine godliness—a lesson the Cretan church needed to learn.

2 The intended connection of v.2 is not quite certain. The NIV translators have added the words "a faith and knowledge" to make clear their understanding of the connection —that the Christian life is grounded in the hope of eternal life. Others hold that the connection is with "apostle" thus giving a further description of Paul's apostleship. But this seems to narrow the thought unduly. It seems best to connect it with all that has gone before.

"Resting on" well renders the original (*epi* with the locative case). "The hope of eternal life" is the basis on which the superstructure of Christian faith and service is built. As with all of God's elect, Paul's life and service were firmly rooted in "hope," which eagerly and confidently awaits the realization of "eternal life"—life not only endless but having an eternal quality. Believers already possess eternal life (John 5:24), but its full and perfect realization awaits the return of the Prince of Life.

This hope is not a vague, pious aspiration but is sure because it is grounded in the absolute trustworthiness of God. The character of the God "who does not lie" (one word in Greek) assures the fulfillment of his promise. This characterization places God in contrast with the notorious deceptiveness of the Cretans (1:12).

God promised this eternal life "before the beginning of time" (literally, "before times eternal"), before the ages of time, begun at creation, began to roll. Some hold that the reference is to the promises made to the OT patriarchs and prophets; others say that the promise reaches back into eternity (cf. 2 Tim 1:9). William Kelly says, "It was a promise within the Godhead when neither the world nor man yet existed" (p.17). The promise is rooted in the eternal purpose of God for man.

3 The reliability of the promise, conceived in the eternal counsels of God, was demonstrated in history through the clear, public revelation it received in the preaching of the gospel. A change in the construction brings out a contrast between the promise of life before times eternal and the manifestation of "his word" at the proper time in history. "His word" is not the personal Christ, the Logos, but rather the saving message of the gospel. This message was made known "at his appointed season," the opportune seasons established by God in his eternal wisdom. All history was the preparation for that revelation. The historical appropriateness of the time is evident from the existence of the Roman peace that gave a favorable setting for the preaching of the gospel and the development of Greek as the linguistic medium of its worldwide proclamation.

The message was brought to the world "through the preaching entrusted to me." This refers, not to the act of preaching, but to the message that was heralded, the message of the gospel. There is no substitute for that message, and Paul was writing so that its purity might be preserved on the island of Crete.

That life-giving message was committed to Paul as a divine trust. He could never escape the wonder that this assignment should be given to him, unworthy as he was (1 Cor 15:9; Eph 3:8; 1 Tim 1:11–13). The personal pronoun is deliberately emphatic, "I on my part was entrusted with" this message. His call was for him a very personal, irreversible experience.

The assignment came to him "by the command of God our Savior." It is a vigorous assertion of his divine commission, underlining the authority behind this letter. "God our Savior" is not used by Paul outside the pastoral Epistles. The original order, "our Savior, God," stresses his saving activity; the One who delivers and preserves is none other than God. The pronoun "our" speaks of the believer's personal appropriation and public confession of him in this capacity. Paul's usage suggests that the reference here is to the Father. In the Pastorals the term is applied to both the Father (1 Tim 1:1; 2:3; 4:10; Titus 1:3; 2:10; 3:4) and the Son (2 Tim 1:10; Titus 1:4; 2:13; 3:6). As the ultimate source of all salvation, the designation is appropriately applied to the Father.

B. The Reader (1:4a)

The recipient is tersely described as "my true son in our common faith." "My true son" ("my" is not in the original) reveals the intimate relation between writer and reader. "Son" is literally "child" and expresses endearment; it implies that Titus was Paul's convert. The adjective "true" (gnēsios), used only in Paul's letters, means "legitimately born, or genuine" and acknowledges that Titus was running true to a parentage that was not physical but spiritual, "in our common faith." "In" (kata) indicates that their relationship was in accord with a "common faith," a faith mutually shared. But "common" reaches farther than writer and reader to denote a faith mutually held by God's elect. This intimate relationship assured that in Crete Titus rightly represented the position of Paul.

C. The Greeting (1:4b)

The greeting with "grace and peace" is characteristically Pauline. "Grace" here is the unmerited favor of God at work in the life of the believer, while "peace" is the resultant experience of harmony and well-being in the life of the reconciled. This double blessing comes "from God the Father and Christ Jesus our Savior." Paul viewed Father and Son as one source of blessing and the one object of every Christian aspiration, thus "from" is not repeated. "Our Savior," in v.3 applied to the Father, is here transferred to the Son. "Our" again signifies the common testimony of believers. This interchange is not accidental; both are involved in bestowing the same salvation. "The Son has brought to us salvation from the Father, and the Father has bestowed it through the Son" (Calvin).

Notes

---

4 As in 1 and 2 Timothy, TR here also reads ἔλεος (*eleos*, "mercy" between "grace" and "peace"). MS evidence, however, strongly favors its omission.

II. Concerning Elders and Errorists in Crete (1:5–16)

The first major division, designed to further the welfare of the Cretan churches, falls into two parts. Verses 5–9 give instructions concerning church officials, whereas vv.10–16 deal with the needed refutation of false teachers in Crete. The presence of the false teachers made more imperative the appointment of qualified leaders.

A. *The Appointment of Qualified Elders*

1:5–9

> 5The reason I left you in Crete was that you might straighten out what was left unfinished and appoint elders in every town, as I directed you. 6An elder must be blameless, the husband of but one wife, a man whose children believe and are not open to the charge of being wild and disobedient. 7Since an overseer is entrusted with God's work, he must be blameless—not overbearing, not quick-tempered, not given to much wine, not violent, not pursuing dishonest gain. 8Rather he must be hospitable, one who loves what is good, who is self-controlled, upright, holy and disciplined. 9He must hold firmly to the trustworthy message as it has been taught, so that he can encourage others by sound doctrine and refute those who oppose it.

Paul's representative in Crete must carry out his commission with the authority shown in the salutation. Verse 5 summarizes the commission given Titus, and vv.6–9 list the needed qualifications for the leaders to be appointed.

1. *The duties of Titus in Crete* (1:5)

5 "I left you in Crete" asserts their joint labors on that island; the time was probably quite brief. Paul's labors in Crete cannot be fitted into Acts 27:7–9 or before. The alternatives are to reject Pauline authorship or to accept that the reference is to a time following his Acts 28 imprisonment. The latter alternative is probable scripturally and is asserted by tradition.

"Left" (*apelipon*) implies that Titus was deliberately left behind in Crete to carry out a specific assignment. Before Paul's departure, the commission was orally delivered; now it is restated concisely in writing. Titus's task was comprehensive: to "straighten out what was left unfinished." The verb "straighten out" (*epidiorthōsē*) denotes that his task was to set things in order; the middle voice implies that he is personally involved in the process, and not merely giving orders to others. "What was left unfinished" points to several serious defects that still needed Titus's attention. The letter points to lack of organization (1:5), unchecked false teachers (1:10, 11; 3:10, 11), and the need for instruction in doctrine and conduct (2:1–10; 3:1, 2). Paul had observed and had begun to correct these matters; Titus must now complete the work. Paul was concerned that the work of grace previously begun in the church should not be left unfinished.

An initial duty was to "appoint elders in every town," in each place where there was a group of believers. Such a plural leadership in the local congregation continued Paul's own earlier practice (Acts 14:23). "Appoint" is preferable to "ordain," as it avoids modern ecclesiastical implication. The verb means "to set down, to put in charge," and does not fix the method of selection. Probably the congregation chose the elders with the encouragement of Titus who had the responsibility of formally appointing them to office.

"As I directed you" recalls that this was in accord with his previous orders. "I" (*egō*) is emphatic, stressing the apostolic authority behind the action of Titus. The middle voice of the verb implies that it would carry out Paul's ideal for these congregations.

2. The qualifications of the elders (1:6-9)

6-9 This list of qualifications corresponds closely to that given in 1 Timothy 3:1-7, yet the differences indicate that it was realistically applied to a contemporary situation. The fact that no deacons are mentioned suggests that the organization of these churches was more primitive than at Ephesus.

6 "An elder must be blameless" marks the basic qualification, demanding an irreproachable reputation in the community. The original, "if anyone is blameless," does not imply doubt but rather assumes that the fact is established. This demand is elaborated in what follows.

Two domestic qualifications are stipulated. The precise implications of "the husband of but one wife" have been debated through the centuries (See Fairbairn, *The Pastoral Epistles*, Appendix B). It has been held to prohibit a second marriage, but this seems improbable (cf. 1 Tim 5:14; Rom 7:2, 3; 1 Cor 7:39). If Paul had meant that the elder *must* be married, the reading would have been "a," not "one," wife. Most natural is the view that he must be the husband of only one living woman.

Since older men would be chosen for leadership, it is assumed that the elder would have children. The latter must "believe," share their father's Christian faith. The original (*tekna pista*) may mean "faithful children" but "believing children," is intended here, referring to those who are old enough to have made a personal decision. If they remained pagans, it would throw into question the father's ability to lead others to the faith. As professed believers, the children must personally fulfill the ethical requirements of the Christian life. They must not be chargeable as being "wild," self-indulgent and wasteful in their manner of life, like the prodigal son, nor be "disobedient," refusing to bow to parental authority. An elder's inability to train and govern his children would place in question his ability to train and govern the church.

7 The leader's true position and personal qualifications are given in vv.7, 8. The switch in v.7 to "overseer" shows that "elder" and "overseer" or "bishop" are interchangeable terms, yet with a different connotation. "Elder" (*presbyteros*) implies the maturity and dignity of the man, while "bishop" (*episkopos*) indicates his work as the "overseer" of God's flock.

The Greek is more literally, "It is necessary that the overseer be blameless as God's steward." "The" is the generic use of the article and signifies the representative of the class. The repeated "blameless" prepares for the further elaboration in vv.7-9, but now the stress is on "it is necessary" (*dei*), because of the elder's position as "God's steward." The steward was the manager of a household or estate, appointed by and accountable to the owner. The picture of the steward embodies one of Paul's favorite concepts of the ministry (1 Cor 4:1, 2; 9:17; Eph 3:2; Col 1:25). The Christian minister is not merely the servant of the church; he exercises his office under God's authority and is directly accountable to him. This high office makes high demands on the character of the man. Five negative and six positive personal qualifications are listed in vv.7, 8.

The repeated negative (mē) rejects any thought of the steward's being (1) "overbearing," arrogantly disregarding the interests of others in order to please himself; (2) "quicktempered," readily yielding to anger, for pastoral work demands much patience; (3) "given to wine," literally, "alongside of wine" (paroinon), as addicted to its use; he must not be an alcoholic; (4) "violent," ready to assail an opponent, either with fists or by bellicose behavior; (5) "pursuing dishonest gain," using his office to profit in an underhanded and shameful way. The laborer is worthy of his hire, but he must not turn his office into a money-making business.

8 "Rather" (alla) introduces the contrasting positive qualifications: (1) "hospitable," literally, "lover of strangers," ready to befriend and lodge traveling or fleeing believers; (2) "one who loves what is good," an ally and zealous supporter of the good, including men as well as deeds and things; (3) "self-controlled," in control of his mind and emotions so that he can act rationally and discreetly, a virtue much needed on Crete and one stressed in the Pastorals (1 Tim 2:9, 15; 3:2; 2 Tim 1:7; Titus 2:2, 4, 5, 6, 12); (4) "upright," or just, conforming his conduct to right standards; (5) "holy" (hosios), denoting his personal piety, an inner attitude of conforming to what is felt to be pleasing to God and consistent with religious practices; and (6) "disciplined," having the inner strength that enables him to control his bodily appetites and passions, a virtue listed in Galatians 5:23 as one quality of the fruit of the Spirit. These last three characteristics may be viewed as looking manward, Godward, and selfward, respectively.

9 Doctrinal fitness is also necessary. The overseer must be known to "hold firmly to the trustworthy message," clinging to it despite the winds of false teaching and open opposition. "Trustworthy" underlines that the Christian gospel is perfectly reliable and completely worthy of his confidence. He must adhere to the Word "as it has been taught" and be in accord with the teaching given by the apostles. Unfaithfulness to the biblical revelation disqualifies a man for leadership in God's church. Doctrinal fidelity will give him a standing ability to perform a twofold task: First, he is to "encourage others by sound doctrine," appealing to them to adhere to and advance in their Christian faith. This can be done by proclaiming "sound doctrine," teaching that is not only correct but healthful, promoting spiritual health, in contrast to the unhealthy false teaching. Secondly, his work also demands that he "refute those who oppose" the true gospel and speak against it as the advocates of error. He must "refute" them be exposing their error and trying to convince them that they are wrong. Christian truth needs not only defense against attacks, but also clear exposition. Effective presentation of the truth is a powerful antidote to error.

B. The Refutation of False Teachers

1:10–16

10For there are many rebellious people, mere talkers and deceivers, especially those of the circumcision group. 11They must be silenced, because they are ruining whole households by teaching things they ought not to teach—and that for the sake of dishonest gain. 12Even one of their own prophets has said, "Cretans are always liars, evil brutes, lazy gluttons." 13This testimony is true. Therefore, rebuke

> them sharply, so that they will be sound in the faith ¹⁴and will pay no attention to Jewish myths or to the commands of those who reject the truth. ¹⁵To the pure, all things are pure, but to those who are corrupted and do not believe, nothing is pure. In fact, both their minds and consciences are corrupted. ¹⁶They claim to know God, but by their actions they deny him. They are detestable, disobedient and unfit for doing anything good.

"For" introduces the justification for the requirement that elders must be able to expound and defend the truth (v.9). This is essential because of the false teachers described in vv.10-13a. Verses 13b, 14 state the necessary action, while vv.15, 16 present the evidence condemning these errorists.

1. *The picture of the false teachers* (1:10-13a)

10 "There are many rebellious people" is a general statement of the external danger facing the Cretan churches. The worst offenders were Jewish, but they were not the only ones. These false teachers, apparently Cretans by birth, are not easily identified with any specific heresy. Apparently they were gnosticizing Judaists who as professed Christians sought to infiltrate the churches with their misguided teaching. They seemingly sought to fasten onto Christianity various aspects of Judaism and to present the hybrid as a teaching containing higher philosophical insights. The view of Gealy (IB, 11:529, 530) that they were Gentile Christians who were attracted to Jewish practices and sought to retain them as obligatory, seems improbable.

Three terms describe these "many" false teachers: They are (1) "rebellious," refusing to subordinate themselves to any authority, rejecting the demands of the gospel on them; (2) "mere talkers," men fluent and impressive in speech that accomplishes nothing constructive; (3) "deceivers," men whose glib tongues exercise a fascination over the minds of their dupes and lead them astray. "Those of the circumcision group" were the most active offenders.

11 Paul demanded that these men "be silenced." "Must" (*dei*) presents this as a moral necessity for the welfare of the churches. "Silenced" translates a rare verb meaning "to close the mouth by means of a muzzle or gag." The offenders must be refused opportunity to spread their teachings in the churches; the term also includes silencing them by a logical refutation of their views, making further dissemination impossible.

Their suppression was necessary because of their seductive work. They belonged to that class of people who were "ruining whole households," disturbing and turning upside down the faith of entire families. They achieved these disastrous results "by teaching things they ought not to teach," things that simply "must not" (*mē dei*) be presented as Christian truth. Committed to God's revelation in Christ, the church may not offer "the freedom of *misleading* speech."

"For the sake of dishonest gain" unveils their materialistic motives (contrast v.7), the desire to enrich themselves at the expense of the spiritual welfare of their victims. In v.7 "dishonest gain" is one compound word in Greek, but here it is written as two words to stress the literal fact.

12 These Cretan false teachers were all the more dangerous because of the known nature of the people on whom they preyed. As evidence, Paul quoted a line from Epimenides (6th-5th century B.C.), who was held in honor on Crete as a poet, prophet, and religious reformer. The NIV rendering, "one of their own prophets," implies that Crete boasted a number of such prophets, a point not raised by Paul. The original, "A

certain one of them, their own prophet," stresses that the quoted verdict came from one who had intimate knowledge of his own people and was esteemed by them as a "prophet." Paul was willing to accept this evaluation in order to underline the authority of his own judgment. The quotation establishes the picture without exposing Paul to the charge of being anti-Cretan. It put the Cretans on the horns of a dilemma. They must either admit the truthfulness of his verdict concerning them or deny the charge and brand their own prophet a liar.

The triple charge—"Cretans are always liars, evil brutes, lazy gluttons"—is supported by other extrabiblical witnesses. The pagan moralists classified Cretans with Cilicians and Cappadocians as preeminent in wickedness. So notorious was the Cretan reputation for falsehood that the Greek word $krētiz\bar{o}$ ("to Crete-ize") meant "to lie." "Evil brutes" stigmatizes them as having sunk to the level of beasts, unrestrained in their brutality, always on a prowl for prey. "Lazy gluttons" underlines their greed as idle sensualists who desired to be filled without exerting personal effort to earn an honest living.

13a Paul's own observations confirmed the adverse judgment. Probably he had some unpleasant experiences on the island that verified the verdict.

2. The response to the situation (1:13b–14)

13b "Therefore," or "for which cause," introduces the action demanded by this situation. Titus must continue to "rebuke them sharply," dealing pungently and incisively with the danger, like a surgeon cutting away cancerous tissue. "Rebuke," the verb rendered "refute" in v.9 above, may here be rendered "convict," effectively showing the error of the teaching that is being opposed. Generally, "them" is taken as a direct reference to the false teachers. They would obviously be dealt with whenever they sought to gain a hearing in the church, but it seems clear that the action demanded would also include those church members who were known to be receptive to the claims of the false teachers. Primary reference to the endangered church members seems clear from the contemplated results of the action commanded.

The positive result aimed at is "that they will be sound in the faith." The verb *sound* means "to be in good health, be healthy," while the present tense indicates that the apostolic concern is their continued spiritual health. "The faith" denotes the truth embodied in the gospel they have personally accepted. Their personal spiritual health will be impaired if they feed on unhealthy doctrine.

14 The realization of this positive aim will involve a twofold negative achievement. They must be led to a position where they "will pay no attention to Jewish myths." Apparently the error is the same as the one mentioned in 1 Timothy 1:4, but here stamped explicitly as Jewish. These myths seemingly were speculative and fanciful inventions drawn from the OT records such as are found in the apocryphal and pseudepigraphical writings of Judaism. The rejected teaching is further characterized as "the commands of those who reject the truth." These commands were evidently Jewish-Gnostic ritual observances that the false teachers sought to make binding on Christians (cf. 1 Tim 4:3–6). They are to be spurned because they are merely the unauthorized "commands of men" (Gr.), men characterized as "those who reject the truth," habitually turning themselves away from the truth embodied in the gospel. The commands are to be rejected because of the character of their advocates. There is a close connection between false doctrine and evil character.

3. The condemnation of the false teachers (1:15–16)

These teachers stand condemned by the test of character (v.15) as well as conduct (v.16).

15 The test of character is stated in the form of a double maxim. "To the pure, all things are pure" embodies a principle enunciated by Jesus himself in dealing with Jewish food laws (Matt 15:10, 11; Mark 7:14–19; Luke 11:37–41) and forcefully impressed on Peter in his vision at Joppa (Acts 10:9–15, 28). These Cretan teachers apparently were engrossed in perpetuating ceremonial distinctions between the pure and the impure. They tended to lay emphasis on outward appearance and judged others on the basis of their own external criteria. Paul teaches that true purity lies not in adherence to nonmoral external rites and regulations but in the inner purity of the regenerated heart. Material things receive their moral character from the inner attitude of the user. Paul's maxim does not mean that nothing is impure unless thinking makes it so. It does not invalidate the revelation that certain things are morally wrong.

The converse of the principle carries the attack into enemy territory. Their attribution of impurity to nonmoral things reveals their character, their inner state of corruption or defilement, as well as their unbelief. White, noting the order of the two elements, comments, "Their moral obliquity is more characteristic of them than their intellectual perversion" (EGT, 4:190). Fellowship with God acts to clarify moral perception, but indulgence in evil stultifies the powers of moral discrimination.

A moral perversion has taken place in their whole being. Their "minds," their rational nature enabling them to think and reflect on things moral and spiritual, have become polluted, and their conscience has lost its ability to make correct moral judgments, leaving them unable to make true distinctions between good and evil.

16 The false teachers also stand condemned by the test of conduct. They publicly confess that they "know God," are fully informed about him, and stand in intimate relations with him. ("God" is emphatic by position.) The claim may be pride in assumed Jewish religious privilege or an expression of the Gnostic claim to an esoteric knowledge of God. Perhaps both elements are involved. But their vaunted claim is belied by their evil conduct. Moral quality of life is the determinative test of religious profession (1 John 2:4) and by it true character is exposed. Three terms describe the corrupt and unbelieving. They are (1) "detestable," loathsome, causing horror and disgust because of their hypocrisy; (2) "disobedient," insubordinate to God's truth because of their willful adherence to their man-made rules and regulations; (3) "unfit for doing anything good," disqualifed by their impurity from performing any morally good deed. They are like coins found, upon testing, to be spurious, utterly to be rejected as worthless.

Notes

10 The editors of UBS add καί (*kai*, "and") as the fourth word in this verse, making it read, "For there are many *and* rebellious people," but put it into brackets to mark the uncertainty. In favor of it is the unusualness of the rhetorical expression. However, the weight of the oldest MSS is against its insertion and it is best omitted (so WH and Nestle).

III. Concerning the Natural Groups in the Congregations (2:1-15)

Chapter two, concerned with the pastoral care of the Cretan Christians, is the second main division. Verses 1-10 give ethical instructions for the different groups in the congregations; vv.11-14 unfold the grace of God as the motivating power for Christian living; and v.15 summarizes the duty of Titus on Crete.

A. The Instructions for the Different Groups

(2:1-10)

¹You must teach what is in accord with sound doctrine. ²Teach the older men to be temperate, worthy of respect, self-controlled, and sound in faith, in love and in endurance. ³Likewise, teach the older women to be reverent in the way they live, not to be slanderers or addicted to much wine, but to teach what is good. ⁴Then they can train the younger women to love their husbands and children, ⁵to be self-controlled and pure, to be busy at home, to be kind, and to be subject to their husbands, so that no one will malign the word of God.
⁶Similarly, encourage the young men to be self-controlled. ⁷In everything set them an example by doing what is good. In your teaching show integrity, seriousness ⁸and soundness of speech that cannot be condemned, so that those who oppose you may be ashamed because they have nothing bad to say about us.
⁹Teach slaves to be subject to their masters in everything, to try to please them, not to talk back to them, ¹⁰and not to steal from them, but to show that they can be fully trusted, so that in every way they will make the teaching about God our Savior attractive.

Paul here stresses the importance of building up the inner life of believers as the best antidote against error. Sound doctrine must lead to ethical conduct in the lives of all the groups in the congregations. Emphasis falls on the family groups; the false teachers there had apparently done their greatest damage (1:11).

The paragraph may be divided into four parts. Paul opens with the instructional duty of Titus (v.1); describes the desired character and conduct of various groups (vv.2-6); reminds Titus of the importance of his personal example (vv.7, 8); and adds instructions for the slaves (vv.9, 10).

1. The instructional duty of Titus (2:1)

1 The opening "you" (*su*) is emphatic, contrasting Titus with the false teachers. He must show the difference by continuing to "teach," orally communicate, "what is in accord with sound doctrine." "What is according to" is more literally "what is fitting, proper to." "Sound doctrine," teaching that promotes spiritual health, requires conduct consistent with the teaching professed. Correct doctrine must result in good behavior.

2. The instruction to different age groups (2:2-6)

These verses lay down some of the Christian attributes to be commended to different groups, divided according to age and sex. In the original there is no finite verb until v.6. "Teach" in v.2 is supplied from v.1.

2 The term "older men" (not the word rendered, "elder" in 1:5) denotes age, not office. The "senior" male members are named first as natural leaders. The value of their example will depend on their moral character. Four qualifications are insisted on; the elders must be (1) "temperate," an adjective basically meaning "abstaining from wine," but

having a wider meaning, "clear-headed," manifesting self-possession under all circumstances; (2) "worthy of respect," revealing a personal dignity and seriousness of purpose that invite honor and respect; (3) "self-controlled," possessing self-mastery in thought and judgment (cf. 1:8); and (4) "sound in faith, in love and in endurance," revealing a Christian healthiness of heart and mind. In v.1 "sound" is applied to doctrine, here to character. The definite article with each of the three nouns in the Greek makes them definite and distinct, apparently carrying a possessive force, "their faith, their love, their endurance." "Faith" may be objective, as the doctrinal content of the faith professed, but the following two items suggest that here it is subjective—their personal faith in the Lord. They must be mature in their exercise of genuine love, not bitter and vindictive, and they must display active "endurance," that steadfast persistence that bravely bears the trials and afflictions of life. Endurance is a much-needed virtue, especially in old age, as revealing personal maturity and strength of character.

3 "Likewise" indicates that the same kind of deportment is expected of the "older women," although the demands on them are related to their own station in life. The basic demand is that they "be reverent in the way they live." "The way they live" translates a noun denoting manner of life as expressive of inner character, while the adjective "reverent" basically means "suitable to a sacred person" and conveys the image of a good priestess carrying out the duties of her office. The conduct of the older women must reveal that they regard life as sacred in all of its aspects.

Their reverential behavior requires that they "not be slanderers or addicted to much wine." As mature Christians, they must not be given to gossip, repeating vicious and unfounded charges against others, and must not overindulge in wine. The union of the two negatives suggests the close connection between a loose tongue and intoxicating drink.

The older women must fulfill a positive role; they must "teach what is good." By personal word and example, they must teach what is morally good, noble, and attractive. The reference is not to public instruction, but to their teaching function in the home.

4 The training of the younger women is the duty, not of Titus, but the older women, qualified to do so by position and character. "Train" means to school in the lessons of sobriety and self-control (cf. vv.2, 5). "Younger" is a positive adjective literally meaning "new" or "fresh" and probably suggests a reference to the newly married.

Paul lists seven characteristics that must be commended to such (vv.4, 5a). "To love their husbands and children" renders two separate adjectives, "devoted to husbands, devoted to children." Such domestic affection stands at the very heart of any Christian home.

5 "To be self-controlled and pure" forms another pair. Self-control is a standing duty for all Christians (cf. 1:8; 2:2, 6). "Pure" denotes not only chastity in their sex life but also purity of heart and mind in all their conduct.

"To be busy at home, to be kind" designates a third pair. The first describes the many domestic activities of the housewife that she must willingly accept as part of her position as queen of the home. The KJV rendering "keepers at home" (*oikourous*) is based on a slightly different text and has less textual support than the rare term (*oikourgous*) behind the rendering above. The latter is the more stimulating concept and agrees with Paul's condemnation of idleness in 1 Timothy 5:13, 14. The devoted wife and mother finds her absorbing interest in the innumerable duties of the home. These demand unsparing self-giving and may subject her to the temptation to be irritable and harsh in her demands on members of her household. She must therefore cultivate the virtue of being "kind," i.e., benevolent, heartily doing what is good and beneficial to others, especially those of her household.

The concluding item, "to be subject to their husbands," stresses her acceptance of the established relationship between husband and wife as her Christian duty. "To be subject to" may be in the middle voice, "subjecting themselves to," as expressing their voluntary acceptance of the headship of the husband (cf. Eph 5:22–24). The requirement to love her husband does not eliminate her duty to yield to his headship. In declaring the spiritual equality of the woman before God (Gal 3:28), Christianity immeasurably elevated her status but did not thereby abolish her functional position as the complement and support of her husband as the head of the home.

The concluding purpose clause apparently relates to all seven items. It is the first expression of Paul's strong sense of a religious purpose behind these ethical demands. If Christian wives ignored these demands and flouted the role their culture demanded of good wives, the gospel would be maligned, criticized, and discredited by non-Christians. Christianity would be judged especially by the impact that it had on the women. It therefore was the duty of the women to protect God's revelation from profanation by living discreet and wholesome lives. For Christians, no life style is justified that hinders "the word of God," the message of God's salvation in Christ.

6 The requirement for the young men is brief but comprehensive: "Similarly, encourage the young men to be self-controlled." As a young man, Titus must fittingly convey his instructions for the young women indirectly, but his age was an advantage in dealing directly with the young men. "Encourage" (parakalei) is the first imperative verb in vv.2–6 and is stronger than "teach" in v.1. It may be rendered "urge" or "admonish" and is an appeal to their sense of personal moral responsibility. "Similarly" implies the same acceptance of responsibility as in the previous instructions. Since young men are inclined to be somewhat impetuous and unrestrained in conduct, their basic need is to be "self-controlled," cultivating balance and self-restraint in daily practice. It was a quality of which Paul found it necessary to remind the Cretan believers (1:8; 2:2, 4, 5).

3. The personal example of Titus (2:7–8)

7 In concluding instructions to the different age groups, Paul reminded Titus that his own conduct must confirm his teaching. "Set them an example" is literally "holding yourself alongside as an example,"—a meaning made clear through the use of the reflexive pronoun (seauton) with the middle voice of the participle. There is no word for "them" in the original and the example is not to be restricted to the young men. "In everything" underlines the comprehensiveness of the duty. Some would connect this phrase with the self-control demanded of the young men (v.6), but a connection with v.7 gives proper emphasis to "yourself." It is expanded in what follows. "Doing what is good," being an example "of good works," places the initial stress on his conduct, reflecting his noble deeds. Personal example must precede effective teaching, but his "teaching" in its manner and content must be of the highest quality. Two qualities, "integrity" and "seriousness," must characterize his work of teaching. The former stresses his purity of motive, revealing that he himself is uninfected by the evil conduct and erroneous views of the false teachers. "Seriousness" points to his outward dignity, reflecting the high moral tone and serious manner appropriate to his sacred task.

8 Titus must also demonstrate "soundness of speech that cannot be condemned." The content of his "speech," his personal word spoken while teaching or in ordinary conversation, must have two characteristics. In the first place, it must be "sound," conforming to healthful doctrine (2:1), a demand made on elders (1:9) as well as members (1:13; 2:2). Such soundness will insure the second characteristic—that is, "cannot be condemned." No critic will be able to point out anything in it justly open to censure or rebuke. The original suggests the picture of a courtroom where the judge can find no basis for the accusation of the plaintiff. Every faithful teacher must at times declare doctrine to which some rebellious hearer may object, but such objection must prove unjustified upon faithful examination.

Paul concluded his personal remarks to Titus with another purpose clause. The expression "those who oppose you" is apparently left intentionally vague to leave room for all types of critics. (The original is singular: "the opponent, one of the opposition.") When the objections are examined, the anticipated result is that the critic "may be ashamed," either feeling personally ashamed of his own conduct or made to look foolish because he is shown to have no case. The latter view seems more probable. He will "have nothing bad to say about us." An accusation of something "bad," morally bad or worthless, "about us," including Paul and Christians generally, will be found to be groundless. If justified, such attacks would bring discredit on Christ's servants and his cause.

4. The instructions to the slaves (2:9-10)

Paul's ethical instructions are now addressed to a distinct social group that overlaps groups divided by age and sex. Slaves formed a significant element in the apostolic churches and the welfare of the faith demanded that they too accept their spiritual responsibility as believers. Paul here makes no distinction between slaves who had Christian masters and those who did not (cf. 1 Tim 6:1, 2).

9 The original has no finite verb in v.9; perhaps it would be better here to use the verb of v.6 and render "encourage" or "exhort the slaves." Their fundamental duty is "to be subject to their masters in everything," voluntarily accepting subjection to their masters as a matter of principle. "Masters" (our English word *despot*) denotes that as owners they had complete authority over their slaves. While "in everything" may be taken with what follows, the parallel in Colossians 3:22 favors a connection with the demanded subjection. It stresses the comprehensiveness of this duty. But patristic commentators were careful to point out the necessary limitation on this demand, for a Christian slave could not submit when his pagan master demanded things contrary to Christian conscience.

The character of their subjection is indicated in the appositional infinitive, "to try to please them." Instead of having a sullen disposition, let them aim to be well pleasing (*euarestous*), giving full satisfaction to their masters. Elsewhere this adjective is always used of men's relation to God. It is the distinctive contribution of Christianity that slaves should govern their relations to their masters by this high principle. Three participial clauses, two negative and one positive, further describe their relationship to their masters.

The first negative requirement is "not to talk back to them," not to dispute their commands and by deliberate resistance seek to thwart their will.

10 The second negative demand is "not to steal from them," not underhandedly to divert to themselves part of anything their masters had not intended for them. Petty theft was common among slaves in Roman households. Employment in various trades and occupations offered slaves ample opportunity to resort to the various tricks of the trade for their own advantage.

Their positive duty is "to show that they can be fully trusted," demonstrating "good faith" in their whole relationship to their masters. They must not only be Christians but actively show this by proving themselves dependable in everything "good" or beneficial to their masters. "Good" naturally excluded any wrongdoing in which their master might order participation.

Such ethical conduct Paul again undergirds with a profound spiritual motive, "so that in every way they will make the teaching about God our Savior attractive." For a Christian there can be no higher motive. A slave's acceptance of the teaching about "God our Savior" must find expression in his transformed conduct. The very difficulty of his position would make such conduct a powerful recommendation of the gospel, proving to the master the power of the gospel. "In every way" (*en pasin*) in the original stands emphatically at the end. Adornment of faith by conduct must extend to every aspect of their lives. Less probable is the view that the meaning is "among all men" as denoting that the testimony of their conduct will permeate all areas of society.

B. *The Foundation for Godly Living*

2:11-14

> [11]For the grace of God that brings salvation has appeared to all men. [12]It teaches us to say "No" to ungodliness and worldly passions, and to live self-controlled, upright and godly lives in this present age, [13]while we wait for the blessed hope—the glorious appearing of our great God and Savior, Jesus Christ, [14]who gave himself for us to redeem us from all wickedness and to purify for himself a people that are his very own, eager to do what is good.

"For" marks Paul's masterly epitome of Christian doctrine as the proper foundation for the ethical demands just made on the various groups. Christian conduct must be grounded in and motivated by Christian truth. The vitality of doctrinal profession must be demonstrated by transformed Christian conduct.

Verses 11-14 unfold the meaning of "God our Savior" in v.10. Paul could not think of Christian truth and conduct apart from God's grace. He speaks of the manifestation of God's grace (v.11), the Christian's present training by grace (v.12), the expectation of Christ's return (v.13), and the aim of Christ's redemptive work (v.14).

1. *The manifestation of God's grace (2:11)*

11 The entire program of redemption is rooted in "the grace of God," his free favor and spontaneous action toward needy sinners to deliver and transform them. In the Greek, "has appeared" stands emphatically at the beginning, stressing the manifestation of grace as a historical reality. The reference is to Christ's entire earthly life—his birth, life, death, and resurrection. The verb *epephanē*, from which we derive our word "epiphany," means "to become visible, make an appearance," and conveys the image of grace suddenly breaking in on our moral darkness, like the rising sun. (It is used of the sun in Acts 27:20.) Men could never have formed an adequate conception of that grace apart from its personal manifestation in Christ, in his incarnation and atonement.

The effect of the manifestation was redemptive, not destructive. The adjective rendered "that brings salvation" (*sōtērios*) asserts its saving efficacy. The dative "to all men" may equally be rendered "for all men," thus stressing the universality of the salvation provided. Salvation is available to all, but its saving effect is dependent on the personal response of faith. Its universal scope justifies the application of its ethical demands to all classes of its professed recipients.

2. The training by God's grace (2:12)

12 "It teaches us" declares that grace also operates in the lives of the saved. Grounded in God's nature, grace makes ethical demands of Christians consistent with his nature. "Teaches" pictures grace, practically personified, as instructing the believer in the things "in accord with sound doctrine" (2:1). The verb basically means "to train a child," hence "to instruct, train, educate." It comprehends the entire training process—teaching, encouragement, correction, discipline.

The negative pedagogical purpose of grace is to train us "to say 'No' to ungodliness and worldly passions." The aorist participle indicates that grace aims to lead the believer to the place where as a definite act he will voluntarily make a double renunciation of the past. He must repudiate and abandon "ungodliness," the impiety and irreverence that characterized his unsaved life, as well as "worldly passions," those cravings characteristic of the world in its estrangement from God. Such an act of renunciation, standing at the beginning of a life of Christian victory, must be maintained in daily self-denial.

This negative work clears the field for its positive aim for believers: "to live self-controlled, upright and godly lives." "Live" (aorist tense) may mean "come to live" but more probably means that our entire course of life should be consistently characterized by three qualities (state as adverbs). In the original these adverbs stand emphatically before the verb. They look in three directions, though sharp distinctions need not be pressed: (1) *inward*, "self-controlled" ("soberly"), already stipulated for different groups (1:8; 2:2, 5) and now demanded of every believer; (2) *outward*, "upright" ("righteously"), faithfully fulfilling all the demands of truth and justice in our relations with others; (3) *upward*, "godly" ("reverently"), fully devoted to God in reverence and loving obedience.

Such a life is a possibility and duty "in this present age." This present evil age (Gal 1:4) holds dangers for the believer (Rom 12:2; 2 Tim 4:10) and stands in contrast to the anticipated future.

3. The expectation of Christ's return (2:13)

13 Those now being trained by God's grace eagerly anticipate the eschatological future. Having renounced their sinful past, they live disciplined lives in the present and look eagerly to the future (cf. 1 Thess 1:9, 10). "Wait for" depicts their eager expectancy as they look "for the blessed hope," the personal return of Christ who will consummate our bliss in eternal glory. The present tense marks this waiting as the characteristic attitude of believers, ever ready to welcome the returning Lord.

In the Greek "the glorious appearing" has no definite article. The use of the dash in NIV assumes that "the glorious appearing of our great God and Savior" is virtually in apposition with "the blessed hope" as a further definition of that hope. The Greek connects "the blessed hope and glorious appearing" under one article, suggesting that the reference is to one event viewed from two aspects. For believers, it is indeed the blessed hope and the longed-for consummation of that hope. For Christ himself, this awaited "glorious appearing" will vindicate his character as the Lord of glory. "Glorious appearing" is more literally "appearing of the glory" and points to his present glorification in heaven. Now unrecognized and disregarded by the world, his glory at his return will be manifested in all its splendor. Verse 11 spoke of his past epiphany in grace; v.13, of his future epiphany in glory.

The NIV rendering, "the glorious appearing of our great God and Savior, Jesus Christ" (cf. also RSV; NEB; NASB; BV), relates the glory to be revealed to Christ alone. The KJV rendering, "the glorious appearing of the great God and our Saviour Jesus Christ" (cf. ASV; Mof), relates it to both the Father and Christ. Either is grammatically possible. In favor of the latter rendering are the facts that in the pastoral Epistles God and Christ are regularly named side by side, that the double glory at the Parousia is mentioned elsewhere (Luke 9:26), and that the term *God* is rarely applied to Christ in Scripture. It is also the view of most of the ancient versions. But there are stronger arguments for referring the entire expression to Christ alone: (1) Grammatically this is the most natural view since both nouns are connected by one article as referring to one person. (2) The combination "god and savior" was familiar to the Hellenistic religions. (3) The added clause in v.14 refers to Christ alone and it is most natural to take the entire preceding expression as its antecedent. (4) In the Pastorals the coming epiphany is referred to Christ alone. (5) The adjective "great" of God is rather pointless but highly significant if applied to Christ. (6) This view is in full harmony with other passages such as John 20:28; Rom 9:5; Heb 1:8; and 2 Peter 1:1. (7) It is the view of the majority of the church fathers. This view takes the statement as an explicit assertion of the deity of Christ. Under the other view his deity is assumed, for the intimate association of his glory with that of God would be blasphemous for a monotheist like Paul if he did not accept Christ's deity.

4. The purpose of Christ's redemption (2:14)

14 From the eschatological future, Paul reverts to the historical work of Christ as Savior as the foundation for present sanctification. "Who gave himself for us" summarizes that work as voluntary, exhaustive, and substitutionary. His giving of himself was the grandest of all gifts. Because of our sinfulness, his atoning work had a dual aspect.

Its negative aspect was "to redeem us from all wickedness" or "lawlessness," that assertion of self-will in defiance of God's standard that is the essence of sin (1 John 3:4). The expression stresses not our guilt as rebels but rather our deliverance from bondage to lawlessness through Christ's ransom. "From" (*apo*) indicates effective removal from that sphere and our deliverance from "all" aspects of its domination.

This negative work is the necessary prelude to the positive work of sanctification, "to purify for himself a people that are his very own." "Purify" points to the moral defilement that man's rebellion produced. Sin makes us not only guilty but also unclean before a holy God. The blood-wrought cleansing (1 John 1:7) enables men to be restored to fellowship with God as "a people that are his very own." Since they have been redeemed by his blood (1 Peter 1:18-21), Christ yearns that they voluntarily yield themselves wholly to him. Such a surrender is man's only reasonable response to divine mercy (Rom 12:1, 2).

"Eager to do what is good" delineates what this relationship involves. "Eager" in the Greek is a noun (*zēlōtēs*) meaning "a zealot, an enthusiast." For those who have been redeemed from the doom of sin and death and brought into a unique relationship with God, the true voluntary response is to be enthusiastic "to do what is good." It is the true badge of his divine ownership. He who eagerly awaits the return of the Savior will be eager also to further his cause by good works until he comes. It is another instance of the union between creed and conduct insisted upon in the pastoral Epistles.

C. *The Restatement of the Duty of Titus*

2:15

> 15These, then, are the things you should teach. Encourage and rebuke with all authority. Do not let anyone despise you.

15 "These ... things ... teach" looks back to 2:1. The same imperative is used. Titus must continually present the practical instructions to the various groups in their proper doctrinal setting. The NIV rendering regards "teach" as Titus' central duty and views the following imperatives as the two major functions of that work. In the Greek the three imperatives are closely connected: "These things teach and encourage and rebuke." All are present imperatives, Paul urging Titus to continue what he has been doing. The three form a climax. He must clearly proclaim the message, "encourage" or exhort the hearers to appropriate and practice it, and "rebuke" or convict those who are slack or fail to respond. He must perform these duties "with all authority," for the message is apostolic and authentic and its authority must be stressed. The gospel must not be presented as an optional opinion to be accepted or rejected as its hearers may please. The minister's authority rests in the nature of his message; he is not raised above the truth but the truth above him.

As the apostolic representative in Crete, Titus must "not let anyone despise" him, look down on him, or belittle his message and authority. He must not permit the message and work to be slighted or disdainfully rejected. Since this letter would be read in the churches, the remark was apparently intended as much for the Cretans as for Titus himself.

IV. Concerning Believers Among Men Generally (3:1–11)

Having dealt with church leaders (ch. 1) and the conduct of believers as members of the Christian community (ch. 2). in this final section Paul insists that believers also have duties to the government and the non-Christian world. The section is in three parts: the duties of believers as citizens (vv.1, 2), the motives for godly living (vv.3–8), and the necessary reaction to spiritual error (vv.9–11).

A. *Their Obligations As Citizens*

3:1–2

> Remind the people to be subject to rulers and authorities, to be obedient, to be ready to do whatever is good, 2to slander no one, to be peaceable and considerate, and to show true humility toward all men.

1 Christians have a duty to government. "The people," literally "them," refers to the members of the churches, not to all Cretans in general. "Remind" indicates that the duties now insisted on are not new to them; the present imperative demands that Titus must repeatedly press these duties upon their consciences. Early Christian preaching was not limited to the way of salvation but included instructions concerning the practical implications of that salvation for daily living. Paul ever desired that the lives of believers should produce a favorable impression on the non-Christian world.

The duty of believers is "to be subject to rulers and authorities." "To be subject" is best taken as a middle-voice infinitive, implying their voluntary acceptance of this position of submission. "Rulers and authorities," two abstract nouns, signifies not the individual rulers but the various forms of human government. This demand for obedience to government is found in other NT letters (Rom 13:1–7; 1 Peter 2:13–17), but the known turbulence of the Cretans made it particularly appropriate here.

"To be obedient" states the result and visible demonstration of their attitude of submission. The compound infinitive (*peitharchein*) denotes practical obedience to particular authoritative orders. The context implies obedience to the particular demands of government, but the practice of obedience is not to be limited to these areas. It is assumed that the obedience demanded does not contradict explicit Christian duties.

As good citizens, believers must also "be ready to do whatever is good"—prepared and willing to participate in activities that promote the welfare of the community. They must not stand coldly aloof from praiseworthy enterprises of government but show good public spirit, thus proving that Christianity is a constructive force in society.

2 Believers also have obligations to pagan neighbors. Negatively, they must "slander no one," abstain from the common practice of hurling curses and vicious epithets at those offending or injuring them. The demand required inner grace but was appropriate for followers of the Christ who did not revile when he was reviled (1 Peter 2:23). In the Greek, "to be peaceable" is another negative demand, "to be nonfighting" (*amachous*), refusing to engage in quarrels and conflicts. The Christian must not adopt the arts of the agitator.

Positively, he must be "considerate," gentle or yielding, not stubbornly insisting on his own rights but acting in courtesy and forbearance. A further positive duty is "to show true humility," an attitude of mind the opposite of self-assertiveness and harshness. "True" is literally "all" and stresses not its genuineness but the greatest possible manifestation of this grace. The present participle rendered "to show" suggests a continuing demonstration of humility as an essential trait of Christian character. It is not to be exhibited only in dealing with fellow believers but must be shown "toward all men," including those who are hostile and morally perverse. It is a difficult test of Christian character but one that effectively proves the genuineness of Christian profession.

B. *The Motives for Such Godly Conduct*

    3:3–8

> [3]At one time we too were foolish, disobedient, deceived and enslaved by all kinds of passions and pleasures. We lived in malice and envy, being hated and hating one another. [4]But when the kindness and love of God our Savior appeared, [5]he saved us, not because of righteous things we had done, but because of his mercy. He saved us through the washing of rebirth and renewal by the Holy Spirit, [6]whom he poured out on us generously through Jesus Christ our Savior, [7]so that, having been justified by his grace, we might become heirs having the hope of eternal life. [8]This is a trustworthy saying. And I want you to stress these things, so that those who have trusted in God may be careful to devote themselves to doing what is good. These things are excellent and profitable for everyone.

Paul's opening "for" in the original (*gar*, not represented in the NIV rendering) again indicates that the required conduct is being undergirded by weighty reasons. His masterly summary of evangelical teaching encourages his readers with the reminder that such conduct is necessary and possible in view of God's transforming work in their own lives. He advances three supporting motives: their own pre-Christian past (v.3), the saving work of God in believers (vv.4–8a), and the necessary connection between Christian truth and conduct (v.8b).

1. The motive from our own past (3:3)

3 The remembrance of our own past should be a powerful motive for gentleness and consideration toward the unsaved. "We were," standing emphatically at the opening of the sentence, implies that what was once true of us is still true of the unsaved neighbor. The added "we too" (*kai hēmeis*) stresses that the condition described in retrospect applied to Paul and Titus as well as to the Cretan Christians; it is, in fact, true of all believers everywhere. It is salutary to remember our own past moral condition when dealing with the unsaved in their degradation.

The picture of our past is vividly and concisely drawn. We were "foolish," without spiritual understanding, lacking discernment of spiritual realities because of the darkening effect of sin on the intellect (Eph 4:18). As outward evidence of our alienated condition, we were "disobedient," wilfully disregarding authority, refusing obedience to God's law and fretting under human authority. "Deceived" pictures active straying from the true course by following false guides. Allowing our conduct to be dictated by a wide variety of personal "passions and pleasures," the inevitable result was our enslavement to them. Never finding true personal satisfaction in their pursuit, we lived our lives in the grip of the antisocial forces of "malice and envy," harboring an attitude of ill-will toward others and enviously begrudging others their good fortune. "Being hated" (*stugē-toi*, only here in the NT, but see the compound form in Rom 12:9) denotes being odious, repulsive, and disgusting to others. It pictures that stage of degradation "when vice becomes odious to the vicious, stands a self-confessed failure to produce happiness" (White, EGT, 4:198). "Hating one another" marks the climax in the active operation of mutual antagonisms that hasten the dissolution of the bonds of human society.

2. The motive from our present salvation (3:4-7)

"But" introduces the familiar Pauline contrast between what we once were and now are (Rom 6:17–23; 1 Cor 6:9–11; Eph 2:2–13; 5:7–12; Col 1:21, 22; 3:7–10). The marvelous salvation that we now know must motivate our dealings with the unsaved. This beautiful summary of the whole gospel mentions the manifestation (v.4), the basis (v.5a), the means (vv.5b, 6), and the results (v.7) of our salvation.

4 a. *Its manifestation.* Our salvation roots in a definite historical event, "when the kindness and love of God our Savior appeared." "Appeared" (the precise form in 2:11) looks back to the salvation manifested in the incarnate Christ. The salvation embodied in him manifested two aspects of the nature of "God our Savior": (1) his "kindness" or "benignity," his pitying kindness that prompts him to bestow forgiveness and blessings; (2) his "love" (*philanthrōpia*), his affection for men seen in his display of love for us in our sin and degradation. (It would have been better to retain the rendering "love toward man" to mark the unique term, used only here in the NT, and bring out the connection with John 3:16; Rom 5:8; and similar verses). Each noun has the definite article, thus making the two concepts distinct, yet the singular verb views them as so closely connected as to form one whole. Through his action in Christ, God is now revealed as "our Savior." "Our" is strongly confessional. The plural associates Paul with all those who have appropriated this Savior as their own (cf. Gal 2:20).

5a b. *Its basis.* "He saved us" simply records the historic fact of his saving work in all who have accepted salvation in Christ. The aorist tense records the past saving act; we now possess his salvation, although it is still incomplete, awaiting its consummation at Christ's return.

The original order stresses the basis of this experienced salvation, "not because of righteous things we had done, but because of his mercy, he saved us." The order eliminates any thought of salvation due to personal merit and magnifies God's sovereign grace.

The negative clause repeats Paul's well-known denial of salvation by works (Rom 4:4, 5; Gal 2:16, 17; Eph 2:8, 9). Our salvation did not arise out of "righteous things we had done," more literally, "out of works that we ourselves had performed in righteousness." As sinners, we did no such works, nor were we able to perform them. The gospel emphatically denies the possibility of attaining salvation by human effort or merit.

Positively, God saved us "because of his mercy." In our wretchedness he graciously withheld deserved punishment and freely saved us. "Because of " is literally "according to" (*kata*) and points to his mercy as the yardstick for measuring the vastness of his saving grace. The pronouns "we" and "his" stand in intentional and emphatic contrast.

5b–6 c. *Its means.* God's salvation was mediated to us "through the washing of rebirth and renewal by the Holy Spirit." "Washing" speaks of our cleansing from the defilement of sin in regeneration. The noun (*loutron*) may mean the receptacle for washing, the "laver," or the act of washing itself. In Ephesians 5:26, the only other NT occurrence of the term, the natural meaning is "washing." Simpson remarks that "*laver* lacks corroboration, except in patristic treatises, coloured by the dogma of baptismal regeneration, and the LXX term thus translated is *loutēr*, which undoubtedly signifies a bathing-tub" (p. 114). "Washing" is thus best understood as denoting the act rather than the place of washing. (The use of *dia* with the genitive clearly asserts the washing as the means of the rebirth). Most commentators take the washing as a reference to water baptism. But if water baptism is the means that produces the spiritual rebirth, we then have the questionable teaching of a material agency as the indispensable means for producing a spiritual result (but cf. Matt 15:1–20; Rom 2:25–29; Gal 5:6). We accept the washing as a divine inner act, although the experience is symbolically pictured in Christian baptism. In the NT the inner experience is viewed as openly confessed before men in baptism, but the rite does not produce the inner experience of spiritual "rebirth," a new state of life in consequence of a new birth. The word *rebirth* (*palingenesia*) occurs elsewhere in the NT only in Matthew 19:28, where it refers to the external material rebirth of creation at Christ's return. Here it denotes the inner spiritual regeneration of the individual believer.

The expression "through the washing of rebirth and renewal by the Holy Spirit" is open to two interpretations grammatically. Both "rebirth" and "renewal" may be regarded as dependent on "washing" to form one concept. Then the washing of rebirth is further described as a renewal wrought by the Spirit. The other view holds that the preposition "through" is in thought also repeated with "renewal." This view sees two separate aspects of salvation. The fact that the preposition is not repeated is in favor of the first view, but the resultant thought favors the second view. Then the washing is viewed as producing an instantaneous change that ended the old life and began the new, while the work of renewal by the Spirit, beginning with the impartation of the new life, is a lifelong activity in the experience of the believer. In Romans 12:2 this renewal is viewed as a continuing process. In Ephesians 5:26, 27 the act of cleansing of the church is followed by the work of sanctification till no spot or wrinkle remains. The spiritual rebirth, taking place at a particular moment, is the prerequisite for the subsequent process of "renewal" (*anakainōseōs*), "a making new," the development of an entirely new nature as contrasted with the old. This process of renewal in the believer is the work of the Holy Spirit. He alone can produce a new nature that finds active expression in an entirely new manner of life.

"Whom he poured out on us generously," or "richly," stresses that God has made ample provision for the development of this renewed life. "Poured out" (aorist tense) had its primary fulfillment at Pentecost, but "on us" marks the pouring out as individually experienced at conversion (Rom 5:5). The Spirit's work in each believer as a member of the Body is a continuation of the Pentecostal outpouring. Every faulty or inadequate experience of renewal is always due to some human impediment, never to God's inadequate provision. "Through Jesus Christ our Savior" states the channel through which the Spirit's renewing presence was bestowed. That bestowal was based on the finished work of Christ as Savior (John 7:38, 39; 15:26; Acts 2:33). The "our" is again confessional. Our acceptance of Christ as Savior is the human condition for the bestowal of the Spirit. Note the Trinity in vv.5b, 6: "the Holy Spirit," "he" (the Father), "Jesus Christ." Each member of the divine Trinity has his own special function in the work of human redemption.

7 d. *Its results.* "So that" (*hina*) here denotes more than mere purpose; the aim has been accomplished. "Having been justified by his grace" relates the result of salvation to our past. Sin had brought guilt and condemnation, but when we received Christ as our Savior, we were "justified," "declared righteous," and given a standing of acceptance before him. "Justified," in reference to man, is always in the passive; it is always the act of God, motivated "by his grace." "His" (*ekeinou*), "of that one," indicates that the reference is to the grace of the Father, his free unmerited favor bestowed on the basis of Christ's perfect work. The condensed comment assumes knowledge of Paul's doctrine of justification.

The second stated result comprehends our present standing in relation to the future. "Might become heirs" denotes not just a future prospect but a present reality. As members of God's family, we now are heirs, but entrance upon our inheritance belongs to the future. Our standing as heirs is "according to" (*kata*), in full harmony with, "the hope of eternal life" (1:2). Our present experience of salvation can give us only a tantalizing foretaste of the nature of our future inheritance.

3. The necessary connection between doctrine and conduct (3:8)

8a "This is a trustworthy saying" clearly looks back to the doctrinal statement in vv.4–7 as a unified whole and stamps it as worthy of full approval. Confined to the pastoral Epistles (1 Tim 1:15; 3:1; 4:9; 2 Tim 2:11), here is the sole occurrence of this formula in Titus. Clearly the application in this case is not restricted to a single pithy utterance. Scholars generally accept the view that the writer is citing a hymn or confessional statement, but there is no agreement about the extent or exact contents of the assumed quotation (see Hinson, Broadman Commentary, 11:273). Whether it is a quotation or

Paul's own composition, no nobler doctrinal statement is found in any Pauline Epistle.

8b It is Paul's definite intention that Titus, as his personal representative in Crete, continue insistently "to stress these things." "These things" apparently looks back to vv.4–7 and views those doctrinal truths in their varied aspects. Their trustworthy character demands that Titus "stress," stoutly and confidently affirm, them. The orthodox preacher must proclaim his message with confidence and ringing certainty.

Such insistent preaching must aim at a definite result in the lives of believers. "Those who have trusted in God" (a perfect active participle, standing emphatically at the end of the sentence) pictures not only their initial acceptance of these truths but also their present personal faith relationship to God. Because of this present relationship, they are obligated to "be careful to devote themselves to doing what is good." The gospel message of free forgiveness for sinners on the sole basis of faith must find expression in a life characterized as taking a lead in the performance of excellent deeds. The practice of good works is the logical outcome of a true apprehension of the grace of God. The original statement can be taken to mean "that they engage in honourable occupations" (NEB), but this rendering is less probable as not strictly relevant to the theme of the passage and not in accord with the usual meaning of the statement in the NT.

Paul's summary evaluation of the instructions just given is that they are "excellent and profitable for everyone." "These things" may refer to his final demand that believers combine faith and practice, but more probably the reference is to the true teachings that Titus must insist on in his work in Crete. By their very nature they are "excellent," good, attractive, and praiseworthy. They are also "profitable for everyone," having a beneficial impact on mankind. The beneficial effects of Christian ethical standards are not limited to believers only. A vital Christianity unites the beautiful and the profitable.

C. The Reaction to Spiritual Error

3:9–11

> [9]But avoid foolish controversies and genealogies and arguments and quarrels about the law, because these are unprofitable and useless. [10]Warn a divisive person once, and then warn him a second time. After that, have nothing to do with him. [11]You may be sure that such a man is warped and sinful; he is self-condemned.

9 "But" introduces the necessary reaction of Titus to matters contrary to the teaching insisted on in v.8. They are described as "foolish controversies and genealogies and arguments and quarrels about the law." The picture looks back to 1:10–16; "about the law" marks the Jewish coloring. All four nouns are without the article and this stresses the quality of these things. The same sort of problems also existed at Ephesus (cf. 1 Tim 1:3–7). They comprise various "foolish" or senseless inquiries, involving speculations about the OT genealogies, and resulted in sharp dissensions and open quarrels.

All such matters Titus must "avoid," deliberately shun and stand aloof from, "because they are unprofitable and useless." They produce no spiritual benefits and lead to no constructive results.

10 Paul now passes from these reprehensible opinions to their perverted advocates. The adjective "divisive" (*hairetikon*), found only here in the NT, essentially characterizes what is a self-chosen opinion or viewpoint; because of their insistence on their opinions, devoid of a true scriptural basis, the dissidents stir up divisions. Simpson characterizes such a man as an "opinionative propagandist who promotes dissension by his pertinacity" (p. 117). When persisted in, this results in the formation of heretical parties.

Such a man Titus must "warn" or "admonish" by faithfully and lovingly pointing out his error. If a second effort to deal with him proves ineffective, let Titus "have nothing to do with him," refusing further to bother with him. Further efforts would not be a good stewardship of his time and energies and would give the offender an undeserved sense of importance.

11 His stubborn refusal of admonition would assure Titus that the man is "warped," the perfect tense marking him as being in a state of perversion, twisted and turned out, wholly out of touch with truth. The passive voice seems to point to the satanic agency behind his condition.

"Sinful" represents a present-tense verb: "he is sinning," deliberately missing the divine standard by his persistent refusal to receive correction. It reveals an inner moral condition of being "self-condemned." He knows that in his deliberate refusal to abandon his self-chosen views he is wrong and stands condemned by his own better judgment.

V. Conclusion

3:12–15

> ¹²As soon as I send Artemas or Tychicus to you, do your best to come to me at Nicopolis, because I have decided to winter there. ¹³Do everything you can to help Zenas the lawyer and Apollos on their way and see that they have everything they need. ¹⁴Our people must learn to devote themselves to doing what is good, in order that they may provide for daily necessities and not live unproductive lives.
> ¹⁵Everyone with me sends you greetings. Greet those who love us in the faith. Grace be with you all.

The conclusion to the Epistle, comparable in length to the opening salutation, consists of three directives from Paul (vv.12–14), mutual greetings (v.15a), and the closing benediction (v.15b).

A. The Concluding Instructions (3:12–14).

12 Verse 12 announces Paul's plans for the future as they concern Titus himself. Another worker would be sent to replace Titus in Crete. Since his assignment to Crete was not permanent, Titus obviously was not the "first bishop of the Cretans" as the scribal subscription has it. When Paul wrote, neither the time nor the final selection of the replacement had been determined. Nothing further is known of Artemas. Tychicus was a trusted co-worker who on several occasions appears as traveling with or for Paul (Acts 20:4; Eph 6:21, 22; Col 4:7, 8; 2 Tim 4:12). When a replacement arrived, not before, Titus was urged to proceed as quickly as possible to Nicopolis (lit., "victory-town"), apparently the city in Epirus on the west coast of Greece. Paul planned to spend the winter there, presumably making it a base of operation for work in Dalmatia. "There" shows that Paul was not yet there when he wrote. The place of writing is unknown, but it may have been Corinth.

13 Zenas and Apollos are almost certainly the bearers of this letter. "Zenas the lawyer" appears only here. His name is Greek, but he may have been a convert from Judaism. If he was of Jewish origin, "lawyer" means that he had been an expert in the Mosaic law;

if a Gentile, it means he had been a Roman jurist. Apollos is the well-known Alexandrian Jew who, having been fully instructed at Ephesus, effectively worked in the Corinthian church (Acts 18:24-28; 19:1; 1 Cor 1:12; 3:4-6; 4:6; 16:12). Their journey took Zenas and Apollos through Crete, and Titus must diligently assist them by seeing that their further needs are supplied. Such generous material assistance for Christian workers on their journeys characterized the early church (Acts 15:3; Rom 15:24; 1 Cor 16:6; 2 Cor 1:16; 3 John 5-8).

14 Titus need not carry the burden alone. By appealing to the churches for further funds, he had an opportunity to train them in the practice of "doing what is good" (cf. 3:8). It would further the gospel and develop their own Christian lives. This situation gave Paul a final opportunity to stress the theme that Christians must be characterized by the practice of noble deeds, thus assuring that their lives would not be "unproductive." Noble deeds are the fruit of the tree of salvation.

B. The Personal Greetings (3:15a)

15a All the workers with Paul joined in sending their greetings. They are left unnamed, since Zenas and Apollos would orally identify them. Titus is to pass on these greetings to "those who love us in the faith," the believers in Crete who are filled with affection for Paul and his assistants "in the faith." "Faith," without an article, may mean the sphere where their affection was operative, or it may simply mean "in faith," that is, loyally. The former view seems preferable.

C. The Closing Benediction (3:15b)

15b The "you" is plural, including all those to whom Titus was to convey Paul's greetings. It suggests that Paul expected the letter to be read in the various churches.

Notes

15 The closing ἀμήν (amēn, "amen"), found in numerous MSS, is very probably a scribal addition. It is absent from many early and diverse textual witnesses. The scribes would be more likely to add this liturgical conclusion than omit it.